20-04-21

The Quest for the Good Life

The Quest for the Good Life

Ancient Philosophers on Happiness

EDITED BY

Øyvind Rabbås, Eyjólfur K. Emilsson, Hallvard
Fossheim, and Miira Tuominen

OXFORD
UNIVERSITY PRESS

OXFORD
UNIVERSITY PRESS

Great Clarendon Street, Oxford, OX2 6DP,
United Kingdom

Oxford University Press is a department of the University of Oxford.
It furthers the University's objective of excellence in research, scholarship,
and education by publishing worldwide. Oxford is a registered trade mark of
Oxford University Press in the UK and in certain other countries

First Edition published in 2015
Impression: 2

Published in the United States of America by Oxford University Press
198 Madison Avenue, New York, NY 10016, United States of America

British Library Cataloguing in Publication Data
Data available

Library of Congress Control Number: 2015933906

ISBN 978-0-19-874698-0

Printed and bound by
CPI Group (UK) Ltd, Croydon, CR0 4YY

Preface

This volume derives from the project *Ethics in Antiquity: The Quest for the Good Life*, at the Centre for Advanced Study in Oslo. We are most grateful to the Centre for funding our project, as well as for its generous hospitality and excellent working conditions during our year there (2009–10). Most of the papers were presented at the concluding conference of our project, in Rome in June 2010.

This project was an interdisciplinary project between philosophy and classics, led by Professors Eyjólfur K. Emilsson and Øivind Andersen. Its aim was to contribute to a better understanding of ancient thought on happiness and the good life. Eight papers from the classics side of the project were published in *Symbolae Osloenses* 85:1 (2011).

We would like to express our gratitude to the editors and the anonymous reviewers at the Press, whose assistance in producing this volume has been unfailing and extremely helpful. Finally, we thank Lars Gjøvikli for invaluable assistance in compiling the indices and in proof-reading, and the Department of Philosophy, Classics, History of Art and Ideas at the University of Oslo for supporting his work.

Ø.R.
E.K.E.
H.F.
M.T.

Contents

List of Contributors   ix

Introduction   1

1. On Happiness and Godlikeness before Socrates   28
   Svavar Hrafn Svavarsson

2. Plato's Defence of Justice: The Wrong Kind of Reason?   49
   Julia Annas

3. Wanting to Do What Is Just in the *Gorgias*   66
   Panos Dimas

4. *Eudaimonia*, Human Nature, and Normativity: Reflections on
   Aristotle's Project in *Nicomachean Ethics* Book I   88
   Øyvind Rabbås

5. Aristotle on Happiness and Old Age   113
   Hallvard Fossheim

6. Aristotle on Happiness and Long Life   127
   Gabriel Richardson Lear

7. Why Is Aristotle's Vicious Person Miserable?   146
   Gösta Grönroos

8. Epicurus on Pleasure, Desire, and Friendship   164
   Panos Dimas

9. How Feasible Is the Stoic Conception of *Eudaimonia*?   183
   Katerina Ierodiakonou

10. The Pyrrhonian Idea of a Good Life   197
    Svavar Hrafn Svavarsson

11. Plotinus' Way of Defining '*Eudaimonia*' in *Ennead* I 4 [46] 1–3   212
    Alexandrine Schniewind

12. On Happiness and Time   222
    Eyjólfur K. Emilsson

13. Why Do We Need Other People to Be Happy? Happiness and
    Concern for Others in Aspasius and Porphyry   241
    Miira Tuominen

14. Happiness in this Life? Augustine on the Principle that Virtue Is
    Self-sufficient for Happiness   265
    Christian Tornau

Bibliography   281
Index Locorum   293
General Index   302

List of Contributors

JULIA ANNAS is Regents Professor of Philosophy at the University of Arizona.

PANOS DIMAS is Professor of Philosophy at the University of Oslo and Director of the Norwegian Institute at Athens.

EYJÓLFUR K. EMILSSON is Professor of Philosophy at the University of Oslo.

HALLVARD FOSSHEIM is Associate Professor of Ancient Philosophy at the University of Bergen.

GÖSTA GRÖNROOS is a researcher in Philosophy at the University of Stockholm.

KATERINA IERODIAKONOU is Associate Professor of Ancient Philosophy at the University of Athens.

GABRIEL RICHARDSON LEAR is Professor of Philosophy at the University of Chicago.

ØYVIND RABBÅS is Professor of Philosophy at the University of Oslo.

ALEXANDRINE SCHNIEWIND is Professor of Ancient Philosophy at the University of Lausanne.

SVAVAR HRAFN SVAVARSSON is Professor of Philosophy at the University of Iceland.

CHRISTIAN TORNAU is Professor of Classics at the University of Würzburg.

MIIRA TUOMINEN is University Lecturer in Philosophy at the University of Jyväskylä.

Introduction

Human beings are distinguished from other kinds of living creature by, among other things, the fact that we not only live our lives, but do so *reflectively*. We can ask such questions as: 'Is my life a good life?' 'What makes a life a good life?' 'What can be done to make my life good/better?' Thus, being reflective, we humans live our lives under an idea of the significance and value of that life. This reflective idea is not theoretical but *practical*. It is not merely a view about some fact in the world, namely, the life lived—it is both constitutive and expressive of the very life it is about. The way I live my life is shaped by the idea I have of my life—of what it is and of what it should be. By living my life in this way, on the basis of this idea, I am in fact endorsing this idea; thus this idea is also *normative*: it involves an answer to the question 'How should I live?' (or 'How should we live?').

Now, all human beings are in a fundamental way reflective in this way, but not all humans engage in reflection as an articulate and reasoned activity. It is one thing to have a fairly inarticulate and implicit idea of one's life and its value, and quite another to actively engage in reflective reasoning about one's life, with the aim of arriving at an idea of how life should be lived that is articulate and well founded, and therefore capable of being justified and defended in argument. Such active reflective reasoning is a central concern in ethics.

Ethics is part of philosophy, and just as philosophy in general originated in ancient Greece, so did ethics. Indeed, a case can be made for the claim that ethics and the quest for the good life is the central part of philosophy in antiquity. Thus, the other parts of philosophy, such as metaphysics and physics, epistemology and logic, are seen as somehow subservient or supplementary to the central concern about the good life. Some scholars have gone further and emphasized the way philosophy, and not only the part of it that we call ethics, is a way of life—indeed, the fulfilment of human nature.[1]

The more systematic tradition of ancient philosophical ethics starts with Plato and Aristotle, and continues through the Hellenistic schools and then into late ancient thought of the commentators and the Neoplatonist schools. In this collection we take

---

[1] See Hadot (2004), Horn (1998), and Cooper (2012) for various, in part opposed versions of this idea.

up important aspects of this tradition all the way down to Augustine, who, despite being earlier than many authors regarded as belonging to late antiquity, occupies a transitional position between the ancient and medieval worlds.

When reflecting on life and the question how it should be lived, one very natural and common notion suggests itself: *happiness*. We want to live a good life, and happiness seems to offer itself as a concept well suited to capture what we are after when we give voice to such an aspiration, and when we reflect on the quality of our life. Ancient ethicists mostly agree in taking happiness to provide the highest good or ultimate end in a human life, a good such that it is the achievement of it that makes life good—indeed, supremely and completely good or valuable/choiceworthy. Thus ancient ethics centered on the notion of happiness (*eudaimonia* in Greek, *beatitudo* and *felicitas* in Latin), and is therefore appropriately described as *eudaemonist ethics*. All—or most, at any rate—philosophers and philosophical schools agreed that happiness was the proper content of the good life.[2] Moreover, they took themselves to be following common sense or the reputable opinions in this. But, as Aristotle points out, to call the highest good or ultimate end 'happiness' is not yet to solve a problem but merely to give it a name, which raises a more substantial question: What is happiness? (*EN* I 4, 1095a18–20) Ancient ethics can be seen as a systematic attempt to answer this question.

Today the questions 'What is a good life?' and 'How do we become happy?' are encountered in all sorts of public and private discourse. They are the material for a large part of the literature on the self-help and alternative shelves of any bookstore. Radio and television programmes highlight the problem of making the right choices in life and address its philosophical and ethical implications. The question of the good life has even reached the political domain; in several countries policies have been proposed and implemented to monitor and promote 'gross national happiness'.[3] In this respect, therefore, modern thinkers share the ancient ethicists' concern with the question of the good life.

The problems concerning happiness have not continuously been at the centre of ethics and philosophy in our tradition, however. As mentioned already, even in ancient thought one may question whether the concern with the good life and happiness was the only, let alone primary, concern for ethicists. Moreover, an important development took place in the Christian Middle Ages, especially in the thirteenth to the sixteenth centuries, with the emergence of the natural law tradition. Here the conception of happiness and the good life was transformed as ethics and politics became a matter of living in obedience to the natural law. This law, whose

---

[2] Exceptions seem to be the Cyrenaics, a minor 'Socratic' school, active mainly in the fourth century BC, focused on what Julia Annas calls 'episodes of pleasure' (1993: 426), and the Cynics, another 'Socratic' school that survived into Christian times, that seemed to reject the whole project of looking for an over-arching end for one's life.

[3] See e.g. the website <http://www.grossnationalhappiness.com>, as well as <http://en.wikipedia.org/wiki/Gross_national_happiness>.

obligatory power was taken ultimately to rest on the authority of God, commands us to conduct ourselves in certain ways, but since God is benevolent, these ways will also be conducive to the realization of our own nature and welfare. So we are, in a sense, commanded to pursue (what in fact will be to) our own good, that is, happiness. Thus, while the conception of the content of proper human conduct may not have changed, the ground or justification for this conception had certainly altered.[4] Arguably, already in late antiquity a significant change had taken place: both pagan and Christian thinkers placed 'the best life' outside the embodied, social human life. A consequence of this is that the strong bonds between virtue, understood as the perfection of the embodied life, and happiness were loosened: it is no longer possible to maintain that the truly happy life simply is the virtuous life, so understood. At least some further theorizing is needed, for example, an argument to the effect that the virtuous will be rewarded. (This is discussed by Tornau in chapter 14.)

At any rate, with the advent of modern philosophy in the seventeenth century,[5] both the content and the ground of ethical thought were altered: the notion of morality was separated from the notion of the good or happiness, and the conception of the good or happiness was itself transformed. One may speculate on why the latter happened.[6] One explanation seems to be the emergence of two broad movements in political and moral philosophy since the eighteenth century: *liberalism* and *utilitarianism*. Both are built upon a rejection of an objectivist and perfectionist view of the human good that characterized ancient thought on happiness and the good life.[7] Utilitarianism identifies the human good with happiness understood in terms of the satisfaction of each person's desires, preferences, and ambitions, and the supervenient positive psychological experience, while liberalism insists on each individual's inviolable right to shape his or her own life in the free pursuit of happiness.[8] Both schools of thought thus tend to oppose the notion of objective standards of happiness.

Recently things have changed again, however, and a new research discipline has emerged: happiness studies.[9] This discipline is interdisciplinary and originates partly in psychology and partly in the social sciences, with somewhat different, but increasingly convergent, tendencies. In psychology there is a turn away from a focus on psychic problems such as anxiety, depression, neuroses, and so on towards the

---

[4] For accounts of this development, see Schneewind (1998); Irwin (2007) and (2008); Darwall (2013).

[5] An earlier date for the shift has been suggested by, e.g. Irwin (2008), who argues that Scotus' criticism of Aquinas was crucial in this development.

[6] For surveys of the history of happiness as an intellectual topic, see White (2005) and McMahon (2006).

[7] This holds for utilitarianism in its 'purest' versions, such as Bentham and Sidgwick, not Mill, whose version of utilitarianism contains objectivist and perfectionist elements.

[8] Cf. the second section of the US Declaration of Independence: 'We hold these truths to be self-evident, that all men are created equal, that they are endowed by their creator with certain unalienable Rights, that among these are Life, Liberty, and *the pursuit of Happiness*.'

[9] Cf. *The Journal of Happiness Studies*, started in 2000.

positive aspects of our psychic life: enjoyment, pleasure, 'flow', satisfaction—in short, aspects of what we call happiness. In the social sciences a parallel recognition comes when one realizes that the notion of welfare, which is of central importance both as a measure for the quality and success of a society, and as the aim of political work, has been surprisingly understudied. While happiness used to be understood as a kind of positive feeling or experience, and welfare as the social aggregate of individual happiness, both these assumptions have started to look suspect, or at least in need of argument.

Despite differences in approach and claims, there are clear common points among the participants in this research. In what is perhaps the most comprehensive philosophical survey of modern research on happiness, Daniel Haybron identifies what he calls the 'Assumption of Personal Autonomy' as the fundamental, shared assumption underlying this modern research.[10] The idea here is that each individual is the sole expert on his or her own happiness. This is supported by two other assumptions: 'Transparency', according to which the individual's actual state of happiness is easily accessible to him or her, and 'Aptitude', the idea that people are on the whole capable of making the choices required to secure their own happiness. The Assumption of Personal Autonomy, which is a psychological thesis about the nature of happiness, is then often coupled with a political thesis, 'Liberal Optimism', which claims that the best political strategy for promoting happiness and welfare in a population is to let people decide for themselves, without any paternalistic interference from the government or other authorities.

Subjectivism and liberalism, or Transparency and Aptitude combined with Liberal Optimism, have thus continued to dominate the approach to happiness to this day.[11] The assumption is that any viable theory of happiness or well-being must satisfy the 'experience requirement', for happiness is a subjective phenomenon in the sense that it makes essential 'reference to the subject's attitudes and concerns', as one prominent thinker expresses it.[12]

We are thus in a peculiar situation. Happiness, well-being, or welfare has once again become a topic for academic study in psychology, social science, and philosophy, and this to an extent it has never had since antiquity. Nevertheless, as we shall see, the current approach to this topic seems to differ in many respects from the way happiness was approached in antiquity. In a nutshell the difference is that ancient ethics fails to acknowledge anything like the fundamental, shared assumptions we

[10]   Haybron (2008), 11–14. This and the next paragraph are greatly indebted to Haybron's excellent discussion.
[11]   This is not to deny any disagreement between various approaches in modern research, however. Thus it is common to distinguish between the *hedonic approach* and the *life-satisfaction approach*. On the former view, happiness is identified with certain positive or pleasant feelings and experiences, whatever the occasions or objects of these feelings and experiences may be, and a happy life is one marked by an overall surplus of positive over negative feelings. On the latter view, happiness is identified with one particular positive feeling, namely the one that has the perceived quality of our life as its object.
[12]   Sumner (1996), 43.

just saw underlying modern approaches to happiness: the ancient concept of happiness is not primarily the concept of a subjective, psychological, or experiential phenomenon. Even if so-called eudaemonism is a recognized position on the contemporary scene, most modern thinkers still tend to find the objectivist character of the ancient conceptions of happiness alien and so do not explore their potential or use these insights to criticize more subjectivist presuppositions. However, it is important to note that even though a contrast between the ancient notion of happiness as (entirely) objectivist and the modern one as (entirely) subjectivist is instructive, it is somewhat simplified.[13]

This volume contains a wide range of studies of ancient discussions of happiness and the good life. Our motivation for collecting this volume is twofold. The first and immediate motivation is to give the readers a sense of how ancient thinkers approached the topic, and in particular how they thought about happiness not only as *a* practical end or value, but as the highest good and ultimate end of all human endeavour. While there are several good general discussions of ancient ethics, there is none, to our knowledge, that takes the notion of happiness as its primary focus. The closest we come is Julia Annas (1993), but even here the focus seems to be more on virtue and morality than on happiness as such. Moreover, while the eudaemonist nature of ancient ethics is well recognized, discussions tend to focus almost exclusively on Aristotle. This is not surprising, given Aristotle's undeniable canonical status, but it has had the cost of making ancient eudaemonist thinking seem more homogeneous than it in fact is. So it is part of our purpose to show that even if the attention devoted to Aristotle's account is reasonable, his account is not the only one, and there are in fact important differences and developments within ancient philosophical reflections on happiness.

Secondly, we are convinced that there is a lot to be learnt today concerning the nature and content of happiness from a proper understanding of the ancient debates. Above all we believe that a deeper appreciation of the complexity and subtlety of the fundamentally objectivist ancient approaches can prove fertile for modern discussions. It may, for example, make us see that our own 'official' approach may not be so unambiguously subjectivist as we may be inclined to think; there may be objectivist strands of our conception of happiness that tend to go unnoticed when we explicitly reflect on the topic.

A further motivation for considering ancient views of happiness derives from the challenges to modern moral philosophy presented in recent decades. It has been argued, for example, that modern ethical theories are 'schizophrenic'.[14] This is because they introduce a necessary gap between motivation and reason: if moral reasons cannot be self-interested, why would anyone be motivated to act morally?[15]

---

[13] See, e.g. Kraut (1979).   [14] In Stocker's (1976) famous expression.

[15] Stocker argues, in his controversial paper, that modern hedonism, utilitarianism, and deontology all suffer from this schizophrenia because they do not manage to incorporate the notion of a person into the

Given that there is a common consensus in ancient ethics that happiness is our ultimate goal, no gap seems to arise between the quest for morality (virtue) and the motivation to act. From this point of view, it is important to consider how exactly the quest for the good life—as both an ethical and a happy one—is articulated in various ancient schools.[16]

Similarly, even though it is common to take the ancient notion of happiness as objectivist and as pertaining to a whole life, in contrast to a modern, more episodic and subjectivist one, several of the contributions in this collection (by Fossheim (chapter 5), Lear (6), Schniewind (11), and Emilsson (12) in particular) to some extent challenge this view, thereby creating an opening for renewed appreciation of continuity with and reflection on current preconceptions. To articulate the contrast between ancient and contemporary conceptions of happiness in terms of the distinction between objectivist and subjectivist conceptions is too crude and potentially misleading because the term 'subjective' can mean different things. On the one hand, by describing happiness as a subjective affair we may mean that each person is the sole arbiter on what counts has happiness for him- or herself: if I say that for me happiness consists in watching sports on television, for instance, nobody is in a position to question that this is happiness for me. No ancient philosopher came close to accepting such a claim, however. On the other hand, there is another sense of 'subjective' according to which the subjective is what relates to experience or the inner mental state of a person. The later post-Aristotelian ancient thinkers generally thought that happiness is subjective in this latter sense without thereby admitting it to be subjective in the former sense. And even Plato and Aristotle recognize an experiential element in happiness, although they do not identify happiness with a particular kind of experience.

Thus, we believe that our collection can both help students of ancient ethics get a better sense of the complexity and variety of ancient approaches and positions on happiness and the good life, and also that modern research, as well as practice, may be conceptually and morally enriched by exposure to the ancient discussions. In the following, we go through some of the most important features of ancient eudaemonist ethics. The aim is to get a preliminary grasp on the contours of ancient ethical discussions of happiness, as a background to the studies that follow. Roughly, we can group these aspects of *eudaimonia* under five headings: (1) *eudaimonia* and 'happiness, (2) *eudaimonia* and virtue, (3) *eudaimonia* and reason, (4) *eudaimonia* and community, and (5) *eudaimonia* and morality.

---

theories, and this is why these theories cannot be directly lived by (1976: 459–61)—or, if one does live by these theories, one cannot achieve the goods of love and friendship, for example. (Cf. this volume, p. 21.)

[16] Annas (1993) makes a strong case for taking ancient ethics as moral theories in a recognizably modern sense, despite the conceptual prominence of the quest for happiness.

1 *Eudaimonia* and Happiness

Aristotle's ethics is generally regarded as the canonical expression of ancient eudaemonist ethics. In his discussion of happiness, Aristotle makes the point that even though everyone agrees that the highest good is *eudaimonia*, there is no consensus on what in fact deserves this name (cf. as discussed earlier). Therefore, ethics must clarify what *eudaimonia* really is, and to do so in a way that will be of practical value.

The term '*eudaimonia*' is usually translated as 'happiness', but this may be misleading.[17] As we have already indicated, in modern thought and language the term 'happiness' and its equivalents tend to be understood as denoting some kind of positive experience or feeling. (In this respect, modern 'happiness studies', as outlined above, for the most part reflect ordinary beliefs.) This experience may be of shorter or longer duration, which means that the experience of happiness can range from momentary feelings of joy or elation to a more enduring contentment or satisfaction with life in general.

Clearly this subjective aspect is not absent from Plato's and Aristotle's conception of *eudaimonia*, but it is secondary to the objective aspect: *eudaimonia* is a *successful* life, *eudaimonia* is what makes a life *valuable* or *worth living*.[18] This life will then surely also (normally, at least) be experienced in a positive way by the person living it, but the notion of *eudaimonia* is primarily the notion of the ethical quality or value of the life, not of the way this life feels. That is why Aristotle can identify *eudaimonia* with living and doing well—*eudaimonia* is understood as a certain kind of *activity* (namely the virtuous one) or *life*, not as the experience of this life.[19]

Etymologically, the term *eudaimonia* is composed of *daimōn*, 'divine spirit', and the prefix *eu*, 'good'. In its traditional use the term would thus mean something like 'blessed with a good spirit' or 'guardian angel'. The idea is that *eudaimonia* is a matter of *success* or *good fortune* in life. This idea has several aspects. First, an individual would succeed in a certain respect, for example, by gaining wealth or political power, by fostering a great and successful family, by doing his city a great service (e.g. laying down one's life in battle), by gaining fame and glory, by winning athletic contests.[20] Secondly, the term '*eudaimonia*' would primarily denote this success, not the experience that such success might bring along with it.[21] Thirdly, the success or prosperity

---

[17] See the classic account in Kraut (1979). This is what led some interpreters to adopt the alternative translation 'human flourishing'; see Cooper (1975), 89f with note 1 for discussion. Kraut argues that we should retain the translation 'happiness' so as not to conceal that there is a genuine disagreement between the ancient and modern conceptions.

[18] Cf. e.g. Plato, *Rep.* IX 580a ff; Aristotle, *EN* I 8.

[19] *Eudaimonia* as equivalent to 'living well [*eu zēn*]' and 'doing well [*eu prattein*]': I 4, 1095a18–20. *Eudaimonia* as 'activity of the soul [*psuchēs energeia*]': I 7, 1098a16.

[20] For various aspects of this, see, e.g. the contributions to the same project as the papers in the present volume, published in *Symbolae Osloenses* 85 (2011), especially those by Andersen, Cairns, Dewald, and Maravela.

[21] Cf. note 17 above.

of the agent was always taken to be precarious; according to the so-called 'Principle of Alternation', no mortal could enjoy anything more than momentary good fortune, so one should always be prepared for the worst, even—indeed, especially—in good times.[22] Fourthly, the traditional conception of *eudaimonia* also included an idea of *divine power and paradigm*. The gods were not only the cause of whatever good fortune man may enjoy, but they also represented the model by reference to which such success was conceived and measured. We live at the mercy of the gods, but our ideal of the good life is the divine life. The idea of *eudaimonia* as *ideal prosperity*, as a god-like life, runs through Greek thought from beginning to end. (Svavarsson discusses this more fully in chapter 1.) Finally, to the extent that it is possible for humans to gain some measure of control over their own life circumstances, this would be through the development of *technē*, craft or expertise, that is, the ability to manipulate reality in a knowledgeable and controlled way for the promotion of the human good. Thus, there was a strong connection, evident in both poets and philosophers, between the idea of *eudaimonia* and the notion of *technē*.[23]

However, the term *eudaimonia* is ambiguous, as just indicated by the phrase '*eudaimonia* is a successful life, *eudaimonia* is what makes a life valuable or worth living'. On the one hand, the term denotes either the happy or successful *life*, the life that is the best one for a human being to live, or, alternatively, the *quality* of this life: its being *eudaimōn*. But, on the other hand, the term also denotes a specific *end or value* within a life, which end or value is such that when it is realized, that life thereby becomes *eudaimōn*: successful, good, worth pursuing.[24] *Eudaimonia* is frequently talked about as if it were only used in the former sense, but the second one seems at least as prevalent. In fact, the second sense may very well be the most important one for ethics, in that it is the notion of *eudaimonia* as a specific end in life that provides (1) the focus for people's *life aspiration*, and for the debate about what this aspiration ought to be, and hence (2) the *criterion* or *ground* for evaluating the quality or degree of success of the life in question. *Eudaimonia* in the first sense depends on the attainment of *eudaimonia* in the second sense. The question, of course, is what *eudaimonia* in this second sense is, that is, what a life's being *eudaimōn* depends on—what that principle or cause is that can make a life *eudaimōn*.

Thus it is clear that the question about the nature of *eudaimonia* is also the question about a choice of life. This is clear already in Presocractic times,[25] where the legendary 'choice of Heracles' depicts this fundamental human predicament.[26] The same idea of a choice facing humans is found elsewhere as well, for example, in

---

[22] Cf. Cairns (2011).   [23] See Heinimann (1961), Kube (1969), Roochnik (1996).

[24] Following Broadie (1991), 26–7. See also Cooper (1999), 219–20; (2004), 289; Broadie (1991), 26–7; Lear (2004), 1 for discussion.

[25] de Heer (1968) gives a useful, though non-philosophical, survey of terminology for and conceptions of success in life in ancient Greece to the end of the fifth century.

[26] See Xenophon (*Memorabilia* 2.1.21–34), who recounts how Heracles was faced with a choice between the life of pleasure and the life of virtue. (He chose the latter.)

Thucydides, where different lives are set up against each other.[27] In the philosophers, this choice is prevalent. A paradigmatic passage is Plato's *Republic*, IX 580a ff, where Socrates makes a direct comparison and ranking of various candidates for being the best life.[28] Similarly, after stating that everybody agrees on *eudaimonia* as the name of the highest good or ultimate end in life, but not on the nature of this good, Aristotle goes on to say that there are three lives that stand out as reputable or respectable and initially plausible answers to the question: the life of pleasure, the life of political activity, and the life of theory or philosophy (*EN* I 5). Similar sets of alternatives can be found throughout ancient thought, down through Roman times and into late antiquity and early Christian thought.

To the extent that the notion of *eudaimonia* is combined with a belief in the Principle of Alternation, the resulting outlook on human life and happiness will tend to be rather pessimistic: no matter what one does, the prospects are dim since how one fares is largely beyond one's own control. Indeed, one may even take the further step into fatalism if one believes that one's fortune is entirely up to the whims of the gods, and thus unrelated to the way one conducts oneself. However, to the extent that one rejects the Principle of Alternation and takes the way one fares in life to be subject to (at least some significant measure of) one's own control, thanks to the development of *technē*, one's conception of *eudaimonia* will amount to a conception of a particular *form of life*, an entire way of living, organized around a certain ultimate end that one aspires to achieve and whose achievement makes life *eudaimōn* or successful. Such a positive or optimistic conception of *eudaimonia* gradually develops in classical times and is reflected in philosophers such as Plato and Aristotle. Thus, when Aristotle raises the question what *eudaimonia* as the highest good consists in, this is the question which kind of life is the best and therefore the one that one ought to aspire to.[29] Achieving *eudaimonia* amounts to *success* in the project which is one's life, which is why regarding someone as *eudaimōn*, unlike describing someone as happy in the modern sense, is not to describe a psychological fact—it is to make a heavily loaded normative (ethical) judgement. Thus, to the noun *eudaimonia* there corresponds a verb *eudaimonizein*, 'to felicitate'. That is why 'regarding someone as *eudaimōn* is more like ascribing a status, or applauding. It is to imply that the person is admirable, even enviable, an exemplar of life at its best.'[30] It has often been argued that the Stoic notion of *eudaimonia* is particularly unrealistic in this respect: that attaining the status of the wise person is simply outside the reach of

---

[27] See e.g. Rusten (1985) for a brief discussion of the choice of life in Thucydides.

[28] Plato conducts a similar comparison and ranking of lives in the *Philebus* 64c–66c.

[29] Cf. the terms used for the alternatives: 'the *life* of consumption', 'the political *life*', 'the *life* of reflection' (I 5, 1095b17, 23, 1096a4; our emphases). Plato does not use the term '*eudaimonia*' the way Aristotle does, but he is clear that the most important question in ethics is 'How one ought to live', and this is the question which form of life is the best, i.e. what *eudaimonia* consists in; see e.g. *Gorg.* 492d; *Rep.* I 352d.

[30] Broadie (2002), 12.

normal human beings and thus the whole notion of virtue is not feasible. Katerina Ierodiakonou addresses this claim in chapter 9 and argues that the Stoic ideal of a sage is no more idealistic and unrealistic than the virtuous person Aristotle describes, for example. From this perspective, all ancient theories have their respective ideal-izations of the virtuous person as an ideal that refers to the best status that a human being can achieve and that such an ideal also has practical value in terms of guiding our action towards that ideal.

We have emphasized the objective nature of the notion of *eudaimonia* and how this makes it different from the modern notion of happiness. However, as noted, Plato and Aristotle recognize an experiential component in happiness and the post-Aristotelian thinkers generally tend to identify happiness with some kind of internal state. For one thing, some thinkers were hedonists, that is, they identified *eudaimonia* with pleasure (*hēdonē*), which is clearly an experiential phenomenon. These thinkers include the Epicureans as well as the 'minor' schools of the Cynics and the Cyrenaics. (The Epicureans, however, did not doubt that their identification of happiness with pleasure is objectively valid nor that there are objective truths about the nature and sources of pleasure.) The Stoic notion of *eupatheia*, the 'good feelings' that charac-terize the Stoic wise person (who alone is happy, according to the Stoics), also clearly contain experiential elements. It is reasonable to hold, however, that even in these thinkers the positive subjective experience is not what *defines* the concept of *eu-daimonia* but, rather, what provides the real *reference* for the term '*eudaimonia*', to be discovered through philosophical reflection. *Eudaimonia* is still the concept of the highest good, the achievement of which makes for a successful life; the innovation is that what makes a life successful is the achievement of a certain kind of subjective experience or psychological state.

Furthermore, even in philosophers who are not hedonists—that is, in the other two main Hellenistic schools (Stoicism and Scepticism) as well as in late antiquity—we see a shift of emphasis from (external) activity and practical success towards internal states of mind, such as *ataraxia*, 'tranquillity' or 'unperturbedness'. (See Svavarsson, chapter 10.) The idea here is that although it is by no means unimportant what one does, and how and to what extent one succeeds in this, what matters is that one's life is free of disturbance, anxiety, and the like, which are clearly experiential states.

A difficulty may be raised concerning the notion of success involved in the concept of *eudaimonia*. If *eudaimonia* is conceived of as the successful perform-ance of a certain task, namely, that of living a human life, then in what does this success consist? Such talk of the good life in terms of success easily invites thinking of virtue as a kind of art or craft, a *technē*. Now, crafts are typically defined in terms of certain external results. But the achievement of these external results tends to depend not merely on the agent and his competence, but also on external factors, referred to under the heading 'luck'. And this highlights a possible ambiguity in the notion of success. For when is a craftsman's action successful? Two answers are possible: (1) when it constitutes the perfectly correct and competent performance of his craft, regardless of whether the external result follows, and (2) when the external result reliably follows. This ambiguity, and the analogy of virtue with craft, make evident two ways of thinking of *eudaimonia* as success, of which the former internalizes the notion—although without psychologizing it to become a matter of mere experience.[31]

The internalization of happiness that we see in post-Aristotelian philosophers is accompanied by a rejection of the approach characteristic of Aristotle that takes happiness to pertain to life as a whole. (The exact meaning of this Aristotelian claim is discussed by Lear in chapter 6 and Emilsson in chapter 12.) Whatever Aristotle may exactly mean, however, the post-Aristotelian thinkers—Epicureans, Stoics, and Plotinus—do not share this 'life as a whole' view. They insist that happiness does not depend on a certain temporal, narrative structure of life but only on the state of the individual at a given time.[32] This does not mean that they thought that the potentially happy person will often vacillate between happiness and non-happiness, not to say unhappiness. All of them agreed, despite quite different conceptions of what happiness consists in, that it is a stable condition. For the Stoics and Plotinus this follows from the fact that virtue is a stable trait; the Epicureans do not speak in such terms but clearly they too think that once internalized the Epicurean outlook on life is stable.

In short, we see that there is clearly development taking place in Epicureanism, Stoicism and Neoplatonism away from a focus on external features towards understanding *eudaimonia* as in one way or other a matter internal to the mind.

2 *Eudaimonia* and Virtue

Most philosophical schools in post-Socratic antiquity agreed that a vital prerequisite for *eudaimonia* is virtue (*aretē*), that is, in order for one to be happy, one needs to be virtuous. However, the articulation and further implications of this claim were (and are) debated, and the schools also diverged as to whether virtue is not only necessary but also sufficient for happiness. Despite the variety of views of what exactly virtue and happiness are, the connection between the two was widely accepted, with some exceptions. The Cynics, for example, rejected general theorizing of virtue and the Cyrenaics seem to have denied the quest for happiness as a distinctive final end.[33] Further, to the extent that the Pyrrhonian sceptics sought happiness, they did not connect it with virtue of character but rather with the sceptical suspension of belief.

---

[31] See Striker (1991), section 3, for a discussion of this problem in Stoicism. Aristotle indicates this ambiguity and makes a distinction between *eudaimonia* and *makariotēs* ('blessedness'), i.e. the state where every virtuous undertaking achieves its external objective (see *EN* I 9–10).

[32] We find contemporary advocates of both positions: contrast Velleman (1991), who defends an Aristotelian type of position, and Strawson (2004), who defends the post-Aristotelian view.

[33] Diogenes Laertius 2.28. See also note 2 above.

What, then, is virtue? Given the assumption just explained, our understanding of how the majority of ancient philosophical schools understood happiness clearly requires some specification of the conditions that make it possible. Virtue was usually taken to be a dynamic state of the individual who has it, a disposition or attitude (*hexis*) that will make the individual act in certain ways. Happiness, on the other hand, was taken as a property of a certain kind of life, that is, as a certain kind of activity, and an individual living such a life was considered happy. As a state of the individual, virtue was not understood as a passing one—such as having one's body in a certain pose—but as remarkably persistent even to the extent that, once acquired, virtue is almost impossible to lose.

A central question with respect to those descriptions is whether or to what extent the virtue of an individual should be defined as an intellectual or cognitive state, as a certain kind of knowledge, or whether virtue requires, or can even be reduced to, non-intellectual components. While nobody (with the possible exception of the Cynics) ever advocated a view that excluded all cognitive elements from virtue, versions of a combined view were prominent in the Platonic-Aristotelian tradition.

Plato's Socrates has traditionally been saddled with the view that virtue is to be identified with knowing the good, and that wrong action is a sign of ignorance. Naturally, if one supposes that virtue is sufficient for happiness and that virtue is knowledge of the good, this implies that in order to attain virtue and thus happiness, one needs to attain knowledge of the good. Plato developed arguments along these broad outlines in several dialogues. However, the tripartite view of the soul in the *Republic* and the *Phaedrus* raises the question of how exactly the lower parts contribute to the overall functioning of the whole, and the answer to this question is disputed. In some dialogues, such as the *Philebus*, the arguments do not seem to operate on the tripartite model at all, and the view that virtue or the good is knowledge of the good yields to a view that the good should be attributed to a certain kind of life that involves a proper mixture of various elements.

Aristotle distinguished between virtues of character and intellectual virtues. The exact role of the two kinds of virtue in human happiness as presented in the *Nicomachean Ethics* is debated. The virtues of character require cognitive achievements and include a stable tendency of the lower desires to habitually 'respect' and even 'want' the proper measure. Thus, for Aristotle, knowledge is not sufficient for virtue. (Fossheim discusses the combined cognitive and non-cognitive impact of old age on Aristotelian virtue and happiness in chapter 5.) However, even the Aristotelian virtues of character require practical wisdom or intelligence (*phronēsis*) and *vice versa*: the cognitive achievement of practical intelligence only occurs in virtuous characters. Such practical wisdom or intelligence, moreover, cannot be reduced to the possession of universal moral principles but is a sort of unfailing expertise at identifying the right kind of action in varying circumstances.

An important element in the Platonic-Aristotelian theory of virtue is that a virtuous soul functions as a unity. Therefore, the dynamic forces of the non-rational animal soul need to be habituated or brought under reason's kingly rule so as to desire the same action or the same measure that reason or practical intelligence recommends. Otherwise the individual will suffer from constant motivational conflicts that do not belong to a happy life. With respect to Aristotle, this causes a particular puzzle: motivational conflict is characteristic of an akratic person who knows what is right but does not act accordingly. However, it is not clear why a vicious person would suffer from a conflict. (This problem is discussed by Grönroos in chapter 7.)

The intellectualist tradition was taken up by the Stoics who consider virtue, understood as wisdom, as sufficient for (if not identical with) happiness. The kind of knowledge or understanding characteristic of a Stoic wise person is related to what is ethically significant and includes a firm understanding of the irrelevance to happiness of the external goods. However, some knowledge of natural philosophy is also required, as well as understanding the human condition in the providential, rationally ordered cosmos. Further, Stoic wisdom includes a certain security concerning the acceptance and rejection of appearances: in addition to the knowledge the wise person has, s/he never assents to a false appearance. The ensuing tranquillity (*ataraxia*) amounts to happiness, and happiness does not depend on external circumstances. (Svavarsson takes up this theme in chapter 10.)

Building perhaps to some extent on Aristotle's distinction between virtues of character and intellectual virtues,[34] Plotinus distinguished between lower and higher virtues, the latter being theoretical—not exactly virtues of the intellect but virtues leading up to the Intellect (*Enneads* I.2). Porphyry developed Plotinus' distinction into a fourfold hierarchy consisting of two levels (political and purificatory) of lower virtue and two levels (theoretical and paradigmatic) of higher virtue, and redefined the cardinal virtues specific to each level. Both of them agreed that it is not possible to perfectly have (and exercise) the lower virtues without the higher ones, and thus theoretical virtue is, for Plotinus, a prerequisite for the virtues of the soul as described in Plato's *Republic* IV and, for Porphyry, for the virtues related to the communal life. (This is discussed by Tuominen in chapter 13.) For Plotinus, human happiness amounts to a theoretical life that, due to his view that the whole soul does not descend to the carnal life, is actually always present in us. However, even though this theoretical life as *eudaimonia* is always present in us, we normally fail to live it because we are identified with our lower soul and preoccupied with its concerns. Only when we fully understand that our true identity is with the Intellect, can we actually live the theoretical life and, thereby, enjoy happiness. (These themes are discussed by Schniewind and Emilsson in chapters 11 and 12.)

One central issue on which the views of the schools diverged was whether virtue has a constitutive role in happiness. The Platonists, Aristotelians, and Stoics agreed

---

[34] See O'Meara (2013).

that it does, whereas the Epicureans countered this consensus and instead took virtue as instrumental to happiness as pleasure, which they understood as the absence of pain. However, the Epicureans also seemed to have agreed that without virtue one is not able to reach life-long pleasure—that is, that virtue is necessary for happiness even though it does not occur as its constituent. (This is taken up by Dimas in chapter 8.)

While agreeing on the necessity of virtue for happiness, the schools could have very different articulations of what happiness is like. Consider for example the difference between the Epicureans and the Neoplatonists, for whom happiness is understood as theoretical life in an eternal atemporal activity of grasping the intelligible forms and thus being involved in the creation of the perceived reality. As regards virtue and happiness, Augustine inherits a number of tenets from the pagan eudaemonism. (See Tornau in chapter 14 for elaboration.) For instance, he agrees that Christian eschatology with its promise of eternal bliss achieves what the philosophers had only attempted. But this view does not sit well with the Stoic and Platonic tenet that virtue is a sufficient condition for happiness.

An important point of divergence among ancient schools relates to the just-mentioned question of whether virtue is sufficient for happiness. While the Stoics and to some extent the Platonists affirm its sufficiency, the Aristotelians deny this. As Aristotle famously argues in the *Nicomachean Ethics* (I 9)—followed by Aspasius in his commentary—if a virtuous person encounters many and severe misfortunes, no one in his or her right mind would consider such a person happy, whereas there is no reason to suppose that virtue is lost. A virtuous person will nobly bear even the greatest calamities, but even though virtue 'shines through' severe misfortunes, a fate like Priam's will destroy his happiness.

3 *Eudaimonia* and Reason

The strong connection between virtue and knowledge implies a certain rationalism as a peculiar feature of the mainstream of ancient philosophical accounts of human happiness or well-being.[35] By 'rationalism' we do of course not have in mind the epistemological position that reason as opposed to the senses is the sole or most important source of knowledge. Some of the ancients, the Platonists in particular, were rationalists in this sense, but this kind of rationalism is not primarily at stake here. What is intended is rather the view that a cultivated reason is the key to happiness. The preoccupation with reason that is so characteristic of much of ancient philosophy seems, at least partly, to have been motivated by concerns about what may secure human beings a good life, or at least make such a life possible. Is it wealth?

---

[35] The content of the following paragraphs on rationalism depends heavily on Frede (1996).

Good birth? Divine grace? Chance or fortune? No, said the philosophers, none of these things will do, but perfected reason will.

Socrates, more than anyone else, seems to have introduced rationalism in this sense. Although he did not profess any particular views, he insisted that the Athenians use their reason to elicit the true beliefs they hold and get rid of the false ones. Clearly he thought this was a prerequisite for leading a decent, happy life. As suggested above, the tradition after him, including Plato, Aristotle and his followers, the Stoics, and the Platonists of the early empire and late antiquity, is characterized by variations on this theme. Even the Epicureans, who in many ways deviated from the mainstream, were to some extent in the grips of this idea in so far as they suggested that human happiness depends on the right use of reason to dispel false views about life, death and the world.

The mainstream thinkers just mentioned agreed that reason is somehow central to happiness, but their views varied on exactly how it is so. As indicated, the majority believed that a cultivated reason actualized as knowledge or as dispositions to know is not only a necessary but also a sufficient condition for having a good life. As indicated, Aristotle and the Aristotelians were alone in holding that reason as such is insufficient for happiness: some external goods are needed in addition, and even a perfectly rational person may suffer calamities that deprive him or her of their happy life. The others, by contrast, thought that the fully rational person needs only what is necessary to sustain life—not in order to be happy but to live—and that his or her happiness is immune to the hard blows of fortune. The question of the sufficiency of virtue for happiness is related to the question of whether external goods are necessary for happiness or not. Further, when considering the role of external goods in a virtuous and/or happy life, we also need to ask whether it is the possession or the exercise of virtue that is crucial for happiness, and whether it is for the former or for the latter that the external goods are necessary. The rationalist tradition tended to claim that having the virtue is sufficient for happiness, whereas the Aristotelians underlined the exercise of virtue, and claimed that the external goods were necessary for the exercise of the virtues of character.

As mentioned, views also differed on the scope of mature reason: is it enough to know about human affairs, that is, to internalize the normative concepts that are central to the ethical life conceived in human terms? Socrates may have argued so, but the subsequent tradition required more: fully rational humans need to know about the basic constitution of the world and in particular about their own nature and place in it.

The role of cultivated reason in securing a good life was not taken to be merely or primarily instrumental, that is, a matter of calculating effectively the best means to achieve some end, or even of identifying the reasonable ends to be pursued. The life of reason—the philosophical or theoretical life—was seen as having intrinsic value and as constituting the best kind of life. This was evidently Plato's view in the *Republic* and many other dialogues, though qualified in the *Philebus*. Aristotle, the

Stoics, and Plotinus also advocated such a view, the latter holding a particularly strong version of it. (See Rabbås, in chapter 4, for a discussion of Aristotle on this.)

Towards the end of the Hellenistic period and in late antiquity we see a weakening of the philosophers' faith in reason. There are undoubtedly many and complex reasons for this, both internal to philosophy and others. In so far as philosophy is concerned, the sceptical philosophical movements, whose agenda consisted primarily in questioning reason's ability to discover truths, must have contributed to undermining faith in the power of reason. In late antiquity, both pagans and Christians also came to regard certain ancient texts as divinely inspired authorities. Rationalism did not disappear entirely but it underwent significant changes in that reason was seen to need divine or at least extra-rational inspiration as its starting point. Once such inspiration was granted, however, reason could ascertain the truths on its own accord. This obviously constitutes a major revision of the claims of classical eudaemonism, which was much more optimistic about reason's ability to secure happiness.

One additional common thread that runs through several rather different ancient accounts of virtue and happiness from early on is that the happy human life is in some sense divine.[36] The Socrates of Plato's *Theaetetus* claims that human happiness (*anthrōpinē eudaimonia*) requires a flight from the sensible world because it is not possible to avoid all evils here (175c5–176b1). This flight is then identified with assimilation to god as far as it is (humanly) possible (176b1–2). At the very end of the *Nicomachean Ethics* Aristotle develops a somewhat similar idea in distinguishing between the properly human virtues, and the happiness particular to their exercise, and the divine theoretical virtue that transcends our human nature (X 7–8). In other words, in order to perfectly realize the human function, and thus the human good, human beings, paradoxically, need to transcend their strictly human nature. Even though Epicurus identified happiness with pleasure properly defined and did not follow Aristotle in positing divine theoretical virtue, he also endorsed a view according to which happy human life in a significant sense embodies the enjoyment that is characteristic to gods, blessed immortal beings who are not concerned or preoccupied with mundane affairs.

Some schools also combined the aspect of divinity with the idea that when human beings realize their highest potential, they are also involved in the co-creation of reality. The perfect rationality of the Stoic sage is a property of god (Zeus) as the reason that creates and guides reality. A variation of this general assumption is also found in Plotinus, who understands the creation of external reality as the Intellect's attempt to understand the highest principle, the One. Since the Intellect understands the One imperfectly, the result is its diversification into multiplicity. Human beings also take part in this diversification when they are engaged in the activity of the Intellect, and thus human beings also contribute to the 'creation' of the perceived

---

[36] See Svavarsson, this volume ch. 1.

reality that has its source in the overflowing abundance of the One. Thus a happy human being who fully realizes all his or her potential is not just involved in theoretical activity but also in the creation of the world.

4 *Eudaimonia* and Community

The notion of happiness as pertaining to human life in a (political) community is of course central in Plato's *Republic* where, in a sense, the whole city is the subject of *eudaimonia*. The communal nature of human happiness is also present in the myth of the *Statesman*, but it is in Aristotle that we find a more systematic although controversial treatment of the topic. Therefore, taking Aristotle as our starting point again, he emphasizes that the perfectly good life of *eudaimonia* is a 'self-sufficient' or 'complete' (*autarkēs*) life. But then he makes clear, in the same breath, that this life is not a solitary life for the individual, but a life lived together with others in a community (*EN* I 2, 1094b7–11; 7, 1097b8–13). This may come as a surprise, and the proper understanding of this has caused a lot of puzzlement among scholars (as it seems to do for Aristotle himself; cf. IX 9). It may be useful to divide the issue into two parts, since the communal life may be located at the level of (a) friendship (*philia*) as well as (b) political society (*polis*).

Friendship (philia)

A conspicuous feature of ancient discussions concerning happiness is the prominence given to discussions of friendship and its value. Thus, Plato devotes a whole dialogue (*Lysis*) to this topic, and Aristotle spends two entire books (VIII and IX) of the *Nicomachean Ethics* on friendship. Among later writers, we find Cicero devoting an entire work, *De amicitia*, to the topic, and it is generally taken as central to the good or happy life even when not made the primary subject of individual works.[37] It is an interesting question why the ancients put so much weight on friendship, for the topic has dropped out of ethical thought since the early modern era.[38]

The terms *philia* and *philos* are normally translated as 'friendship' and 'friend' but this can sometimes be misleading. When we talk of friendship, we tend to talk about an emotionally charged relation between people who have more or less deliberately chosen to enter into and maintain the relationship. The Greeks would certainly include such relationships, and even regard them as paradigmatic of *philia*, but the extension of their term was considerably wider. It is reasonable to take the term *philia* to cover a field of concentric circles representing various degrees of interpersonal

---

[37] See e.g. Seneca, *Moral Epistles* 3 and 9; Epictetus, *Discourses* 2.22.

[38] This does not mean, of course, that friendship has ceased to be of importance to people; we are here talking about the place of friendship in philosophical reflection. One may wonder why friendship has dropped out of philosophy. A speculative answer: as happiness came to be conceived of in subjective terms, and reduced to a private matter, friendship fell beneath the radar of moral and political philosophy.

relationship, ranging from the deepest and most intimate to the more superficial and impersonal.[39] But we can also identify the conceptual core, as it were, of the notion of *philia* in the ideas of loyalty, commitment, reliability, and community, rather than in emotional attachment and personal sympathy. The relation of *philia* is, in a wide sense, a moral relation, defined in terms of a certain community of actions and ends, as well as of corresponding obligations and entitlements.[40] Even so, however, the notion also had emotional connotations: friendship was perceived as deeply satisfactory, and it involved such emotional bonds as empathy and sympathy.

The important issue in the present context is why friendship should be a part of a happy or *eudaimōn* life. This may seem obvious since most (normal) people in fact value friends more than almost anything else. But ancient ethicists, starting with Aristotle (at least), emphasized that the *eudaimōn* life was a complete or self-sufficient life, in need of nothing (*EN* I 7, 1097b6–16). So how could a person who is *eudaimōn* need others to make his life more complete? To the extent that the best life was identified as the life of wisdom and theoretical contemplation, this problem might seem to find a solution, for this activity is one that one could arguably claim might be carried out in splendid isolation, and such that association with others, even—perhaps especially—friends, would merely represent sources of distraction. But the philosophers discussing the topic of friendship emphasize not only human imperfection and need for others, but also the way friendship can extend the self. A person with friends can accomplish more because his friends can extend himself so that he can do things he could not have done had he been alone. And 'what comes about through our friends in a way comes about through us'.[41] Moreover, there are several things we are clearly better able to do in the company of friends, such as play, develop our character, and engage in politics. Finally, Aristotle claims that living with a friend enables one to better know oneself.

Later authors were faced with the fact that Aristotle's views in particular were closely connected to the cultural practices of a Greek *polis*, and this also affected his notion of friendship. In his commentary on the *Nicomachean Ethics* from the early second century CE, Aspasius (briefly discussed by Tuominen in chapter 13) recognizes this and makes some moves to show that Aristotle's views of friendship can be transposed into the social and political context of imperial Rome. For example, overthrowing a tyrant—a paradigm of a virtuous act after Cicero—is only possible with help from friends (*In Eth. Nic.* 24.9–11).

Political community (polis)

Friendship is a special case of community (*koinōnia*), for in a friendship we live together with one or more others. And it seems essential to human beings to be living

---

[39] For this idea, see Blundell (1989), 39ff. See Konstan (1997) for a general survey of friendship in antiquity.
[40] Cf. Bordt (1998), 42–4.   [41] *EN* III 3, 1112b27–8.

in community with others. However, there are many other animals that are social, in that they live their characteristic lives in groups that act in concert.[42] Humans are unique in that their way of living in a community is distinct from that of the other social animals. Again, Aristotle provides the classic statement, that 'the human being is more of a political [or social: *politikon*] animal than bees or any other gregarious animals' because 'the human being is the only animal who has the gift of speech [*logos*]' (*Politics* I 2, 1253a7–18), that is, the ability to represent to themselves what they are doing, what they are aiming at, and why, and what they need to do in order to achieve what they are aiming at. Aristotle takes this to amount to a conception of justice. Hence, unlike animal associations, a human association or community is rationally organized, and what organizes it is a conception of the just (*to dikaion*), or justice.

To the extent that it is part of human nature to participate in a political community, actually living in such a community will be a necessary condition for—indeed, part of—the achievement of human *eudaimonia*. Here it is important to keep in mind that the purpose or end of political activity—that is, both of the common project of politics, and of each individual's participation in this project—is this activity itself. Political activity is not (primarily) a means to some end given prior to and independently of politics, such as securing the welfare of individuals, but, rather, an essential part of being human.[43] It is only through political activity (living the political life) that many of our most important human ends are made possible, and it is only through politics, that is, rationally organizing our life in common, that we can fully realize ourselves as human.

The political life is constituted by laws, whose principle is justice. Aristotle says that the laws, and in particular the constitution, is a determination (or interpretation, as we might say) of justice in and by that community.[44] Therefore the systematic development of the principles of political community is a necessary and essential part of working out what the happy (*eudaimōn*) life for a human being is. Which principles these are, and exactly how they are to be related to the ultimate end of *eudaimonia*, is one of the major questions addressed by ancient thinkers. (See, most directly, the chapters by Annas (2) and Dimas (3), but indirectly also Rabbås (4) and Tuominen (13), on this.)

5 *Eudaimonia* and Morality

Ancient ethical philosophy is eudaemonistic. That is to say, ancient ethicists agree that there is such a thing as a *highest good* or *ultimate end* to be pursued in action,

---

[42] See *History of Animals* I 1, 488a7f: 'social [*politika*] animals are those that have as their function [*ergon*] some single thing that they all do together.' (See all of 487b33–488a14.)

[43] See Cooper (2010) for an argument along these lines. Here we see another obvious difference from most modern conceptions, although so-called 'communitarian', as well as 'republican', positions may be exceptions.

[44] See e.g. *Politics* III 1, 1274b38; 3, 1276b1–15; IV 1, 1289a15–18.

and that this good or end is *eudaimonia* or happiness. Their main task, as they see it, is to work out a valid answer to the question 'What is *eudaimonia*?' Given this task, ancient philosophers develop their ethical theories by incorporating concepts such as *virtue, practical wisdom, pleasure, friendship*, and *justice* within the eudaemonistic framework. Their theories differ, sometimes significantly, but they all start from the same point and develop within the same framework defined by that starting-point.

Now, these notions—'virtue' and 'justice', in particular—seem to be moral notions, notions that by themselves contain moral standards or norms as to how we should act, whether we are so inclined or not. In particular, justice also contains a dimension of how we should conduct ourselves towards others, and such a dimension is certainly recognizable as specifically moral from the point of view of most modern moral theories. However, it is unclear exactly how ancient ethics with its focus on *eudaimonia* fits within moral philosophy as we understand and practice it today. Moral philosophy today is concerned with articulating and justifying principles for deciding what to do, how we are to solve conflicts of interest arising in the course of communal life, and on what grounds we should be concerned with the welfare of each other. This project ranges from the most fundamental and general matters of principle in ethical theory to concrete, more or less realistic problems in applied ethics. But the purpose is all along to provide the grounds for making the morally right decisions.[45]

However, it is hard to see how ancient ethics has much to offer by way of moral guidance in such questions. For one thing, we search pretty much in vain for rules or injunctions telling us what to do in such situations, and the conceptual apparatus does not seem designed for that purpose. Secondly, and perhaps even more seriously, to the extent that we *can* find guidance for the conduct of our lives in the ancient ethicists, this guidance seems grounded in the wrong kind of principle. For, on ancient theories, the ethical values highlighted are all based in one ultimate value, *eudaimonia*, or happiness, and that seems to threaten to make all the ancient ethical theories varieties of egoism (the view that all actions are to be justified by reference to the agent's self-interest), which strikes most modern moral philosophers as objectionable. This discomfort with the alleged egoism of ancient ethics has spurred several attempts to exonerate the ancients, but suspicion is still lingering that there is something fundamentally wrong about the starting point of ancient ethics.[46]

---

[45] Interestingly, an exception to this tendency—where the purpose of ethics is taken to be that of providing rules for solving conflicts of interest—has developed over the past few decades: so-called 'virtue ethics'. It is noteworthy that the initial impetus, as well as much of its driving inspiration, comes from ancient ethics, especially Aristotle. However, there is reason to question the assimilation of modern virtue ethics to the ancient ethical theories. This collection also contributes to this discussion by articulating important aspects of the ancient notion of *eudaimonia*. It has also been argued that, independently and decades before Anscombe's seminal 'Modern Moral Philosophy' (1958), phenomenological ethics developed alternative analyses to modern ethics that also resemble some forms of ancient ethics, most notably Aristotle and the Stoics; see Drummond (2014) and Heinämaa (2014).

[46] Julia Annas' magisterial (1993) is witness to this. See also her contribution to this volume.

The objections to the eudaemonism of ancient ethics operate with the assumption that modern ethics is, at least on some level of generality, right about the relationship between morality and self-interest. However, in the past few decades there have been several attempts to show that this is not necessarily a correct starting point. Rather, as mentioned, it has been argued that modern ethical theory is 'schizophrenic' because it severs the connection between motivation and moral reasons. Therefore, one of the motivations for this collection is to show that there in fact is something that modern ethics and theories of happiness that proceed separately from each other can learn from ancient theories arguing for the necessary link between *eudaimonia* and morality. As Simon Blackburn puts it, to solve the issues around the question of whether, why, and how being just benefits the just person is 'the holy grail of moral philosophy'.[47] This holy grail might have been lost to some of Plato's and Aristotle's opponents, but they themselves certainly argued that virtue or virtuous action is not only vital but even constitutive of *eudaimonia*, which clearly is beneficial to the just agent. We suggest that the ancient conceptions of virtue or virtuous action as constitutive of *eudaimonia* offer us a much needed opportunity to reconsider the modern separation of happiness or well-being from morality.

When one considers the problem mentioned above that ancient ethics does not seem to offer much in terms of guidelines on how to act in particular situations, one might try to solve it by explaining it away, as it were. This can be done by pointing out that ancient ethics is not really about morality at all but, rather, about happiness and individual well-being or welfare. The problem with this solution, however, is that it does not seem quite right to take the Greek concept of *eudaimonia* to be the same as our concept of happiness or well-being, as we saw at the outset. In fact, the ancient ethicists do not seem to have much to say about happiness in the modern, psychological sense—as mentioned, they may claim that *eudaimonia* will result in such experience, but they do not define *eudaimonia* in terms of it, nor do they seem to have carried out their investigations with such experience in mind. One might try to meet this objection by making a distinction between happiness in the sense of subjective well-being, on the one hand, and welfare or well-being in a broader sense, on the other, and then identify *eudaimonia* with the latter.[48] However, there are problems with this as well, since the modern notion of welfare still seems too subjective, tying welfare as it does to the satisfaction of the autonomously defined interests of the individual.

---

[47] Blackburn (1984), 222. For a recent argument to the effect that justice is self-interested because it is necessary for genuine self-respect, see Bloomfield (2011). It should be pointed out that the opposition between morality and self-interest is not accepted by all modern moral theories: hedonist theories as well as those following Kant are exceptions. Thinkers such as Christine Korsgaard (2008: chs. 1 and 2) and Joseph Raz (1999: chs. 11–13) deny that there is such a thing as a genuine and morally significant opposition between morality and self-interest. (Cf. also this Introduction, p. 5f with note 15.)

[48] See Darwall (2002), as well as Haybron (2008), for important attempts to work out this distinction.

One might respond to this by claiming that what ancient ethics is about is the proper organization and formation of one's life as a whole, a task that requires articulating everything one takes to be valuable and then balancing these values into a coherent whole. In short, ancient ethics, on this interpretation, is about 'making sense of one's life as a whole', in Julia Annas' memorable phrase.[49] Now, this take on ancient ethics may certainly seem attractive to many modern ethicists, as well as to students, but it is doubtful whether this will solve the problem. The notion of something's making sense is essentially related to a subject *for* whom—and presumably also *by* whom—the sense is made, but this seems to be a notion far too modern and existential. Ancient ethics revolves around a kind of objective notion of the good that cannot be captured in talk of making sense of life.

Another response to the alleged mismatch between ancient eudaemonism and modern ethics would be to point out that perhaps our modern intuitions are not as exclusively subjective and feeling-oriented as one often claims. If one imagines, say, a medicine that makes one feel good all the time irrespective of what one does (or whether one does anything at all), some might suspect that this is not quite what was meant by happiness or well-being even in the modern context.[50] This suggests the existence of a common ground that one is more likely to find if one takes the ancient reflections seriously.

One place to start, if we want to see the relevance of ancient ethics to modern morality-centred concerns, is with Aristotle's emphasis on the practical nature of ethics: its purpose is action, not knowledge (*EN* II 2, 1103b26–31). This is surely to be taken as implying that the purpose of ethics (and political philosophy) is to provide some kind of practical guidance. This guidance, moreover, must be based on a grasp of the best or right way to live, the way that will in fact contribute to happiness or *eudaimonia*. The point can be generalized to pertain to other ancient schools as well: if we read ancient ethics, it invites us to consider what kind of persons we are and whether there are ways in which we might correct how we act and organize our lives as wholes.

But which way is this, and what kind of guidance is this? One way to see this might be to assume that everybody as a matter of fact desires to become *eudaimōn*, the question is how. The normative force of the guidance provided by ethics could then be conceived of as supplied by an antecedently given desire for *eudaimonia*, which only needs to be channelled, as it were, in the right direction, towards the right objects, and then the task of ethics is precisely to clarify the nature of these objects such that they can be effectively pursued. One problem with this interpretation, however, is that it seems to reduce ethics to prudence, which seems to deflate its normative import. A second problem is that, to the extent that *eudaimonia* presupposes or includes living the life of moral virtue as a necessary condition, and also

[49] Annas (1993), 27f.
[50] Cf. Robert Nozick's famous thought-experiment with the 'experience machine' (1974: 42–5).

justifies the value of this life, it becomes very hard to acquit the ancient eudaemonist position of the charge of egoism.

Alternatively one might hold that *eudaimonia* is the *telos* or final end of human endeavour in the sense of being what we *ought* to pursue (and not what we *in fact* pursue). This way of postulating *eudaimonia* as the ultimate end of human endeavour would not amount to a claim about empirical facts of human psychology but, rather, a normative claim about what our psychology should be like and what we ought to strive for, that is, what kinds of things or activities actually are *worth* pursuing. On this reading, *eudaimonia* would be something that human beings ought to pursue. The problem, of course, is to account for how this is to be understood, and a crucial factor here would be the emphasis that most ancient ethicists put on the idea that *eudaimonia* is based on our nature as rational beings. (Rabbås addresses this point in chapter 4.)

Finally, we should once again recall that ancient eudaemonist ethics does not make up a monolithic whole but, rather, a cluster of theories that develop and differ among themselves. Thus, while an emphasis on obligations to others is more prominent in classical authors such as Plato and Aristotle, and perhaps the Stoics, it is much less articulated in later authors, especially in late antiquity. Whether this should be taken as a change within moral philosophy or, rather, as a sign that the 'ought of morality' (understood as a principled concern with our obligations to each other) recedes to the periphery of ethical thought, yielding to a more general, metaphysical conception of an 'ought of rationality', is an open question.[51]

All in all, this collection shows how much variation the general eudaemonistic framework allowed for ancient philosophers, and why their reflections concerning the connection between happiness and morality are still highly pertinent.

6 Summary of the Chapters

In chapter 1, Svavar Hrafn Svavarsson provides an introduction to 'happiness before Plato'. The idea of happiness, or *eudaimonia*, was ever since the beginning and down to the times of Plato and Aristotle taken to be something divine. But the notion then underwent a twofold transformation: internalization and intellectualization. First the focus shifted from external success to internal qualities responsible for this success, and then the relevant qualities were increasingly interpreted as intellectual rather than physical. Svavarsson traces this development from the beginnings in Homer and Hesiod, through Solon and Pindar, to Heraclitus.

---

[51] The points made in this and the previous two paragraphs should alert us to the crucial move away from ancient eudaemonism that takes place when practical teleology is identified merely in terms of the pursuit of the actual objects of desire. In this way practical reason is reduced to mere prudence, and morality comes to seem like an imposition on what is now termed 'self-interest'. A central figure in this development is surely Hobbes. (Cf. note 48.)

The next two chapters deal with Plato. Plato's thought is a peculiar case in our story. On the one hand, Plato never subjects the problem of *eudaimonia* to the same kind of systematic scrutiny that Aristotle does in the *Nicomachean Ethics*; this is why it is Aristotle and not Plato that stands as the canonical thinker of ancient eudaemonist ethics. On the other hand, the problem of determining the nature of the good life, the truly successful and admirable life, is clearly central to his thought. Plato's concern with *eudaimonia* is evident in several passages. Most directly we see this where he has Socrates state without argument that everybody pursues *eudaimonia*: *Euthydemus* 278e–282e; *Symposium* 204e–205a; *Philebus* 20b–23a, 60a–61a. In other passages he explicitly has Socrates raise the question 'In what way ought we to live?' (*hontina tropon chrē zēn*) (*Gorgias* 472c–d, 492d; *Republic* I 352d). Thirdly, we also see the concern with *eudaimonia* more indirectly in those passages, for example in the early dialogues, where the hunt for a definition of some virtue invariably leads to considerations of the good life and the role of virtue in that life (e.g. *Euthyphro*, *Charmides*, *Laches*). Finally, one of Plato's greatest concerns is with justice (*dikaiosunē*) and whether the just (*dikaion*) life is better than the unjust (*adikon*) life; the treatment of this question in effect amounts to an investigation of what the good and successful life, namely *eudaimonia*, is. (See *Gorgias* 473a, 474b; *Republic* II 358c–d, 362d–e, 367b.)

Julia Annas, in chapter 2, addresses precisely the topic of justice and the good life in the *Republic*. In Book II of that dialogue, Socrates is challenged by Glaucon and Adeimantus to provide a justification for the claim that it is better to live the just life than the unjust, namely, that a successful life requires—or is identical with—living the just life. The form of Socrates' answer to this challenge has been much studied. Socrates' answer aims to show that justice is good for the just person. However, an important objection claims that this answer in effect provides the wrong kind of reason for why we should choose the just life, and thus fails to meet important 'everyday moral convictions' about justice of Socrates' audience. What this old but revived challenge threatens is thus no less than the acceptability of a eudaemonist answer to Glaucon's challenge. Annas explores this challenge and provides Socrates' answer with a new defence.

In chapter 3, Panos Dimas discusses Plato's *Gorgias*. He starts from the assumption that, ultimately, the main theme of this dialogue is justice and its proper place in the good or successful life. The dialogue falls into three parts, in which Socrates is confronted by three interlocutors: Gorgias, Polus, and Callicles. While Socrates, ostensibly, holds his sway in these successive discussions, Dimas argues that the way Plato has crafted the dialogue shows that Socrates is genuinely at a loss how to understand justice and its value. In particular, he is unable to provide a valid refutation of Callicles' position since his own position is deeply unclear. We should therefore read the dialogue as an implicit criticism of Socrates, and that is why Plato had to write the *Republic*.

Aristotle provides the canonical investigation of *eudaimonia*, setting the agenda for the following discussions in ancient ethics. It is therefore natural that he should receive a lot of attention, and the following four chapters are devoted to him.

The topic of Øyvind Rabbås' discussion in chapter 4 is closely related to Annas' account. Aristotle takes there to be an ultimate end of human endeavour, *eudaimonia*, and he identifies this as excellent rational activity. Thus he may be regarded both as a naturalist and as a rationalist in ethics: we ought to do what we can to actualize our natural end: reason. But how can an ethical theory, which is supposed to be practical and normative, have this form? Rabbås approaches this question through a reading of the so-called '*ergon*-argument', and argues that, properly understood, this enables us to understand how Aristotle can be a non-reductionist naturalist of sorts.

Hallvard Fossheim, in chapter 5, takes up Aristotle's view of the relation between old age and happiness. After outlining the physiological and psychological background, he sums up Aristotle's view in three points. (1) Human life is divided into temporal stages, each of which has its characteristic strengths and weaknesses as well as suitable activities. (2) The stages are determined partly by nature and partly by what one does with what nature provides. (3) How one fares at a later stage, when it comes to its strengths, weaknesses, and activities, depends partly on what one did at an earlier stage. Fossheim ends by suggesting that Aristotle implicitly takes *extreme* old age to entail a gradual exclusion from activities that define *eudaimonia*.

In chapter 6, Gabriel Richardson Lear asks why Aristotle insists that happiness takes time, as he does when he likens it to spring (*EN* I 7, 1098a16–20). Rejecting an interpretation relying on Aristotle's distinction between activity (*energeia*) and process (*kinēsis*), Lear argues that virtuous action is something habitual: only as a form of life can it amount to happiness. Furthermore, even if the parties might want to become friends more quickly, developing the knowledge of the other's goodness in the habitual, stable sense that characterizes virtue friendship is something that takes time. Similarly, knowing one's own stable and good qualities too takes time, and without such self-knowledge as an integral aspect of one's activity, one is not fully *eudaimōn*.

In chapter 7, Gösta Grönroos asks why the vicious person is miserable, that is, why he feels bad about himself in the very real way that he is full of remorse, hates himself, and even contemplates suicide. Grönroos argues that the vicious person must be seen in contrast to the akratic person. Whereas the latter has access to and is able to reflect on and articulate the right action and the values attendant on it, the self-hating bad person, by contrast, is someone who lacks any clear and conscious access to the values spurned by his lowly acts. Nevertheless, he feels he is not only missing out on goodness, but that he is degrading himself, without being able to spell out exactly what is wrong with his choices and acts. Such a person senses that something is missing (a life in the light of the values upon which he does not build his life), but has no conception of them beyond what might be allowed through so-called 'natural virtue'.

The next three chapters take up themes in the thought of the three Hellenistic schools of thought: the Epicurean, Stoic, and Sceptical schools.

The Epicureans stand out among the major schools in ancient ethics for being hedonists, that is, they take the highest good to be pleasure (*hēdonē*). However, there is little clarity as to what being a hedonist really amounts to for Epicurus, or even whether he is a fully committed hedonist. In chapter 8 Panos Dimas presents an account of Epicurus' axiology and an interpretation of his notions of pleasure, as well as his views on rational choice and desire. He concludes that he is an unwavering hedonist of the egoistic sort and tests this conclusion on his view on friendship, that is, the part of his theory that has seemed hardest to align with an interpretation of him as a hedonist.

According to the Stoics, human beings can in principle attain *eudaimonia* by becoming virtuous and wise. But was their optimism justifiable and realistic? The Stoics have been severely criticized, both in antiquity and in modern times, for presenting an extremely demanding theory, since they claimed that as long as ordinary people do not realize in full their rational nature, they cannot be said to be virtuous and reach happiness. In chapter 9, Katerina Ierodiakonou argues that, although the Stoics do not admit of degrees of virtue and vice, the notion of moral progress is perfectly consistent with their ethical principles. Moreover, even if the Stoics' demands seem to have been more stringent than those made by other ancient philosophers, the Stoic conception of *eudaimonia*, as an aspiration towards an ideal, was no less feasible than that of any other ancient ethical theory.

In chapter 10, Svavar Hrafn Svavarsson considers the specifically Sceptical understanding of the relation between suspension of judgement and happiness as tranquillity, starting with Pyrrho of Elis who advocated a nihilist attitude towards reality and knowledge, according to which a thing is neither knowable as something specific nor is it really anything specific. This attitude should deprive its holder of all beliefs (save this insight) and above all furnish him with tranquillity. Neo-Pyrrhonists interpreted Pyrrho's philosophy as radical Scepticism as opposed to Academic Scepticism. They also appropriated Pyrrho's promise of tranquillity. Of our Neo-Pyrrhonist sources, Sextus Empiricus makes the most of Sceptical tranquillity, in a complex and perplexing attempt to explain that the Sceptic aims at tranquillity but attains it by chance. His attempt may be indebted to the Empiricists, the Pyrrhonists' medical counterparts, according to whom the origins of successful treatments of diseases could be based on chance.

With the four last papers we move to late antiquity: to Neoplatonist and early Christian thought.

In chapter 11, Alexandrine Schniewind discusses the sketchy criticisms Plotinus advances against several well-known notions of his predecessors at the beginning of his treatise on happiness, *Ennead* I. 4. Schniewind argues that this should be taken less as a refutation of certain systematic views than as arguments aiming at showing that it is wrongheaded to start an account of happiness from notions such as pleasure or affection, or even life, unless these are properly understood. She sees these first critical chapters as clearing the way for Plotinus' own definition of happiness as the life of the intellect.

In chapter 12, Eyjólfur K. Emilsson takes up a theme first broached by Lear in chapter 6, namely, the relation of happiness to the passage of time. Emilsson considers the contrasting views of Aristotle, on the one hand, and, on the other hand, post-Aristotelian thinkers such as the Epicureans, the Stoics, and Plotinus. The latter consider the length of happy time lived and the direction for the better or the worse as irrelevant to the question whether somebody is happy at a given time, whereas Aristotle thinks this matters.

Ancient ethics, especially the ethics of late antiquity, is often considered rather self-centred. Miira Tuominen considers this commonplace in chapter 13 and argues, first, that Aspasius departs from Aristotle in an interesting side-remark he makes to Aristotle's claim that happiness requires a complete life, and introduces things done also to other people into the requirements of happiness. Further, even though in Porphyry's Neoplatonic hierarchy of virtues, the higher virtues are not formulated in other-regarding terms, it would be exaggerated to take them as particularly egoistic. This is because the higher virtues are also the preconditions for full possession of the political virtues interpreted by Porphyry as pertaining to communities. The higher virtues are also required for the full understanding of the good as well as for the detachment from bodily desires, and both can be seen as requirements for genuine other-regard from the Neoplatonic perspective.

In the final chapter, Christian Tornau discusses Augustine's views on the relation between virtue and happiness. Augustine seems to be committed both to the traditional pagan view that virtue is sufficient for happiness and to the view that happiness is strictly confined to the eschatological future and an exclusive gift of divine grace. Tornau argues that Augustine seeks to solve this dilemma by introducing a distinction between 'teleological virtue' and 'operative virtue' and then limiting the validity of the axiom of self-sufficiency to the former.

1

On Happiness and Godlikeness before Socrates

Svavar Hrafn Svavarsson

1 Happiness as Godlikeness

Plato and Aristotle share an idea about happiness. It is this: Happiness as the final good of human beings consists in being as like god as possible. Consider this passage from Plato's *Theaetetus* (176a5–e4):

But it is not possible, Theodorus, that evil should be destroyed—for there must always be something opposed to the good; nor is it possible that it should have its seat in heaven. But it must inevitably haunt human life, and prowl about this earth. That is why a man should make all haste to escape from earth to heaven; and escape means becoming as like God as possible; and a man becomes like God when he becomes just and pure, with understanding. But it is not at all an easy matter, my good friend, to persuade men that it is not for the reasons commonly alleged that one should try to escape from wickedness and pursue virtue. It is not in order to avoid a bad reputation and obtain a good one that virtue should be practiced and not vice; that, it seems to me, is only what men call 'old wives' talk. Let us put the truth in this way. In God there is no sort of wrong whatsoever; he is supremely just, and the thing most like him is the man who has become as just as it lies in human nature to be...My friend, there are two patterns set up in reality. One is divine and supremely happy; the other has nothing of God in it, and is the pattern of the deepest unhappiness.[1]

In the *Timaeus* god as the designer of the world is above all intellect and as such he is the object of our emulation. For anyone attending to it, Plato submits (*Timaeus* 90c):

there is absolutely no way that his thoughts can fail to be immortal and divine, should truth come within his grasp. And to the extent that human nature can partake of immortality, he can in no way fail to achieve this: constantly caring for his divine part as he does, keeping well-ordered the guiding spirit [*daimōn*] that lives within him, he must indeed be supremely happy.[2]

---

[1] Translation from Burnyeat and Levett (1990).   [2] Translation from Zeyl (2000).

Such is Plato's stance.[3] Aristotle follows suit in the *Nicomachean Ethics* X 6–8. Although he rejects god as designer, god as intellect is still the paradigm of happiness.[4] Submitting that supreme happiness consists in theoretical contemplation, as opposed to the political life, Aristotle specifies the attributes of happiness (X 7, 1177a12–b34):

> If happiness is activity in accordance with excellence, it is reasonable that it should be in accordance with the highest excellence; and this will be that of the best thing in us... For, firstly, this activity [contemplation] is the best (since not only is intellect the best thing in us, but the objects of intellect are the best of knowable objects); and, secondly, it is the most continuous, since we can contemplate truth more continuously than we can *do* anything. And we think that happiness ought to have pleasure mingled with it, but the activity of philosophic wisdom is admittedly the pleasantest of excellent activities... And the self-sufficiency that is spoken of must belong most to the contemplative activity... And this activity alone would seem to be loved for its own sake... And happiness is thought to depend on leisure... But such a life would be too high for man; for it is not in so far as he is man that he will live so, but in so far as something divine is present in him; and by so much as this is superior to our composite nature it is activity superior to that which is the exercise of the other kind of excellence. If intellect is divine, then, in comparison with man, the life according to it is divine in comparison with human life. But we should not follow those who advise us, being men, to think of human things, and, being mortal, of mortal things, but must, so far as we can, make ourselves immortal, and strain every nerve to live in accordance with the best thing in us.[5]

This difficult passage invites contrary approaches to Aristotle's notion of happiness.[6] At all events, for both philosophers god is above all intellect. Human happiness, it seems, consists in being as much intellect as possible.

Eminent scholars of ancient philosophy have begun to emphasize this aspect of Platonic and Aristotelian ethics, which has received limited attention in modern times, perhaps because it is considered to have little or no relevance to modern ethics.[7] David

---

[3] For different statements in Plato's works to the effect that happiness consists in godlikeness, see especially the *Symposium* 207d–9e, *Republic* 613a–b, *Phaedrus* 252d–53c, *Timaeus* 90a–d. The godlikeness thesis expressed in these passages has been discussed by Sedley (1999); cf. his (2004), 74–81. The *Theaetetus* passage has recently been the subject of some discussion; see e.g. Rue (1993), Mahoney (2004), Armstrong (2004), Giannopoulou (2011), Lännström (2011). Annas (1999) concentrates on the ancient interpretation of Platonism that emphasizes the godlikeness thesis as central to Plato (see e.g. Alcinous, *Handbook* 28), as does Baltzly (2004). See also Russell (2005), ch. 5, on the ideal in antiquity. For the history of the idea, cf. Merki (1952); for a general account, see Passmore (1970), chs. 2–3.

[4] For the different teleological roles of god in Plato and Aristotle, see Sedley (2007), 167–73.

[5] Translation from Ross and Brown (2009). I use *excellence* and *intellect* for the translators' *virtue* (*aretē*) and *reason* (*nous*).

[6] The literature on contemplation as happiness in Aristotle is vast. For recent discussions of the problem, with references, see Irwin (2007), 149–52; Long (2011).

[7] The otherworldliness of Plato's ethics has long been acknowledged, while godlikeness as the final end has not, at least not since antiquity. Aristotle's ethics, however, has been used as groundwork for modern virtue ethics. His godlikeness thesis hardly squares with the emphases encountered in that kind of ethics. Nussbaum (2001 [1986]), 373–7, finds Aristotle's godlikeness thesis 'in contradiction with the *EN's* overall enterprise' and 'oddly out of step' with it. For the connection of happiness and deity in Epicureanism and Stoicism, which to my knowledge has not received much scrutiny, cf. Long (2004: 128); see e.g. Seneca, *Letters* 92.3; Epicurus, *Letter to Menoeceus* 135.

Sedley suggests that by disregarding or trivializing it we risk misunderstanding Greek ethics. Anthony Long submits it as an example of Greek remoteness. He presents the idea thus: 'the final good the different schools all propose (the universal objective of life in the Isles of the Blessed, as it were) is a state of godlikeness, which we can achieve only by cultivating that which actually is divine or quasi-divine in us—that is to say, our rational faculty.'[8]

In the writings of the moral philosophers, godlikeness is presented as the essence of happiness. Human beings become godlike, for the philosophers, if they exercise in as unadulterated a form as humanly possible their intellect, their rational self; happiness is above all the intellectual life of reason. This is because god is, for them, intellect. The moral philosophers, then, explain in what sense human beings can be like god. Their conception of god is very different from the one Xenophanes famously found grotesquely absurd. But their explanation of the possibility of god-likeness is expressed primarily in terms that nevertheless draw on the Greek trad-ition, even on Homer himself. It is expressed in terms of excellence (*aretē*). The aspirations to happiness as godlikeness can be realized, if at all, only by possessing the excellence of knowledge that would enable human beings to elevate themselves towards the divine.

We can sketch the historical background to this philosophical conception of happiness as godlikeness. The Greeks traditionally contrasted divine power and immortality with the feeble status of human beings. Zeus controls the fortunes of humans inscrutably if justly. Humans do best if they avoid provoking divine anger and receive divine (but seemingly arbitrary) favor; their prosperity is never up to themselves.[9] Then, with the moral philosophers a shift occurs; they make use of the emerging notion of internal goodness, excellence of character and intellect, which becomes the criterion of human prosperity. The importance of external goods and divine dispensations for this prosperity all but vanishes; human prosperity is for the most part up to human beings themselves. But the shift is not only ethical, but also theological; the all-important internal goods conceived as purely rational are either divine or divinely sanctioned.

2   Excellence Internalized and Intellectualized

Consider the following account of the ethical shift, according to which the moral philosophers' mold-breaking contribution consisted in conceiving of the agent's

---

[8]   Long (2004), 126.
[9]   The only historical general study of the godlikeness thesis known to me is Roloff (1970). Long (2011) is mainly concerned with the importance of the philosophical term *eudaimonia* as indicating a close connection with the divine. He suggests (2011), 97, that 'philosophical *eudaimonia*...is presumed without argument to be a godlike or quasi-divine existence. The presumption does not need argument because this connotation of the word is a cultural datum.'

happiness as being up to himself rather than to external deities.[10] This notion of happiness as up to the agent himself then dominated Greek philosophical discussions of human agency.

The moral philosophers assumed that the good life would be the life that every human being sought and ought to seek; happiness was seen as the correct goal of desire and action, as the human good. The idea that human beings should aim at happiness, as that idea is spelled out in Greek moral theories, also presupposes that the goal at which human beings should aim is ultimate and unified, as opposed to a collection of disparate goals that each could be a reason for action.[11] This presupposition is important for understanding these theories, offering as it does a picture of the happy life as a single whole; it has been described as the Greeks' entry point for ethical reflection.[12]

So long as the individual believes himself to be at the mercy of external forces, whether necessities of Zeus or contingencies of luck, or both, he lacks the resources to impose seriously on his own life a coherent, unified and goal-directed pattern which renders his life meaningful. When his happiness is under his own control and depends on his own self-cultivation, the individual is set to realize himself by enhancing his excellences according to such a pattern. These excellences, as the conditions of the good life, had traditionally been conceived as the objects of human desires.

The question of overriding importance for the moral philosophers becomes: What single goal is happiness? Achieving this goal is, then, if not completely then at least to a considerable extent—it depends on the philosophical school—up to the agent himself. For if the agent has little or no control over whether he reaches what he aims for, acquires what he desires—and is well aware of his powerlessness—his actions should hardly be determined by the goal. At best he can attempt to pacify and sway the powers that do control the fulfillment of his desires; thus he can attempt indirect control, presumably by pious and just behavior. In order for the achievement of happiness to be up to the agent himself, happiness—or the goods the possession of which secures happiness—is gradually internalized; the condition of happiness becomes internal to the agent. This internal condition is excellence. Such is the view we find in early Plato and later Greek philosophy.

But we do not only find this internalization of excellence, but also its intellectualization. According to all the major schools the moral excellences are necessarily tied to the dominating intellectual excellence, the right reason that orders all mental matters, knowledge itself. For Socrates as for the Stoics, excellence simply is knowledge; for others, moral excellences are dispositions that follow right reason.[13] And it

---

[10] For another account of the shift, see Kahn (1998), 28–37.

[11] For the importance of this claim, see Striker (1998), 171–2.

[12] For an account of this idea, see Annas (1993), 27–34.

[13] Even some of the Sophists intellectualize excellence, although in a way challenged and opposed by Plato's Socrates.

is above all this ruling excellence that amounts to happiness. Thus excellence, having been internalized, so as to make happiness attainable, is additionally intellectualized. And insofar as excellence is intellectualized, happiness itself is intellectualized. This intellectualization of excellence and happiness can be taken to imply two views. It can be taken to imply that moral excellence always requires rational support and leadership if it is to lead to happiness. This is a reasonable understanding. But it can also be understood to imply that real happiness consists in unadulterated rationality where other kinds of excellences are left behind.

Now one might reasonably ask what motivates the intellectualization of excellence. Let us assume that the internalization of the excellences that are supposed to secure happiness is motivated by the wish to bring happiness under the control of the agent himself. But it seems that it is not sufficient to make these goods internal to the agent if the purpose is to bring them under his control, although it is no doubt necessary. For even if internal, the realization of the goods in question may still depend on things external to the agent, such as his financial situation, parents, opportunities, that is, the luck and contingencies the power of which the internalization was supposed to eradicate. By emphasizing the sovereignty of reason the moral philosophers suggest that only the agent's rationality is beyond the ambit of luck and contingency.[14]

As mentioned above, there are two ways of understanding this sovereignty. Can intellectual excellence secure happiness by controlling the practical? Or can happiness only be realized in the absence of those things that are the subject matter of practical excellences? Both Plato and Aristotle can and have been interpreted as leaning towards the second option, namely in those passages where they explain human happiness as likeness to god, who is conceived as pure intellect. In order to secure the possibility of happiness being up to the human being itself, excellence as its sufficient condition is in turn internalized, intellectualized, and finally made godlike.

There is tension in Plato, then, as to the status of the moral excellences with regard to supreme happiness conceived as godlikeness. Godlikeness does not exclusively consist in intellectually excellent activity but includes being morally excellent. Accordingly the *Theaetetus* (176b) includes being just and pious in being like god. And in the *Timaeus* (29e), likewise, god as intellect is depicted as entirely good. The *Republic* (613a) further includes justice in godlikeness. Plato's guardians seem to sacrifice their happiness by not pursuing contemplation (519c–d).[15] On Aristotle's conception god could hardly be conceived as expressing other-regarding social qualities. For him such a presumption is absurd: 'But that complete happiness is a

---

[14] I take Nussbaum's *The Fragility of Goodness* to examine this attempt, 'the aspiration to rational self-sufficiency in Greek ethical thought: the aspiration to make the goodness of a good human life safe from luck through the controlling power of reason' (2001), 5.

[15] This issue is much discussed; cf. Irwin (2007), 105–9.

contemplative activity', Aristotle says (*Nicomachean Ethics* X 8, 1178b8–15), 'will appear from the following consideration as well. We assume gods to be above all other beings blessed and happy; but what sort of actions must we assign to them? Acts of justice? Will not the gods seem absurd if they make contracts and return deposits, and so on? Acts of a brave man...? Or liberal acts?...And what would their temperate acts be?'[16] So, what about the moral excellences? Evidently they retain their importance, but their place in happiness as godlikeness is unclear.

We have suggested that, for the moral philosophers, the goods, the possession of which secures happiness, are internal, intellectual, and godlike. By the time of Socrates, there was an established conception of five cardinal kinds of excellence. Apart from knowledge (*sophia*) and courage (*andreia*), there were the two other-regarding moral excellences of justice (*dikaiosunē/dikē*) and restraint (*sōphrosunē*), in addition to piety (*hosiotēs*), which in Plato was subsumed under justice.[17] Plato's *Republic* is an extended attempt to explain the sense in which their happiness requires agents to be just. It is usually assumed that Greek moral theory takes shape when philosophers discuss the connection between happiness and the moral excellences, and attempt to clarify the thesis that these excellences, an elucidation of which they offer, are indeed necessary for happiness. Most Greek philosophers from Plato onwards did argue that people could only be happy if they were morally excellent—whether or not that moral excellence was co-extensive with moral excellence as commonly conceived; for Aristotle the two seem to have been co-extensive, while the early Stoics appear to have been unconventional in their understanding of moral excellence, leaving quite some room for the morally indifferent. Moral excellence, at all events, is a salient feature in philosophical accounts of happiness.

This is one account of the ethical shift. But by connecting happiness with godlikeness the philosophers are not thinking in a vacuum, but rather following the traditional conception of happiness as divine and beyond the reach of human beings except insofar as they partake in the divine. Long suggests the following: 'The project of Greek ethics is both conservative and revolutionary. It is conservative in the sense that it retains the traditional belief that long-term prosperity presupposes divine favor or a condition of godlikeness. But, instead of treating such favor or godlikeness as the unpredictable gift of fickle deities, it overturns that conception by proposing that *eudaimonia* is largely or entirely up to us.'[18] Consider what I suggest are the main facets of the traditional conception of happiness, facets that are not static, but rather gradually coalesce into a conception that makes the individual ever more in charge of his lot.

---

[16] Cf. Sedley (1999), 322–8, and (2007), 167–73, for a discussion of the underlying differences in teleology between Plato and Aristotle.

[17] On Platonic piety, see McPherran (2006).   [18] Long (2004), 127.

3 Evolving Conceptions of the Relation between the Human and the Divine

Whether as philosophical discourses on the conditions of happiness, poetic exhortations to just living in the hope of immediate or transcendent happiness, or tragic lamentations over human powerlessness to achieve happiness, Greek approaches to happiness have one point of reference in common. Where there is happiness, there is deity, invariably the paradigm of happiness, to which all inferior states are compared. The deity deserves a special term, *makar* (blessed), used of human beings by analogy in exceptional cases, when a person in some respect transcends human limitations, becomes like god. For the Greeks, supreme happiness belongs to god. For most of them, human beings are inevitably wretched in comparison to god, more or less depending on divine favor and the excellence that enables them to approach godliness; such a being was usually termed *olbios* (prosperous), in philosophical literature *eudaimon* (happy).[19] For some of them, human beings can hope to achieve transcendent happiness on their own in a future divine state by correctly making their souls as excellent as possible. For the moral philosophers, as we have seen, human beings can attain happiness in this life on their own insofar as they manage to be like god, engaged in the activity of their intellect, their divine element, and ruling excellence.

One aspect of the supreme happiness of the deity is its utter excellence. As conceptions of god differ, spanning a spectrum from Homeric anthropomorphism to the intellectualism of Plato and Aristotle, so there are different notions of the excellences that promote divine happiness. And as the notion of excellence changes, being increasingly restricted to goods of the soul, so conceptions of happiness are altered. But for poets and philosophers alike, there seem to be three clusters of attributes that characterize god: (i) God is excellent above all others, and endowed with those qualities that afford him supreme honor. (ii) Unlike humans god is self-sufficient and immortal. (iii) All these attributes afford him pleasure and the serenity that accompanies the carefree life. We find these attributes—excellence and honor, self-sufficiency, pleasure—associated with god in Homer as well as in Aristotle.[20] They are presented as objects of human desire, as perfect happiness, some more than others, depending on the author and his view of human possibilities. God possesses them and human beings covet them. These divine attributes might be seen as the externalization of idealized human attributes. Insofar as human beings aspire to the

---

[19] The term *eudaimōn* seems to occur first in Hesiod (*Works and Days* 826), and in fifth century BC literature usually refers to material wealth; see Dover (1994), 174. In relating the discussion of Solon and Croesus concerning happiness, and material wealth as a serious candidate, Herodotus uses *olbios* (1.30).

[20] We can discern these clusters for example in the passage from Aristotle's *Nicomachean Ethics* (X 7, 1177a19–b31), quoted above, where he enumerates the acknowledged characteristics of happiness, and god. On their occurrences in Homer, see de Heer (1968), 4–11, whose work has proved very useful.

good life, that is, a life of excellence and honor, self-sufficiency, and pleasure, they aspire to be like god.

On this account, human beings stand in a twofold relationship with god, characterized by dependence and emulation. On the one hand, god bestows gifts on human beings; it is through his gifts that human beings can become excellent, whether by endowment of enabling qualities or good fortune. On the other, human beings seek and emulate divine qualities. As we have seen, the moral philosophers attempt to minimize human dependence and maximize the emulation of godliness for the attainment of happiness.

There are different ways in which to follow and describe the changes of the conception of happiness and its connection with the divine. I propose to trace the barest outline of four stages in the development of the conception of this relationship of human beings and god in terms of dependence and emulation. I have in mind the Homeric poems, the poetry of Hesiod, the lyric poets, and finally early philosophical ideas. We could consider other aspects and authors, not least the tragic poets, but these allow us I suggest—at least to describe the important factors in the development of the conception that then finds expression in the moral philosophers' idea of happiness as godlikeness.

4 Homeric Happiness

The Homeric epics offer descriptions of divine attributes and of human endeavors to partake in these attributes through human excellence and thus lead the good life. In this way Homeric man aspires to happiness as godlikeness through excellence. He is hindered by his mortal limitations, and he must always abide by the justice of Zeus, who invariably allots some misery to man. Man's dependence on god is complete.[21] Human beings are certainly the most miserable of all creatures in the Homeric epics: 'For truly there is nothing, I think, more miserable than man among all the things that breathe and move on earth' (*Iliad* 17.446–7).[22] Such is the view of man from the vantage point of Zeus.

In Homer reflection on human behavior presupposes that the immediate object of men's pursuit is excellence, which secures honor or worth (*timē*). In a way it seems legitimate to take honor to be the Homeric notion of happiness.[23] Aristotle did suggest it as a serious candidate for happiness and was no doubt aware of the

---

[21] The Homeric poems are brimming with epithets such as 'god-like', 'resembling the immortals' etc. For a discussion of these epithets and their uses, in particular with regard to the heroes' mortality, see J. Griffin (1980), 81–102.

[22] Translations from the *Iliad* are from Murray and Wyatt (1999).

[23] In their very influential studies, Moses Finley (1979 [1954]) and Alasdair MacIntyre (1981) posit a union of morality and social structure in Homeric society through the notions of excellence and honor. The latter suggests (123): 'There is only one set of social bonds. Morality as something distinct does not yet exist. Evaluative questions are questions of social fact.'

importance of honor in Homer, and elsewhere in Greek culture; he made it the end of the political life (*Nicomachean Ethics* I 5, 1095b22–3). The possession of honor, for Homeric man, should reflect the possession of excellence, as indeed Aristotle went on to observe, immediately commenting that, if such is the case, perhaps excellence itself is a better candidate (1095b26–31).

Honor also belonged to the gods; theirs was the greatest honor, unchallenged by any human being, because theirs was the greatest excellence, as for instance Phoenix makes clear in his appeal to Achilles (*Iliad* 9.496–8): 'So Achilles, master your proud spirit; nor must you have a pitiless heart. Even the very gods can bend, though theirs is even greater excellence and honor and might.'

As incessant self-assertion of the agent who surpasses others, excellence could relate to many things in the Homeric epics.[24] That a man possesses excellence in something entails that he is very good—*aretē* would mean 'bestness'—with respect to that something. He has striven for and succeeded in being better than others. This kind of success has reasonably enough been viewed as success in competition.[25] But further, there does not seem to be a clear distinction between the quality or skill that enables an agent to excel and the success that results from his abilities.[26] Material wealth as a man's excellence indicates honor, and sometimes (for instance as a warrior's booty or gifts) it is a manifestation of honor. Physical prowess and courage are likewise excellences, as is swiftness of feet, as is beauty. But good council—which is conciliatory and cooperative in origin and intent—is also regarded as an excellence, as are other quiet qualities.[27] Whatever its kind, excellence is a prized good that is supposed to secure a man's honor; it is meant to give content to honor that reflects the good life of the excellent agent. But there is not an explicit duality of the external and the internal. Wealth and prowess are not differentiated by these categories. Further, the gods' excellences are superior to those of human beings. Divine beauty and strength, opulence and wisdom, is always beyond the human grasp, and worthy of ultimate honor.

There is another source of honor in the Homeric epics that is less competitive and more akin to cooperative and conciliatory excellence, less indicative of self-assertion (and even inhibiting self-assertion) than a sense of shame (*aidōs*) based on regard for others, a regard that is in turn based on the honor due to others no less than the

---

[24] See for instance *Iliad* 15.642, on Perephetes, who is better in all kinds of excellences, whether pertaining to feet, fighting, or thinking. For a seminal discussion that in some ways set the terms of the debate, and elicited considerable criticism, see Adkins (1960), 31–9, and then Cairns (1993), 100–2.

[25] Adkins (1960) famously stresses the competitive side. The *locus classicus* is *Iliad* 11.783–84: 'Old Peleus charged his son Achilles always to be best (*aristeuein*) and preeminent above all.' Indeed, the agonistic element of Greek culture in general has long been recognized, and perhaps first emphasized in the works of the nineteenth-century historian Jacob Burckhardt.

[26] Cf. Adkins (1960), 32–3. The lack of this distinction between an internal quality as a disposition to act in some manner and actions or results of actions makes it difficult to disassociate excellence as a disposition (say, courage) from certain excellent actions (such as good fighting) or results of actions (such as wealth).

[27] On *euboulia*, see Schofield (1986).

honor due to oneself.[28] Aspects of the sense of shame would later merge with the excellence of self-restraint (sōphrosunē), but at this stage may not have been conceived quite as an excellence, but perhaps as the emotion that gives rise to prudent tempering of a cooperative kind.[29]

Connected with this sense of shame is respect for the justice of Zeus, the paradigm for the justice of kings.[30] In order to obtain from the gods what they desire men must show the gods the respect and awe that they deserve, as lesser men must show kings respect. Men must be pious and just in accordance with divine will. This means that they must observe the correct behavior towards the gods, and each other, not least through self-restraint and just actions. Here, justice (dikē) dictates to men becoming behavior. As in the case of self-restraint, for Homeric man justice is not a competitive excellence as for instance physical prowess could be, but nevertheless an important value that decides his behavior and happiness.

Although justice may not have been an excellence of the same kind as physical prowess, and perhaps more akin to quieter qualities, it does not follow that justice was not conceived as necessary for the good life. Although the meaning of aretē changed drastically from the Homeric epics to the moral philosophers, it was always associated with notions of the good life. For the Homeric man, being excellent secures honor (timē), by far the most important factor of the good life. But honor was also secured by justice, even if justice was not conceived as a competitive excellence. Indeed, an excellent agent could act unjustly without losing his excellence, while his honor would nevertheless suffer, as the suitors of Penelope experienced. The tension between the two, competitive excellence and justice, can result in conflict. It could therefore be maintained that the idea of the good life from Homer to the moral philosophers is the stage for the conflict between the kinds of goods that best serve this life.

However one construes the content of and the relation between excellences, a prudently tempering sense of shame, and respect for the justice of Zeus—and there have been different approaches—these seem to be the requisites of timē. It was suggested above that the possession of timē, for Homeric man, is happiness, which can be juxtaposed with another notion of the good life that lies beyond honor. This goal would be the easy life, the emulation of attributes of divine happiness ideally characterized by riches, pleasure, absence of care and toil, and as much security from human evils as possible. The positing of two distinct notions of happiness in Homer may be misleading.[31] The possession of timē, for Homeric man, amounts to a public recognition

---

[28] Cairns (1993), 12–14, clarifies the term. The flip side of shame is the feeling of failure of self-assertion. One of the more famous attempts at clarifying contemporary ethical thought with the help of Greek notions such as that of shame is that of Williams (1993).

[29] See North's study of sōphrosunē (1966), 5–7, and Cairns (1993), 104.

[30] The justice of Zeus is the subject of the influential study by Lloyd-Jones (1971).

[31] Pace de Heer (1968) and Andersen (2011), who see honor and the good life as two independent objects of pursuit.

of excellence and other-regarding qualities and actions. The good life, for him, consists in possessing these attributes. This is the human approximation of divine blessedness (*makaria*), reflected in their supreme honor. Being rich, for Homeric man, is one important way of being excellent. And riches indicate might and leisure. But it is always an excellence that brings *timē* in its wake. As Sarpedon vaults (*Iliad* 12.310–12):

> Glaucus, why is it that we two are most held in honor, with a seat of honor and meats and full cups, in Lycia and all men gaze on us as on gods? And we possess a great estate by the banks of Xanthus, a fair tract of orchard and of wheat-bearing plough-land. Therefore now we must take our stand among the foremost Lycians and confront blazing battle so that many a one of the mail-clad Lycians may say: 'Surely no inglorious men are these who rule in Lycia, our kings, and they eat fat sheep and drink choice wine, honey-sweet: but their might too is noble, since they fight among the foremost Lycians'.

The *timē* of Sarpedon and Glaucus is based on qualities and actions that ensure their (relatively) easy life. Consider the excellence of material wealth. It indicates honor as a sign of prestige. But wealth also, not least in the *Odyssey*, underlies the security of the prosperous; that is what generates the honor due to the rich. As such wealth and material prosperity secure splendor, keep toil at bay, and grant the wealthy an easy life, which is another characteristic of the gods. And since it keeps care and toil at bay, it gives rise to enjoyment and untroubled pleasure. The idea is that being wealthy increases your chances of enjoying a future of a pleasant and easy life. Wealth also gives the rich an opportunity for leading a life of splendor. The ideas of the carefree and pleasant life as well as that of splendor are not difficult to associate with the admiration mortals have for the gods. In conceiving of splendor and untroubled pleasure, men refer to the everlasting gods.

It is always up to divine will, Zeus and the fates, whether the agent manages to put his qualities to such use that he becomes successful and receives his due honor. We find the idea that gods are responsible for human misery and intermittent prosperity (as we read towards the end of the *Iliad*), or that they are unfairly held so responsible (as suggested at the beginning of the *Odyssey*). Even if human beings emulate the qualities that characterize the gods, they are also completely dependent on the gods. The man who possesses honor through goods is prosperous (*olbios*). He receives from the gods things that are *olbia* (wealth, children, and status). These benefits are not *ipso facto olbia*; they need the sanction of the gods. Only with such sanction is the prosperity permanent, or at least more permanent and secure than without it.[32]

5   Hesiodic Damage Control

The poetry of Hesiod (around 700 BC), as expressed in the *Works and Days*, presents a darker and less elevated world than that of Homer. In Hesiod's myth of the races,

---

[32] Cf. the analysis of the terms in de Heer (1968), 12–14.

Homeric heroes are fourth: 'more just and superior, the godly race of men-heroes, who are called demigods' (158-60).[33] As opposed to that race, the fifth and last race of ordinary human beings like Hesiod himself 'will not cease from toil and distress by day, nor from being worn out by suffering at night, and the gods will give them grievous cares' (176-8).[34] There are perhaps fleeting moments of pleasure, but human misery can be mitigated, inevitable damage can be controlled, by adhering to divine justice. Homeric excellence, ideally tempered by a sense of justice, has expanded and clearly includes justice.[35] Thus human beings have been given a slight measure of independence in their quest for, if not the good life, then the minimizing of the bad life.

The view that human happiness is divinely dispensed may give rise to despair and pessimism. Human life is in varying degrees bogged down by the human condition and external factors over which agents exercise limited control; they are continually thwarted in their search for the good life. Some authors, in particular many of the lyric poets, came to think that happiness, being divine, was not only beyond the power of man to achieve; life was in fact a series of more or less painful miseries, allotted by the divine, whether justly or arbitrarily. Other writers brought human beings closer to the orbit of the divine, so that they could temporally share in divine happiness and even transcend their human condition by association with the divine. If people are to act in order to become happy, then they must play at least some role in securing their own happiness; this is where excellence enters. If, however, their happiness is not at all up to them, if their happiness is purely a matter of divine will or fate, their actions need not be based on considerations of happiness. But if happiness depends on divine beings, people can attempt to sway these beings in their favor (or at least attempt to avoid their ill will) by behaving piously, justly, and meekly, at all events so that the divine favors them. This seems to be the way Hesiod envisages the possibility of prosperity in the *Works and Days*.

For him, the *makares* are not only the blessed gods we find in Homer, but also and perhaps in particular *daimones*, numinous beings, at least some of whom are 'guardians of mortal human beings . . . givers of wealth' (124-6); these are the dead of the first two races. People now call them *makares* or blessed in order to ward off their ill will towards them.[36] Even if they are an extension of the justice of Zeus, they

---

[33] The translation of Hesiod is from Most (2006).

[34] I refer to Hesiod's *Works and Days* since it is concerned with the human condition, as opposed to the very different *Theogony*. See Clay (2003), 85-95, for a discussion of the myth of the races, and of other aspects of the Hesiodic universe.

[35] I assume that Hesiod is later than the Homeric poems, and that, even if he was not much later, the Homeric poems reflect older values. In *Works and Days* 190-2 the good and the just are, even if juxtaposed, closely connected, while in 274-92 (where the poet addresses his brother Perses), excellence presupposes justice. On justice with respect to excellence in Homer and Hesiod, see Clay (2003), 36-44, 144-8, and the seminal works of Lloyd-Jones (1971), chs. 1-2, *contra* Adkins (1960), ch. 4, and Dodds (1951), ch. 2, and cf. Cairns (1993), 100-3, 152-6.

[36] Cf. de Heer (1968), 22-3, and West (1978), 186, as well as Clay (2003), 88-90.

are chthonic powers that can generate misfortune and have to be pacified in various ways. They can give men wealth, and as such they are *daimones*. Being as happy as man can be, then, implies that a man has successfully dodged the displeasure of the *daimones*, and enjoys their favor. Being *olbios* is still to possess wealth, which is the visible manifestation of being *eudaimon*. The honor of the Homeric poems is all but absent, and the morality at stake, the *sōphrosunē* element, may be understood in relation to the *daimones*; be wary of the *daimones*. Show circumspection so as not to incur divine ill will. This is another entry point for the cooperative values that we saw in tension with competitive ones in the Homeric poems. This Hesiodic notion of restraint and circum-spection is often associated with the Delphic mottos of *mēden agan* (nothing too much) and *gnōthi seauton* (know yourself), which underline the importance of being aware of one's mortal limitations. As fear of divine beings it is more religious. It is not quite the political and social value of shame of the Homeric poems.

As a result of material well-being the fortunate enjoy freedom and a carefree life devoid of trouble. In that way they may resemble the gods. This prosperity as the basis of a carefree and toil-less life is created by work. According to Hesiod (*Works and Days* 286–92), the gods have inserted between mortals and excellence (conceived as wealth and high status) labor and sweat. This excellence is not an internal quality, and it can only be gained if sanctioned by the gods. This sanction requires the agent to be just. At all events, labor is up to oneself as a necessary, although far from sufficient condition of prosperity.

The justice of Zeus that we found in the Homeric epics is more pronounced in Hesiod. The poet writes that he has suffered injustice in the form of dishonest testimonies and bought-off judges at the hand of his brother, which results in an improper distribution of wealth (the source of happiness). Hesiod's gods are guard-ians of justice when rulers full of *hubris* act on selfish grounds. Justice is rewarded by prosperity (*olbos*) and injustice punished (*Work and Days* 280–8):

Perses, lay these things in your heart and give heed to justice ... this is the law that Cronus' son has established for human beings: that fish and beasts and winged birds eat one another, since justice is not among them; but to human beings he has given justice, which is the best by far. For if someone who recognizes what is just is willing to speak it out publicly, then far-seeing Zeus gives him prosperity. But whoever willfully swears a false oath, telling a lie in his testimony, he himself is incurably hurt at the same time as he harms justice, and in after times his family is left more obscure; whereas the family of the man who keeps his oath is better in after times.

Just behavior in Hesiod can result in some share in the divine attributes of happiness. Justice as an excellence is up to the agent himself, and insofar as justice contributes to prosperity, prosperity is up to the agent.[37]

---

[37] The difference between Homeric and Hesiodic man is not that in Homer we find only competitive values behind views of the good life while in Hesiod we see introduced and emphasized excellence that we

6 From Solon to Pindar: Excellence Internalized

Human beings must fail to achieve the good life, say the lyric poets, simply because they are not gods. Witness Solon, poet and politician, writing in the early sixth century BC (fragment 14): 'Nor is any mortal blessed (*makar*), but miserable (*ponēroi*) are all those down on whom the sun looks.'[38] The good life of human beings is as ever measured against the divine standard. The human life is always found wanting. However, in the later, brighter, and aristocratic world of the poetry of Pindar (born perhaps 518 BC), we find that the different excellences, canonized as internal qualities, enable human beings, at least with divine aid, to attain fleeting godlikeness in this life and, crucially, divine company and even godliness in the next life.[39] Human beings are more independent in the quest for happiness, the necessary conditions of which include the internal excellences.

The lyric poets have long been associated with pessimism regarding the possibility of happiness. They tend to stress the imperfections of human beings as compared to divine beings, who have absolute control over human affairs.[40] According to this *Weltanschauung* one's happiness is completely dependent on god. Further, especially for the older lyric poets, human beings are miserable and cannot hope to become like god or emulate him in any way. The relationship is one-sided, so that god can grant to the excellent favors and a measure of fleeting prosperity. Hence one should grab what enjoyment is on offer, with those means one has at one's disposal. There arose, with this pessimism, a kind of hedonism that advocated the savoring of the few pleasures afforded. These pleasures are different from those attributed to god. His enjoyment and easy life rest on complete self-sufficiency, while these are uncertain moments of sensuality. So, many of the poets advocate the taking of pleasure when it is on offer: 'What are wealth and respect to me? Pleasure combined with good cheer surpasses everything' (Theognis 1067–8; cf. 765–8).[41] The pleasant life is nevertheless based on material prosperity, which is always temporary; one should enjoy what it gives when possible. Unlike Hesiod, many lyric poets suggest that the *daimones* who control our lives are themselves utterly uncontrollable.[42] Therefore we are not independent agents with regard to our happiness: 'No one, Cyrnus, is responsible on his own for ruin or profit, but it is the gods who give both' (Theognis 131–2).

At this early stage we nevertheless witness a tendency to internalize excellence by juxtaposing it with bodily goods like beauty or health and external goods like wealth;

---

can now call cooperative. Rather Hesiodic man is warier of divine beings in a way that is absent from Homer, in whose epics there is not the same fear of divine beings. This wariness is expressed in just and pious behavior, in the hope for prosperity.

[38] Translations of Solon and Theognis are from Gerber (1999).

[39] See Currie (2005), ch. 9, who discusses the idea of the *theios anēr* historically.

[40] Cf. Griffith (2009), 75–83, on the relations between humans and gods in the lyric poets.

[41] The poetry attributed to Theognis (perhaps mid sixth century BC) was composed by different authors. I disregard the attendant complexities.

[42] For *loci*, see de Heer (1968), 39–40, 45–7.

together, these different goods make a man fortunate, says Theognis (933–5): 'Excellence and good looks go hand in hand with few men. Fortunate (*olbios*) the one who is allotted both of these. All honor him.' And (129–30): 'Don't pray for outstanding excellence or wealth, Polypaïdes: the only thing a man can have is luck.' We witness a devaluation of material prosperity as an expression of excellence, which here may take the colorings of moral excellence (incorporating justice and restraint) and the internalization of excellence. There is a contrast between being prosperous (*olbios*) and being excellent (having *aretē*). This contrast may reflect a different status of excellence, which now leans inwards, to character traits.

For many of the lyric poets, *olbos* connotes pleasure, secured by enduring wealth, which belongs only to the just. The gods can give man this prosperity. As part of that prosperity, wealth is an object of pursuit. Solon's views on wealth, revealed in his hymn to the Pierian Muses, as a part of human prosperity, are interesting. Following Hesiod, he believes that only justly acquired wealth can lead to happiness, while unjustly acquired wealth inevitably leads to divine retribution and the psychic disintegration of the individual. Divinely sanctioned wealth is enduring, for what is not divinely sanctioned does not endure.

For Solon, Zeus acts as an omniscient avenger, although he need not react quickly. Those who act unjustly can expect punishment either instantly or in the future, or that the punishment is saved for their (innocent) children and kin. The view that prosperity includes wealth as a main and necessary part is unsurprising in view of the tradition. One can acquire prosperity and wealth in two ways, justly or unjustly. Acquired in the latter way prosperity is unstable and gives rise to divine retribution. So, according to Solon, *olbos* as prosperity also needs justice as a necessary part.[43]

In fragment 15 (cf. frg. 24) we find Solon actually disassociating wealth and human excellence: 'Many base men are rich and many good men poor: but we will not take their wealth in exchange for excellence, since this is always secure, while wealth belongs now to one man, now to another.'[44] Here one clearly sees a tendency to differentiate excellence and wealth as the most important external good. Solon goes further in this direction, and even suggests an internalization of excellence in his description of the ages of life (frg. 27.11–16):

In the sixth [age] a man's mind is being trained for everything and he is no longer as willing to commit acts of foolishness. In the seventh and eighth, a total of fourteen years, he is far the best in thought and speech. In the ninth he still has ability, but his speech and wisdom give weaker proof of a high level of excellence.

---

[43] Vlastos (1946), 65–83, argued for the bifurcation of justice in Solon, on the one hand of the private sphere, and on the other of the political; Solon's radical views concerned only the political sphere. According to Vlastos, Solon introduces political justice (but not private) 'as a natural, self-regulative order' (65). The idea that injustice forestalls prosperity, as opposed to guaranteeing success, whether for individuals or state, becomes of course the subject matter of Plato's *Republic*.

[44] See the seminal discussion of Solmsen (1949), 122.

At the very least the distinction between excellence as ability and success, absent from Homer, is clear to Solon. Prosperity, however, reliant on human justice, stands in need of divine favor.

This sentiment of human helplessness becomes conspicuous in the lyric poets. Human limitations and consequent imperfections can be of different kinds. Since human beings never have complete excellence, in the sense of having all of them, their happiness can never be complete; it is interspersed with ills; it does not last; it is not self-sufficient but stands in need of divine help. We find this conception of man ripe and mature in perhaps the most famous lines of Pindar (*Pythian* 8.95): 'Creatures of a day (*epameroi*)! What is someone? What is no one? A dream of a shadow is man. But whenever Zeus-given brightness comes, a shining light rests upon men, and a gentle life.'[45]

Pindar differs from earlier lyric poets in that he does not appear to emphasize human dependence on the divine to the same extent as earlier poets. The gods are superior, as in the Homeric worldview, but it is possible to approach the divine through natural endowments, that is, the excellences, although divine favor is needed.[46] The excellences that in Pindar have become the cardinal virtues,[47] notably along with piety (useful for securing the good will of gods), need divine intervention in order to give rise to exceptional success, and create the *eudaimones*; they give victory as honor. But this *eudaimonia* cannot endure and clearly depends on the will of Zeus: 'Truly the great mind of Zeus steers the *daimōn* of men who are dear to him' (*Pythian* 5.122–3).

Excellences reside in a soul that is immortal and gives access to lasting although transcendent happiness (fragments 131b and 133). This can happen if the soul, at some point, gets to rest in a transcendent world with divine beings. In that way it can return to its divine origin, for human beings and divine have the same origin (*Nemean* 6.1–7):

There is one race of men, another of gods; but from one mother we both draw our breath. Yet the allotment of a wholly different power separates us, for the one race is nothing, whereas the bronze heaven remains a secure abode forever. Nevertheless we do somewhat resemble the immortals, either in greatness of mind or bodily nature, although we do not know by day or in the night what course destiny has marked for us to run.

In these lines Pindar acknowledges the traditional conception of the nullity of man as compared to god, as well as its distance from the self-sufficiency of the immortal gods.[48] He suggests that, even though there is resemblance between the two

---

[45] Translations of Pindar are from Race (1997). See Fränkel's classic essay (1960) on the term *ephemeral* as a code for human nature.

[46] It should be borne in mind that, whatever one can say of the other lyric poets, Pindar's epinician poetry is highly religious, expressing dominant ideas about the divine and its relation to the human; cf. Lloyd-Jones (1990), 65–6.

[47] See especially *Isthmian* 8.24ff. on the cardinal virtues.

[48] See also for example *Isthmian* 3.18: 'As the days roll by, one's life changes now this way now that, but the sons of the gods remain unwounded.'

(suggesting the possibility of emulation), human beings are dependent on external powers. Pindar depicts different sides of human imperfections, on which human vicissitudes are based. So long as the principle of alternation really works on happiness, internal excellence is not enough.[49] Human prosperity is always imperfect because unsafe and based on fate.

Excellence as the internal quality we found in Solon is clearly disassociated from external goods. This sentiment is clear in the important *Olympian* 2.51–6:

Winning releases from anxieties one who engages in competition. Truly wealth embellished with excellences provides fit occasion for various achievements by supporting a profound and questing ambition; it is a conspicuous lodestar, the truest light for a man.

It is equally clearly stated in *Pythian* 5.1–4: 'Wealth has wide strength, when conjoined with flawless excellence, a mortal man receives it from destiny and takes it as a companion which brings many friends.' And in *Olympian* 10.20–2 Pindar juxtaposes human excellence with divine favor: 'By honing someone born for excellence a man may, with divine help, urge him on to prodigious fame.' Even if divine succor is always needed, human excellence, which itself is god-given, seems at times to be sufficient for happiness, although not in this life, where it can easily be thwarted. *Pythian* 5.12–14: 'Truly, wise men sustain more nobly even their god-given power. And as you travel the path of justice, great prosperity surrounds you.'

Happiness is found in the afterlife. And it consists in being like god. Eventually the divine attributes are attainable, even if only after death. Pindar elaborates in *Olympian* 2.56–72:

If one has it [wealth and excellence] and knows the future, that the helpless spirits of those who have died on earth immediately pay the penalty—and upon sins committed here in Zeus' realm, a judge beneath the earth pronounces sentence with hateful necessity; but forever having sunshine in equal nights and in equal days, good men receive a life of less toil, for they do not vex the earth or the water of the sea with the strength of their hands to earn a paltry living. No, in company with the honored gods, those who joyfully kept their oaths spend a tearless existence, whereas the others endure pain too terrible to behold. But those with courage to have lived three times in either realm, while keeping their souls free from all unjust deeds, travel the road of Zeus to the tower of Kronos, where ocean breezes blow round the Isle of the Blessed.

7 Xenophanes, Heraclitus, and Transcendental Adumbrations

The transcendent happiness of epinician poetry is the subject of transcendent philosophies that explain the supreme happiness of divinities and man's association

---

[49] See e.g. *Isthmian* 4.6–7: 'At different times different winds rush upon all humans and drive them on.' See also *Ol.* 2.30–6, *Pyth.* 9.76–7; 7.19–21.

with the divine through pure living, which seem up to human beings themselves. The conditions of happiness have been internalized, but happiness is still beyond reach in this life, while godliness itself, as opposed to godlikeness, is the transcendent goal.

The Greeks had originally conceived their gods in the likeness of man. This conception was in part demolished by the sixth-century Xenophanes, whose critique of the traditional attributes of the Olympian gods laid to rest Homeric anthropomorphism as a viable philosophical option. His god nevertheless is a recognizable continuation of the traditional one, even if he is not of human form. First, according to Xenophanes, god is self-sufficient and neither generated nor destructible (B14, 23, 26). Secondly, he is all-seeing, all-knowing, all-hearing, and steers all through the power of his intellect (B23–5). Nor is wisdom his only excellence, for, given the government of intellect, god's rule is just (B11, 12, B1.13–16). Thirdly, god's self-sufficiency indicates his leisure and freedom from disturbance (B25–6). Walter Burkert submits: 'Thus in essence the old epithets of the everlasting, stronger, blessed gods are preserved and made absolute, only the spiritual element has been introduced in place of naïve anthropomorphism.'[50]

Slightly younger than Solon, Xenophanes may also be taken to prefigure the division of goods into mental and non-mental, when he claims that 'better than the strength of men and horses is our wisdom . . . it is wrong to prefer strength to noble wisdom' (B2).[51] We witness an emphasis on human knowledge as an internal excellence. But Xenophanes is famously ambivalent about the possibility of gaining knowledge, at least about the gods. Nevertheless he states (B18): 'Not from the beginning have the gods revealed all things to mortals, but in time by seeking they come upon what is better.' With Xenophanes we have hints about the epistemological relationship of god as intellect and man seeking understanding.[52]

The internalization of excellence requires a contrast between the internal and the external. We need a notion of an inner life, soul, self, that can serve as the conglomeration of the excellences conceived as mental capacities and traits. Xenophanes does refer to the soul in his remarks about Pythagoras (B7): 'And once when he [Pythagoras] was passing a puppy being beaten they say he took pity and said this word: Cease beating him; for surely it is the soul of a friend which I recognized when I heard it howling!' Perhaps this passage from Xenophanes indicates a conception of the soul or of an inner self possibly constituted of excellences. But there is clearly such a mention of the soul as the seat of the excellences in Heraclitus (active around and after 500 BC), who not only internalizes excellence but intellectualizes it as well.

---

[50] Burkert (1985), 318–19. At around the same time Xenophanes is at work, Anaximander, in spite of his rejection of anthropomorphic conceptions, preserves the traditional predicates of god; his divine being is eternal, and he is the omnipotent administrator of justice.

[51] Translations of Presocratic texts are from Graham (2010).

[52] Robinson (2008), 489, plausibly suggests that the gods have a role 'as the indispensable, firm, and incontrovertible underpinning for rational inquiry about the world.'

Intellectual and practical excellences reside in the soul.[53] We possess an important explanation of the excellences (B112): 'Sound thinking (sōphronein) is the greatest excellence and wisdom: to speak the truth and act on the basis of understanding of the nature of things.' However one reads this passage, it is clear that intellectual excellence is the greatest. Heraclitus' statement (B119) that a man's character is his *daimōn* would seem to indicate that an agent's prosperity was up to the agent himself. Insofar as the agent's character is a product of his soul, and of his excellences, one might infer that, according to Heraclitus, the excellences decided the agent's prosperity.

Heraclitus' god, the new Zeus, 'the wise one alone' (B32) governs the universe through his intellect (B41). The order that god maintains is justice (B94). As before, man compares badly to god, who is absolutely wise; man can attempt to find wisdom, but, as man is to god, so an ape is to man (B82–3 cf. B79). Even acknowledging the divide between the human and the divine, Heraclitus stresses the rational account of reality as a way to approach truth, which is divine.[54] One might even suggest that insofar as man is able to get hold of this account, he becomes like the divinity itself.[55]

There is another tradition that puts less emphasis on the pursuit of such an account than on a religious and pure lifestyle as a way to salvation and actually becoming god, as opposed to becoming like god. For Heraclitus is straddled by Orphism and Pythagoreanism on the one hand and Empedocles (ca. 492–32 BC) on the other, who in turn is influenced by Pythagorean and Orphic traditions. Mystery cults associated with Orphism and Pythagoreanism promised the deceased initiate a divine status, an actual state of blessedness: 'Prosperous and blessed one (*olbie kai makariste*), you shall be a god instead of a mortal.'[56] In the *Purifications*,[57] Empedocles counted himself 'an immortal god' (B112) sentenced to mortal existence because of sinning through murder or perjury. His account is highly mythical, no doubt drawing on earlier literature and practices. Recalling Pindar's fragment 133, he envisions a return to divine immortality through a series of more or less unhappy lives.

8   Conclusion

As suggested at the outset, the Greek philosophical conception of happiness refers to excellence—and intellectual excellence above all—as the necessary (even sufficient)

---

[53] For an argument for this claim, see Kahn's commentary on B118 (1979), 245–54; for a general study of the notion of *psuchē* before Plato, see Claus (1981).

[54] For an account of the originality of the Heraclitean ideal of rationality, see Long (2009).

[55] Democritus also plays an important role in the early history of Greek moral psychology, not least by internalizing and intellectualizing the excellences. His approach, though, judging from preserved fragments and testimonies, is not characterized by referring to the divine. Once he says (B189): 'Best for a person is to live his life being as content and as little disturbed as possible. This will occur if he does not take his pleasures in mortal things.'

[56] DK1[Orpheus]B18. On the Pythagorean notion of soul, see most recently Huffman (2009). The mystery cults aim at 'salvation through closeness to the divine'; Burkert (1987), 12.

[57] I leave aside the issue of whether the *Purifications* and *On Nature* are one or two poems.

condition of happiness and, finally, to godlikeness as the state of happiness. The emulation of god is the goal. Among the predecessors of the moral philosophers, three connected attitudes made it impossible to formulate the idea that intellectual excellence—and the successful emulation of god—secures happiness. First, there was the received opinion—even platitude—that the agent's happiness is not up to the agent himself. Evidently this opinion does not require the thesis that the agent plays no part in his own prosperity. The accepted view was that happiness depended on higher powers, divinities that could secure a stable and good fortune. The attitude of these divinities towards human beings is not altogether up to the human beings themselves, even not at all. But their happiness nevertheless depends on these divinities. Secondly, the notion of excellence is such that it is not clearly internal to the agent. Given the philosophers' view, moral and intellectual excellence is a good of the soul, an internal good, the possession of which is a necessary condition for happiness. This conception of the philosophers is the result of a gradual change in the meaning of the term. For their predecessors, excellence as a human quality is at first distinguished from the successful results of its activity. And thirdly, such a distinction is in need of a conception of a soul or self that encompasses such human qualities. This soul to which the philosophers refer the excellences only gradually became capable of containing such an entity.

It is commonly acknowledged that Greek ethics emerged as an attempt to argue that the moral life is necessary for happiness, which is and should be the final aim of our desires and actions.[58] This is not the whole story, since it stops short of including the idea that human happiness is godlikeness. If this godlike intellectual activity is given pride of place, the story might perhaps have a different plot, or at least an important subplot. Greek ethics might then be viewed as an attempt to explain how human beings attain godlikeness as self-sufficient possessors of wisdom and true pleasure. At any rate, the idea of happiness as godlikeness is a noticeable feature of ancient ethics. As such it is obviously an important subject for the historian of philosophy. We have traced in the barest outline antecedents of this philosophical idea and suggested that it is part of a traditional Greek idea of happiness. According to this idea happiness—defined by excellence, self-sufficiency, and pleasure—is measured by notions of the divine. As far as I know the idea that happiness is godlikeness has not been defended in modern (secular) ethics, or in virtue ethics. This ethics has nevertheless looked to the ancient schools for inspiration and guidance, as a legitimate source for understanding morality and agency, not least through the notions of excellence and happiness. Given this difference between ancient and modern ethics, questions arise concerning the modern appropriation of these ancient ideas. Is it possible to mine the ancients and disregard their

---

[58] See e.g. Annas (1993), ch. 14.

idea of happiness as godlikeness without distorting their enterprise? That may well be possible. And even if that is not the case, what distortion there is may not matter for modern ethics. But the fact that the godlikeness idea, integral to ancient ethics, has seemingly not proved tractable within modern ethics indicates an important difference between the two.

2

Plato's Defence of Justice
The Wrong Kind of Reason?

Julia Annas

Socrates' Answer to Glaucon's Challenge

In book 2 of the *Republic* Glaucon makes a famous challenge to Socrates: defend justice for its own sake. The answer which Socrates gives (and which he explicitly relates to the challenge at the end of book 9, at 588b1–4) is a eudaemonist one—that is, it is in terms of *eudaimonia*, which I will translate as happiness.[1] To the question, 'Why should I be just (more generally, virtuous)?'[2] Socrates' answer is that being just will lead to my living a happy life; it is also said to be in my interests, and to benefit me.[3]

To contemporaries this may sound unfamiliar and unconvincing, and it is often met by what are claimed to be obvious counterexamples: people who are recognizably virtuous (for example, just) but obviously not happy. This is to miss Plato's point, however. He is the first example of a consciously eudaemonist philosopher; his ethical framework is one in which the central concepts are those of virtue and happiness or *eudaimonia*. The ancient conceptions of virtue and *eudaimonia* differ from our unreflective notions of virtue and happiness, and Plato is the first to think philosophically about these notions and their roles in an ethical framework. He does not set this framework out explicitly as Aristotle will do, but it can be clearly seen in some passages.[4]

---

[1] I am not here taking up the question of whether *eudaimonia* should be translated as *flourishing*. There is no one translation of *eudaimonia* which suits all contexts.

[2] *Dikaios* is familiarly not as narrow as *just*, and would be better translated as *virtuous* in the *Republic*, but since the philosophers I am discussing use the term *just* I shall follow them, indicating where I think a broader term is required.

[3] *Lusitelein*, to be in one's interest, is prominent in book 1 and in the response to book 2 in book 9, 588b1–92b5. The judgement of lives is posed in terms of happiness; I will not take up here the issue of whether the comparative language in the judgement of lives passage shows that Plato has in mind the weaker thesis, that the just person is happier in this life than the unjust, rather than the stronger thesis, that the just person is happy in this life, regardless of circumstances.

[4] For the legitimacy of finding such a framework in Plato's dialogues, see Annas (1999) ch. 2. Democritus has a claim to be the first philosopher with a eudaemonist ethical framework (see Annas 2002a) but he is not self-consciously aware of it as an object of reflection.

In Plato *eudaimonia*, though often translated as happiness (and corresponding terms in other languages) is not happiness as often understood today—feeling good or getting what you want. It is what we all pursue, and we pursue other things for the sake of it. It's silly, Plato has a character say, to ask whether someone wants to be happy; of course he does. It is the overarching goal that we have for the sake of which we pursue everything we want and value; it is also called 'living well', and it is also taken as obvious that being happy benefits the individual, and is in her interests. Similarly obvious is the point that to be happy we need good things; it would be equally silly to query that. The point that needs investigation, then, is the question of what things are good, since we need to get that right to pursue happiness successfully. Plato himself rejects the ordinary answers to this: money, health, status and so on. It's virtue that we require for happiness, he insists, and without it nothing else will render our lives happy. This thesis (the exact form of which is open to interpretative dispute)[5] shows that Plato is willing to reinterpret, sometimes radically, our evaluations of things as good, but he leaves untouched the fundamental point that we pursue everything for the sake of happiness, understood as *eudaimonia*, and pursue everything else for the sake of it.[6] The ordinary ancient understanding of *eudaimonia* includes virtue, but only as one component among others. Plato not only rejects this, as noted, but gives his own account of virtue as a state of the individual in which the various sources of motivation are harmonized, so that desires and evaluation are integrated.[7]

For both happiness and virtue, then, Plato's account differs from our contemporary unreflective view. His claim, argued most famously in the *Republic*, is that being just, and in general being virtuous, will clearly benefit you and be in your interests, and lead to the happiness of a life well lived that satisfies the person living it.[8]

A Complaint

There has been a great deal of argument as to whether Plato's answer in the *Republic* succeeds in its own terms. Some philosophers have more radically felt uncomfortable with the answer itself. In the last century the English intuitionist philosopher

[5] Plato never formulates his claim with the kind of precision to be found later once it becomes the topic of philosophical discussion. It has been claimed both that he holds that being virtuous is sufficient for being happy and that other things are good and so make us happy only on condition of being put to use in a virtuous life. Each of these claims has texts that support it and texts that do not, or conflict with it. The issue does not have to be settled prior to the present discussion, since both these claims go beyond what ancient common sense holds.

[6] The argument briefly indicated here can be found at *Euthydemus* 278e–82e; analogous points are at *Symposium* 204e–5a and *Philebus* 20b–3a, 60a–1a.

[7] The *Republic* account of the 'divided soul' is the most famous; the account in the *Laws* is similar in spirit but less theoretical. For present purposes we do not need to consider the issue of whether dialogues with a more intellectualist-sounding account do or do not represent a change of position on Plato's part.

[8] That *eudaimonia* requires satisfaction emerges in the *Republic* from the arguments in book 9 which show that the just individual's life is many times more pleasant than that of the vicious.

H. A. Prichard made a complaint, famous in its day, against Plato among others: in appealing to the person's own good they were making a fatal mistake which derailed their theories.[9] For, Prichard claimed, such an answer conflicts with the ordinary moral convictions that people have, namely that appeal to one's happiness (or more generally one's good) misses the point. Ordinary people, the claim goes, recognize that a reason for being just[10] should not appeal to one's happiness or good; it should appeal to its being the right thing to do, or one's duty or obligation, and about *this* there is no more to be said; it is just an appeal to a kind of value (*moral* value, according to Prichard) utterly distinct from one's good.

Prichard is not well known outside the anglophone philosophical world, and his particular form of this complaint has lost much of its influence. It has recently been revived, however, and its interest remains, because it is a forceful version of the thought that the answer which Plato gives to Socrates in the *Republic* to the question, 'Why should I be just (or virtuous)?' is the wrong *kind* of answer. If this can be made out, then the *Republic* turns out to be a misguided project, and with it the mainstream of ancient ethical thinking, which is similarly eudaemonist. The care that has gone into the many explorations of Plato's main argument in the *Republic* would emerge as of strictly historical interest, since the argument itself would be merely an ethical dead end. Further, recent projects of reviving eudaemonist theories of ethics would likewise appear to be a waste of effort. This would endanger the recent revival of kinds of virtue ethics which are eudaemonistic in form. So it is important to examine a contemporary form of this objection, and to see whether Plato has the resources to answer it.

The 'wrong kind of answer' objection has been revived by Lesley Brown and Nicholas White. It is important to examine their version, particularly Brown's, because it is stronger and more defensible than Prichard's, both philosophically and from a scholarly perspective.[11] They do not simply appeal to the idea that eudaemonism does not fit 'ordinary moral views', as though there were such a thing as a clear idea of 'morality' available timelessly from Plato through Prichard to the present day. Rather, they point to indications *in Plato himself* that Socrates' answer to Glaucon's challenge ignores a different kind of answer, one actually available to Plato's own audience.

This is an important challenge. For one thing, it does not depend on particular interpretations of eudaemonism—the claim, for example, that eudaemonism is egoistic. Brown holds that Socrates' 'rational eudaemonism' just is 'rational egoism', an interpretation which is controversial (and which I reject); but her objection would hold of non-egoistic eudaemonism too. For Socrates does appeal to the person's good,

---

[9] Most notably in McAdam (ed.) (2002b), 21–49.

[10] Prichard fails to see that *dikaios* is much broader than *just*, and thinks of it in terms of right and wrong action in a way reflecting his own deontological position.

[11] Brown (2007), White (2002).

and it is this which forms the basis of objections that Plato is appealing to the wrong kind of reason.

More importantly, however, if the challenge is successful, it would establish that when Plato defends justice in a eudaemonist way he is ignoring an alternative available to his audience. This would undercut the widespread approach to ancient ethics which holds that eudaemonism is the default ancient approach to ethics, since it takes over and develops everyday thinking about how to live. On this widespread view, the differing ethical theories provided by Plato, Aristotle, Epicurus, the Stoics, and later thinkers are variations on a common structure: eudaemonism develops, in a variety of theoretically enriched ways, an approach to ethics which is, in everyday life, the obvious default. If Plato is ignoring an alternative plainly available to his audience, then eudaemonism is not so obviously the ancient default way to think about ethics. And this would be a particularly striking result where Plato is concerned, since it is passages in Plato which provide our best examples of eudaemonism as an everyday way of thinking, before philosophy gets going.[12] So, although the challenge here concerns aspects of Plato's text in *Republic* 1 and 2, it is a powerful challenge to the argument of the whole *Republic*, and has important repercussions.

I shall focus on Brown's challenge, since it is the most careful and sophisticated version of the Prichard objection. There are four aspects to it. Firstly, Brown claims that Socrates' interlocutors in the *Republic* show awareness of people who are regarded as admirable, though 'oddballs', because they act in ways that do not contribute to what is good for them, and may indeed go against it. Secondly, she claims that the challenge to Socrates is set up, at the beginning of book 2, in 'egoist' terms which make an answer in terms of the agent's good seem inevitable. Thirdly, she argues that when Socrates sets up the judgement between the lives of the completely just and completely unjust people, this is slanted towards the kind of conclusion he draws by the fact that he focuses only on good or harm to the agents themselves, whereas ordinary moral judgement would think it also relevant what the good or harm is that the person produces for other people. Fourthly and finally she claims that ordinary people of the time, in Plato and elsewhere, think that acting 'for the sake of the just' (*tou dikaiou heneka*) is quite distinct from acting for the sake of something good for you.

These are far from minor points. She concludes that Socrates 'fails to recognise that a just person has reasons for just action *of a quite different kind* from an appeal to one's own good'.[13] The first and second points depend on interpretation of

---

[12] *Euthydemus* 278e–82e, *Symposium* 204e–5a and *Philebus* 20b–3a, as we have seen. The first especially emphasizes the way in which people assume it to be completely obvious that we all seek *eudaimonia* in everything we do, so that reflection will take the form of giving us a better account of what *eudaimonia* is, rather than an alternative to it.

[13] She continues: 'What I have called ordinary moral convictions (glimpsed in the oddballs who are scorned in the brothers' speeches) recognize this, and I agree with Prichard that it is a fatal flaw in Socrates' account in the *Republic* that it does not do so' (Brown (2007), 59).

passages in the text, and concern the exact form of what Plato is claiming. The third and fourth are more directly concerned with what Plato, and we, take to be the appropriate kind of argument when defending justice (or virtue) for its own sake.

I greatly appreciate Brown's insightful argument, and the incisive way that it detaches Prichard's central and important point from other considerations with which it has often been misleadingly bundled. Nonetheless I am still not persuaded that Socrates' eudaemonist answer to Glaucon does offer the wrong kind of reason, nor that the passages she and White point to compel us to their interpretation.

1 The oddballs

The 'oddballs' are people whose views are mentioned, only to be rejected, in books 1 and 2 of the *Republic*. They are said to give us a glimpse of a position held by ordinary people, namely that justice is valuable for its own sake, not for benefits it may bring the agent. This is the alleged ordinary view allegedly ignored by Socrates in his response to Glaucon.

THRASYMACHUS' EXAMPLE

Thrasymachus in *Republic* I is confronted by Socrates at 348c5–d2:

SOCRATES: So you don't think that justice is a virtue (*aretē*), and injustice a vice (*kakia*)?

THRASYMACHUS: Is that likely, do you think, since I say that injustice is profitable, while justice isn't.

SOCRATES: So what is it?

THRASYMACHUS: The opposite.

SOCRATES: So you say that justice is a vice?

THRASYMACHUS: No—it's very noble simplicity (*panu gennaia euētheia*).

SOCRATES: So you call injustice duplicity (*kakoētheia*), then?

THRASYMACHUS: No—it's prudence (*euboulia*).

White (2002, 166–71) claims that Thrasymachus is here recognizing that some ordinary people do not think of justice as being a matter of one's own interests, but rather something one should value for itself even if it is against one's own interests. Thrasymachus himself despises this view and people who hold it, since their 'simplicity' allows them to be taken in by unjust rulers, who, under the cloak of justice, get them to do what is in the rulers' interest but against their own. This is a practice Thrasymachus takes himself to be unmasking with his account of justice as being another's good rather than yours.

The 'simple' people, however, might be being taken in by unjust rulers even if they did think that justice was a matter of their own interests in some way; their simplicity might be a failure to realize that the system the rulers set up is not in everyone's interests, but *only* in that of the rulers. Indeed, this seems the obvious way to read the passage. White complains (170) that this would not account for the 'noble' aspect of the simplicity. 'Whence would the thought of high-mindedness even arise, if we were dealing here with a simple strategic or tactical error about what happiness might result from?' Dispute therefore arises here over the force of the *gennaia* in *gennaia euētheia*. White thinks that it straightforwardly means that the person is admirably noble and high-minded, and is supported by Brown.[14] A more obvious reading, though, is that *gennaia* here just means 'naïve', and is no indication that the position in question amounts to anything more than naïve failure to see how the rulers' actions are failing to work to the benefit of their subjects.[15]

Whether we have a distinct, non-eudaemonistic position here, then, appears to depend rather precariously on whether *gennaia* here means 'noble, high-minded' or is used ironically, with the implication here of 'naïve, foolish'. Obviously it is easy to find examples of *gennaios* where the word straightforwardly does praise what is thought to be noble. And we can also find examples where the word is clearly being used ironically, with no intention to praise.[16] Whether the word is being used straightforwardly or ironically in this passage is hard to determine independently.

We may, however, get some help by looking at a longer discussion in Plato of people who are both *gennaioi* and *euēthēs*, at *Laws* 678e9–9e4. Plato is discussing the first generations of people surviving one of the periodic great floods, and living in small groups on high ground in conditions that later societies consider primitive. These people, he says, were friendly to one another, being neither poor enough to fight over necessities nor rich enough to covet possessions. It is in societies lacking both poverty and riches that the noblest characters (*gennaiotata ēthē*) are to be found. The people at that time were good (*agathoi*) because of this, and also because of what is called simplicity (*hē legomenē euētheia*). Plato uses the word *euēthēs* several times in describing how these people believed what they were told about good and bad, lacking the modern 'wisdom' to suspect falsehood, and unlearned in modern forms of hostility like lawsuits and civic conflicts. Compared with modern people, these early people were 'more simple (*euēthēs*), braver, more temperate and altogether more just' (679e2–3). Here, I think, *euēthēs* can reasonably be understood as *unsophisticated*. It is linked with nobility and virtue, but the link is set very firmly in a simple and 'primitive' context utterly unlike the 'modern' one in which people do lie and are hostile to one another.

The *Laws* passage strongly suggests that Thrasymachus is not straightforwardly praising some people as high-mindedly recognizing the value of justice distinct from their own interest. Rather, he is saying that some people are 'nobly' unsophisticated[17] in a world where (as he thinks is the case) people do lie and are hostile to one another.

[14] Brown (2007), 48. 'In calling their conduct high-minded, he implies that they take the fact that certain conduct is just as a reason for doing it, independent of its being in their interest to act that way; perhaps even in spite of recognizing that it is not in their interest to act that way.'

[15] See, for example, Irwin (2004), 857–8.

[16] As, for example, when Socrates addresses Polus as *O gennaie Pōle* at *Gorgias* 473d3.

[17] It is the lack of sophistication which makes the nobility require scare quotes in English.

This might make them admirable in a more friendly and less devious society, but as it is they are too unsophisticated to deal with the actual world. In short, the force of the term here is to call people naïve and foolish, and the passage does not establish that Thrasymachus recognizes an ordinary admirable non-eudaemonist attitude to justice.

GLAUCON'S EXAMPLE

There are two more 'oddballs', Glaucon's and Adeimantus'. Glaucon says the following at 360c6–d7:

And yet some might say that this is a great indication that nobody is just willingly, only under compulsion, justice not being privately a good: whenever someone thinks that he is able to be unjust, unjust is what he is. For everyone thinks that injustice is much more profitable than justice privately; and they are right, as the author of this argument will say. If someone got hold of such an opportunity but was not willing to do anything unjust, nor to touch other people's property, he would seem most wretched by those aware of it, and utterly foolish. But they would praise him in front of one another, deceiving one another because of their fear of being wronged.

This is counterfactual—people are aware of a situation which *ex hypothesi* requires that nobody be aware of it. Still, Brown (51) and White (172–3) hold that here we find the exceptional just person, who, though admittedly thought an oddball, shows that there are people who refrain from injustice because of what injustice is, not because it isn't in their interest—indeed in the case envisaged it is likely that injustice *is* in their interest.

What does the passage actually show, however? The person envisaged refrains from doing what is unjust—taking someone else's property, for example, in a situation where he could get away with it. Why does he do so? We are not told what his reasons are, except that he is not 'compelled' by what 'compels' other people—presumably fear of bad consequences. This leaves open more than one reason for him to refrain from acting unjustly. He might refrain from injustice because of blankly finding injustice something to refrain from, without further justification. Or he might refrain from injustice because he understands, at some level, that injustice is not actually beneficial to him. Glaucon's example leaves it open which kind of reason is in question here. The example is merely meant as support for the thesis that even an exception to the rule that nobody is willingly a just person turns out to be someone whose life is not enviable, since he is thought to be wretched and stupid. (Why would you want to be like that person?) The passage simply does not concern itself with the person's reasons here, so as it stands it does not give us an alternative to eudaemonist assumptions.

ADEIMANTUS' EXAMPLE

Adeimantus' example, at 366c3–d4, does mention reasons, and is the most interesting of the three:

Suppose someone can show that what I said is false, and that he has adequate knowledge (*hikanōs egnōken*) that justice is best: he will feel great forgiveness and not anger for the unjust, knowing (*oiden*) that apart from someone who is repelled by injustice because of a divine nature, or refrains from it having achieved knowledge (*epistēmēn labōn*), none of the others is just willingly, but only faults injustice because of cowardice or old age or some other weakness, being incapable of doing it. It's clear that this is so: among people like this, the first to acquire power is the first to do wrong, as much as he is able to.

The only reasons, it appears, why people as they are refrain from injustice, because of the kind of thing justice is rather than because of bad consequences, are either a divine nature (that is, a nature for which no merely human explanation is adequate) or that they have knowledge. These are alternatives presented elsewhere by Plato to explain why someone can do something or get something right. It is sometimes hard to know whether the 'divine' alternative is seriously or ironically meant.[18]

At any rate, we here have people who get something important right, either through a kind of divine good fortune or through knowledge. Plato, however, can't have thought that some Athenians already had *knowledge* about justice adequate to show Glaucon and Adeimantus' theory false, to show that justice is best, and to recognize that some others also have this knowledge. If he had thought that, he would hardly have written the *Republic*. Adeimantus is merely assuming that some people do know about justice and injustice, even though he himself has no view here as to what kind of knowledge they have. (We, of course, can't help noting, once we have ourselves read the rest of the *Republic*, that we do get an account of the kind of knowledge that the just person has, of what justice is in itself—and it is precisely the knowledge that being a just person constitutes living a happy life—it is, that is, the eudaemonist answer.)

The people who refrain from injustice here, then, either do so because their nature has something inexplicable about it, or they have knowledge of some kind. But someone with no reasons to offer in support of his or her claim about justice would scarcely be an example of knowledge, however—particularly in the *Republic*, where the account we do find of knowledge and its objects is arguably the furthest in all Plato from ordinary assumptions about what it is to know something.

We don't find, then, in the three passages from Thrasymachus, Glaucon, and Adeimantus, evidence of an alternative non-eudaemonist position about justice, one held by ordinary people who can be assumed to be part of Socrates' audience for his theory.

2 Egoism in the framework?

There are two places in the passage at the beginning of book 2 where it may look as though the framework of Glaucon's challenge encourages, or tilts the discussion towards, Socrates' answer in terms of justice being a good for the agent, neglecting

---

[18] Ion, the rhapsode, has to be divinely inspired, since he is so stupid that he certainly lacks knowledge, and in the *Meno* the statesmen who get things right without knowledge are called divine—but along with poets, prophets, and soothsayers! (*Ion* 541e–2b, *Meno* 99b–d). I agree with Brown that it is unlikely that the knowledgeable person is here meant to *be* either Socrates or Plato, as Vegetti claims (1998, 45 note 57).

alternatives. Right at the start Glaucon distinguishes three kinds of good: a good we welcome for its own sake and not for its consequences, a good we welcome for both, and a good we welcome only for its consequences.[19] Justice is to be shown to be the second kind, the 'finest'. These three kinds of good are all good for the person who is asking whether she should be a just, virtuous person; it is never envisaged that someone might welcome a good because it is good for someone else, not herself. This, it is claimed, narrows the options in a way that makes it appear more obvious than it should, that justice is to be defended as a good for the just person.

But does this build egoism into the framework? That I welcome something as a good for me does not at all imply that I welcome it as good *for only me, me as opposed to other people*. Whether what is good for me is good for me to the exclusion of others depends on whether I have a view of my own good as being *only my* good. So the framework of the three kinds of good is not egoistic just because of the way it is set up.

Does the view that Socrates develops in the *Republic* show that he does in fact think of what is good for the agent in a narrow way opposed to the good of others? Hardly; the good life turns out to be a life which in the ideal conditions of the ideally good city would exclude anything we recognize as self-centredness, and notoriously tries to erase many boundaries between one's own perceived good and the perceived good of others. Even apart from the extreme positions of book 5, we can note that a eudaemonist theory that takes a happy life to be constituted by living justly does not just imply egoism; a eudaemonist theory might be egoistic (as Epicurus' hedonism arguably is) but it might not, and Plato's theory in the *Republic* goes in the opposite direction from egoism.

Glaucon goes on, secondly, to sketch a social contract view in which justice appears as a compromise among people all of whom are motivated by *pleonexia*, the desire to have *more*, often well translated as 'greed'.[20] This assumption about motivation is not an essential part of the social contract idea; Epicurus revives the social contract, but assumes that people are naturally cooperative rather than naturally competitive, so that the social contract turns out to be a coordinating mechanism rather than a compromise. The assumption that greed is the motivation leading to the need for a social contract to establish justice looks like a deliberate choice of Plato's here.

There is no need to assume, however, that Glaucon takes it that *pleonexia* is, as the world stands, the only or even the dominant motive that people have. The social contract is, like the Ring of Gyges, a thought-experiment to help us see how justice

---

[19] *Republic* 357b4–8a3. 'Consequences' is here used in an everyday sense, not to mark the kind of state of affairs that figures in consequentialist theories.

[20] More than I already have, or more than other people? This is not specified, but the assumption appears to be that the first will require the second, since people are assumed to be in competition for limited resources.

might come about in a society. People may have all sorts of admirable motives, but to explain why society sets up a system of justice we need to assume, not just these admirable motives, but the motive of *pleonexia*, since this is the one that needs the constraints of a system of justice. Glaucon is thus not assuming a universal egoistic motivation of greed, merely assuming that greed, and hence competitiveness, is sufficiently widespread among people to explain why we have systems of justice.

Glaucon's assumption here is more realistic than Epicurus' (and arguably Protagoras' in his long speech in the *Protagoras*). If we assume that humans are naturally cooperative rather than competitive, as Epicurus does, then we sorely need an explanation of how people can go so wrong about their own interest as to end up competing for things that there is, in ideal Epicurean circumstances, no need to compete for. It is significant that Epicurus, or at least Epicureans, rejected the thought-experiment of the Ring of Gyges, dismissing it as too unrealistic to be taken seriously.[21]

But even if Glaucon's assumptions here did presuppose egoism, that would not show that *Socrates'* answer to the question of why I should be just would have to be forced into the same mould. Socrates' answer, as it unfolds over the course of the *Republic*, rejects the assumptions made here in setting up the social contract account of justice. We can, Socrates claims, come to understand that justice is valuable in itself precisely because living justly constitutes the happy life. Hence it is a mistake to think of us as limited to seeking our own good as opposed to that of others—whether this is thought of as a universal assumption about human nature or merely an assumption needed to explain a social contract account of justice.

3 The judgement of lives

Brown points out two interesting and neglected points about Glaucon's judgement of lives. This comes in a passage (360e1–1d3) where we are to judge which is the happier of two lives. On the one hand we have the completely just person stripped of everything but justice, including the reputation for being just, and suffering horrible torture and death. On the other hand we have the completely unjust person given every advantage of justice, including the reputation of being just, and meeting with universal prosperity and approval.

The first point is that the unjust person is said to do the greatest injustices, but we are not told what these are; 'since these do not accrue to him, but to others, why— Plato seems to ask—should we be interested in them in judging which life is preferable?' (Brown, 52–3). In judging the person's life, that is, Plato assumes that we ignore the bad effects of his actions on others. We take into account only what he has gained from his unjust actions, not what others have lost by them. Secondly, when the just person is stripped of everything but his justice, the question is never

---

[21] Cicero *De Officiis* III 37–9.

raised, what the just person achieves for others through his justice, for which he falsely loses the credit. As with the unjust person, we are to take into account only the impact on the just person, not on others, of his just actions. We take into account only what the person loses by his justice, not what others gain. As Brown forcefully puts it (54): 'It seems to be *of not the slightest relevance* what the just person achieves by the ... practice of his *dikaiosunē* (justice). Any good he achieves is another's good, and why should anyone care about that?'

This is an important point, neglected (as far as I know) in the abundant literature on the topic of Glaucon's challenge.[22] It raises a very reasonable query: shouldn't our judgement between two lives take into account the impact on others, as well as on the people themselves, of the way the lives are lived? When Plato tacitly ignores the effect on others of the just person's justice and the unjust person's injustice, is he not thereby tacitly introducing an egoist assumption: that justice must be shown to be a good for the person in a way which in fact shows it to be good *only* for the person, excluding its being a good for others?

Here we need to make an important distinction, one which is not prominent in contemporary ethical theories. Plato's judgement of lives can be taken in two quite different ways. In one way of understanding it, we are thinking of the person's life *in its circumstances*. That is, we are judging the person in a way which takes into account what he achieved in the situation in which he lived, including his effect on others, both positive and negative. In this sense a person's life includes his impact on others—the bad effects of his wrongdoing and the good effects of his just actions—others' deaths and disasters, or benefits conferred.

In the other way of understanding it, when we think of a life, we are thinking of *how the person lives his life*, what he makes of the circumstances he is in. Here the circumstances in which he finds himself determine whether his justice succeeds in benefitting others, or his injustice succeeds in harming others. But these circumstances are distinct from his *life* in this sense, that is, the way he *chooses to live his life*.

Which of these does Plato have in mind: your life including your circumstances or the living of your life as distinct from the circumstances you live it in? Clearly he intends the latter. He has to—he wants to show, after all, that it will be to your benefit to be just in *any* circumstances, including the worst circumstances of the actual world. It is to your benefit to be just, he claims—you will actually be happier—even if you are despised as a wrongdoer, ruined, tortured, and put to death. Circumstances don't get much worse than that, so this is, as he recognizes, an extremely strong claim to make about the benefits of living your life justly rather than unjustly. You can, Plato thinks, choose to live your life this way, to the extent that you can come to grasp what justice and goodness are. Plato does not try to show that it will be to your benefit to be just and to find yourself in circumstances in which you happen to be able to

---

[22] At least, I am not aware of anyone else who has made use of this point to challenge the ethical relevance of Plato's eudaemonism.

benefit others—since obviously whether or not you find yourself in these circumstances is not the kind of thing you can choose. What you can choose is to live in a
way which will enable you to flourish in any circumstances.

Plato is, then, entirely right, in the judgement of lives, not to take account of the
impact on others of the just and unjust people's justice and injustice. For this is not
part of the way they choose *to live their lives*, namely justly or unjustly; it is due to the
circumstances they happen to live in. One unjust person, for example, might live in
circumstances in which he was unable to do harm to anyone; another might be an
absolute ruler, and turn out to wreak as much destruction as Genghis Khan or Vlad
the Impaler. One just person might have little money; another might have a lot, and
use it to benefit a large number of people. This is a matter of the circumstances in
which they find themselves, and these obviously cannot make one life more just or
unjust than the other. What the just person achieves for others by exercising his
justice is important, but it isn't part of how he lives his life; *he* lives his life, justly or
unjustly. This is not in any way egoistic; it is merely the point that only he can live his
life, and the impact on others of his living his life isn't part of his living his life, which
is what the judgement of lives is about.

Brown says that 'ordinary moral convictions' (as opposed to those of Kantians and
Stoics) would naturally value more highly a scenario where a just man, even though
falsely deprived of his reputation, produces benefits for others, to a scenario where a
just man is not only falsely deprived of the reputation of having benefitted others but
has not in fact, because of systematic bad luck, benefitted them. This is interesting
and puzzling, since the alternatives are not clear. What is it that we value more highly
in the first case? Is it the state of affairs where more people are benefitted than in the
other? How do we value states of affairs? We can't *choose* between states of affairs, as
we are supposed to choose between the two lives, for example. We might choose to
bring a state of affairs about, but that is a different matter. To the extent that it is not
clear what it is to value a state of affairs, I think that 'ordinary moral convictions' here
are, to the extent that they rely on it (if they do), not clear. We can, however, give
sense without much difficulty to the idea that we prefer the circumstances in which
the just man benefits others to that in which he does not, or the circumstance in
which the unjust man fails to harm others to that in which he does. This seems
indeed to be both reasonable and a widespread phenomenon. It is, however, a
preference between lives thought of in certain circumstances, and is clearly distinct
from judging lives in the sense of *living* those lives. We can make the difference
clearer by distinguishing, as the Stoics were to do, between preferring some circumstances to others, and choosing to live one kind of life rather than another. And
clearly it is the latter which concerns Plato here.

Brown claims that the way that the judgement of lives is set up removes from
consideration matters which are relevant when we pass a judgement on a life—
namely the impact on others of the way the life is lived. This bears on eudaemonism
in that she thinks that it is by setting up the judgement in the way that he does that

Plato makes Socrates' answer, in terms of justice constituting the happy life, seem the natural response to the question of how best to live, implicitly excluding alternatives that would focus on lives other than the agent's. I have argued that Plato is right to set the judgement up in the way that he does, since he distinguishes the way a person lives her life, justly or unjustly, from the circumstances, preferable or not, in which she does it. This is a defensible and important distinction, though of course it has not been fully defended here. Hence there is no clear alternative here which Plato has failed to consider in setting up the judgement.

Brown's article makes it clear that contemporaries might well find alternatives here, and some do. Much contemporary ethical thinking is perfectly comfortable with valuing states of affairs, for example. If we do find it obvious, and a matter of ordinary moral convictions, that we judge lives including their circumstances, and that we prefer a life including circumstances with more people benefitted to a life including circumstances with fewer, then we are obviously not making the distinction Plato does, namely between life and circumstances. But this is not a problem *for Plato*, or for his formulation of eudaemonism. And to the extent that we find Plato's kind of eudaemonism attractive, we might find it useful to enlarge the options of contemporary ethical thinking by making use of the distinction between the living of a life and the circumstances in which it is lived.

4 Acting 'because it's just'

Glaucon demands that we remove the just person's reputation for justice, because only so will we be able to see whether his reason for being just is 'for the sake of the just (*tou dikaiou heneka*) or for the sake of the rewards and honours' (361c1–4). Brown foregrounds the point that what is to be shown is that the just person acts 'for the sake of the just'. What does this amount to? At the least it must mean that the just person does just (and generally, of course, more broadly virtuous) actions without being compelled to them, and without any ulterior motive; her reason is simply that the actions in question are just.[23] Such a person can reasonably be said to value justice 'for its own sake' or 'in itself'; they value justice for what it is and not for the wrong kind of reason, whatever the wrong kind of reason may be. But most people, according to Brown, think that they understand perfectly well what this amounts to without also thinking that valuing justice for its own sake involves valuing justice as an intrinsic good for themselves (Brown (2007), 55–7).

The same goes for a passage referred to by White,[24] namely 363e4–4a4, where Adeimantus says that poets and people all agree that justice and temperance are fine (*kalon*) but difficult and burdensome. People here simply hold that justice is

---

[23] I pass over here issues of the exact form of motivation; of course the just person will not normally have to tell herself explicitly that she is acting in order to do a just action, or to become a just person. Her reasons will normally take the form, 'I owed the money' and the like.

[24] White (2002), 173 note 56.

something fine, even though they also think that valuing it, and doing just actions, is not as pleasant as being unjust, and even if they are induced to think that the shamefulness of injustice is not as important as they have been brought up to think. Again, it seems clear that when people have this thought about justice they are not thereby having the thought that valuing it as something fine involves valuing it as an intrinsic good to oneself.

Brown points out that we easily find cases (she gives one from the orator Lysias) in ordinary discourse in which people describe actions as done simply because they are just or for the sake of the just (*tou dikaiou heneka*), where all that this implies is that the person did what justice required without thought of reputation or the like. If this is how the idea of valuing justice for itself is naturally understood, then, she claims, Socrates is introducing a new idea, one not required by 'ordinary moral convictions', in insisting that justice be shown to be a good for the just person. In fact, the objection runs, Glaucon's speech will turn out to introduce an idea not given in the assumptions of 'ordinary morality' in producing a eudaemonist answer to the question, why one should be just.[25]

Let us assume that 'ordinary morality' does stop at the point of recognizing that we can act in ways that show that we value justice for itself and act *simply* 'for the sake of the just' (*tou dikaiou heneka*). Does this show that 'ordinary morality' recognizes a kind of reason for action which is distinct from acting for your own good or happiness, and that Glaucon's challenge shows failure to accept this—or even failure to understand it?

If 'ordinary morality' does just stop at the idea of acting 'for the sake of justice', then Glaucon's challenge arguably shows that Plato understands it all too well. For what kind of reason for acting is it, that it is 'for the sake of the just', *tou dikaiou heneka*, full stop? It doesn't sound much like a *reason*. Suppose we ask someone who acts in the supposed exemplary fashion, why she does so, what her reason is. If she can do no better than to repeat that she is acting simply because that kind of thing is just, and that she values the just because it is just, we have a failure to give a reason rather than the ability to give a distinct kind of reason.

Plato, as is notorious, has Socrates require his interlocutors over and over again to 'give an account' (*logon didonai*) of what they claim to know, or even to have good grounds for. For unless you can explain what the object of your concern is, and explain your reasons in acting on it, you are clueless as to what you are talking about. Plato is (at least in his own terms) correct, rather than missing something, in not taking seriously as an alternative kind of reason the kind of thing that would be said by someone who could *only* say that she was acting *tou dikaiou heneka*, and give no further reason. If you cannot give an account of what you are doing when you act

---

[25] Again, this is not dependent on the questionable claim that Glaucon is introducing an 'egoist take on the matter' (Brown (2007), 57). Eudaemonism is clearly introducing a new kind of context for the issue of valuing justice for its own sake, even if it is not egoist.

justly, and can give no account of *what justice is* that you should value it for its own sake, then you are not in possession of a distinct kind of reason for being just; you are only someone who has not thought about what justice is.

This is the kind of person who, according to Plato, is vulnerable to sophistical reasoning that undermines his commitment to justice. In a passage later in the work (538d6–e5) Socrates describes a person who has picked up his views about the fine (and the just and the good) from 'the lawgiver'—that is, from traditional teaching and behaviour. He is tempted, but not yet deeply, by a lifestyle that ignores or opposes these traditional values. Then someone asks him what the fine and just are, and he has no resources to defend the views he has got from tradition about them, and fails to give an answer that can withstand criticism of them. So he gives up on them and ceases to respect them. Plato regards this process as one that leads many people to abandon traditional values that they themselves don't find fault with, because they lack reasons and arguments to meet criticisms from others.

The person who merely values justice for its own sake and goes no further, then, is someone who has no reason to give as to why he is acting as he is. And this is a dangerously fragile position. We do not, then, find a non-eudaemonistic alternative kind of reason for valuing justice for its own sake; we merely have people who stop at that point because they have no kind of reason; they have thought no further than what tradition or 'the lawgiver' said. Of course people who act justly without being able to give an account of why they are acting as they do, are preferable to people who act unjustly; but they are not an acceptable alternative to people who *can* give an account of justice, what it is and why we should value it for its own sake.

Plato's own account, developed in the *Republic*, tells us that we should value justice for its own sake because it constitutes the happy life. This rejects the kind of reason that 'ordinary morality' also rejects, namely rewards, respect, and the like. It also explains to us what it is about justice that makes it reasonable to value it for its own sake, even in the worst circumstances the world can throw at us. We may, of course, reject Plato's kind of answer. What I have tried to show here is merely that it is an answer that explains the benefits of justice not only to people who are tempted to be unjust but also to people who, even when not seriously tempted to be unjust, lack the resources to explain why this is reasonable, and so cannot get beyond the mere claim that they value justice 'for itself'. Plato, then, does not neglect an available alternative kind of reason here; there is none for him to find.

Giving a Reason

Many critics of Plato (and Aristotle, and other eudaemonist ethical thinkers) hold that appeal to one's own good in any way gives us the wrong kind of reason for acting justly. I will here lay aside the issue of whether Plato's claim about one's good can be reasonably defended; I am here focusing rather on what the alternative is supposed to be. Brown claims that her arguments 'vindicate' Prichard (Brown 57, 59) in claiming that Plato neglects the availability, to his audience, of a completely distinct, non-eudaemonist kind of reason for being just. What is this distinct kind of reason?

As is clear by this point, the people claimed by Brown and White to have a non-eudaemonist viewpoint are people who do just actions because they are the just thing to do (and presumably with the other virtues), and who value justice for its own sake; in general, they act 'for the sake of the just', *tou dikaiou heneka*. Does it follow that they have and act on a different kind of reason, a viable alternative to eudaemonism? Not yet, I have argued; their position is better interpreted as that of people who act and think in certain ways because they were well brought up, but who lack the resources to explain what they are doing and why they value what they do. This is why they simply stop at the idea of what is just.

It is worth pointing out that Prichard is a problematic ally here, since he is an intuitionist about ethics, which he takes to be centrally a matter of morality, duty, and right action. He insists that it is radically mistaken to ask for an argument or reason as to why we should be moral and do the right thing: this is, he claims, 'self-evident' since it cannot rest on anything further. His own objection to Plato is not merely that Plato offers the wrong kind of reason in giving eudaemonist grounds for being just; Plato is among (virtually all) philosophers who have given us reasons for something for which, Prichard thinks, reasons cannot be given without changing the subject or missing the point.[26]

There are two major reasons why Plato could not possibly do what Prichard demands. One is that Plato thinks that ethics is centrally about virtue, virtuous action, and the virtuous person, and that being virtuous involves sensitivity to reasons; that is why in the *Republic* there is so much stress on the guardians' education. It is not enough for them to follow the laws and do the right thing; they must understand why they do it.

The other, already touched on, is that for Plato the person who acts justly and can even talk about justice, but cannot give an account of what justice is, is so far defective; he needs to reflect on what he does and what he thinks, and to come up with a defensible account of it.[27] Until he can do this, we cannot take his position seriously. So, given that Prichard actually makes a virtue of *not* coming up with an account of exactly what Plato thinks we do need an account of—what justice is and why we should be just—Plato has nothing to fear from Prichard.[28]

Meeting this kind of criticism—the objection that Plato offers us the wrong kind of reason for being just—makes it clear how important it is for Plato that we understand why we are just, when we are, and that we understand what it is about justice that

---

[26] See especially Prichard's remarks (2002), 19–20 and 38–9.

[27] Cf *Meno* 80a–b, where Meno recalls how he used to pontificate about virtue in front of large audiences, before realizing that he could give no account of it and thus did not understand what he was talking about.

[28] A fuller discussion of Prichard's own methodology in comparison to that of ancient ethical thinkers in general can be found in LeBar (2010).

makes it reasonable to value it for itself rather than for its conventional rewards. It also shows how vast is the distance between Plato and an intuitionist like Prichard, who simply rejects the demand that we reflect on and come up with understanding of *why* we do our duty, when we do, and *what it is* about duty and obligation that enables them to make their demands on us. In my view, appreciating this distance leads us to see what is lacking in intuitionists like Prichard, and encourages us to appreciate the importance of Plato's kind of demand, namely that we understand why we are acting as we do, rather than remaining at our starting post and refusing to go further.[29]

[29] I am grateful to my audience at Oslo for very helpful comments, to my colleague Rachana Kamtekar for comments and discussion, and to the *Happiness in Antiquity* project for stimulating interaction which greatly improved my thinking on ancient eudaemonism.

3

Wanting to Do What Is Just in the *Gorgias*

Panos Dimas

I

Socrates wins acceptance from Gorgias for the view that doing what is just is what people want, but when this is challenged by Polus, he fails to back up this view with substantive content. At the end he only succeeds in opposing the one substantive account offered in support of such a view in the *Gorgias*—that is, the view that people want to do what is just—namely that of Callicles. Socrates' elenctic efforts notwithstanding, none of his interlocutors admit to having been refuted. Though they seem unable to defend themselves and are often caught in contradiction, the position underlying their views is not adequately shaken and too entrenched to have suffered a blow. To have any hope of dislodging it, Socrates needs to offer a positive alternative, and this he seems unable to do.

Nominally the subject matter of the *Gorgias* is rhetoric. However, its main theme, I believe, is the demands that justice makes of us and our attitudes, and the part of justice in human happiness. This is explored in the argument Socrates conducts with three different interlocutors: Gorgias, Polus, and Callicles. Since rhetoric is the occasion for introducing the main theme, I will say a bit about it, mainly to indicate my scepticism that Plato is as hostile toward rhetoric as Socrates' remarks might be suggesting.[1] I will not argue this, however, but instead focus on the disagreement concerning the proper role of justice in the happy or good life.

More precisely, I will be arguing in some detail for the following. The point of the discussion between Socrates and Gorgias is not merely, as is usually thought, to reduce Gorgias to a contradiction.[2] True, following Socrates' questioning, Gorgias agrees to a proposition that is in conflict with a statement he has made previously. But the point of philosophical interest in this is rather that each of these conflicting

---

[1] Cf. Stauffer (2002), 656.
[2] See, e.g. Cooper (1999), 29–51; Kahn (1996), 134, for this view.

statements Gorgias accepts seems plausible in its own right. What this discussion between Socrates and Gorgias succeeds in doing, I argue, is bring out an aporia of the genuine Aristotelian type: on the one hand there is ample empirical evidence, and hence also reason, to hold that people often choose not to do what is just in circumstances that call for just action, despite knowing what the just thing to do is; on the other hand, there is also reason to think that, knowing what is just, one would want to do it. Polus enters the discussion denying the second horn of this aporia, that is, the one Socrates defends, namely that people want to do what is just.[3] When it becomes clear that Polus is unable to support his view with argument, Callicles comes to his defence by offering a view on justice, which in fact makes it possible to assert the second horn of the aporia, that is, the one acceptable to Socrates. However, Socrates finds this view unacceptable. Despite appearances, Callicles' view is not hedonism, I argue. I offer an interpretation of this view by Callicles, and indicate reasons for which Socrates is unable to dislodge it.

II

The discussion with Gorgias falls into two parts, each at either side of 458b4–c2, where Gorgias tries politely to excuse himself from the conversation, but is obliged to continue, following a request by Callicles and Chaerephon. The first part concerns itself mostly with rhetoric and lays the groundwork for the attack that will reduce Gorgias to aporia.

In Gorgias' view, the task of the orator is to be persuasive (*peithein*) to jurors in court, councillors in the council, assemblymen in the assembly and any other political gathering (452e1–4). Having restated the argument that rhetoric is the art (*technē*) engaging solely in producing conviction (*peithous dēmiourgos*) (452e9–3a3), he asks the following question: since teachers of other crafts, such as mathematics, can also claim to produce persuasion in the subject matter specific to their art, to set the craft of rhetoric apart from them we must identify the specific subject matter in which rhetoric produces persuasion. To this Gorgias responds that rhetoric is the persuasion taking place in courts and other large gatherings and is concerned with what is just and unjust.

Socrates now draws a distinction between two kinds of persuasion, one produced by learning (*mathēsis*), the other by conviction (*pistis*). Learning and teaching are said to be of knowledge (*epistēmē*), and hence of what is true (454d6–7). Conviction, on the other hand, is agreed to be either true or false (454d4), and the persuasion produced by rhetoric in courts is of this kind (455a1). With Gorgias' agreement, Socrates accounts for rhetoric as the producer of persuasion of the kind produced by conviction about what is just and unjust (454e9–5a2), and goes on to argue that,

---

[3] For a good discussion of the implications of this claim, see Segvic (2000).

being such, rhetoric is redundant (455a8–d5). Rather than an orator politician, we should have experts possessing knowledge in the various fields, able to produce knowledge-based conviction by addressing the assembly when decisions need to be made: an expert physician, when a chief physician is to be hired, an expert ship-builder when the decision concerns ships, the master builder when it is about walls, and in general the master craftsman of whatever craft in relation to which a decision needs to be made.

However, Gorgias is able to deflect this criticism, and at the same time drive home a valuable point, which Socrates never discusses. Gorgias himself has often been more successful in convincing his brother's patients to follow the treatment prescribed by his brother, who is the expert physician (456b–c). Rhetoric benefited patients when the expert physician was not able to do this with his expertise alone. To the extent that this point can be generalized, it suggests that rhetoric is valuable. It has the capacity to convince people to do what is good for them in cases where the expert on the issue under discussion might fail. Matters of state are a case in point. As Gorgias points out, it was not on the advice of expert craftsmen but on that of Themistocles and Pericles that the walls and dockyards of Athens were built (445d–e). Admittedly, it seems much more plausible, intuitively, that it is the politicians and generals who should advise on these matters rather than the master builders. On this basis, it seems true that rhetoric is an expertise, or skill, that is distinct from any expertise in particular scientific fields. It would also seem intuitively plausible that an expert in any one of these other scientific fields who possesses this skill in addition would be likely to be better equipped to advise non-experts more effectively than one who lacks it. Socrates does not take this consideration up for discussion.[4]

More importantly, in many, if not most, of the areas of civic life in which an assembly would be called upon to reach a decision, the knowledge that according to Socrates would be required to produce knowledge-based conviction is not possessed by anyone, even by Socrates' own lights. Crucially, on Socrates' account, an expert scientist in justice would be required to advise on issues concerning what is just and unjust, and it is not clear who that would be. The same would be the case with respect to matters pertaining to military strategy, economic policy, and so on. In such contexts it would seem more reasonable to proceed by offering proposals and inviting people to consider them. Naturally, those with rhetorical skills will be more forceful than others in presenting their case. And it may well be that the case they make is a poor one in its substance, although they manage to present it forcefully, even convincingly. It is such cases Gorgias has in mind when he says (456c–7c) that there is no way of knowing how rhetoric might be used, if it will be used well or badly. But its questionable use is not sufficient to rob it of all value. Even if there were an

---

[4] He offers no comment at least at this point. Much later, at 519a, in an emotional monologue against these leaders, he calls the walls rubbish. Surely Plato does not expect this to be taken seriously, given the strategic importance of the Athenian Walls.

expert scientist in some of these areas that mostly interest Socrates, the people this expert would often need to address and persuade would be non-experts, and it is reasonable that he should think that it would not be as effective if he were to address them with arguments and considerations designed to address other experts.[5]

III

Without further discussion, Socrates generalizes the point that, not knowing medicine, the orator may still be more successful in persuading than the expert physician, and asks whether the orator, without actually knowing about the just and the unjust, the good and the bad, the noble and the shameful, would appear to those who do not know about these things to know more than the one who actually does know. Gorgias is never given a chance to respond; instead he is put on the spot with a further question: would he take in students who do not know about these things and simply go on to teach them rhetoric, or would he begin by giving them instruction on what is just and unjust first? (459c8–e)

   Usually Socrates wants to know what something is before he allows himself or anyone else to say anything about it, such as for instance whether it can be taught or not.[6] Ignoring this question completely, as Socrates does here, leaves it unclear whether by 'justice' Socrates and Gorgias refer to the same thing. Socrates speaks about justice as something of which one can have knowledge, by which we know he means a rigorous science, and, more importantly, as something of which people actually lack knowledge (459e). Gorgias, on the other hand, sounds astounded when Socrates asks him whether he would teach justice to a prospective student of rhetoric who does not know about it. 'If he really does not have this knowledge, I suppose I'll teach him.' (460a2–3) Part of the reason for Gorgias' response seems straightforward. To be effective, the orator must be sensitive to the sensitivities of his audience. Should Gorgias receive a student who is clueless about justice, it is imperative that he should teach him, if he is going to be successful in teaching him rhetoric, and given that rhetoric is a skill that aims at making the student effective in debates that involve the concept of justice. More interestingly, however, with his answer Gorgias indicates that, his age and experience as a teacher notwithstanding, he has not come across anyone who does not know sufficiently about matters pertaining to justice, and that he would be very surprised if anyone came to him without knowing. Quite unsurprisingly, therefore, he assumes that any adult would know enough about justice, without Gorgias or anyone else having to instruct him, and that, quite generally, a properly socialized adult probably knows all that can be said to be known about it. Even though Gorgias does not reflect on the issue, 'knowledge' might even be a misleading term in this case, if it suggests that the one who knows about justice is an

---

[5] As Socrates himself points out at 458e–9a.
[6] Think, for example, of his insistence on defining virtue before discussing its teachability in the *Meno*.

expert in a science that has the same kind of structural arrangement as, say, the science of mathematics. Justice for Gorgias is most likely not the sort of thing one needs special instruction to acquire, but rather a competence one acquires through ordinary socialization.[7]

As far as Gorgias is concerned, then, we would be correct in assuming, the case of medicine is not comparable to that of justice. Medicine or mathematics are sciences in which there are only few experts. Most people do not know much about either, nor would they be expected to know. That physicians are placed apart from non-physicians with respect to their knowledge of medicine cannot imply, or even suggest, that there is similarly a kind of knowledge about justice possessed by some but not by others and that it is such as to place those who possess it apart from those who do not.

Furthermore, Socrates appears illegitimately to conflate being convincing and claiming—or misleadingly, but intentionally appearing—to have knowledge of what one does not. So he describes the trained orator as one who gives the impression of having knowledge about justice even though he is ignorant about it. It is unclear what warrant his discussion with Gorgias may have provided for him to make this claim. Nowhere does Gorgias say or imply that he had appeared to his brother's patients to be more knowledgeable about medicine than is his brother. He only said that he was more successful than his brother in convincing his brother's patients to follow the treatment prescribed by his brother. Socrates' remarks concerning the treatment of justice by the trained rhetorician is even more problematic, given that the context Gorgias most probably has mind is one where the participants negotiating matters of justice assume that they all share whatever competence there is to be had about it. Quite likely, in such a context no participant will even be inclined to think that the orator is an expert on justice as opposed to those who are not, for the simple reason that no participant will believe that there are experts on justice.

IV

Upon Gorgias' response that he would teach his students about the good and bad if they did not know, Socrates begins on the line of questioning that will lead to what is universally thought by commentators to be a refutation of Gorgias, and eventually Polus' entrance onto the scene. What Socrates' line of questioning results in at this point, however, is not a refutation, but an aporia of the kind we have become used to finding in Aristotle. The discussion has revealed two positions, each one of which seems plausible, but which are mutually exclusive. Socrates makes the point that if someone learns carpentry, he becomes a carpenter, if he learns music a musician, medicine a doctor. Based on this reasoning, he makes the further point that if

---

[7] A view that is actually defended by Protagoras in his great speech in the dialogue that bears his name.

someone learns about the just he becomes just. But the just man, Socrates goes on to say, does just things, and if this is true, it cannot also be true, as Gorgias has asserted, that the rhetorician cannot control how the student will eventually use rhetoric, justly or unjustly.

This is clearly a tricky piece of argument. Initially, it is plagued by the lack of clarity as regards the reference of 'just' or 'justice'. If what Gorgias' students would learn from him about justice is what every other adult knows, it is doubtful that this alone would make them just in the sense Socrates has in mind, or any more just than any other adult Athenian. However, Socrates' point affords a more charitable reading. When he says that the one who knows about justice is just, he does not have to be using 'just' in the sense we would be inclined to take it, namely that to be just simply means to be doing what is just. More likely he uses it to designate the possession of a capacity; being 'just' merely indicates that one knows what the just or unjust thing to do is in circumstances that call for just action.[8] To the extent that he draws a parallel between this case and those of the knowledge of carpentry, music, and medicine, this is precisely what he ought to be doing. Indeed, Socrates confirms that he thinks of the case of justice in the same way when he says, not simply that the just person would be doing what is just, but that he would be doing so because he would *want* (*boulesthai*) to be doing what is just (460b8–c6). He actually makes this point, that the just person would want to act this way, three times in the course of four lines. In other words, he seems careful not to imply that knowledge of what is just generates just action *by itself*. In fact, what he implies is the contrary, for he says, unequivocally, that knowledge of the just is able to secure just action on account of the fact that the agent who possesses it *wants* to be doing what is just. In the very least, this statement delineates, and therefore implies, the existence of two distinct psychic capacities, one epistemic and one volitional, both of which need to cooperate for just action to take place. But it also implies that knowledge of justice is such that, once one has it, one does want to do what is just.

It is not entirely clear on the basis of what view exactly Socrates supports what he has just said. It could be that knowledge of what is just, even though it is not itself what makes the agent do what is just in circumstances that call for just action, is by itself sufficient to make him want to do what is just. Or it could be that this knowledge explains to the agent that an independent motivation of his that is linked to his personal well-being is best served by putting this knowledge into practice whenever circumstances call for it. We will have the opportunity later to reach a decision on this. For now we need only notice that Socrates' position that the agent who knows what is just will also want to do it is not easy to reject off hand. People do generally consider justice an important value. They expect leaders to cherish it and to pay heed to it when they lead. They expect their legislative assemblies to respect it when they legislate. And they expect the courts of law to follow it when they pass

---

[8] This is a move Socrates clearly makes in the *Hippias Minor*. See Dimas (2014a).

judgment. More crucially, people expect—actually assume—this kind of attitude from individuals to whom they have relations, be those of friendship or of any other kind. They have contempt for those individuals who knowingly violate the commands of justice and, more interestingly, they are likely to be uncomfortable about doing so themselves, also in those cases where they in fact happen to do it. It seems fair to say that a properly functioning society depends on the individuals' comprising it observing the commands of justice, and it is rather taken for granted that individuals want to be members of such a society. It is simply not easy, therefore, philosophically or otherwise, to deny that humans would want to do the just thing when they know it, and it is definitely not easy for Gorgias to deny it. But quite apart from whatever reasons Gorgias might have for not denying it, the fact is that what we have here is a genuine aporia. On the one hand, it seems reasonable to hold that people would want to do what is just, when they know it. On the other, there are facts in great supply supporting Gorgias' view that people, orators included, often do not act in accordance with what they believe is just.

V

It is at this point that Polus intervenes. He accuses Socrates of leading Gorgias to the kind of inconsistency Socrates takes delight in, the inconsistency in this case being the aporia facing Gorgias and the remainder of the dialogue. Gorgias, it is reasonable to expect, is, as most people, inclined to hold both that it is possible that one might not do the just thing even though one knows it, and that the one who knows what is just wants to do it. According to Polus, Socrates exploited that Gorgias was too ashamed not to agree that he would teach his students about justice if they did not know about it.[9] Polus may of course be right that this is the reason Gorgias never engaged Socrates on the issue of the need to teach justice to someone nearing adulthood, but the problem that Gorgias—and with him the discussion—faces is not this. It is that, thanks to Socrates, there has emerged a view that conflicts with the one Gorgias originally expressed, and which Gorgias has good reason to acknowledge that he also finds attractive.

At this point there comes an interlude in which Socrates offers his views on rhetoric (464b2–6a3). He distinguishes between body and soul and claims that there is a craft that sees to the fitness of each. In the case of the soul this craft is politics and has two parts, legislation and justice. The craft that sees to the fitness of the body is not given a name, but it too is said to have two parts, gymnastics and medicine; gymnastics corresponds to legislation, and medicine to justice. To each of these four crafts there corresponds a form of flattery, which pretends to see to the fitness of soul or body, but is actually doing nothing other than producing pleasure

---

[9] The concept of shame runs through the dialogue. For a discussion of it as a central motif in the *Gorgias*, see Race (1979).

without consideration for what is good. Pastry baking masks itself as medicine, pretending to know the foods that are best for the body. Rhetoric is to justice what pastry baking is to medicine.

Though impressive in its articulation, this speech is unconvincing, and seems carefully calibrated to satisfy Socrates' own account of rhetoric, with Socrates actually being the one performing as the seasoned rhetorician. The correspondence between crafts and flatteries may be pleasing to the ear, but the claim that rhetoric is a kind of flattery the sole aim of which is to produce pleasure is never subjected to scrutiny, nor are other statements made in this section that sound outright false. It is not clear that baking presents itself as medicine, and it is never established that rhetoric presents itself as justice. One might even have thought that knowledge of food preparation and culinary pleasure can be a useful complement to medicine. More subtly, Socrates is careful in this speech to withhold relevant information that could jeopardize a rhetorical advantage he enjoys already from the outset. Polus is the one who will attack popular justice, and this is likely to alienate the audience—which is confirmation of the horn of the aporia stating that justice is a value. But Socrates never discloses any of the misgivings we know he has with this conception of justice, and which, if known, could also alienate the audience.

Be that as it may, Socrates' views fail completely to excite Polus' interest, or change his mind. He flat-out asserts that he believes rhetoric is good and admirable because it gives the orator the power to do whatever he wants, even to banish or put to death whomever he wants and confiscate his property (465b–d). What Polus denies is one of the two conflicting claims Gorgias accepted, namely that those who know what is just want also to do it (cf. 460b–c). Considerations of justice are irrelevant. People often want to do what they want, even if what they want goes against justice, and rhetoric is good because it empowers them to do these things (469a).

There are two things to notice here. First, by denying the view that Gorgias had come to accept, Polus opts for the one of the horns of the aporia at which the discussion with Gorgias had ended. According to him, knowing what the just thing is does not in any way make the knower want to do it. Second, by having Polus flat-out deny the view Socrates asserted, Plato signals his view that the position Socrates has just asserted is in need of defence.

The defence Socrates will mount for it is merely an attempt to refute Polus, with the attack coming in two stages. In the first, Socrates tries to throw doubt on Polus' claim that the tyrant who banishes and kills does what he wants. Here is the argument.

When we do things we do them not for what they are descriptively. We do not do medicine for the sake of mixing foul-tasting herbs and convincing people to swallow them, or for the sake of performing surgical burnings on them. Nor do we walk for the sake of moving our legs the one after the other. To the extent that doings such as these represent actions of ours, the work we complete by doing them can make sense only against the background of the value context to which the agent is attentive when performing them. It is this that makes them be the actions they are. No full account of these doings as actions can be offered independently of this context. These doings are actions of an agent because they are incorporable in that agent's system of values, and can be accounted for only in that light. Now the value context in which the agent's actions are incorporated represents, quite reasonably, the agent's view of what is good, or rather what is good for him (467d–8c).[10] Ultimately, each action that any agent performs represents a particular way in which this agent aims at realizing his good, as he understands it.

Socrates then goes on to say, plausibly, that since it is not for the sake of the particular doings themselves, considered descriptively, that the agent does them, it is not these doings in and of themselves that he declares a wanting for by doing them. Rather it is the good that these doings contribute to accomplish. Hence, if the agent thought that such doings would result in something that is bad for him, he would not be interested in performing them. This, of course, is true on the assumption that the agent is rational, given the premise Socrates endorses that seeking what is good is an axiom of rationality. Nor would the agent be interested in performing them as his actions if they were neither good nor bad. The rational agent's volition, according to Socrates, responds only to what has value significance for him (468c5–7). Therefore, it is not the actual banishing or killing of people or the confiscation of their property that the tyrant wants but the good which he thereby (believes he) accomplishes. And if (he believed that) the outcome of doing these things was bad for him, he would not want to do them.

As ought to be clear already, Socrates distinguishes between what is good (*agathon*) and what seems best to one (*ho dokei autō(i) beltiston einai*). Distinguishing in this way between what is good and what one believes is good implies that good is understood to be an objective property, one to which, as the case is thought to be with such properties, humans respond epistemically. On this view, their epistemic powers are the only means humans have available for identifying what is good, or good for them. These powers may now be deployed successfully or unsuccessfully. When they are deployed successfully, that which one believes is best, or best for one, and what is really good and good for one refer to same thing (470a10–12). But they may also be deployed unsuccessfully to arrive at an erroneous view of what is good, with the result that the agent will often be mistaken in believing that something is good for him, even though it is actually bad. Still, and this is the crucial element in this view, deploying their epistemic powers to obtain views about what is good, successfully or unsuccessfully as it may be, is the only rational means available to humans for attending to and directing themselves toward it.

---

[10] This is no evidence that Plato holds an instrumental view of virtue, as claims Irwin (1995: 67–8). All Plato does here is draw the reasonable distinction between the merely behavioural aspect of an action and the value its agent attaches to it, and points out that it is its value that is of interest in value contexts.

Now, according to Socrates, what everyone wants (*bouletai*) is the good (*agathon*). Since humans depend on their epistemic powers for identifying the good, their volition depends on the views these powers deliver. Our wanting can, on this view, obtain an object to be directed at only by making use of our views of what is good. Socrates says that one only wants the good and that one does not want that which is not good. But he clearly does not mean by this that, in the case one is mistaken in his belief that something is good, one does not want that thing while having this belief, even though one does this thing while believing that it is good. What he does mean is that, although he wanted it and for this reason did it, he would not have wanted *it* if he had had the correct belief that not it but something else is good. Believing that something is good, I submit on Socrates' behalf, is sufficient to make one want it. As he clearly implies at 470a9–12 together with 466d7–e2, if what one thinks is best coincides with what is really good, then what one believes is best and what one truly wants. Since the only way one can approach the good is through one's epistemic powers, the only way one can also direct one's volition toward it is through one's view of what the good is.[11]

All this seems intuitively plausible, which is probably also the reason Polus has no problem accepting it. Accepting it, however, does not imply accepting also that people want what is just. So, Polus disagrees that what people want is what is just. Whether one will accept the latter or not will depend on whether one will accept that what is just is also good, and good for whomever does the just thing. It is therefore incumbent on Socrates to convince him that this is so. For the first time in the dialogue what has been assumed all the while is made clear: 'good' here means 'good with a view to (contributing toward) making one happy' (470e8–11). Notice that Socrates now offers an explanation for the position he had succeeded in making Gorgias accept, namely that people want to do what is just if they know it. For if, as Socrates now reveals, being just is what makes one happy (470e), and, obviously, all rational beings want for themselves to be happy, it follows unequivocally that one would want to do what is just.

But also, this passage makes it possible to decide between the two positions articulated earlier. It seems clear now, or so I claim, that, according to Socrates, the agent's wanting to do what is just when he knows it is not internal to his knowledge of it. The motivation to do what is just is not internal to this knowledge in that it is not this alone by itself that makes the agent want to do what is just. Socrates is explicit in offering a reason for why we want justice, and this is that it makes us happy, in his view. So, Socrates does not think that the knowledge of the just takes over, as it were, the agent's volition. He clearly thinks that the agent's volition is, and remains even after the instalment of the knowledge of the just in the agent, a distinct source of

---

[11] Though compatible with an instrumental view of virtue, this position does not, in itself, imply it. For it leaves open the possibility that the content of happiness just is virtuous action, in which case the knowledge of what virtue is constitutive of happiness; cf. Dimas (2002).

motivation for the agent, focused as it is on the agent's happiness. However, he also thinks of the knowledge of the just as integral to the agent's happiness because he thinks of it as the only source of rational guidance for the agent's volition in its aim to realize the agent's goal, namely happiness.

The positions of Polus and Socrates have now become clearly demarcated. They both agree that the chief human goal is happiness, and that humans perform their actions with a view to achieving this goal. However, Polus holds that human happiness has nothing to do with justice and just action. In Socrates' view, on the other hand, the way to happiness is exclusively through justice; the good and admirable person who is also just is good and happy, whereas the unjust one is wicked and miserable (470e). On this basis Socrates holds also that committing injustice is worse than suffering it. We can understand why. His position is that one's own happiness depends on one being oneself just, and not, for instance, on another's being just toward one. Committing injustice corrupts the integrity of one's own justice and therefore also one's happiness as a result; suffering injustice does not involve doing anything oneself, and therefore does not affect this integrity. Hence, it has no bearing on one's happiness.

But Socrates also claims that those who have committed injustice and have not been punished for it are more miserable than those who do get punished. This too is supposed to be a consequence of his view, though it is less clear why, and Socrates does not explain. In fact Socrates never argues in this dialogue for his view on the connection between justice and happiness or these two alleged consequences of his view. What he does instead is argue for these two consequences of his view by attacking Polus who is sceptical about this view on happiness (470e8) and denies these consequences. For Polus holds that committing injustice is better than suffering it and that one can be very happy even after having committed horrendous crimes, as long as one gets away with it (473a–b).

However, Polus agrees that committing injustice is more shameful than suffering it (474c–d), and to the following account of shamefulness: of two shameful things, the more shameful is that which surpasses the other either in pain or badness. This is all Socrates needs to refute him. For Polus also holds that doing injustice is less painful than suffering it, for which reason he must accept that it is more shameful because it is worse in terms of badness, and hence that doing it is worse than suffering it (475b–d).[12]

Next, and somewhat more trickily, Socrates equates paying one's due (dikēn didonai) with being justly disciplined (dikaiōs kolazesthai). Having agreed that all just things are admirable in so far as they are just (476a7–b2), Polus also agrees that whatever way someone acts upon something, this something gets acted upon in precisely the same way (established inductively, and problematically, on the basis of examples among which is also this: when the surgical burning performed is deep, the surgical burning suffered is also deep; 476b3d–4). So if the acting upon is disciplining

---

[12] For discussions of Socrates' refutation of Polus, see Vlastos (1967); Archie (1984); Johnson (1989); Segvic (2000) 40–5.

someone justly, the one being disciplined gets acted upon justly. Since, as Polus accepts, what is just is also admirable, and it is the latter not because it is pleasant, it must be admirable because it is good. Whoever is being justly punished, then, has a good thing done to him (476d5–7a4), the good thing being that justice is inserted in his soul, since it is agreed that the quality of what is suffered by something is exactly the same as the quality of the action inflicting the suffering. But injustice cannot coexist with justice in the same soul, and so Socrates is able to infer that punishment rids the one who is punished of the worst thing that can affect his soul, injustice (477a7–8), and instils in it the greatest good, namely justice.[13] Putting this result together with the claim that justice in the human soul is what makes a human being happy, Socrates goes on to conclude that punishment makes the perpetrator happy.

Throughout this refutation Polus has been disciplined enough to follow the argument and accept whatever he believes his answers to Socrates' questions commit him to, but he does not believe any of Socrates' conclusions. As he puts it, 'I think these statements are absurd, Socrates, though no doubt you think they agree with those expressed earlier' (480e). One can only guess why Polus remains unconvinced, but the fact of the matter is that Socrates' argument is weak. For one thing, not many would accept that disciplining rids the soul of its injustice and instils justice in it, and Socrates' argument to this effect is demonstrably poor. It is not even clear how this can be made to fit with a position, which is clearly his, that one must make *oneself* just, and it is doing *oneself* what is just that is good for one. It is the one who punishes justly who commits the just act in this case, and, obviously, not the one who is punished, who, by Socrates' own admission, actually resists it. The preamble to this refutation is even trickier. It hinges first on the claim that doing what is unjust is shameful, while doing what is just is admirable, and then on the claim that what is admirable is also good. Polus accepts the first and denies the second (474c7–d2), but Socrates uses the first to force him to concede also the second. Socrates and Polus appear to share common ground when saying that committing injustice is shameful and doing what is just is admirable, but it is more likely that they mean different things. Polus probably thinks something along the lines that committing injustice is shameful because, and for whatever reason, there is a generally shared expectation that agents ought to be doing what is just, and people badmouth and renounce those who do the opposite. (Recall one of the two horns of the aporia in which resulted the discussion between Socrates and Gorgias.) Had Polus had any philosophical training

---

[13] Injustice is also the *most* shameful thing, and since it is not so because of pain it must be because of badness. Being the cause of the greatest shame, injustice must be the worst thing that is (i.e. worst is established through most shameful; 477c2–5). Polus agrees that by receiving just punishment, the soul receives benefit (477a5–7) because he has already admitted that, being less shameful, being punished is also good (476e3–7a4). Having received benefit, though, it has received something good which means it must have gotten rid of something bad. The bad thing that it had, being the most shameful, was also the worst possible. Hence it has gotten rid of the greatest bad. On the other hand, having gotten rid of that implies that it has received something good.

or had he been given more time for reflection, he could accept, as he did, that things are shameful because they cause pain or are bad, and object that doing what is unjust is shameful not because it is bad, but because it is painful, given how those who do so are treated.

Most importantly, even if Socrates' argument that suffering injustice is better than committing it and that it is good to receive punishment if one commits injustice than not were successful, it would still do nothing to support what is his main claim, namely that only justice in the agent's soul makes the agent happy.

V

It is in particular the grounds for extracting from Polus the concession that committing injustice is shameful that lashes Callicles into accusing Socrates of grandstanding and acting like a real crowd-pleaser (*dēmēgoros*, 482c5). He accuses Socrates of being more intent on winning points by making Polus look bad than addressing the issue in its substance. Though Socrates says he seeks the truth, he nonetheless has shifted the focus of the discussion without mention, and extracts from Polus admissions that concern things that are admirable by law but not by nature. More precisely, Callicles accuses Socrates of exploiting an equivocation on 'just' in refuting Polus. There are two senses of 'just', Callicles claims: just by law and just by nature. So, as he sees it, when Polus had said initially that it is better to commit injustice than to suffer it, he was talking about what is just by nature (*phusei*). When he said later that it is more shameful to commit injustice than suffer it, the discussion had by then moved to what is just by law (*nomō(i)*). Had he stuck with what is just by nature all the way, he would have said not only that suffering injustice is worse, but also that it is more shameful, for in nature bad and shameful go together (483a).

According to Callicles, there are two kinds of people and, relatedly, two different things to which 'justice' refers. There are the weak or inferior people, who are the more numerous by far, and the strong or superior people. Correspondingly, there is what is just by law, which is to follow whatever the many who are weak agree to and prescribe as law. Their motivation for their agreement is to prevent the few strong ones from getting a greater share. It is only according to this law, the sole legitimacy of which is that it is agreed upon by the many who authored it, that getting a greater share than the law prescribes is to commit injustice. To this Callicles contrasts, and declares himself an adherent of, what he calls the 'just by nature' (*phusei dikaion*). According to what is just by nature, the superior few have the right to secure a greater share for themselves by subordinating the inferior and treating them as befits their interests. As signalled by the characterization 'natural', this view of justice is claimed to have an objective basis, one that, according to Callicles, may be confirmed by mere observation of what is going on among both beasts and men (484c).

It is to be noticed now that this distinction provides Callicles with the resources to offer his own resolution of the aporia in which Socrates' discussion with Gorgias had ended. Though we may reasonably suppose that the view of which he is an adherent is, in its substance, not different from the one to which Polus would subscribe, Callicles' resolution opts for the horn Polus rejected. Polus, we recall, opted for the horn that people often do what they know is unjust, essentially denying that, when they know what is just, they also want to do it. Interestingly, Callicles opts for the same horn as does Socrates: what people really want to do is the just thing. For Callicles, however, 'just' in this case is 'just by nature'. At the same time Callicles can offer an explanation for the statement of the other horn that people often want to do things that they know or believe are in conflict with what is unjust. The just thing that in these cases is in conflict with what they want to do is just by law, while what they want to do is just by nature.

To provide an objective basis for this view, Callicles must support the claim that it is justified that the superior ones subordinate those who are weak, and as importantly, present impartial criteria for distinguishing the superior from the inferior ones. The former he does by pointing to what he takes to be a fact of nature. Human activity has its source in the appetites (*epithumiai*), and the appetites are the sole provider of the human psychic energy. The goal of human activity is to satisfy them (*plērōsis*), and it is by satisfying them, and in the activity that aims at satisfying them, that humans can achieve happiness. On the other hand, frustrated appetites result in unhappiness.

If left unrestrained, the appetites will grow large until they peak (cf. *megiston*, 492e). Therefore, Callicles does not hold that the appetites an agent has will be increasing forever if uncurbed, which is reasonable, since it is hard to imagine that anyone's appetites for food, drink, and sex, for instance, could be increasing for ever. But he does leave open the possibility that one's appetites may unceasingly become more diverse, if uncurbed. Now, the agent who does not curb his appetites and has the ability to provide the resources for satisfying them is the one who is truly happy. Anyone's appetites would grow if they were allowed. However, due to the limited resources available, not every single individual's appetites could be adequately fulfilled, if left uncurbed, and unfulfilled appetites cause unhappiness. Aware of the risk that, if allowed to grow, their appetites might be left unfulfilled, most individuals do not allow them to grow. Here is where the difference between the two kinds of people mentioned above becomes relevant. Superior are those who are by nature intelligent (*phronimoi*) and thus able to unearth resources for fulfilling uncurbed appetites. The superior are also brave enough (*andreioi*), by nature, to do what is required of them to acquire these resources. Confident that their intelligence and bravery will enable them to satisfy their appetites, they let them grow. The big majority of people, however, are weak and populate the ranks of the inferior. They are weak because they lack intelligence and courage necessary to serve uncurbed appetites; being aware of this, they curb them. At the same time they want to protect themselves from the superior ones, and for this reason they get together to agree upon and author laws that declare it unjust and shameful for anyone to want to allot a greater share to himself.[14]

---

[14] Not everyone who has the natural capacity to lead the life of the superior ones does so. Some are duped by the weak to adopt their conventional view of justice, thus preventing their appetites from

Epithumia here must not be thought to have the sense it is usually thought to have in the *Republic*. Here, the term refers not only to a specific type of desires, those associated with one particular part of the soul in the tripartite psychic model of the *Republic*. In this dialogue, the reference of the term covers everything we would call desires. Though in this part of the discussion Socrates mentions exclusively appetites for food, drink, or scratching, his reason cannot be that Callicles confines the reference of *epithumia* just to those types of desire. His reason is more likely that in this way his polemic becomes more venomous. Be that as it may, Callicles points out explicitly, in a retort aimed at correcting Socrates' mention of hunger and thirst only, that he talks not only about these, but also about 'all other appetites' (*allas epithumias hapasas*, 494c2–3).[15] Callicles' hero is the successful tyrant, such as Peisistratus or Cleisthenes, or the successful orator such as Pericles. The desires of such men, one might expect, will, apart from being for food, drink, and sex, include strengthening their country as well as their own reputation, providing adequately for their family, friends, and fellow citizens. We would expect them to have desires for intellectual accomplishments, such as outwitting their opponents in debate or even battle, and, why not, for appreciating beauty in art, architecture, and theatre. Notice also that Callicles is careful to make the point that the truly happy life consists in maintaining a high pace of activity aimed at fulfilling desires. Clearly, as already mentioned, however much the desires for food, drink, and sex are allowed to grow, they are likely to be easily and quickly satiated, thus providing zero opportunity for a high pace of activity aimed at fulfilling appetites. Charitably to Socrates, the reason he mentions only desires for food and drink in his discussion with Callicles is to make it apparent that Callicles' view leaves open the possibility that someone may want to devote oneself to satisfying only this type of desires, in which case this view is vulnerable to the objection that such a life is unlikely to be deemed good. It is unfortunate if commentators have taken this as evidence that Callicles' view is only concerned with a rather limited subset of desires. So, I will henceforth be using the terms 'appetites' and 'desires' interchangeably.

On Callicles' view, then, Polus must have been on the right track to claim that the tyrant acted admirably in acquiring what he desired. The tyrant did also what he wanted (*bouletai*), in Socrates' sense of 'want'. Callicles can grant that we want what is truly good for us and claim that what was good for the tyrant was to act so as to satisfy his desires, because satisfying one's desire is what is good for one, as it is what makes one happy. The more desires one satisfies, the happier one becomes.

---

becoming large (492b2–8). But that does not change the fact that living rightly (ὀρθῶς) and in accordance with what is by nature just and admirable is to let one's appetites grow without curbing them and be able (ἱκανὸς) to serve them (ὑπηρετεῖν) with one's intelligence and bravery (491e6–2a1). And this is by nature just even though very few are able to, and actually do it, because the psychological makeup of all humans is such that every individual would want to be satisfying large appetites, if he could, but nature endows with intelligence and bravery only few.

[15] But see Gosling and Taylor (1982) 71–2 for a different view.

Moreover, he would claim that doing so is to be doing what is just by nature, thus paradoxically being in agreement with Socrates' position that the just is what is good for one, and makes one happy.

No sooner has Callicles' view taken shape, than Socrates begins to attack it. First he presents an alternative kind of ideal life with the help of two images. According to the first image, which Socrates attributes to a wise Sicilian, the appetites of fools are insatiable, and the part of their soul where these appetites reside is likened to a leaking jar. With insatiable appetites, their soul is undisciplined and, for this reason, according to him, their life miserable. The orderly and disciplined souls, on the other hand, the life of which he claims is happy, he likens to a tight jar (493c–d). In the second image he compares a man who possesses jars sound and full to a man who possesses perforated jars full of holes. Having filled his jars once, the first man can relax and never think about them again, whereas the second man has to find the resources to be filling his jars continuously, or sustain great pain if they are not full.

These two images serve two distinct purposes. The first is to depict two life-ideals, whereas the second is to explain why the first life-ideal is good according to Socrates, and the second bad. Both images together are intended to depict the role Socrates assigns to desires with respect to human happiness. In Socrates' view, appetites are clearly an impediment to happiness, and to have a good and happy life, the agent must do what he can do to eliminate them completely. If he cannot eliminate them completely, he must do what he can to reduce them to no more than what he can fulfil with the resources available to him and with minimal effort. On the other hand, Socrates and Callicles agree that, in the view of the latter, desires are the fundamental psychic energy, and dedicating one's life to fulfilling them is vital to being happy. One's intelligence and bravery are, on this view, the agent's tool with which to serve them.

To summarize, three elements are indispensable for the happy life according to Callicles: (1) to have as many appetites as one can have, (2) to have intelligence and bravery that can be put to work in order to serve them, and (3) to serve them with the aim to fulfil them. At 494c2–3 he puts it unequivocally: To be happy, one must have all appetites and rejoice in his ability to fulfil them. Notice that, as conceived by him, the ideal life will also, and inevitably, contain a lot of pain. Socrates actually points this out in his images, and, more importantly, Callicles accepts it without blinking: the man with the leaky jars will have to work day and night to fill them, or suffer extreme pain. Since filling them presupposes that they are at least partly empty, and as long as they are not full they are the cause of pain, pain is unavoidable. Callicles fully recognizes this implication and endorses it in his retort. So he says that the life of the man in Socrates' life-ideal will be like that of a stone, and the reason he gives for this is that this life will contain neither pleasure nor *pain*. Hence pleasure and pain are central components of the ideal life as Callicles envisages it.

Though Callicles has said that, to live the best life possible, one would have to have *all* appetites, Socrates sets off on his attempt to refute Callicles by considering someone who spends his life getting pleasure from scratching an itch. Callicles is frustrated to have to concede that such a man will be happy, but he is right to think that he has to face this objection because he has, in his answers to Socrates' questions, made himself vulnerable to it (494d1). For Socrates saddles him with the view that the good and pleasure are the same thing (495a2–4), which Callicles agrees to, although grudgingly, and only in order to keep his statements from being inconsistent, as he says (495a5–6). Socrates then raises two objections against this view.

Callicles agrees with Socrates that desire is accompanied by pain and that pleasure is gotten only for as long as there is a desire in place. Being thirsty, that is, having a desire to drink, is painful, and one gets pleasure out of drinking only as long as one is thirsty. But then, one can only have pleasure while also having pain. So, in the course of satisfying a desire there is co-presence of pleasure and pain, and since pleasure is good and pain bad, there is co-presence of good and bad in the agent, which Callicles agrees is impossible.

With Callicles completely unimpressed, Socrates offers a second argument, in which he uses something to which Callicles agreed previously: the good and pleasure are the same, whereas knowledge and courage are different from the good and from each other (495d4–5). Callicles has also claimed that the courageous and intelligent (*phronimoi*) persons are good, and by implication that the cowardly and foolish (*aphrones*) ones bad (498c2–3; 499a1–2).[16] However, as regards intelligence, Callicles must concede that foolish children enjoy pleasure, as do also foolish men, and in general that foolish people are no worse at enjoying pleasure, and need not enjoy less of it than do intelligent people. Being intelligent cannot therefore play any part in the acquisition of pleasure (498a1–5). The same is true of bravery. In war, both the brave and the cowardly feel pleasure when the enemy retreats, the cowardly maybe more. And when the enemy approaches, both feel pain to the same extent, more or less. On this basis Socrates puts it to Callicles, in full generality, that the cowardly seem to enjoy, on the whole, no less pleasure than do those who are brave (put forward at 498b7–c3 and 498e5–8).

If 'the good' and 'pleasure' refer to the same thing, there is no basis for holding that intelligence and bravery are good. Callicles could abandon the latter claim and maintain the former. But does not, because he has no interest in hedonism. This is a view he has been saddled with, not one he cares to defend. What he is interested in is what he calls natural justice, his view on which would collapse without the claim that intelligence and bravery are good. It is intelligence and bravery, not enlarged appetites, that distinguish the superior from the inferior. The superior people obtain the right to impose their rule from the fact that everyone's aim is to satisfy desires, and they possess the intelligence and bravery necessary to be able to serve enlarged

---

[16] Though Callicles has said that the courageous and intelligent are good he is not being inconsistent when he also says that intelligence and courage are different from what is good. The latter claim is merely that they are not the same as the good, but that does not prevent them from being good derivatively, say, insofar as they are indispensable for the acquisition of what is good.

appetites, which also the inferior people would have come to have, if they had sufficient confidence in their intelligence and bravery to allow them to grow.

Callicles does not hesitate to admit, and becomes impatient with Socrates for not being able to take it into his head (499b4–8), that he, as do all reasonable people, believes that some pleasures are better than others. There are good and bad pleasures and Callicles does not care in the least that this, as Socrates points out, contradicts the claim that the good and pleasure are the same (500d6–8), thus refuting hedonism. Callicles agrees also that pleasure and the good are different and that it requires a craftsman to distinguish the good pleasures from the bad ones. Compatibly with this he also accepts that orators in general take aim at producing pleasure in their audience, and that some, though not all, do so considering what is good for the audience (502a–3a).

Not hedonism, but, as Callicles puts it at 494c2–3, the view that to be happy one must have appetites and rejoice in his ability to fulfil them is what attracts him. I suggest that the view Callicles puts forward in the *Gorgias* is a desire-satisfaction type theory, which is other than hedonism.[17] By identifying the good with pleasure, hedonism makes welfare consist in psychological states alone. By further claiming that the happy life consists in having as much pleasure as possible, it claims that being happy amounts to spending as much time as possible in these states. In a desire-satisfaction type theory, value is desire-dependent. Something is valuable because it is linked to the satisfaction of a desire one has. If it is an action, one has reason for doing it because by doing it he would satisfy a desire, and if it is a thing, he has reason to want because by acquiring it he would again be satisfying a desire. Of course satisfying a desire produces pleasure, but this in no way, of course, implies that the agent seeks to satisfy that desire because of the pleasure that satisfying it would be producing. The desire-satisfaction account of value places the weight not on having experiences of a certain kind but on *being* a certain kind of person and on *doing* certain kinds of things as a result of being that kind of person. On this desire-satisfaction theory that Callicles proposes, on my view, experiences of pleasure are not in any way what makes the agent happy, but side effects of being happy. For, on Callicles' theory, it is entirely possible that one may lead a happy life even though this life may end up containing more pain than pleasure overall. Indeed Callicles' hero is hardly someone who would plan his life based on how to maximize pleasure. The tyrant is more likely to, and knows that he is more likely to, expose himself to circumstances in which the risk of getting more pain than pleasure is greater than the expectation of getting more pleasure. And he may in fact get more pain than pleasure overall, while still being happy because he was able to satisfy the desire of being a tyrant.

---

[17] Callicles' view is typically understood as hedonistic; see e.g. Irwin (1979), 196–7; Klosko (1984), 129–30; Berman (1991); Kahn (1996), 137. Stauffer (2002) sees Callicles as a weak hedonist, for 'he also displays a sense of shame that is incompatible with thoroughgoing hedonism' (642). For an example of the view that Socrates' refutation of Callicles is unsuccessful, see Irwin (1979), 203 or Klosko (1984); for the opposite view, see Jenks (2007).

This position is not vulnerable to Socrates' criticisms, and if it is the one under-pinning Callicles' statements it explains why it is incomprehensible to him that he should be impressed by those criticisms. By denying that the good is to be equated with psychological states, this position is obviously not susceptible to the 'scratching' type objections. It also remains unscathed by the second objection that desire is painful and pleasure is felt only as long as the desire is not fulfilled. Finally, Callicles can say, consistently with this view, as he in fact does, that there are good and bad pleasures. He may say, for instance, that good are the pleasures felt when one satisfies the desires one has planned to satisfy and bad are the ones that, if indulged in, would end up frustrating those desires. More importantly, he would say that good are those pleasures that would result from satisfying the noble desire of subordinating one's inferiors, and infinitely less good are the pleasures gotten from scratching an itch, or pleasures that would end up frustrating the noble desire. As Callicles indeed agrees, to know which pleasures are good, that is, what desires it is best to have and seek to satisfy, and experience pleasure as a result, would require a true craftsman.

VI

At 505d Callicles announces that he will no longer cooperate with Socrates. He tells him to either stop or carry on the discussion with someone else. Since no one present is willing to take over from Callicles, Socrates performs the remarkable feat of going it alone for almost another twenty pages. For the largest part of the remainder of the dialogue he asks and answers his own questions—a peculiar picture, unparalleled in Plato's writings. Even if we were to think that Plato's sympathies lie with Socrates, it is hard not to think that Plato here presents an alienated character who fails to convince his interlocutors, and becomes gradually unable even to engage them in substantive philosophical conversation. I will conclude by reflecting shortly on reasons Plato might have for doing this.

In other Platonic dialogues, the ones commonly called aporetic, Socrates engages individuals without himself having a view to present or defend. His task is almost exclusively to make interlocutors think about important issues and he succeeds in showing not only that they had not reflected on them adequately on their own, but also that these are issues about which sustained philosophical reflection is needed. In this dialogue he presents views on rhetoric and, much more importantly, on happi-ness and its dependence on justice. Moreover, he meets with interlocutors who have views, considered ones, even if they have not developed them in the way expected from a philosopher.

In such an environment the Socratic practice of the elenchus is of limited utility. Though Socrates is able to make his interlocutors contradict other statements they have made, it is not clear that this is philosophically productive in the present context. First of all, catching others in contradiction does not in itself advance one's own views. It does not necessarily even refute the views of those caught in contradiction. In this regard, Socrates' long remarks about refutation in his discussion with Polus are of interest (471e1–2d4; 473e6–4b5). He does not think much, he says, of the kind of refutations where a majority speaks against a view, or the value of a position adopted because a majority adopts it. He only cares about the testimony of the man with whom he discusses, disregarding what the majority might say. Whatever the rhetorical appeal of these remarks, it is not clear that the refutation of a single person is philosophically preferable to the facts, the *gegonota* as Polus calls them, if the facts point in the opposite direction (470d1). Even more so if the one refuted is still attracted to his view, or this view enjoys widespread appeal, its refutation notwithstanding. Without further comparison, it is significant that Plato has Euthydemus and Dionysodorus take pride in the *Euthydemus* in their success in refuting anyone they care to, even if their view is not true. No matter whom they manage to refute, no one would take this as proof that they have refuted anything.

Plato at any rate is not, I submit, satisfied that Socrates' refutation has done anything to deal a blow to Callicles' view. The second book of the *Republic* is proof of that.[18] As we recall, the entire discussion on justice is motivated there with Glaucon asking why it is not the case, as most people think, that committing injustice is naturally good (*pephukenai gar dē phasin to men adikein agathon*, 358e3), and that suffering injustice without avenging it is bad, the very claim that Callicles begins his speech with.[19] Adeimantus only sharpens this question with the further point that it is only by reputation that suffering injustice is nobler than doing it (363a). This is precisely the view that Plato has Callicles tell us is Polus', even though the latter was unable to defend it. The question Adeimantus puts to Socrates in the *Republic* is pressing for Plato to give an answer to, because it is underpinned by what most people seem to think about justice. It is precisely this point Plato makes in the *Gorgias*, when he has Socrates say that Callicles' view expresses what most people think but do not dare admit (492d).

Plato readily concedes that by having Socrates engage Callicles he engages a deeply embedded view. More importantly he concedes he engages a view that enjoys intuitive strength. It is a trivial psychological fact that humans have desires, and it seems true that the wish to fulfil them is the chief motivating source of human action. It seems also a fact that individuals more often than not seek a greater share for themselves and those close to them, and this is even reflected in the way laws tend to be aligned to the interest of those in power. The strong, be they strong because they constitute a majority, or be it a single man, seek power to safeguard their interests, and when in power they make laws that draw lines that determine what is to be considered just or unjust, at least by law.

Plato is also clear that, as things stand in the *Gorgias* regarding the issue of justice, Callicles has the upper hand. Socrates wants to defend the view that people want to

---

[18] Cf. Kahn (1996) 144–7.
[19] 359e–60d is an eloquent presentation by Glaucon of Callicles' position.

do what is just, and he explains why in his discussion with Polus. What people want is to be happy: this is the fundamental premise all discussants agree on, and, in Socrates' view, it is only justice that can secure this goal for them. This is a bold thesis, and no doubt one Plato endorses. Still, most people, as the evidence supplied by Plato himself suggests, would think it is false and would definitely find it counterintuitive. More importantly, defending such a position presupposes not only that one has a view of justice, but also that one has a view of happiness. At the same time, to have a decent hope of reaching a plausible account of happiness, one needs an antecedent understanding of the human psyche. Not to mention that any account of happiness, if it is to enjoy intuitive plausibility as such an account, must present something that is recognizable as happiness. It must draw out conditions such that when agents realize them they can truly be said also to be feeling happy. This is further confirmation that an account of happiness cannot be reached independently of a proper understanding of human psychology. And if one is also to claim, as Socrates does here, that justice is what makes one happy, a proper understanding of the human psyche becomes also a precondition for a successful theory of justice.

Callicles makes precise, seemingly plausible claims about human psychology, that even Plato admits are prima facie appealing. Obviously humans have desires and, more importantly, these do seem to constitute the source motivating human action. Callicles' actual account of justice may seem repugnant and we can safely assume that this is what Plato thinks it is. Still, Callicles' psychological account represents, maybe even unbeknownst to him, an interesting philosophical move, which points to the requirements that an account of the kind Socrates would want to defend must observe. If it really is a fact of human psychology that humans have desires and care about satisfying them, and, as Socrates claims, doing what is just is to be something people want, then a workable account cannot avoid being linked to human desires.

On the other hand, the picture offered by Socrates is hazy. Though already in his discussion with Gorgias he recognizes that the soul is by its nature responsive to more things than simply reason, and confirms this in his discussion with Polus when he says that the orator can successfully sway his audience by producing pleasure in them, he ignores this aspect of the human psyche when he presents his life-ideal to Callicles. His only rational recommendation, coming late in the dialogue in the form of an image, is that the agent should minimize the importance of desires as much as possible. More radically, he recommends that agents ought to try and extinguish virtually all motivating power emanating from them by training themselves to be satisfied by whatever they have available. The only thing he can offer in response to Callicles' comment that one would not notice if an individual leading a life such as the one Socrates recommends is dead or alive is that Callicles' ideal is intolerably demanding. Maybe so, but that does not necessarily make it less appealing, nor Socrates' own recommendation more attractive. Later on (503c–d), Socrates appears to be moving away from the recommendation of his images and to allow for the importance of desires by distinguishing between good and bad pleasures, and advising that one should go for those that make one better and avoid those that make one worse. But this is not something that can decide the issue between himself and Callicles. As 503d3 indicates, this statement is one Callicles himself could readily endorse, as he is also prepared fully to endorse that the disciplined soul is the better one (506c–7e). In his case we could also have a view of what he might mean. Though there is nothing to suggest what discipline and order (*taxis*) would be for Socrates, there is plenty to suggest that for Callicles it would be the order and priorities that would serve the aim of the shrewd tyrant.

Finally, but no less importantly, it is unclear what Socrates means by justice. His argument with Polus and Callicles gives no reason to anyone, certainly not to Polus and Callicles, to think that he thinks anything other than what most people mean by it, whatever this is. At the same time we should not lose sight of the fact that he may be exposing a deep incoherence in the view, one that Plato will expertly exploit in the *Republic*. The many, whose view of justice this is, would obviously not hesitate themselves to undermine it, believing as they do that it is often attractive to do what is unjust. Evidently, one crucial thing that Socrates' performance in the *Gorgias* achieves is to expose the need for a coherent theory of justice. The *Gorgias* as a whole on the other hand demonstrates that there can be a promising theory of this sort only if based on a proper understanding of human psychology, which requires a richer and more adequate conceptual apparatus than Socrates appears to have at his disposal in this dialogue.

4

Eudaimonia, Human Nature, and Normativity

Reflections on Aristotle's Project in *Nicomachean Ethics* Book I

Øyvind Rabbås

It is not particularly controversial to take Aristotle's ethics to be the canonical expression of ancient ethics.[1] Aristotle systematizes and develops Plato's thought and sets the agenda for philosophical ethics in the centuries to follow. In his ethics we find the central feature of ancient ethics: eudaemonism, that is, the view that there is such a thing as a *highest good* or *ultimate end* to be pursued in action, and that this good or end is *eudaimonia* or happiness, as it is commonly translated.[2] The task of ethics, as the ancients see it, following Aristotle, is to determine the precise nature of eudaimonia and, in the course of so doing, to incorporate concepts such as *virtue, practical wisdom, pleasure, friendship*, and *justice* into the eudaemonistic framework.

Aristotle is also canonical for ancient ethics in the way he bases his conception of eudaimonia as the ultimate end on a view of human nature; his ethical theory is thus a form of *naturalism*. At the same time, however, he takes the essence of human nature to be reason or rationality, *logos*. Thus, his ethical theory is not only naturalistic, but also (at least partly) *rationalistic*.

From a modern point of view this way of doing ethics has seemed highly problematic. One reason to worry is the way Aristotle, and the ancients in general, base

[1] Thanks to the audiences at the two conferences (in Rome, June 2010, and Erice, March 2012) organized by the project from which this collection derives, as well as at the University of Western Ontario (November 2011). In addition I am grateful to comments from and discussion with Håvard Løkke and Will Small.

[2] Since this translation is controversial and can be rather misleading (for reasons that will become clear in section 1), I shall leave the Greek term untranslated throughout, and since it occurs so frequently, I shall also leave it unitalicized. For discussion of translation, see the classic account in Kraut (1979), as well as Cooper (1975), 89f with note 1, who proposes the alternative translation 'human flourishing'.

their ethics in a conception of human nature. This has appeared to many to jeopardize the integrity of ethical theory as a normative enterprise, and to do so in two important ways. First, ancient theories—and here Aristotle may seem to be in a particularly exposed position—threaten the legitimacy of ethics by holding it hostage to a metaphysically dubious, no longer credible biology.[3] Secondly, even if the biological framework should be scientifically respectable as such, the project of basing ethical theory on any conception of human nature would be guilty of committing the so-called 'naturalistic fallacy' by trying to reduce the normative to the descriptive. Man's nature is reason. But reason is clearly a normative concept, and the role of practical reason is to guide us in deliberation and action. This, however, seems to defy reduction in naturalist terms, so how can we have a naturalistic theory of reason?

In the following I shall try to outline a way of understanding eudaemonist ethics in its Aristotelian version that can be seen as both naturalistic and rationalistic, that is, as based in a conception of human nature as a rational being, and at the same time as capable of accounting for the normativity of ethics.

The core of Aristotle's eudaemonist ethics is the 'function [*ergon*] argument' (I 7), the culminating point of Book I of the *Nicomachean Ethics*, where Aristotle lays out the premises and outline for his entire eudaemonist project. The function argument is also the main ground for taking Aristotle's eudaemonism to be a naturalist ethics. I shall therefore articulate the main structure of this argument, as I read it (section 2). But I start (in section 1) with some preliminary remarks on the teleological structure of human endeavour and the place of the notion of eudaimonia within that structure, in order to clarify the nature of Aristotle's project in ethics. Then (in section 3) I address the question of the normativity of eudaemonist ethics. The aim is to end up with a non-reductionist interpretation of Aristotle's eudaemonist ethics as both naturalistic, in a sense, and rationalistic, in a sense.

1. Eudaimonia and Ethics

Aristotle begins his ethics by pointing to the teleological structure of human activity (from *telos*, 'goal' or 'end'): 'Every sort of expert knowledge [*technē*] and every inquiry [*methodos*], and similarly every activity [*praxis*] and undertaking [*prohairesis*], seems to seek some good' (I 1, 1094a1–2).[4]

This statement should cause us to puzzle—to the extent that 'we' are modern readers approaching the text against the background of a conception of ethics as the study of the right principles for action. For here at the beginning of his main ethical treatise Aristotle does not talk, the way modern ethicists do, about individual actions,

---

[3] Prominent representatives of this line of criticism include Alasdair MacIntyre and Bernard Williams in several writings.

[4] Translations of the *Nicomachean Ethics* are from Rowe (2002), sometimes slightly emended. Here I have replaced 'action' by 'activity' for *praxis*.

such as switching on the light in order to read or supporting an old lady across the street in order to help her, but rather about certain kinds of structured activity or practice such as the *technai* (crafts or fields of expert knowledge). This is reflected in the terminology and examples Aristotle employs, as well as in the claims he makes.

When Aristotle talks generally about human action, he consistently uses terms that normally denote examples of what we might call 'activity' or 'practice'. These terms include *technē, methodos, praxis, prohairesis* (cf. I 2, 1094a18–22, 25–6; I 4, 1095a14–17; I 7, 1097a16–22). When he gives examples to illustrate general points about human activity and its teleological structure, he first mentions medicine, shipbuilding, generalship, and household management (1094a8–9), then adds bridle-making and horsemanship (a10–14) and, finally, political expertise (in I 2). Each of these examples is a distinct *technē*, constituted by reference to a fundamental good or end. Aristotle mentions these ends as well: health, a ship, victory, wealth.

The central claims Aristotle makes in the opening chapters are also concerned with such organized practices. Thus, some activities are said to be subordinate to others because the constitutive ends of the lower ones are subordinate to those of the higher ones, but again he uses the same range of examples to illustrate his point. The next important claim that Aristotle makes is that the chain of subordination will stop at the highest good or end, and the task is to find out what this end is and 'to which sort of knowledge [*epistēmē*] or capacity [*dunamis*] it belongs' (I 2, 1094a25–6).[5] This kind of knowledge seems to be 'the most sovereign [*kuriōtatē*], that is, the most 'architectonic' [*architektonikē*]' (a26–7). It belongs to this highest form of knowledge or practice to 'set out [*diatassein*] which of the expertises there needs to be in cities, and what sorts of expertise each group of people should learn, and up to what point' (1094a28–b2), and hence,

since it makes use of [*chrōmenēs*] the practical expertises that remain and furthermore legislates [*nomothetousēs*] about what one must do and what things one must abstain from doing, the end of this expertise will contain those of the rest; so that this end will be the human good. (I 2, 1094b4–7)

So the puzzle is this: Why start a treatise on ethics by talking about more or less institutionalized, and hierarchically organized, practices or professions, rather than about individual actions? The answer, as I see it, is that for Aristotle ethics is not a matter of finding the criteria for determining the right thing to do on particular occasions. Rather, ethics is the study of how we should live our lives, what the best life is for a human being,[6] and the *Nicomachean Ethics* is the canonical work of ethics thus understood. Given this starting point, it is reasonable for Aristotle to think of

---

[5] Note that Aristotle here uses yet another word, *epistēmē*, which also indicates a kind of organized activity or field of endeavour, sc. something like the practice of science. I have changed Rowe's translation, which has 'expertise or productive capacity' for *epistēmē*.

[6] Cf. Plato's question 'how one ought to live [*hontina tropon chē zēn*]'; see *Gorg.* 492d; cf. 472c–d, 487e–8a, 500c–d; *Rep.* I 352d; cf. 329d, e, 344e, 347e.

individual actions as embedded in such practices. Although a human being performs a vast number of particular actions in the course of living his life, only some of these are what we might call 'ethically significant': These are the actions by reference to which his life is judged, by himself as well as by others, to be good or successful. These actions, moreover, are actions done by him in some specific capacity, that is, qua doctor, shipbuilder, general, and so forth, and they must be understood within the framework of that practice. Thus, activity engaged in as part of such organized practices constitutes a significant portion of the substance of the individuals' life: they define (in his own eyes as well as in others') who he is, and provide the criteria for judging how well his life goes.

But there is a second reason for starting with the *technai*. Aristotle seems to regard the various practices, including the *technai*, as the substance of civil society. What is the 'function' of society? Surely to provide safety and prosperity for its citizens: the common good.[7] The medical profession, the crafts, navigation, the military, and such like, are all there to safeguard the lives of the citizens, and they have been developed historically for the purpose of enabling humans to improve their lot and to take destiny into their own hands; they all aim at ensuring the good life for human beings. Since all of these practices that constitute the life of civil society are of joint interest to the citizens, and somehow have to be managed as part of a common project, the hierarchical structure of the various *technai* and other (more or less) institutionalized practices will be of the greatest political concern. Politics is the supreme activity since it 'makes use of' and 'legislates' about the other activities. And the end of politics is, simply, the good life.

However, the good life is not merely the ultimate end of politics, and of all those practices that are organized under the supervision of politics; it is also the ultimate end for those individuals who engage in these practices. Obviously there could be no crafts and sciences without craftsmen and scientists, but it is also the case that those persons who are craftsmen or scientists would have no substantial life without the organized practices of their craft or science. Hence the activity of each craftsman and scientist qua craftsman or scientist indirectly aims at the same end as his craft or science, and since the ultimate end of each craft or science is the good life for human beings, the ultimate end of politics and of ethics are one and the same: the good life (see I 2, 1094b7–10; VI 8, 1141b23–4).

So human endeavour is directed towards a single highest good or ultimate end: the good life. The task of ethics is to determine what the nature of this highest good or ultimate end is. In I 7 Aristotle points to two criteria that any answer to the question 'What is eudaimonia?' must satisfy. The first of these he calls 'finality' (*teleion*): the

---

[7] In the *Politics* Aristotle says that in a minimal sense the *polis* exists for the sake of life, i.e. the bare subsistence of its citizens, but in the strict and primary sense it exists for the sake of (i.e. its *ergon* is) living well (*eu zēn*), i.e. the good and virtuous life of its citizens. See I 2, 1252b28–30; III 9, 1280a31–2; 12, 1282b14–18; VII 8, 1328a35–7.

highest good is that which is sought because of itself and never because of anything else, while everything else is sought because of it (1097a25–b5; he mentioned this earlier, in I 2, when he discussed the teleological structure of human endeavour (1094a18–22)). The highest good, in short, is the terminus for every chain of justification, that is, every sequence of answers to the question 'Why do you do/ pursue X?' The highest good or ultimate end, in other words, is the ultimate reason for action, and the concept thus belongs within the context of practical reason and justification.

Now, various practices—crafts, sciences, and so on—are organized in teleologically nested hierarchies. That means that a particular practice, such as the craft of bridle-making, occupies an intermediate position, as both an end and a 'means' (something that is 'towards [pros]' the end). On the one hand, the craft of bridle-making is an end. Or rather, the craft is constituted by an end—the production of bridles—and everything involved in the practice of bridle-making is 'towards' this end. Every particular action performed by the individual bridle-maker aims at the production of bridles, and he exercises his knowledge and skills, and employs various materials and instruments, for the sake of that end. The practice of bridle-making gets its shape and direction from this ultimate end, and this end is never a topic for deliberation within the practice (cf. III 3, 1112b11–15). There may be discussions about how the constitutive end should be understood—one could imagine 'schools' within bridle-making—but not whether the production of bridles is the end of the craft. This end is thus ultimate ('we wish for [it] because of itself, while wishing for the other things we wish for because of it' (I 2, 1094a19–20)) within the craft of bridle-making.

On the other hand, the craft of bridle-making is there because bridles are necessary in other contexts, such as the cavalry, and there has to be someone who produces these bridles. Bridle-making, like any other techné, is thus 'normatively insufficient':[8] it gets its value from some higher end the realization of which it is 'towards'.

We thus get the following picture of human endeavour, as Aristotle conceives it at the beginning of the EN. Most actions performed by individual agents are part of certain practices, such as the crafts and sciences—we could say: professions and other socially defined roles. These practices thus provide people's activities and lives with their sense and direction. Furthermore, these practices themselves, qua practices, are part of more comprehensive teleological hierarchies, hierarchies that, ultimately, constitute life as a whole for society as well as for its individual members. The question then is: What is the ultimate frame of reference for this all-encompassing life-activity? Is there an ultimate end that the entire structure is 'towards'? Aristotle's answer is 'Yes: eudaimonia', and the purpose of ethics is to work out a conception of the nature and implications of this ultimate end or highest good.

---

[8]   Barney (2007), 298.

We can get a firmer grasp of the nature of this project if we attend to the second criterion Aristotle claims that any satisfactory account of the highest good must satisfy. This is the criterion of 'self-sufficiency' (*autarkeia*). Aristotle explains: 'the "self-sufficient" we posit as being what in isolation makes a life desirable and lacking in nothing' (I 7, 1097b14–15). If one succeeds in attaining the highest good, then there is nothing more to be sought for in order to improve one's life: life is complete or self-sufficient. Aristotle then proceeds to claim that only eudaimonia satisfies this criterion, and that this is why the highest good is eudaimonia. The quote above continues:

> and we think happiness [eudaimonia] is like this—and moreover most desirable of all things, it not being counted with [*mē sunarithmoumenēn*] other goods: clearly, if it *were* so counted in with the least of other goods, we would think it more desirable, for what is added becomes an extra quantity of goods, and the larger amount of goods is always more desirable. So happiness is clearly something complete [*teleion*, 'final' as I have rendered it] and self-sufficient, being the end of all practical undertakings [*tōn praktōn ousa telos*]. (1097b15–21)

Let us look more closely at this crucial passage.

Aristotle says that eudaimonia is the 'most desirable of all things, it not being counted with other goods'. This means, first, that he is taking eudaimonia as a specific end serving as the central good in a life—the good which is such that when it is realized in a life, that life thereby becomes *eudaimōn*: successful, good, worth pursuing.[9] But secondly, he is also claiming that this central good is not one good among others, for if it were, one could add more goods to it and this would make the life correspondingly more *eudaimōn*. But eudaimonia as the highest or central good is not like that. Rather than being just another element in a life, one that can be counted in with the others in a quantitative sense, the central good is the one that constitutes and defines the life as that very life, and thereby makes it good and desirable or choice-worthy.

If *E* is the highest or central good of a life, we can call this life the '*E*-life'. This life is constituted by the pursuit of *E*, and organized around that pursuit (so the *E*-life is the 'life-in-pursuit-of-*E*'). The relation between *E* and the other goods or ends in the *E*-life may be instrumental, but does not have to be: it may be 'constitutive' or 'approximative' as well.[10] However, whatever the relation is between *E* and the other goods, *E* is not a good among the others; rather, it is what makes the whole (the *E*-life) and all its parts (the other goods) something good. That is how the central good is 'the one which the agent values most and without which the other goods would be pointless to him'.[11] The *E*-life is constituted as this very life by *E*, and if, and to the extent that, *E* is realized in that life, this life as a whole is good—and complete

---

[9] See the Introduction, this volume, p. 8, for discussion of the ambiguity of the term 'eudaimonia'.

[10] See, e.g. Cooper (1975), 18–22 on 'constitutive' means/ends relations, and Lear (2004), ch. 3 on 'teleological approximation' of means to ends.

[11] Broadie (1991), 27.

or self-sufficient: nothing is lacking, nothing could be added to make it better, sc. better as this life (the *E*-life).

The crafts may serve as illustration. A craft is constituted by a certain fundamental end—in the case of bridle-making: bridles; in the case of medicine: health; and so on. Thus, everything done by a craftsman as part of his practicing his craft is done because of, or for the sake of, this constitutive end. This constitutive end is therefore an ultimate end, relative to the practice of the craft: everything refers to it, while it does not itself refer to anything else but is taken as given. Moreover, if, and to the extent that, this ultimate, constitutive end is realized, everything is achieved: there is nothing more to do. Nothing that is not grounded in the constitutive end of the craft (i.e. is not 'towards' this end) has any value or relevance whatsoever qua part of the craft. Thus, if and to the extent that the bridle-maker successfully produces bridles, his activity is complete and self-sufficient: he does all he should do, and nothing else matters. Similarly with the doctor: all that matters is promoting and preserving the health of the patients; all else is irrelevant and without value as part of medical practice. Of course the bridle-maker and the doctor may have other aims they are pursuing, and they may even succeed in achieving these aims, for example, making money or becoming admired for their work. However, the pursuit and achievement of these latter aims are external to the practice of their craft, and therefore completely irrelevant to the evaluation and success of the bridle-maker or the doctor qua bridle-maker and doctor.[12]

When Aristotle introduces the criterion of self-sufficiency he is generalizing this point from the determinate and limited context of a craft, or other practice, to life in general. And his thought is that just as the successful performance of a craft is complete and leaves nothing more to be desired within the context of the craft, so the successfully lived life is complete and leaves nothing more to be desired within the context of that life. The reason is that a certain life is a whole constituted by a central good that defines it as that very life. Moreover, when this central good is realized, through the living of the life that it constitutes and defines, then that life, with its central good, is complete: there is nothing more to be desired. Here, however, a difference emerges between life in general and any specialized practice such as the crafts. In the case of such practices there is always an 'outside'; the bridle-maker might be in it for the money, and his pursuit of that end may interfere with his commitment to producing bridles, or good bridles. But in the case of life in general there is no external end to aim at: life is complete and self-sufficient, it encompasses and exhausts all possible human activity. When it comes to life as such, we can't be in it for the money, or anything else.[13]

---

[12] Plato makes this point in *Republic* I 345e–6e. Note that pursuit of such external ends may interfere with and even corrupt the pursuit of the internal and constitutive end of the craft—we are all too familiar with that.

[13] We could compare life to an organism such as the human body. All its organs are there, and they function as they should, doing their job in concert. Hence, nothing is lacking; the body is complete.

But that leaves us with the problem of ethics: What is this highest good?

In the two first chapters of the *EN* Aristotle defines his topic as 'the topmost of all achievable goods' (which is the object of political expertise and is called 'the human good' at the end of I 2). He then continues by stating that people agree on what to call this highest good: 'both ordinary people and people of quality say "happiness" [eudaimonia], and suppose that living well [eu zēn] and doing well [eu prattein] are the same thing as being happy' (I 4, 1095a18–20).

Aristotle here follows tradition in taking eudaimonia to be a matter of *success* or *good fortune* in life. To ascribe eudaimonia to a person and his life is to judge it successful, and the notion of eudaimonia is therefore the notion of an *objective, ethical property of a life*, not a subjective, psychological state.[14]

We see this when we look ahead to I 8. Here Aristotle refers to several 'things people say [ta legomena]' (1098b10) about eudaimonia. These include the view that the *eudaimōn* man 'both lives well and does well' (b20–1; already stated in I 4, 1095a18–20). Moreover, eudaimonia belongs to the goods of the soul, rather than to the goods of the body or the external goods (b12–18), and it is said to be 'virtue, or some form of virtue' (b30). However, eudaimonia concerns virtue not qua disposition but insofar as it is an activity (b33). Furthermore, while eudaimonia is not to be identified with pleasure, it will in itself involve pleasure, that is, be enjoyable (1099a7), in addition to being both good (*agathon*) and noble (*kalon*) (a22). Finally, although eudaimonia does not consist in wealth, political power, or other external goods, it will require some such goods in addition (b31–2). In sum, these points show that Aristotle follows tradition and common sense in taking eudaimonia to amount to some kind of success in the activity of living one's life. Eudaimonia is a matter of the activity one engages in and the way one does so, not about whatever results this activity may produce. Such results may be signs or manifestations of the successful performance of this activity, but are not themselves the criteria for such success. The question therefore is to determine what the criterion for such success really is.

To the extent that one takes the way one fares in life to be subject to (at least some significant measure of) one's own control, one's conception of eudaimonia will amount to a conception of what is of primary and ultimate value as an end that it makes practical sense to aim at in life (to have as one's *skopos*).[15] The conception of this value will provide the agent with a practical principle for organizing his life as a particular *form of life*—his way of life, organized around the ultimate end to which he aspires and whose achievement he thinks will make his life *eudaimōn* or successful. Such a positive or optimistic conception of eudaimonia gradually develops in classical times, thanks to the development of *technē* as the primary means for humans to

---

Nothing could be added to the body, no new organs, for the body is, from nature's side, self-sufficient—not only does nature do nothing in vain, but she does everything completely.

[14] See the Introduction, this volume, p. 7f, on the etymology and history of eudaimonia.

[15] Cf. *EE* I 2, 1214b6–11, quoted below p. 110.

gain some measure of control over their own life circumstances. This development is reflected in philosophers such as Plato and Aristotle. Thus, when, in I 4 and 5, Aristotle raises the question what eudaimonia as the highest good consists in, this is the question which kind of life is the best and therefore the one that one ought to aspire to. Achieving eudaimonia amounts to *success* in that project which is one's life, which is why regarding someone as *eudaimōn*, unlike describing someone as happy in the modern sense, is not to describe a psychological fact—it is to make a heavily loaded normative (ethical) judgement, one that normally licences certain 'reactive attitudes', such as applause, admiration, respect, honour.[16]

Aristotle's philosophical conception of eudaimonia should thus be seen as a constructive interpretation of the traditional notion: it articulates presuppositions already present in the tradition, and develops and grounds these presuppositions in a systematic, philosophical conception. The pursuit of eudaimonia amounts to *undertaking the project of living one's life in a certain way*, defined and guided by a conception of an overall end that constitutes the project, or life-form, as that particular project, and hence that determines the criteria for judging its success or failure.[17] This presupposes, as we saw, a recognition of the *possibility* for humans to take their fate in their own hands, as well as their *responsibility* for doing so. In addition, however, it presupposes both a *clear idea* of what the nature of the project is, and a *firm commitment* to undertake this project. This opens up the possibility of failure on two counts: one may have the wrong idea of what eudaimonia and the proper project of life is, and one may fail to make the required commitment to pursue this project. Of course, one may fail on both counts—which, no doubt, is what most people do, on Aristotle's view. The task of ethics is to clarify the nature of eudaimonia, in order to help us achieve it.

2. Eudaimonia and Human Nature: The *Ergon* Argument

Aristotle presents the core of his view on eudaimonia in the so-called 'function [*ergon*] argument' (I 7, 1097b22–8a20), where he determines the nature of the best

---

[16] This also explains how the individual whose life is in question is not in a privileged position with respect to making this judgement: an individual not only may be mistaken in judging his life successful or *eudaimōn*—he may be deluded about the value of his own life—but often will be.

[17] The term 'project' may strike someone as misleading since it may suggest the idea that this project could one day be completed, in the sense that one's ultimate end might be reached and one might then spend the rest of one's life in leisurely retirement, resting on one's laurels, as it were. This is of course misleading; the ultimate end of life, as Aristotle sees it, is the leading of one's life in a certain way, and this end is not 'achieved' until life itself is over (i.e. death). In Aristotelian terminology: the living of a life is an *energeia* (an activity), not a *kinēsis* (a process), and eudaimonia is living life in a certain way, namely, well or successfully. Even so, however, I have chosen to retain the term 'project' since it connotes the kind of commitment and ambition that I take to be central to the classical conception of eudaimonia as the ultimate end in life (cf. previous paragraph on eudaimonia as a way of living one's life). Thanks to Will Small for pressing me on this.

human life on the basis of a clarification of what man's 'function' or *ergon* is. His answer is that the human function is *logos* or reason—'a practical sort of life of what possesses reason' (1098a3–4)—and that the best human life is the life in which reason is actualized to the greatest extent: eudaimonia is 'the activity of the soul in accordance with virtue' (a16–17), that is, the life of virtue. He claims that this answer fits well with reputable pre-philosophical beliefs about the best life or eudaimonia (I 8; cf. above p. 95), and then makes some further clarifications (I 9–12) before he lays the ground (in I 13) for the more detailed—although still schematic—discussion of the best life for humans that is to fill the following nine books of the *EN*.

Aristotle develops his account of the human *ergon* against the background of his biology.[18] The core of this biology is *teleology*: the nature of biological organisms can only be understood within a teleological framework. Aristotle assumes that each biological species, S, is defined by a distinctive activity or way of life, ϕ, such that to be an S is to ϕ, that is, *to be active ϕ-ing*. The way an organism is organized (its anatomy and physiology), develops (growth and maturation), and lives (behaviour) must be described and explained by reference to the activity of ϕ-ing, as various forms of contribution towards the end (*telos*) of successfully performing this activity.

Now, organisms are commonly divided into three categories or kinds of life: plants, animals, and humans. Each species of organism belongs to one of these categories, and each category is distinguished by a common fundamental function or activity: its generic *ergon*. This comes out in the opening lines of the *ergon*-argument:

For being alive [*to zēn*] is obviously shared by plants too, and we are looking for what is peculiar to human beings. In that case we must divide off the kind of life that consists in taking in nutriment and growing [*hē threptikē kai hē auxētikē zōē*]. Next to consider would be some sort of life of perception [*aisthētikē*], but this too is evidently shared, by horses, oxen, and every other animal. There remains a practical sort of life of what possesses reason [*praktikē tis tou logon echontos*]; and of this, one element 'possesses reason' in so far as it is obedient to reason, while the other possesses it in so far as it actually has it, and itself thinks [*dianooumenon*]. (I 7, 1097b33–8a5)

Plants take in nutriment and grow—this is definitive of life, as is the fact that all organisms reproduce. But there are many different ways of performing the activities of taking in nutriment, growing, and reproducing, and correspondingly many different kinds of physiological constitution to make possible these activities. Each

---

[18] Actually, the immediate context for the *ergon* argument is provided by two kinds of case: bodily organs and crafts. Rachel Barney makes a strong case for taking the crafts to carry most of the argumentative burden (Barney (2008), on the 'preparatory argument' (1097b22–33)). While I agree with a lot of what she argues, I do not think we need to go as far as she does in opposing the two contexts, for they seem to me to share the most important feature, namely, teleological organization. This allows Aristotle to move between the two, although the technical case may ultimately be more illuminating. But they also both have their limitations, as we shall see.

individual species of plant is defined by the distinctive form that these activities and constitution take. This is its specific *ergon* or life-form.

Animals are also living creatures, so they too perform the basic biological functions of taking in nutriment, growing, and reproducing. However, animals are distinguished by a further set of fundamental biological activities: desire, perception, and motion. As living creatures they need nutriment, but animals have the capacity to feel this need and to be motivated to acquire whatever will satisfy it, that is, food. Moreover, unlike plants, animals are capable of detecting through perception what, in their surroundings, will satisfy their needs, and they are able to move towards these objects and appropriate them. These basic capacities and activities are distinctive of animals as opposed to plants, and, just as with plants, the various animal species are distinguished from each other by the peculiarities of how they perform these activities, that is, by their specific *ergon* or life-form.

It is important to see that when we move from plant life to animal life, the basic vegetative activities are *transformed*; it is not the case that the animal capacities are simply added on to the capacities of plants.[19] Thus, all living creatures need, and seek, nutriment. But in animals, as opposed to plants, this need appears in the form of a *desire* for what will meet the need, and when they seek nutriment, they do not merely select and appropriate whatever will meet the need, they *perceive* it, and they then proceed to actively *do* whatever (undertake whatever motion) is needed for the purpose of nutrition.

A teleological conception of biological nature allows us to accurately *describe* and, on that basis, *explain* the physiological constitution and behaviour of individual plants and animals by reference to their nature. But teleology also makes it possible to *evaluate* the characteristics and behaviour of each individual plant or animal. To be an S is to be active ϕ-ing: this is its *ergon*. Each specimen of S is so constituted that it will naturally attempt to ϕ, that is, to display the behaviour characteristic of its species S: it will *strive* towards ϕ-ing. As a consequence, if a is a member of S, then a will be a good S if, and to the extent that, it regularly and reliably ϕ's well, that is, is good at ϕ-ing.

This has a couple of important implications that are relevant for us. First, the definition of a species in terms of its *ergon* involves an element of *ideality*. Aristotle makes this point explicit with an example from the human sphere: the cithara-player, but the point holds for all categories of organism (and artefact):

The function, we say, of a given sort of practitioner and a good practitioner of that sort is generically the same [*to d'auto phamen ergon einai tō(i) genei toude kai toude spoudaiou*], as for example in the case of the cithara-player, and this is so without qualification [*haplōs*] in all cases, when a difference in respect of excellence [*prostithemenēs tēs kata tēn aretēn huperochēs*]

---

[19] See Boyle (2012) and (n.d.) for clarification of this.

is added to the function (for what belongs to the citharist is to play the cithara, to the good citharist to play it well). (I 7, 1098a8–12)

Membership of a kind or species is defined in terms of a certain activity or 'work' ('function', *ergon*). All members of the kind/species, qua members, have, or should have, the capacity to engage in this activity. But some members have developed this capacity to a higher level than others; they are better ('differ in respect of excellence') than average. Conversely, some members may have this capacity to a deficient extent, or even lack it altogether, which underwrites the description of them as diseased, injured, or impaired. If we want to grasp what it is to be a member of this species, then we should look to the best, most excellent members, for there we see the essential capacity/activity displayed in the clearest form, and we also see what the other, ordinary (less successful) specimens are measured against, and strive but fail to achieve. The conception we have of the *ergon* of such a species or kind is thus not based on any statistical survey of what most members do; it is to that extent a conception of an ideal entity.

Secondly, in the case of an individual plant or animal, a, to say that it is good at ϕ-ing (good at being S) is not merely to say something *about* it, namely, evaluate it from an external point of view, it is also to say something that is of significance *for* it. The reason for this is that being good at ϕ-ing (good at being S) is also *good for a* insofar as a is S. Moreover, if being S is the essence of a—and we are assuming this since S is the species to which a belongs, and the essence of an organism is defined by reference to its species—then being good at ϕ-ing is *good for a simpliciter*.[20] The point is familiar: when an individual plant, a, grows and blossoms in its natural habitat, we say not only that a's living this way makes it a good specimen of its kind, but that this (i.e. a's living this way) is good for a—it *thrives*. And conversely, if the plant grows under unfavourable circumstances, such that it is unable to thrive as it should, this is said to be bad for it—it *suffers*. Thus, plants can thrive as well as suffer, depending on whether they are able to live the life characteristic of their species; this is reflected in our use of terms such as 'health' and 'sickness' of plants no less than of animals and humans. The teleological perspective thus makes it possible to move from an external, 'third-person' perspective, measuring the particular specimen's life against its *ergon*, to an internal, 'first-person' perspective, as it were, where its life is seen from the point of view of the organism itself. To the extent that we can ascribe to the organism a striving towards ϕ-ing, we can also say that it strives towards maintaining itself, and that it does so for its own sake, because this is good for it.[21] The standard constituted by the *ergon* is thus not an external standard imposed on the organism; it is the organism's own *internal* standard.

---

[20] See Barney (2008), section 4, for a similar, more extended argument to this conclusion.

[21] Needless to say, the notion of ϕ-ing being good for a does not imply that a must *experience* ϕ-ing as being good for it, e.g. by being pleasant or invigorating: plants clearly do not have any such kind of experience, for that would presuppose a capacity for consciousness and mental life that plants lack.

The general teleological conception just outlined applies to all biological organisms, and a fortiori also to humans. That is why Aristotle assumes that even human beings qua species have a distinctive *ergon* or way of life. This is what sets up the *ergon* argument in I 7. However, since human beings are different from other species, their specific *ergon* has to be determined, and when Aristotle undertakes to do this, he assumes that we must look elsewhere than to those more basic biological activities or functions mentioned so far: taking in nutriment and so on, and perception and so on. Rather, we must look to what is distinctive of human beings, what marks them off from the other living creatures. This, he claims, is that they lead 'a practical sort of life of what possesses reason'. So the human *ergon*, the characteristic feature of human beings that makes them human, is reason, *logos*.

This claim might cause some scepticism: Are there not other features of human beings that uniquely characterize them—such as, for example, empathy, a sense of humour, or even cruelty? This misses the point, however, for what Aristotle intends is to identify the feature of human beings and their way of life that gives this life as a whole its distinctive character: the human life-form. This feature will then also collect and explain all the other features and their precise nature by accounting for their place within the integrated, functional whole that is a human life. Thus, while human beings are (I take it) alone in having a sense of humour, this sense cannot be taken to define the human life-form, for we cannot explain everything human beings do, including, for instance, deliberation and other forms of reasoning, by its place within the human life-form, if this is defined by reference to our sense of humour—on the contrary, we explain our sense of humour by reference to our rational capacity. Furthermore, human beings do things that other organisms also do, animals as well as plants. But while it is, in some sense, true to say that we share these activities and functions with the lower kinds of organism, they are *transformed* when they are part of human life, and that is because the way we perform these activities is informed by reason.[22]

Human beings are unique in that we are *practical*, and thereby *rational*, creatures. We share with the animals the ability to desire things, but when we move to satisfy our desires, we do so on the basis of deliberation and decision, which are exercises of *reason*. In an animal a need for nutriments will result in a felt desire for food, and this desire will result in behaviour to acquire food and ingest it. The behaviour of the animal is governed by instinctual patterns and so is not, in a strict sense, up to the individual animal. When a human feels a desire, on the other hand, this desire manifests itself as a representation of the object as something to be appropriated, something that will satisfy the need that grounds the desire. This representation, moreover, amounts to a proposal to move to appropriate the object. Thus, the human agent must decide whether he should endorse the proposal and move to satisfy his

---

[22] Cf. Nagel (1980), 10f, for a succinct statement of this point. See also Devereux (1981), as well as the works by Boyle cited in note 19.

desire now, or whether it would be better to wait, or perhaps it would be best not to satisfy it at all. In short, we can *set our own ends*, whereas in animals the ends are set by instinct.

Thus, a human desire is not a mere urge or impulse towards a certain object; rather, the desire itself partly consists in a logically structured representation of the object as connected in a certain way to its appropriation and the satisfaction of a need. Only a rational creature—a *zōon logikon*—is capable of such representation, and in such creatures even the most basic desires, such as the desire for food and drink, are structured representations of this kind. That is how in human beings reason, *logos*, is not something added on to the desires that we share with animals, with the further difference that we have the capacity to step back from and take a stand towards these desires; rather, reason fundamentally transforms these desires themselves and makes them rational desires, or the desires of rational creatures.[23]

Now, of course human beings have a whole range of desires that animals cannot have, such as desires for art, technical mastery, or scientific understanding, or, more relevantly for present concerns, the desire for justice or proper respect. Moreover, we may have appetitive desires for such things as foie gras and vintage wines (and not just generic food and drink), and thumotic desires for honour and respect (and not just for self-assertion). The desires of human beings are thus the products of reason in two ways: (1) for the most part, the *content* or *object* of human desires presupposes reason, and (2) the *form* of human desires is always rationally constituted, even when their content is 'vegetative' or 'animal'. Since reason is always as such normative, human motivation and action are normative phenomena. Thus, we *perceive* (or *conceive*) the particular situation we find ourselves in (or confronted by) by correctly applying concepts and norms that are constitutive of our practical life. Secondly, we *respond* immediately emotionally and conatively to this perceived/conceived situation in ways that are adequate to the actual features of the situation, as well as to our own condition/position. Thirdly, we *figure out* and *decide*, on the basis of deliberation, what is the best/right thing to do in the situation as we perceive/conceive it and respond to it. And, fourthly, we *act* on our decision. In all of these ways human motivation and behaviour are not the products of causal mechanisms the way animal motivation and behaviour are, not to mention the growth and reproduction of plants. Rather, they are the outcome of a 'causality of reason'—or perhaps, as we might say, of a free will.[24] That is why they are the legitimate subjects of criticism and the demand for justification. (More on this in section 3.)

---

[23] That is to say, rationally (or cognitively) informed desires. These should not be confused with desires that constitute what Aristotle calls 'rational wish [*boulēsis*]': these are a subspecies of human desires, defined in terms of the particular way they are formed (see III 2 and 4).

[24] The concept of a free will is complex and highly contested, as is the idea that there is such a notion in antiquity. Here I have in mind a weak and everyday notion that I take to be universally present among human beings.

So the human *ergon* is *logos*, reason, which in the context of ethics means: practical reason—'a practical sort of life of what possesses reason', as Aristotle puts it. But the content of the work of reason is more complex than so far specified. I want to highlight two points here: first, the way reason manifests itself in desires and emotions, on the one hand, and in deliberation, on the other; and, secondly, the way reason involves not only the ability to deliberate, on particular occasions, towards concrete decisions to act, but also the ability to reason 'upwards' to an articulate and adequate conception of the content of the highest good.

Immediately following the definition of the human *ergon* Aristotle goes on to make a distinction within reason, between two ways in which reason can 'work' or manifest itself in human life: 'of this [sc. what possesses reason], one element "possesses reason" in so far as it is obedient to reason, while the other possesses it in so far as it actually has it, and itself thinks' (I 7, 1098a4–5). This distinction is further elaborated in I 13, where Aristotle divides the soul into two parts: the one that concerns desire (the appetitive part), and the one that concerns thought (the rational part).[25] These parts correspond to the two ways in which reason can manifest itself, and they each have their own set of virtues or excellences: the intellectual and the ethical virtues, respectively. The ethical virtues define the relevant ethical considerations and attunes the agent to them, while practical wisdom (as the ethically relevant intellectual virtue) enables the agent, through deliberation, to determine the best way of preserving these concerns. Human life tends to be of such a degree of complexity that it is not immediately obvious how one's concerns are to be taken care of, which is why deliberation is often needed. The good person, therefore, who succeeds in living his life rationally and is therefore *eudaimōn*, will have to have both kinds of virtue: ethical and intellectual.[26] Thus, eudaimonia is defined as success as a human being, that is, as the successful exercise of ethical and intellectual virtue.

The second point I want to elaborate now concerns the complexity of the purely intellectual function of reason or *logos*. So far we have looked at the directly deliberative function of reason: determining the best course of action under the circumstances, given one's perception of the relevant general considerations. But this perception is itself a rational product, based in some kind of grasp of what the highest or central good of one's life is. So it is a further function of reason to sustain this conception of the highest good.

---

[25] Aristotle actually reckons with three parts of the soul: in addition to the two mentioned, there is also the part that deals with reproduction, growth, and nutrition. However, this third part is irrelevant for ethical purposes since nobody is called virtuous or *eudaimōn* on account of his digestion or reproductive capacity.

[26] The precise relation between virtue and practical wisdom is controversial. In one place Aristotle says that 'virtue makes the goal correct, while [practical] wisdom makes what leads to it correct' (VI 12, 1144a7–9). This passage, along with some others (see I 13, 1145a5–7; VII 8, 1151a15–19; *EE* II 11, 1227b23–5), may seem to suggest an instrumentalist view of this relation. For a good discussion, and a provocative interpretation, see Moss (2011).

We have seen (p. 91f) that eudaimonia as the highest good is the terminus for all chains of justification of action: it provides the single ultimate standard or criterion for deciding what to do. In that way it ensures the coherence of a human life and the justification of each individual action. This is the full implication of Aristotle's remark that 'it is for the sake of [eudaimonia] that we all do everything else we do, and we lay it down that the principle and cause of goods [*tēn archēn kai to aition tōn agathōn*] is something honourable and godlike' (I 12, 1102a1–4). However, a life can be made coherent and given a certain shape in many different ways, depending on the particular conception of the highest good or ultimate end, eudaimonia, that serves as its principle and cause. Now, Aristotle is a realist about ethics, so he believes that there is an objective fact of the matter as to which conception of the highest good is the *right* one, and reason only completely actualizes itself when it grasps this right conception and uses it as the principle for deliberation and conative-emotional response to one's particular circumstances. It is, as we shall see, the purpose of ethics to articulate and justify this *right* conception of eudaimonia, the one that can provide a person with the right principle for leading his life. Thus, acquiring, and working out, this conception is a further task for a person's reason.

So the *ergon* of *logos* is threefold. First, it informs the character of the agent in such a way that his conative and emotional responses to his circumstances are rational, that is, rationally defensible on the basis of a valid conception of the highest good. Secondly, *logos* enables an agent to deliberate well about what to do in a particular situation, again on the basis of his conception of the highest good. Finally, *logos* manifests itself in articulating and justifying a valid conception of the highest good— the one that provides the basis for his conative-emotional responses and his deliberation.

3. Eudaimonia, Human Nature, and Normativity

Aristotle places ethics within the wider framework of his teleological biology. Just as it is good for a plant to grow and unfold in its natural habitat, and for an animal to develop and live its life in the way characteristic of its species, so the good life for a human being is to realize the natural *telos* of human being: 'a practical sort of life of what possesses reason' (I 7, 1098a3–4), and to do so to the optimal extent: eudaimonia is 'the activity of the soul in accordance with virtue' (a16–17). So *human* goodness is a species of *natural* goodness.[27]

However, ethics is also, according to Aristotle, a *practical* discipline—it is to provide people with *guidance* for how to live their lives by showing them the *right* way to live, the way they *ought* to live.[28] The question is how ethics can be both: based

---

[27] This is the starting point for the so-called 'Aristotelian naturalism' in modern ethics, whose main representatives include Philippa Foot, Rosalind Hursthouse, and Michael Thompson.

[28] See II 2, 1103b26–31; X 9, 1179a33–b4; cf. also the analogy with the archer, I 2, 1094a22–4.

in a teleological conception of our *nature* (i.e. biology) and practically *normative*. This seems to lead into all sorts of difficulties associated with naturalism in ethics. In our context, where we are trying to understand Aristotle's eudaemonist ethics, there are two urgent problems: First, (1) what sense can we give to the idea of the human *telos* or human nature as an *authoritative* practical (ethical or moral) end, that is, an end that we *ought* to pursue? How are we to understand this 'ought'? The solution, we shall see, lies in grasping precisely how Aristotle understands the nature of the human *telos* and its normative status; once we reflect further on this, we will see how and why this *telos* is genuinely normative for human beings. The second problem we need to address is (2) how a conception of the human *telos* can be really practical, that is, provide us with the *substantive guidance* needed to help us see how we are to live that is the proper task of ethics. How can eudaemonist ethics be of any practical use? Let us look at the two problems in turn.

(1) Authority. Aristotle assumes that human beings have an *ergon*, a way of living or a life-form that is characteristic of them qua human beings, the way dogs and roses have their specific *erga* or ways of living. The realization of this *telos* is what the creature really is, and to the extent that it fails to realize its *telos*, it fails at being itself—it is itself to a deficient degree or in a deficient way. However, an individual organism will by nature be so constituted that it will aim to realize this *telos* by actually living its specific life-form. Such a *telos* thereby shapes the life (as well as the physical and psychic constitution) of the individual, and the individual's life conduct is measured by reference to this *telos*. In the case of plants and animals an individual automatically strives to actualize this specific *telos*—they are *causally* determined to do so, by biological tropisms or by instinct. But in the case of human beings the situation is different, for we are agents who *intentionally* live the way we do because we have chosen to do so—how we live is 'up to us'. However, since choices must be justified—we act for reasons—the specifically human *telos* (or *ergon*) is normative for us in a way that the *telos* of a plant and an animal is not for them. This raises the question: Why should we humans feel obliged to pursue our *telos*?

This is where the problems start, for it seems that the claim that there is a natural *telos* that we are somehow normatively obligated to pursue, commits us to a version of the naturalistic fallacy—in addition to presuming a dubious, no longer viable metaphysical biology. But I want to claim that something has gone wrong in the way the problem is set up in the preceding paragraph. If we grasp the situation aright, we will see that there is no naturalistic fallacy here, nor any metaphysically dubious biology.

If we go back to the beginning of the *ergon* argument, we see Aristotle using two different contexts to lead up to his identification of the human *ergon*. After introducing the two criteria that any adequate account of eudaimonia must satisfy, Aristotle says:

Perhaps it appears somewhat uncontroversial to say that *happiness* is the chief good, and a more distinct statement of what it is is still required. Well, perhaps this would come about if one established the *function* [*ergon*] of human beings. For just as for a flute-player, or a sculptor, or any expert, and generally for all those who have some characteristic function or activity [*holōs hōn estin ergon ti kai praxis*], the good—their doing well—seems to reside in their function, so too it would seem to be for the human being, if indeed there is some function that belongs to them. So does a carpenter or a shoemaker have certain functions and activities, while a human being has none, and is by nature a do-nothing? Or just as an eye, a hand, a foot, and generally each and every part of the body appears as having some function, in the same way would one posit a characteristic function for a human being too, alongside all of these? (I 7, 1097b22–33)

One of the striking things with this passage where Aristotle articulates the 'function thesis'[29]—apart from the fact that Aristotle seems to take himself to be entitled to assuming it pretty much without argument—is that it appeals to two different contexts that provide him with grounds for articulating the human *ergon*: the crafts (*technai*) and biological organs. It seems clear that both contexts are important, but their distinctive contributions to a proper conception of the human *ergon* do not seem entirely clear. Let us look at the *technē* context first.

As we have already seen, every *technē*—and, indeed, any organized practice (cf. Aristotle's expression at b26: 'for . . . any expert, and generally for all those who have some characteristic function or activity')—is constituted by a certain overall end towards which every part of it is directed. This end is pursued by the craftsman or practitioner in all his activity, and achieving this end is what obligates and motivates him to do what he does. This end is thus internal to, and constitutive of, the craft, and it is rationally normative for the practice of the craft. Qua practitioner—carpenter, doctor—a person is bound to pursue the end that constitutes the craft, otherwise he just isn't practicing the craft but doing something else.

However, the end that constitutes the craft and that is normative for all practice of the craft, is not merely internal to the craft. It is also grounded in something external to the craft, for the craft as such exists—it has been developed and shaped the way it has—because it contributes to the safety and prosperity of humankind. This was one of the main points in the first two chapters of the *Nicomachean Ethics* (cf. section 1). This means, however, that any practitioner of a craft may at any time ask himself whether he should take up the craft or not—and if so, why—or whether there are, in any particular situation, considerations that override the demands of his craft and thus might lead him to act contrary to these demands. So the end of a craft, or the obligation to pursue this end, is always—ultimately—conditional upon pursuit of some further end towards which it contributes: the end of a craft is *contingent* or *hypothetical*.

Now, when Aristotle, in introducing his function thesis, draws on the fact that crafts have an *ergon*, he clearly relies on an important and uncontroversial similarity

---

[29] As Rachel Barney calls it; see Barney (2008), 295. I am indebted to her excellent discussion, though my conclusions are not identical.

between practicing a craft and being a human being, and hence between a craft and human life. This similarity is not hard to see: it is the normative organization internal to the practice. There is a constitutive end to be realized, the activity in question (the *ergon*: task) is defined and regulated by this end, and this end is never questioned within the practice.

But this, of course, leads to the major difference: the end of a craft can always be questioned, and it may be set aside (or justified) by reference to some higher end that overrides it (or that justifies it). The practice of human living, however, has no such higher end, and thus its end cannot be justified by reference to anything higher. The end is therefore necessary: the end of life is *necessary* or *categorical*.

This universal or categorical character of the end of human life comes out in the distinction Aristotle makes between *poiēsis* (technical action) and *praxis* (true or ethical action). In Book VI he distinguishes between the two intellectual virtues that correspond to these two kinds of activity—*technē* and *phronēsis* respectively—and says of the latter:

It is thought characteristic of a [practically] wise person [a *phronimos*] to be able to deliberate well about things that are good and advantageous to himself, not in specific contexts [*ou kata meros*], e.g. what sorts of things conduce to health, or to physical strength, but what sorts of things conduce to the good life in general [*to eu zēn holōs*]. (VI 5, 1140a25–8)

The scope of ethical action, or ethical deliberation, is universal in that there is nothing that falls outside of it, whereas this is the case with technical deliberation. Qua doctor, a person may deliberate whether this or that treatment is the right one, but not whether he should aim to promote the health of the patient. However, qua human being, he may precisely deliberate whether he should try to cure this particular patient or, more generally, whether he should practice medicine at all. So there is an area inside as well as outside of the 'deliberative field' of a technical practice such as medicine. But this is precisely not the case with ethical deliberation: everything belongs within this field, and there is therefore no standpoint outside of, or beyond, the ethical standpoint, from which ethical deliberation and its conclusions may be assessed and overridden. There is no room for the question 'Should we go in for ethics or not?' for ethics is the 'deliberative field' of life as a whole. So ethics is inescapable.[30]

This leads us to the second context for the function thesis, which is biology. Any bodily organ is defined as the organ it is by its contribution to the functioning of the body (organism) as a whole. Thus the eye enables the organism to see, the hand to manipulate objects, and so on. Each organ exists as the organ it is—it is there, is

---

[30] The case here is analogous to the one we find in logic and epistemology. The norms of thought and knowledge are not only normative for reasoning and the formation of our beliefs about the world—they are constitutive. Whoever violates these laws and principles just is not thinking—at least if these violations become too many and too grave.

formed, and has developed in its distinctive way—because of (for the sake of) its contribution to the whole organism and its function. Moreover, and this is the crucial contribution that biology makes to the function thesis, the organs and their *erga* are given by nature: they are not for the sake of something further beyond the organism as a whole. So the end of the organism as a whole is, as it were, *categorical* from the point of view of the organism itself. The various organs of which the organism is composed, exist for the sake of it, while the organism itself does not exist for the sake of anything further—the organism simply exists and cannot but do so: it is complete or self-sufficient (*autarkēs*) (cf. p. 93f).

Now, where does this leave us with our worry that Aristotle is guilty of the naturalistic fallacy in his ethics? I said there was a natural way to misunderstand Aristotle's thought in postulating a naturally given *ergon* or *telos* for human beings. The error was to think of this *telos* as something we are somehow forced or obligated to *choose*. But we can now see that this error is grounded in a confusion between the two contexts for the function thesis: biology and the crafts. Our *ergon* or *telos* is given to us by nature: the human species has a certain way of being that is constitutive for it, just as the life-forms of roses and dogs are for roses and dogs. This is the biology part of Aristotle's line of reasoning. But the particular content or character of the human *ergon* is normative in a way that is closely analogous to—although not identical with—what we find in the crafts. So we are biologically so constituted that we cannot but develop and exercise the capacity for rational normative activity—we are causally determined to be free under the norms of reason.

The source of error is to think as if we had a choice whether to perform the human *ergon* or not, that is, be rational (a *zōon logikon*). Although it is true that humans are special in that they perform their *ergon* intentionally, this does not mean that what they intentionally do is to *opt for* (enter, take up) the human *ergon*, rather than something else (or than doing nothing). Rather, what they intentionally do is to perform their *ergon* the *way* they do. That is to say, performing the human *ergon* (being rationally active) is not the *object* of choice, that is, the alternative (among several) that our choice picks out, and that thereby provides its substantive content and distinguishes it from other choices we might make. Doing the human thing is the *form* of our choices and actions, that is, what makes them precisely that: choices and actions, rather than mere animal behaviour (not to mention vegetative growth). A substance cannot 'opt for' its form, that is, settle *whether* it is to perform its *ergon* and thereby actualize its form, for that would mean that it could choose to exist, which is absurd. What it can do, however, is to settle *how* (in what way, when, where, etc.) it is to do so. Of course, organisms settle this in different ways, depending on what kind of organism they are. The vegetative behaviour of plants is settled by tropisms, while animal behaviour is settled by instinctual patterns of motivation. As for human beings, they settle how, when, where, and so forth they actualize their form by perceiving their situation, responding to it, and deliberating their way to a decision about action. Thus, human beings cannot choose *whether* they should be rationally active, for that is their form: in so far as they are human, that is, exist (are alive), they simply *are* rationally active. To think that they could *choose* to be rationally active would be to introduce an ontological gap between being human and doing the thing that constitutes our form and essence qua human, and thus to imply that they could choose to be human, that is, to exist. But that is where the absurdity becomes apparent, for what would the alternative be? Clearly: to belong to another species! (Or: suicide—but then that is not the alternative to *becoming* human but, rather, to *continuing* to be human.) The error here is to assimilate rational agency as such to the specific kinds of rational activity that we find for instance in the crafts.

To see clearly the implications of this we need to distinguish two levels of activity. On the one hand, we have (I) the activity or practice of performing one's *ergon* or actualizing one's form. This is one's given biological nature, and for human beings this is rational activity as such. This activity consists in our perceiving (or conceiving) our particular current circumstances and the values at stake therein, in deliberating about what to do in these circumstances, in deciding what to do, and in actually doing this (that is, carrying out the decision).

On the other hand, we have (II) the particular way we perform our *ergon*, that is, how, when, where, and so on, we do so, as well as why. Thus, I perceive (or conceive) my particular circumstances in a certain way, rather than another; here I may be challenged, and it may turn out that I should have perceived (conceived) it otherwise—I made a mistake, I was irrational (failed to actualize my rationality), and may accordingly be held accountable. Moreover, I deliberate in a certain way about what to do but, again, I may be challenged, and justly so. Similarly, I make a decision, but it may be right or wrong, well grounded or not. And my action, finally, may be consistent or inconsistent with my decision—I may have displayed a weak character, and so be liable to criticism.

The human *ergon* is *logos*, we have seen. As such it is given by our nature: qua human beings we are always already engaged in the activity of reason. Now, the term '*ergon*' is often translated as 'function' or 'work'. But in the case of human beings, whose *ergon* is *logos*, it may be more illuminating to talk of it as a 'task'. The human *ergon* has in common with the *erga* of plants and animals that it is essential to or constitutive of our being what we are. It is thus normative in the general biological or metaphysical sense. But the human *ergon* is unique in that it is also normative in a further sense: it is a task that it is up to the individual to perform or not. Performing this task presents the individual with a challenge, a challenge that is difficult to meet in a satisfactory way because it makes demands on the individual. These demands are partly intellectual (we may go wrong, fail to understand what is demanded of us, or how we are to do what is demanded) and partly volitional (we may fail to discipline ourselves and make the required effort to do what is required). So while even plants and animals may fail to perform their *ergon*, in humans this failure takes the form of an error, that is, something for which the individual is appropriately held responsible.

With this in mind we can see a sense in which we can, after all, talk about the good life as a matter of choosing, or 'going in for', performing our *ergon*. This choice is not a matter of opting for *logos* rather than something else, but of committing oneself to actualizing this *ergon* in the appropriate way and to the fullest extent. It is up to me whether, and to what extent, I take my constitutive task seriously—by being conscientious about perceiving, deliberating, deciding, and acting rationally, and by disciplining myself and making an effort to do so, and even by trying to make myself someone who is disposed to do so without particular effort or cost to oneself. This is where there is scope for failing or being deficient as a human being, the way there is scope for failing/being deficient as a horse or a rose. However, in humans this failing/deficiency is something for which we can be held accountable, and be made the subject of various reactive attitudes, such as respect and admiration, or disrespect and contempt. Moreover, it is possible to ask the justificatory question about the choice of acting rationally in sense (II): 'Why should I be rational?' And the correct answer to this question is: 'Because you are a human being, and if you don't act rationally, you fail yourself and make yourself less than you are: an animal!' Living the ethically right life is a matter of *being serious about oneself*.[31]

This is where the space—and need—for ethics opens up.

(2) *Substantive guidance.* So our nature as human beings presents us with a challenging task: to be rational, to perform the characteristically human activities of cognition and practical deliberation. This task is difficult, so there is plenty of space for falling short with respect to these norms and standards. We sometimes, some of us, violate the norms and prove poorly capable of performing these activities properly. That is why we need guidance through correction and education, and ethics is one way of providing such guidance. Ethics starts from the fact that humans fall short of the norms and standards of reason, those very norms and standards that constitute us as human beings.

As we saw, such failure can take many forms, corresponding to the various aspects of the human *ergon* of rational activity: perceiving, deliberating, deciding, and acting rationally, as well as disciplining oneself and making an effort to do so, and even making oneself someone who is disposed to do so without particular effort or self-discipline.

---

[31] It is thus no coincidence that Aristotle often uses the term '*spoudaios*' as a synonym for '*agathos*' ('good'); the term is often rendered 'serious', and that is exactly what virtue is about. The opposite might be 'playful' (a common antonym), but more appropriately 'indifferent' or 'frivolous'. Again, a comparison with the case of logic and epistemology may be pertinent (cf. note 30): qua rational we are constitutively necessitated to abide by the norms and standards of logic and belief formation. To the extent that we fail to do so, this is due to inability but also, often, indifference and lack of commitment, which is, in effect, a moral failure. I am grateful to Jonathan Lear and Will Small, who at different stages and in different ways pressed me to make clearer how we humans can fail to actualize our nature and still be human, as well as what it might be, in practice, to strive towards such actualization, i.e. have it as a practical end we see ourselves as obligated to pursue.

Aristotle is quite explicit that such failure is possible—indeed, ubiquitous. For instance, he says that ordinary people have no articulate, that is, explicit and reflective, and therefore clear and stable, conception of what eudaimonia is; instead, they focus merely on the most immediate needs and concerns, and the available ways and means of addressing these, and then, it seems, 'hope for the best' (cf. I 4, 1095a21-6). The same point is implied in a later passage where he claims that most people live ('to judge from their lives') *as if* they had a clear conception of the highest good or eudaimonia, namely, as pleasure (I 5, 1095a14-22). This conception—of pleasure as the highest or central good in life—manifests itself in the way they live. But this conception is not something they have adopted through reflection—they merely have it, or find themselves having it. Consequently, they have no idea why this conception is worth basing their life on, nor do they display any commitment or discipline: they fail both in their perceptual and emotional-conative responses to their circumstances, and in their deliberation about what to do under those circumstances. As a result, their living consists in a mere catering to whatever appetites present themselves to their mind. These people are incapable of living a successful and admirable life—they fail to fully actualize the human *telos* or *ergon*, which is *logos*, reason.

That this is a failure, and a failure of reason, is clear from a passage in the *Eudemian Ethics* where Aristotle says that

everyone who can live according to his own choice [*prohairesis*] *should* adopt[32] some goal [*skopos*] for the fine life [*tou kalōs zēn*], whether it be honour or reputation or wealth or cultivation—an aim that he will have in view in all his actions; for, not to have ordered [*to mē suntetachthai*] one's own life in relation to some end [*telos*] is the mark of extreme folly [*aphrosunē pollē*]. (I 2, 1214b6-11)

The point is that the wise thing to do is to set up a goal for one's life, but that not everybody in fact does this. By 'adopting a goal for the fine life' Aristotle here means articulating for oneself a conception of eudaimonia, that is, interpreting what eudaimonia consists in, and then making this conception their effective aim (*skopos*) in life. But most people fail to do this; they simply drift along in life without any definite purpose, so they do not *pursue* eudaimonia (or anything else for that matter). Thus they fail as rational agents, and therefore as human beings. They are just not very good at being human, and so they fail to achieve eudaimonia.[33]

How is the goal for the fine life set up? Aristotle's view of moral learning is a vast topic which I cannot go into here.[34] What seems clear, however, is that a crucial part

---

[32] Following Woods (who follows Gigon) in reading *dei thesthai* at line 7, by supplying *dei* from line 11. See Woods (1992), 185f for discussion; cf. also Cooper (1975), 94 note 5.

[33] In fact, very few people seem to pass muster on Aristotle's view. He also considers other groups of human beings to fall short in this respect. These include women, children, and natural slaves (cf. *Pol.* I 13, 1260a9-14), as well as akratic people, i.e. people who are incapable of holding on to their beliefs about what would be the right thing for them to do in the situation, and who thereby fail to actually pursue the good.

[34] See Burnyeat (1980) for a classic, highly influential account. A provocative alternative account if provided by Curzer (2012), chs. 15-16.

of such learning is the setting up of a goal for the fine life, that is, a central good or ultimate end that serves as the focus point and principle of one's responses to one's circumstances and one's practical endeavour. At the most basic level, this 'setting up' must take place through the non-argumentative shaping of the young person's sensibility and personality structure. But gradually and increasingly the young person becomes receptive to reason, and then arguments—and hence ethics—may have an effect.

This allows us to see how ethics as an argumentative enterprise can make a contribution to shape and/or improve a person's life.[35] This is not to be achieved by providing specific rules and instructions for the right way to live—a blueprint that can be used as a recipe for success.[36] Rather than providing such a blueprint, what Aristotle is doing in his ethics is to provide a sketch of the good life. He does so, first of all, by clarifying what the central good (the highest good or ultimate end) of a human life is; it is eudaimonia, that is, the successful living of the 'practical sort of life of what possesses reason', that is, the completion of our constitutive task (*ergon*) as human. This clarification involves delineating the contours of such a life, and what the character and intellect of the good person leading this life must look like, given this conception of eudaimonia. Thus, his ethical treatises point to general and typical features of a human life, both the kinds of challenge that we are faced with and the difficulties we have in meeting these challenges. Moreover, this sketch highlights the concerns that we should bear in mind when trying to meet these challenges. In this way ethics serves to strengthen the three aspects of our practical reasoning: it helps us to develop our deliberative capacity so we will be better prepared to find the right way to act in particular situations, and it will also help us see clearer the overall picture of life— what is at stake, what the ultimate end is, and what our priorities ought to be. It may also, finally, help consolidate the agent's character in such a way that he will be more stably disposed to respond perceptually and emotionally-conatively in the correct ways.

The purpose of ethics is to lead creatures—human beings, us—who are always already agents, and hence engaged in the enterprise of actualizing the human *telos*, from the modest degree of rational activity that characterizes any human agent as such, to the highest degree that characterizes the fully good and wise human being. This human being embodies the complete actualization of human nature, that is, *logos*. Only this person will truly merit the epithet *eudaimōn*, for only he

---

[35] Here lurks a problem I cannot address in this paper: Who is to shape and/or improve a person's life? Is it (1) the person himself, (2) somebody else, namely, the one responsible for educating him (his parents? the politicians and lawmakers?), or (3) both (first his educators, then—to an increasing extent—himself)? I incline towards the third answer.

[36] See I 2, 1094a22–6; 3, 1094b11–27; 7, 1098a21–33; II 2, 1103b34–4a11; IX 2, 1164b27–33; 1165a12–14.

(or she, as we would say) is 'an exemplar of life at its best'.[37] The way ethics does this, according to Aristotle, is by sketching the structure of human nature and the essential features of human life. In this way ethics will strengthen our deliberative capacity and help us articulate and consolidate a true conception of the ultimate end of human life: success as a human being—that is, eudaimonia.

[37] Broadie (2002), 12: 'Regarding someone as *eudaimōn* is more like ascribing a status, or applauding. It is to imply that the person is admirable, even enviable, an exemplar of life at its best.'

5

Aristotle on Happiness and Old Age

Hallvard Fossheim

Although the end of a life doesn't have to be old age, old age is always at the end of a life. In spite of this fact, the relation between happiness and old age in Aristotle does not receive much attention. This is unfortunate not only because old age is the final stage of a complete life, but also because old age and ageing are privileged issues when it comes to revealing how nature fits into ethical matters in Aristotle.[1]

Aristotle implicitly suggests that old age is of unique importance in relation to happiness. And so in book I of the *Nicomachean Ethics*, he quotes Solon's words with some approval: if you wonder whether someone really is *eudaimōn*, then *wait to see the end*.[2] The idea is that if someone meets with a really bad end, it is more difficult to say that he was *eudaimōn*, that he had a happy or successful life. As in a tragedy, how it ends has a significance that is irreducible, and of a whole other weight than whether the protagonist was doing well at the beginning of the story. It is no coincidence that we ask 'How did it go', and not 'How did it start', when we want to know whether something was a success or not. The end of a life too is asymmetrical in comparison to its beginning or middle. If the final stage is bad, then this affects how that life as a whole should be judged, in a way that isn't quite true of some middle part.

In what follows, I first sketch Aristotle's take on the relationship between experience and old age, before presenting in some detail his theory of nature's part in ageing. I spell out the ethical implications of this process further by breaking it down in terms of *epithumia* and *thumos*. I then combine the results concerning nature's relevance with Aristotle's view of how experience contributes to ethical forming. This combination I sum up as his 'sowing and harvesting' view.

---

[1] Earlier versions of this chapter were presented at the Ancient Philosophy Society's meeting in Sundance (2010) and at the Ancient Happiness workshops in Rome (2010) and Erice (2011). Thanks to Erin Stackle, Svavar Svavarsson, and Håvard Løkke for their prepared comments on these occasions. I am also very grateful to Sarah Broadie for her detailed and constructive responses to an earlier draft of the paper.
[2] *EN* I 10, 1100a11.

Finally, I will suggest what may be Aristotle's implied understanding of how happiness relates to *extreme* old age.

1. The Tradition

A few brief words about the background are in order. As is usually the case for the other age groups when it comes to Aristotle, the material I will look at concerns primarily males. Generally speaking, the major age division among Greek males was between *neoi* and *presbuteroi*.[3] But around the age of 60, there was a further shift in status for the individual, from *presbutēs* to *gerōn*.[4] As life expectancy may have been around fifty, getting old was certainly not something everyone could expect.[5]

Two features in particular seem to be quite defining in the ancient tradition when it comes to old age. One is the close link between old age and wisdom. The two seem at times to be strictly proportionate. Greater age means greater wisdom.[6] Thus the Seven Sages, as well as any other wise men, are as a rule reported to have lived to a great age, from Homer's Nestor on. Part of the reason for this way of thinking, and part of its interest, lies in seeing wisdom as a function of experience.

Another feature of old age in ancient thought is the notion that each age in a human life has its characteristic possibilities and challenges, and that how one fares in one age is partly decided by how one fared at an earlier age. Especially in later thought, this is sometimes worked out in terms of an analogy with sowing and harvesting. This way of thinking is particularly interesting because it combines what we might call biological or natural aspects of human development with its more strictly ethical aspects.

2. Old Age and Experience

When we turn to Aristotle, we certainly recognize both these dimensions of ageing. The *Metaphysics*, *Posterior Analytics*, and *Nicomachean Ethics* all tell us about how knowledge and wisdom are reached through a process of experience which takes time.[7] Also, from his ethical–political writings it is quite clear that life occurs in stages, and that how one fares in one stage is partly determined by what one did at an earlier stage.

Aristotle does not explicitly go to any extremes concerning the first dimension of ageing I mentioned from the tradition. Experience *is* a requirement for wisdom.[8]

---

[3] The individual entered the ranks of *presbuteroi* around his thirtieth year.

[4] The change from *presbuteros* to *gerōn* was probably associated with being 'no longer liable for military service at around fifty-nine'. Cf. Garland 1990: 243.

[5] Ibid. 244.   [6] Cf. e.g. Dover (1994), 102.

[7] *Metaphysics* Alpha i, *Posterior Analytics* Beta xix, and *Nicomachean Ethics* I 9.

[8] Although certain sorts of exact knowledge that do not require much experience with messy particulars, such as mathematics, can be obtained relatively quickly by those who are sufficiently clever.

Observing about some of the practical intellectual virtues that they depend on perception, Aristotle says:

Hence these states actually seem to grow naturally, so that while no one seems to have natural wisdom [*sophos*], people seem to have natural consideration, comprehension and judgment [*gnōmēn . . . kai sunesin kai noun*]. A sign is our thinking that they also correspond to someone's age, and the fact that understanding and consideration belong to a certain age, as though nature were the cause. We must attend, then, to the undemonstrated remarks and beliefs of experienced and older people [*presbuterōn*] or of intelligent people, no less than to demonstrations. (*EN* VI 11, 1143b6–13; Irwin's translation)

The point to take home here is that certain virtues *seem* to grow naturally, because they grow with experience, and experience increases over time. As Aristotle famously concludes the discussion, 'experience has given them an eye' (*EN* VI 11, 1143b13–14).

But Aristotle does not claim that people get ever wiser with increasing years. His paradigm of practical as well as epistemic wisdom does not appear to be the old person, but rather the mature or perhaps middle-aged one. At one place, he specifies 49 as the age of maximum intellectual merit.[9] Does this tell us something about the limited complexity of the relevant spheres? Or about the limited potential of human beings? Or perhaps only about who in Aristotle's world could as a matter of fact be seen to approach the ideal most fully?

Of course, there is a fourth possibility as well. Aristotle's own achievements were carried out before old age. So it would be pragmatically difficult for him to claim that only old age has the authority of wisdom. Accordingly, some readers have calculated that Aristotle was around 49 years old when he wrote that man reaches his intellectual zenith at 49.[10] But that is not, perhaps, a *philosophical* argument.

Aristotle does provide a hint of an alternative conclusion, however, one that privileges old age at least when it comes to ethical experience and insight. It is unclear how exactly *empeiria* relates to habituation or *ethismos*, but I will here only note that in the *Rhetoric*, Aristotle stresses that old people are pessimistic and cautious because of their experience of life's vicissitudes.[11] Now the simplest understanding of the claim would be that when one is old, one will have had so much experience that one has necessarily reached an insight into how risky things really are. However, among other things, if one is virtuous and lives with a view to the noble, pessimism does not entail caution. And Aristotle in the *Rhetoric* is not talking about the virtuous ideal that occupies much of the *Ethics*, but about the people one needs to persuade in the assembly and the courts.[12]

---

[9] *Rhetoric* II 14, 1390b9–11.
[10] In spite of these cynical calculations, scholars still take the dictum seriously. Cf. e.g. Kraut (1997), 108.
[11] *Rhetoric* II 13, 1389b15–18, 21f.
[12] The *Rhetoric* still gives us an indication that, although they are not identical, what one experiences in the practical field will be partly a function of one's habituation, once this is beginning to get into place.

What this passage from the *Rhetoric* might suggest, then, is that Aristotle does see a possibility that old age constitutes an accumulation of a lifetime of experience. And if this is true of *hoi polloi*, there is nothing to a priori rule out something like it in the case of the *kaloi kagathoi*. That is, one's basic ethical habituation may co-determine what conclusions to reach from later experience. If old age constitutes an accumulation based on experience, it may do so in the direction of perfection as well. So old age for someone virtuous can be an ongoing widening and deepening of one's ethical insight or know-how, just as old age spells further corruption for the many. Beyond this indirect hint in the *Rhetoric*, I have not found that Aristotle anywhere comes out and says this, however. And, as indicated earlier, it goes counter to what seems to be his paradigm of the wise individual.

3. The Challenge of the Season

But ageing is anyway not only a matter of lived experience. Nature definitely plays a part too. Accordingly, after a consideration of nature's role in the ageing process, I shall say something about how nature and experience (in a wide sense, including *ethismos*) combine in the metaphor of sowing and harvesting. As in the origin of the metaphor, part of our development is defined by nature, giving conditions for what each age can harvest and what challenges one meets. Quite literally, according to Aristotle, one is also a seed from nature's part. And in old age, this comes to constitute a particular set of challenges to virtue, and so to happiness.

As a natural being, the human organism is constructed by the individual's vital heat or *pneuma*.[13] This sort of heat is a form of organized motion. Aristotle likens it to the movements defining a craft. These are structured motions that transform suitable material into an ordered entity. While the motions of carpentry can produce a table, the products of *pneuma* are ensouled natural substances like us.

Throughout the human being's life, it is in a way the *pneuma* that *is* the human being's life. In Aristotle's system, *pneuma* seems somehow to be the natural philosopher's form, providing shape and determining functions without contributing materially: *pneuma* is that which, among the tangible and material aspects of the world, comes closest to explaining the order and ordering of organisms.[14] Vital heat provides a physiological counterpart to, or aspect of, the *explanans* that we know in terms of 'nutritive soul'. To quote from *De Anima*,

---

Something like this seems true about the *EN* as well. It is only those who have had a taste of the noble, and are no longer simply living by their emotions, who can gain from Aristotle's course of ethical reflection. The *ethismos* phase of ethical formation will of course have been completed long before anything like old age can enter the picture: Aristotle is clear that the job is pretty much finished when one is around 17, for better or for worse.

[13]   The following exposition is deeply indebted to the brilliant study offered in Freudenthal (1995); for further references, cf. Freudenthal (1995), 40–4, 155–7.

[14]   It also explains their participation in eternity through regeneration.

we must ask what is the force that holds together the earth and the fire which tend to travel in contrary directions; if there is no counteracting force, they will be torn asunder; if there is, this must be the soul and the cause of nutrition and growth. (*DA* II 4, 416a6–9; J. A. Smith's translation in Barnes' edition)

A primary job for *pneuma* is the concoction or *pepsis* of material, to make it conform to the demands of the organism.

To put a paradoxical spin on the quote, we are our own worst enemies. The elements from which we are built have no inherent drive towards the unity in which our being dresses them. Even though it is present only potentially, the earth in us has a natural tendency to move downwards, the air and fire in us upwards, the water to an in-between place. It is only by constantly working on itself that the organism remains an organism. So *pneuma* does not just produce the human being and then disappear, but is vital heat also in the sense that it is what keeps us alive. It not only builds, but does maintenance work as well.

For our purposes, what matters is that old age partly consists in losing this battle. The physical weakness and decay that Aristotle attributes to old age he explains in terms of a dwindling of vital heat. On an elemental level, *pneuma* 'masters' the wet or moist.[15] When the wet starts winning over the hot-and-dry, this is what we recognize as decay and decomposition. The moisture is no longer an integral part of the organism, and is thus free to evaporate. (This is one point where external forces as well enter the scene, for it is external heat that is responsible for the evaporation.) The ultimate drying out leaves the object as earth or dust.

So the explanation of physiological old age is that vital heat leaves us. This means that old age is by definition a state of loss. Although Aristotle is adamant that substance does not come in degrees, its physiological counterpart does. And so old age is, after a fashion, 'metaphysically bad', because it can be defined in terms of a loss of one's principle for being. Being old means being at a stage where the unifying principle is retreating, and the manifold and unorganized forces of decomposition have become unruly.

This tells us something about the things with which we should expect Aristotle to connote old age. This rather depressing picture is not something one could easily wrest from his ethical writings, however, although there are side remarks in the *Nicomacehan Ethics* like 'older people and sour people do not appear to be prone to friendship. For there is little pleasure to be found in them' (VIII 5, 1157b14–16; cf. 6, 1158a2–11).

But the *Rhetoric*, as I said earlier, is a text that cannot afford to be about how people *should* be. In order for persuasion to be efficient, one must take the audience of the day—what people are actually like—as a point of departure. And in the *Rhetoric*, we

---

[15] According to Aristotle's Greek view of things, the hot is active, while the moist is passive. *Pepsis* is a process whereby the moist is brought under the rule of heat as organized motion.

find the assertion that old people are cautious and prone to worrying and fearing all sorts of things. I have mentioned the part of Aristotle's explanation of this that is in terms of *empeiria*. His further explanation goes as follows. The old 'are chilled, but the young are hot, so old age has prepared the way for cowardice; for fear is a kind of chilling' (*Rhetoric* II 13, 1389b31f; Kennedy's translation). 'Prepared the way' is a translation of *proōdopoiein* (b31). The same biological point, about the relation between chilling and fear or timidity, is made in *Parts of Animals* II 4: 'too great an excess of water makes animals timorous. For fear chills the body; so that in animals whose heart contains so watery a mixture the way is prepared for the operation of this emotion' (650b28f; Ogle's translation).

What does it mean to 'prepare the way'? A cause or condition which 'prepares the way' is not identical to the sort of direct or immediate cause that holds centre stage in the *Physics*. Rather, it prepares the way *for* the effect of such a more immediate cause. Support for this interpretation is found in a parallel usage in the *Problems*. 'For it is not the same cause which prepares the way and creates a favourable condition for a series of effects and then begins to produce the effect, but a different one.' (*Problems* II 11, 867a38–9; E. S. Forster's translation.) The greater argument at this place in the *Problems* is surprisingly difficult to sort out. At any rate, the question is about perspiration, and a main point seems to be that a small quantity of heat prepares the way by predisposing the body to perspire better than a large quantity (*Problems* II 11, 867a39–b1): so 'another and a greater proportion is required actually to produce the perspiration' (*Problems* II 11, 867a39–b1).[16]

A cause prepares the way by modifying or affecting a disposition, without quite bringing the matter to actuality or activation on its own.[17] Aristotle also uses the expression to characterize, in his discussion of education in *Politics* VII, the relation between what stories children hear and how they fare later in life. The educators 'should be careful what tales or stories the children hear, for all such things are designed to prepare the way for the business of later life [*panta gar dei ta toiauta proodopoiein pros tas husteron diatribas*]' (*Politics* VII 17, 1336a32–4). Similarly, in chapter 13 of the *Rhetoric*, where the claim is that old age has prepared the way for cowardice, the expression indicates a certain relation between nature and culture: biological old age does not necessitate cowardice, but it has prepared the way, by affecting one's dispositions.

Nature's part in modifying one's character is different for each age. Thus Aristotle introduces this characterization of the old by saying that 'their disposition is the opposite [*enantiōs ... diakeintai*] of the young' (II 13, 1389b30). For the young, their

---

[16] Cf. also *PA* II 5, 651b10; *GA* IV 4, 770b3.

[17] A similar analysis suits the use of the verb *proōdopoiein* at *Problems* XXX 1, 954b12ff, according to which 'the announcement of something alarming, if it occurs at a time when the temperament is rather cold, makes a man cowardly; for it has already prepared a way for the entrance of fear, and fear has a chilling effect (as is shown by the fact that those who are greatly alarmed tremble)'.

violent vital heat makes them prone to anger and emotion. In fact, on Aristotle's theory, being young is a bit like being drunk, in that wine too has a form of semi-organized heat (presumably from the sun, a living being). For the old, however, the corresponding ethical challenge lies in the *dwindling* of natural heat. Thus, the natural chilling prepares the way for cowardice.

Here we have a way in which biological old age presents a challenge when it comes to happiness. It is a main tenet of Aristotle's that being happy or *eudaimōn* presupposes that one is good: that one is virtuous. So to the extent that a tendency to cowardice enters the picture, and courage is threatened, so too is happiness.[18]

Could this challenge from nature's part really affect the virtuous? The *perfectly* virtuous person, who also possesses the by definition never-failing virtue of *phronēsis*, may not be perturbed by the chilling of old age. Like Plato, Aristotle seems to think that perfect goodness has a sort of inherent stability. Somehow, living by reason in this complete way entails that one is integrated internally to the fullest extent—as well as in relation to the rest of reality.[19] And this amounts to a unique degree of solidity or strength. But most people are not such perfect paragons of virtue. Possessing virtue, and having the virtues integrated in us, will be something that comes in degrees. The discussion of forms of courage in *Nicomachean Ethics* III displays how non-paradigmatic virtue is a matter of degree. Citizen's courage, for instance, is graded by the extent to which the individual is moved by the noble rather than by the risk of punishment.

To get clearer about how Aristotle envisions a reduction in vital heat as ethically relevant, it is necessary to introduce his concepts of *thumos* and *epithumia*. In the argument just referred to, he mentions *thumos*, since it is courage that is in question.[20] But the same story applies to *epithumia*. *Thumos* and *epithumia* are both expressions of, and depend on, vital heat, and are both affected by the chilling of old age. A reduction in *thumos* means not least a reduction in feelings and actions that express or affirm the individual's worth or status. *Thumos* is paradigmatically expressed in competitions. *Epithumia* has a less complex structure, and concerns itself primarily with objects of appetite or desire. So while *thumos* in humans has an important social dimension, and then includes other individuals as well as some contested object, basic appetite simply relates to the object of desire. Again very broadly, we can also say that

---

[18] Now just how serious a threat this might be, will depend not least on how we understand the unity of virtues to be in Aristotle's ethics. This is not the place to go into detail on that question, but his view includes a type of reciprocity of the virtues. So falling short in one virtue might have negative effects even outside that virtue.

[19] I put to one side whether or to what extent one could have, or approach, this stability in cases where 'according to reason' (*kata logon*) is to be taken in an external sense, i.e. the sense according to which one's actions and motivations track complete practical reason, but one does not fully possess the ability to provide the relevant reasons.

[20] To say that, for the young, their violent vital heat makes them prone to anger, is to say that *thumos* is naturally strong with them.

while *epithumia* or appetite is only concerned with the pleasant and painful, *thumos* or spirit has a view of the noble and thus of the good.[21]

With the single exception of rational desire or *boulēsis*, all the desires and emotions Aristotle recognizes in his writings are variations upon these two types of motivation.[22] The specifications are defined not least cognitively, depending on the objects and actions involved, and in terms of the combinations of various pleasures and pains they constitute.

To consider one example of each, if we take the *Rhetoric*'s definition of anger (II 2), this is an emotion which includes a desire for retaliation after an apparent slight. In being about the agent's position and self-esteem, anger is a form of *thumos*. The *EN* harmonizes with and follows up on what is said in the *Rhetoric*. The virtue or mean state that consists in being well off with regard to anger, is mildness (*praotēs*, *EN* IV 5). Failing in the direction of excess with regard to anger is a sort of irascibility (*orgilotēs*), while the opposite shortcoming consists in not being pained enough when it comes to matters where one should defend oneself. As Aristotle says, such willingness to accept insult to oneself and to overlook insults to one's family and friends is slavish (*EN* IV 5, 1126a7–8).

To give a corresponding illustration of *epithumia*, we have desires for basic bodily pleasures. Paradigmatic to Aristotle are those that are concerned with touch (*EN* III 10): the pleasures of food, drink, and sex. The glutton is someone badly off in the direction of excess when it comes to the natural basic appetites.[23] The other extreme would be some sort of insensitivity. (Aristotle does not seem convinced that it exists.) Being in a mean and well-off state with regard to these basic desires is having the virtue of temperance (*sōphrosunē*).

As stated, Aristotle's analyses in terms of how vital heat and emotion dwindle with age seem not to make any major distinction between *thumos* and *epithumia*. They are the forms of the individual's non-rational desiderative states, and both are reduced with age. But this is not of course to say that the distinction does not matter to the individual's happiness. We have already looked at how the chilling of old age can affect *thumos*, and so prepare the way for cowardice. To get a clearer view of how the chilling works in relation to *epithumia*, we can turn to another description in the *Rhetoric*. With old age, he says, comes a reduction in desires (which must here mean the flowing of *pathos* generally, not least *epithumia*: 1390a11–14). And this makes the old *seem* as if they're self-controlled. This means that, where an individual used to give in to appetite, or to some specific appetite, he now has less trouble checking

---

[21] Cf. Lear (2004), esp. ch. 6 (123–46); Cooper (1999), 253–80; Rogers (1993).

[22] Or perhaps it is better to say that they are the raw material or genera of all non-rational desires and emotions.

[23] In support of the claim that touch is really the basic medium here, Aristotle reports that 'a glutton [*opsophagōs*] actually prayed for his throat to become longer than a crane's, showing that he took pleasure in the touching' (*EN* III 10, 1118a32–b1). In a wider sense, i.e. concerning appetites for other things than the natural objects of appetite, it is the intemperate person (*ho akolastos*) who desires and acts to excess.

himself. However, it is his lack of desire that allows him to choose his acts and omissions through calculation, rather than the choices being more direct expressions of character.

This is a claim about nature's role in relation to one's happiness. But in admitting that role, one is also admitting that one was never entirely in charge of oneself. To the extent that there is a battle between appetites and rational wish in a soul, and those appetites are functions of one's biological age, one is not only in internal conflict. One is also revealing the fact that one's virtue is not supreme in relation to one's nature. This makes for a sort of cynical perspective on things, where you are more prone to seeing what is worse. With money, for instance, you now know that 'it is difficult to acquire and easy to lose' (1390a11–14). You will also be much more hesitant about making strong assertions for the same reason.

Now this is a most interesting point, because it exemplifies a complex interaction between natural causes and causes that have to do with experience. In the case last described, nature has paved the way for a calculating stance. Natural chilling has the effect of making the old worry and fear things, and so it makes sense for their calculations to be directed towards personal safety and gain.

But old age in a non-biological sense too plays a crucial part. For it is not least their *experience* that has taught the old to be cautious. If you have lived a long time, says Aristotle, it will not have escaped you that 'most things turn out badly' (II 13, 1390a4f). And again, behind *this* level of experience there may be a hint, in Aristotle, of how ethical upbringing in its turn can come to shape experience.

In what Aristotle treats as typical old age, nature and experience play on the same team with respect to *thumos*, in supporting a tendency to focus on the advantageous at the expense of the noble. The point to bring home is that according to Aristotle, old age creates a tendency in a certain direction, a tendency that can affect one's happiness for better and for worse.[24]

4. Sowing and Harvesting

It is time to relate the preceding features of his theory to what I take to be three main tenets of Aristotle's view of human development and ageing. To us, one of the most famous examples of this sort of talk about life's stages is Cicero's *Of Old Age* (*De senectute*).[25] Aristotle does not avail himself of a developed vocabulary of sowing and harvesting like Cicero does. But a model along similar lines is present in his writings.

---

[24] Generally speaking, Aristotle has no qualms about acknowledging two levels of analysis, and then proceeding as if each level could be treated as autonomous. As for old age, we have one physiological and one psychological exposition. And beyond the link I have just unearthed, the psychological exposition goes on in splendid autonomy. (Just as it should be able to do, according to the methodological discussion in *De Anima*: cf. Aristotle's famous example of anger as boiling about the heart.)
[25] Cicero combines talk of the fruit of the age or season with metaphors of life's long road, and of performing on a theatrical stage.

We can call it 'the sowing and harvesting (SH) view'. I take the SH view to include at least the following three features.

(i)   Human life is divided into temporal stages, each of which has its character-istic strengths and weaknesses as well as suitable activities.
(ii) The stages are determined partly by nature, partly by what one does with what nature provides.
(iii) How one fares in a later stage, when it comes to its strengths, weaknesses, and activities, depends partly on what one did at an earlier stage.

All three features of SH come together in Aristotle's theory of human development. He introduces his discussion of the process of habituation by contrasting humans to stones. According to the opening lines of *EN* II 1, one could not make a stone change its natural direction downwards by throwing it upwards a thousand times. But we can be altered in this way, and that is what Aristotle refers to as *ethismos*. As the illustrating contrast also informs us, this crucial phase is still codetermined by nature, however. For the relevant difference between humans and stones lies precisely in their natures. It is human nature to reach perfection not only by nature, as an activation of the substance's internal principle of motion and standstill, but by habituation and reason as well. And on top of our species' nature, differences that are sub-species are thought by Aristotle to be important as well: whether one is a man or a woman; European, Asian, or Greek; well born in the sense of not having a slavish nature; and so on.[26]

To Aristotle, the all-important basis of character forming will in the main have been completed early on. The *Nicomachean Ethics* and the *Politics* seem to concur in this judgement. If one has not gotten into the right habits by one's late teens, it is unlikely that one will ever become virtuous or happy. So the rest of our life is a harvesting of what we and others sowed earlier—in the biological sense, of natural generation, and in the ethical sense of habits, the choice of words and stories, customs, practices, and the outlook on life that goes with them.[27]

To make more concrete sense of how the three features of the SH model contribute in old age, it will be helpful to see them in relation to Aristotle's rough and ready distinction between the fully virtuous, the enkratic, the akratic, and those who live by passion. As indicated, perfectly good, rational individuals would not be heavily affected by a reduction in *thumos* and *epithumia*. Their motivational structure and identity have the stability Aristotle attributes to rationality as a source of goodness.[28]

---

[26] All of these are instances of how nature co-determines for the individual whether he or she can reach virtue and happiness.

[27] Cf. Fossheim (2006).

[28] There is a real question here, however, about the individual who steers by *to kalon* but does not possess reason in the way required to see the reasoned account that Aristotle in these contexts calls *to agathon*. This individual is probably identical to the one who knows the that (*hoti*), but lacks the why (*dioti*). Will such a one be affected by the *pathos* reductions of old age due to his lack in reasoned

But people who, in Aristotle's terminology, have 'lived by *pathos*' will presumably be drastically affected by this reduction in affect. Whether they have been irascible or gluttonous, the shape of their lives will change. Those who have affirmed the drives of *epithumia* and/or *thumos* as their guides, will probably lament that their sources of joy are gone. Taken to the extreme, these individuals may even feel that they no longer have anything to live for. They see old age purely as a loss, in motivation or in ability. Perhaps we can imagine Callicles in the *Gorgias* to end up as one such person. His example is particularly interesting because he illustrates a way in which appetites can combine with *thumos*, in a misguided sense of personal greatness.[29]

But 'living by *pathos*' is ambiguous. In the extreme, it will mean the sort of affirmation of appetite or spirit I have just sketched. Less extreme, and more common, is the akratic, who lives by *pathos* in the sense that his life is de facto ruled by and shaped by irrational desires, but without the same sort of affirmation.[30] There is a continuum here, both when it comes to the degree of affirmation, and when it comes to how much of one's life is affected. But with respect to standard cases of *akrasia*, ageing seems to be good news. For in ageing, the akratics rid themselves of an aspect of their own motivations, thoughts, feelings, and actions, with which they have never ultimately identified. As an illustration of how the chilling of old age can affect *epithumia*, Plato's old Cephalus of *Republic* I is highly instructive. As is well known, Cephalus is grateful that old age has rid him of a lot of disturbing desires, and quotes Sophocles to express the sentiment. As Cephalus approvingly reports,[31] Sophocles was 'very glad to have escaped from all that, like a slave who has escaped from a savage and tyrannical master'. To these individuals, 'old age brings peace and freedom' (*Rep.* I 329bc).

The same goes for *thumos* as for *epithumia* in this respect. Aristotle's qualified akratic, such as the akratic-with-a-view-to-anger, will be someone who has always recognized his own tendency to see degradations of his person in the wrong places, or that he overreacted even when there was in fact an affront. To someone like this, a smoother temperament can come as something of a salvation.

All this will be true of the enkratic too. Although he has not allowed *pathos* to rule his actions, a loss in the relevant appetite or spirit will surely provide peace of mind

---

motivation, or will the fact that his motivations are in fact reasonable—that he possesses something like (but not perfect) ethical virtue—be sufficient to safeguard him?

[29] I do not wish the notion of an appetite-rider to depend on one's reading of the Callicles character. But Plato is so much better than Aristotle at providing examples that I will have to use him for the next category as well. Another example might be Mimnermus, or at least the poet's persona (1 *IEG*): 'What kind of life, what kind of joy is there without golden Aphrodite? May I die when I no longer take any interest in secret love affairs, in sweet exchanges and in bed' (as translated by Garland (1990), 252–3).

[30] The expression also ambiguates between living by *pathos* in a calculating or non-calculating way. What I say applies to both these ways of living by *pathos*.

[31] Cephalus is said to be 'on the threshold of old age' (*epi gēraos oudō(i)*, 328e6), which could mean both that he is getting old (the most likely interpretation according to Garland (1990: 250–1)) and that he is on the brink of death.

and an experience of being at one with oneself. For akratics *and* encratics have continuously been shaping, or at least seeing, their lives in terms of, as it were, two different recipes. Taking away one of the chefs, the messy one, holds promise for a dessert more successful than the main course. This is to say that while a reduction in *thumos* can prepare the way for cowardice, it can also make a difference for the better. More generally, with respect to both *epithumia* and *thumos*, nature's contribution can actually make one come closer to happiness in old age. (Although, to the extent that their lives have been base or bad, they will be haunted by bad memories.)

5. The Final Stages of Old Age

But old age is not all hunky dory, even for the good. The moderate reduction in vital heat is followed by further reduction. Ultimately, Aristotle explains the phenomena discussed above and the geriatric's more complete loss of activity by the same process. Longevity is not without trouble for humans, as Tithonus learned when Eos procured eternal life for him without eternal youth.[32]

Let us briefly concretize this age-related loss by relating it to the political and the theoretical lives, respectively. As for the political life, Aristotle explicitly stresses that success requires much effort. This is a life which offers little leisure. And so in the *Politics*, Aristotle signals his support for what seems to have been common practice. The old are relieved of their duties, and Aristotle even contrasts them with what he calls 'citizens in an unqualified way' (*Pol.* III 1, 1275a17–23). Concerning the theoretical life, we already have the report from the *Rhetoric* that intellectual powers are on the wane from around the age of 49. Since the theoretical life is characterized by leisure, dialogue, and reflection, however, it does—unsurprisingly—seem a better investment for old age.[33]

One passage in particular seems to condense much of what Aristotle thinks about old age. In book VII of the *Politics*, Aristotle goes through the various public offices. His list ends with the class of priests. Concerning 'the service of the gods', he says, 'it is appropriate for those who have retired because of age [*tous dia ton chronon apeirēkotas*] to render service to the gods and find rest [*anapausis*]'. So, 'the priesthoods should be assigned to them' (*Pol.* VII 9, 1329a28–35).

This is a significant passage because it positions the old (or very old) in relation to life in the city, and it is again clear that the decline in powers is of decisive significance

---

[32] (He still babbles on in a closet somewhere.)

[33] It is also of relevance that *Pol.* VII 16, 1335a30, informs us that bodily decline sets in around after the zenith of thirty-seven years. Taking a step back, it is also clear that the choice of a life—political or theoretical—is necessitated partly because each constitutes a specialization, not only a commitment. That is to say, one reason why Aristotle presents them as mutually exclusive alternatives is that each requires much time for developing and upholding the investments made. This means that success in either requires a lifetime of commitment, and is a choice that will already have been made by the time one reaches old age.

to Aristotle's ordinances.[34] Earlier in the *Politics*, he has said that 'that judges of important causes should hold office for life is a disputable thing, for the mind grows old as well as the body [*esti gar, hōsper kai sōmatos, kai dianoias gēras*]' (*Pol.* II 9, 1270b38–1271a1).

The *Politics* VII passage also resonates because, according to Aristotle, rendering service to the gods has affinity to both theoretical and political activity. As an appointment or office, the priesthood is political activity for those no longer politically active. And at the same time, to Aristotle, theoretical activity is also a religious service of sorts: moving closer to the divine by making oneself god-like.[35]

There are other hints as well in the Ethics pertaining to more extreme old age. The reduction in spirit or drive anticipated by Aristotle will slow one down and ultimately exclude one from the strenuous activities required by virtue. Aristotle's discussion of self-sufficiency or *autarkeia* in Book I of the *EN*, as a defining feature of happiness, can perhaps be seen as one way of grappling with this issue. Aristotle makes it clear that he does not intend self-sufficiency to be defined in terms of the single individual.[36] Ageing as a fact of life may be part of Aristotle's thinking here. For the idea of self-sufficiency surely is something which is threatened by extreme old age. This is the time when one can no longer take care of one's family, one's business or economic welfare, or, ultimately, oneself. In Aristotle's political theory, of course, it is true of everyone that the good life is life in the city, and life in the city means mutual dependence. But old age is when self-sufficiency can no longer be thought of in any way in terms of the single individual. On the Greek model, it is one's children who are responsible for securing one's old age.[37] This is a fact which, I think, is in the background when Aristotle a little later in Book I emphasizes that we do not altogether have the character of happiness if we are

solitary or childless, and have it even less, presumably, if our children or friends are totally bad, or were good but have died. And so, as we have said, happiness would seem to need this sort of prosperity added also. (*EN* I 8, 1099b4–7)

It is not only that having children is the respectable thing to do, or that descendants are part of one's life's work, or even that progeny constitutes the animals' way of participating in eternity. Children had a function that was crucial to how one would

---

[34] Although '[p]riesthoods in Greek cities were positions of considerable social prestige,... priests were not regarded as moral leaders or as advisers' (Kraut (1997), 108).

[35] Cf. Broadie (2003).

[36] 'Now what we count as self-sufficient [*to d'autarkes*] is not what suffices for a solitary person by himself, living an isolated life, but what suffices also for parents, children, wife and in general for friends and fellow-citizens, since a human being is a naturally political [animal]. Here, however, we must impose some limit; for if we extend the good to parents' parents and children's children and to friends of friends, we shall go on without limit; but we must examine this another time. Anyhow, we regard something as self-sufficient when all by itself it makes a life choice-worthy and lacking nothing; and that is what we think happiness does' (*EN* I 7, 1097b8–16).

[37] Plato brings in the need in old age of having someone look after one economically or due to reasons of health at *Laws* XI 931a; his respect for the elderly, and in fact for the oldest, is also obvious at *Laws* II 659d.

fare in old age. Keeping this in mind also gives added significance to the fact that Aristotle lists parents among the things we honour, the highest things, above even the things we praise, like virtue. Whether one had gone in for political or theoretical happiness, ethically dependable offspring would be required for enjoying one's old age in a way Aristotle could count as *eudaimōn*. This provides one added reason, if such be wanted, why self-sufficiency as a requirement for a happy life transcends the individual.

6. Conclusion

I hope to have shown that Aristotle thinks old age presents challenges and opportunities vis-à-vis happiness that are all its own. I have suggested that there is one challenge that comes in as a potential wedge between the individual and virtue, while another wedge comes in between virtue and *eudaimonia*. The one between the individual and virtue consists in a reduction in vital heat. The dwindling in *epithumia* may be good riddance for most, but the reduction in *thumos* prepares the way for a loss in virtue. The wedge between virtue and *eudaimonia* takes two forms. One is the general reduction in vitality, both as a reduction in motivation and as a reduction in physical prowess, placing limits on the individual's active life. The other is the loss of friends, which makes it more difficult to make good decisions with a view to a good life.

6

Aristotle on Happiness and Long Life

Gabriel Richardson Lear

> *And there is no plot in that; it is devoid of poetry.*
> —Donald Justice, 'Pantoum of the Great Depression'

Aristotle claims that we must live a long, 'perfect' (*teleion*) length of life in order to be happy. The happiness he has in mind is not a purely subjective condition of contentment or 'flow.' He is talking about *eudaimonia*, commonly translated 'happiness,' 'well-being,' or 'flourishing' and literally meaning something like 'being blessed by a god'. His point, then, is that a person counts as flourishing and fully successful (Aristotle compares *eudaimonia* to victory in the Olympic games (*EN* I 8,1099a3–7)) only if he lives for a long, 'perfect' length of time. Long life does not suffice to make for happiness on its own, of course. A long life may well be miserable. The point, rather, is that we need to have whatever it is that makes life successful— what the Greek philosophers called 'the good'—for a certain perfect length of life. How long is that?

One answer that would have been familiar to Aristotle's audience is: forever. Central to the ethos of Homeric epic is the wish to live as the gods do, in unending bliss. This is an impossible wish, of course. In fact, Homeric heroes face the impossibility of their wish in a particularly acute form, since central components of happiness as they conceive it—bodily vigor and the political power it makes possible—are hard for us to hold on to for long, much less forever. The problem is not just that we die, but that we decay before we die. From this point of view, epic song and memory promise some compensating relief. The hero who goes down in a blaze of glory has his youthful manhood preserved in fame, a fame which, if he is lucky, outlasts the span of ordinary, peaceful life.

In the *Symposium*, Plato takes up and radically transforms this idea. According to Socrates, all mortal things desire happiness, the unending possession of the good. Since we cannot literally hold onto the good forever, we seek to cast a shadow of ourselves as far into the future as we can by having children or by being remembered

(206aff.). At first it seems as if Plato, like Homer, thinks that the object of our desire for immortality is to accumulate as many days of happiness as possible. But when Socrates contrasts mortal flux with the astounding beauty of the unchanging Forms, we discover that temporal extension is not really the most fundamental point of our desire for immortality in Plato's view. The point is rather to be in a *permanent* condition of possessing the good, by contrast with the fleeting brushes with happiness that are the lot of our finite, changeable nature. In other words, whereas the Homeric heroes desire immortality as a temporal condition, the Platonic desire for immortality aims at an ontological condition—permanent being, by contrast with becoming—and only derivatively at a temporal one.

We will see that Aristotle, too, is influenced by ontological aspirations in his discussion of how much time we need to be happy. But unlike Homer and Plato, he is not in any obvious way motivated by a conception of happiness as transcending our mortal capacities. Aristotle does conceive of happiness as a godlike mode of existence, but he insists that it is 'practicable' by human beings. He seems instead to be talking simply about having enough time; not as much time as humanly possible, much less forever, but some finite 'perfect' length of time within the grasp of mortals to achieve. How long is long enough?

Aristotle's remarks in the *Eudemian* and *Nicomachean Ethics* on the temporal character of human happiness have not been much discussed, but he is right to see that something needs to be said about it. We are temporally extended beings, so we might expect our possession of happiness to have some specific temporal character or other. Philosophers who think about the narrative structure of human life are alive to this concern.[1] Unfortunately, Aristotle says almost nothing to explain himself. And as we will see, there are aspects of his theory of happiness that make it hard to understand why he thinks time matters. He may even have been unsettled on this question. That means that my attempt to make sense of this aspect of his view will inevitably be exploratory. Still, I hope this effort of philosophical imagination will be fruitful, even in its false starts, for helping us think about the various ways we exist in time and about why, from an Aristotelian point of view, having enough time might matter to us.

1. The Perfect Life Lasts a Perfect Length of Time

Let us begin by surveying the passages where Aristotle states the perfect life requirement explicitly:

---

[1] See e.g. MacIntyre (1981: ch. 15); Nagel (1979); Velleman (1991); and Williams (1973). One might believe, however, that extension in time is an accidental feature of our nature, in which case the extendedness of the happy life will be equally contingent and unimportant. Plotinus seems to have held such a view. See Emilsson (2011).

The human good is activity of the soul in accordance with virtue, and if there are several virtues, in accordance with the best and most perfect (*teleiotatēn*).[2] And further, in a perfect life (*en biōi teleiōi*). For one swallow does not make spring, and neither does one day. Likewise one day does not make someone blessed and happy, and neither does a short time. (*EN* 1098a16–20)

In this passage Aristotle says that happiness is virtuous activity in a 'perfect life'. The word *bios* often refers to a mode or manner of living, the farming *bios*, for example, and so does not necessarily have a temporal sense (*Politics* I 8, 1256b5). It is clear from the argument of this passage, however, that the perfect life requirement is a temporal one. The argument turns on an analogy between spring and happiness. It is not spring unless there are many swallows and many warm days. So too with happiness. Notice that when Aristotle explicates the analogy between spring and happiness, his focus is solely on length of time. A short time of virtuous activity does not suffice to make a person happy.

Later in *EN* I, he restates the perfect life requirement explicitly in terms of time:

What, then, prevents our calling that person happy who is active in accordance with perfect [*teleian*] virtue and adequately supplied with external goods, not for some chance time [*chronon*] but in a perfect life [*teleion bion*]? (*EN* I 10, 1101a14–16)

This passage concludes a discussion of whether one can lose happiness and what it would take to regain it. Interestingly, Aristotle says that performing a succession of great and glorious deeds can make a person happy, provided they occur 'not in a short time, but...in a great and perfect one [*pollō(i) tini kai teleiō(i)*]' (*EN* I 10, 1101a11–13). This suggests that the time specified by the perfect life requirement is fairly long and not simply not-short.

When Aristotle returns to the topic of happiness in *EN* X, he is again clear that 'perfect life' refers to a certain length of time:

[2] The word '*teleion*', which I have translated as 'perfect', might also be translated as 'end-like', i.e. 'having the character of an end (*telos*)'. This alternative translation would make clear how what I am calling 'the perfect life requirement' continues a line of reasoning that Aristotle has been articulating for the past seven chapters of the *EN*. In these chapters, he argues that happiness is the human good because it fits the criterion of being an ultimate, most 'end-like' (*teleiotaton*), end of action. This finality criterion allows Aristotle to rule out possible substantive accounts of the human good (e.g. wealth is not the highest good because it is instrumentally valuable, *EN* I 5, 1096a5–7). It also provides the rationale for the so-called 'function' (*ergon*) argument, since a thing's *ergon*, if it has one, just is its defining end (cf. *EE* II 1, 1219a8). (Baker (2014), ch. 2 explains the inaccuracy of 'function' as a translation of *ergon*.) So, in requiring that virtuous activity last a *teleion* length of time, Aristotle is presumably thinking that in lasting so long, virtuous activity will be more end-like than it would otherwise be. I will have something more to say about this point later in the chapter. Nevertheless, for the purposes of this chapter, I prefer to translate '*teleion*' as 'perfect'. It is a more fluid translation. And it keeps our attention focused on the question why it is valuable to live virtuously for a certain *teleion* length of time. By contrast, translating *teleion* as 'end-like' would direct us to the related but nevertheless distinct issue of the teleological relations between living virtuously for a *teleion* length of time and the subordinate goods worth choosing for its sake.

So the perfect happiness of a human being would be this [namely, contemplation], provided it has a perfect length [*mēkos*] of life. For none of the features of happiness is imperfect [*ateles*]. (*EN* X 7, 1177b24–6)

Turning to the *Eudemian Ethics* we find that there, too, a perfect life is a life that lasts a perfect amount of time:

Since happiness was something perfect (*teleon*), and life (*zōē*) is both perfect (*telea*) and imperfect (*atelēs*), and likewise virtue (for the former is a whole and the latter is a part), and since the activity of imperfect things is imperfect, happiness would be the activity of perfect life (*zōēs teleias*) in accordance with perfect virtue. The opinions of all people bear witness to us that we do a good job of formulating (*legomen kalōs*) the genus and definition of happiness. For . . . one cannot be happy for one day nor can one be happy as a child or at every stage of life. (And this is the reason why Solon had it right, that we should not congratulate a living person on his happiness, but should do so when he has reached his end (*telos*). For nothing imperfect (*ateles*) is happy, for it is not a whole.) (*EE* II 1, 1219a35–b8)

This discussion differs from its counterparts in the *EN* by speaking of perfect *zōē*— biological aliveness—rather than *bios*—mode of life. It also appeals to the wholeness of the happy life, an idea we do not find explicitly in the *EN*. (We will return to this.) Nevertheless, the *EE* passage agrees with the *EN* passages in framing the issue as a matter of time: the perfect life lasts, not one day or some short period, but for a long, perfect length of time.

I emphasize this so as to ward off a very common temptation to interpret the perfect life as a life replete with external goods. When Aristotle requires that virtuous activity extend through a 'perfect life,' he is referring in the first instance at least to an amount of time.

Now I admit that *some* philosopher (not Aristotle) might ground the desirability of a long life in the desirability of external goods. Someone (not Aristotle) might suppose that there are certain external goods central to happiness that can be achieved only later in life or only after a long time. For example, one might think that having children or grandchildren or a position of influence is intrinsically valuable and that a person cannot be happy without it. Since these goods are not available until one has reached a certain stage of life, a person with this conception of happiness must conclude that a happy life necessarily lasts a fairly long length of time. But Aristotle denies that external goods or indeed any gift of fortune are components of *eudaimonia*.

Let us be clear about this. It is often claimed that Aristotle espouses a so-called inclusivist conception of happiness in the *Eudemian Ethics*.[3] That is to say, he

---

[3] But does he in fact? Aristotle says in the *Eudemian Ethics* that happiness is composed of the activities of all the parts of virtue, rather than of the one of them that is the best (*EE* II 1, 1219a37–9). This sounds like an inclusivist conception. Recently, however, Baker (2014: 189–90) has made the obvious point that, in Aristotle's view, parts are teleologically subordinated to the whole. (We see this assumption in play in the passage quoted above: the activity of an individual virtue is imperfect because the virtue, qua part, is

conceives of happiness as a whole made up of parts. The parts in question are, however, parts of virtue or, more correctly, the distinctive activities of the different parts of virtue. He does not suggest there that happiness is composed of anything external to the soul's own excellent activity. He holds the same view in the *Nicoma-chean Ethics* where he does not maintain an inclusivist conception of *eudaimonia* at all.[4] Whether in the *EN* Aristotle identifies happiness with the activity of the single best virtue, theoretical contemplation, or instead identifies it with the activity of all the virtues, it remains the case that *eudaimonia* consists in nothing but virtuous action. The virtuous, happy person cares about having health, good looks, friends, prestige, and positions of power. He takes steps to possess them, where that is in his power and is consistent with virtue. But these goods are not themselves the cause of his being happy. They are at most instruments for or adornments to the highest human good, virtuous action (*EN* I 8, 1099a31–b7). The perfect life requirement does not presuppose or imply that happiness is partly composed of goods or events whose value is independent of or exceeds the role they play in virtuous action.

Perfection in life is perfection in time. A perfect length of time will not be short and, in particular, it will last past childhood. (*EN* I 9, 1100a2 concurs with the *EE* passage quoted above on the point that children cannot be happy.) Now, I assume that time does not have any positive value simply in itself. Time is valuable because of what happens during it. So, when Aristotle says that a person needs a perfect span of life in order to be happy, his point must be that having this time makes a difference to the quality of virtuous action.

Let me explain this point more fully. Aristotle thinks that happiness is the highest good and goal of every action. By this, he means in part that happiness sets the normative standard by which the goodness of all other things in human life is to be measured.[5] Among other things, then, happiness is the goal of virtuous activity itself. We see this idea reflected in Aristotle's description of practical wisdom as the settled ability to figure out what courses of action conduce to 'living well (*eu zēn=eudaimo-nia*, I 4, 1095a18–20) generally' (VI 5, 1140a28). The implication is that an individual action is desirable to the extent that it realizes or conduces to happiness. This may at first appear to be a hopelessly consequentialist conception of virtuous action, but as we have seen, Aristotle believes that happiness is constituted by virtuous activity alone. In being aimed at *eudaimonia*, virtuous activity is not aimed at some goal other than itself; it is, on the contrary, worth choosing for its own sake. So virtuous action aims at a normative standard, *eudaimonia*, that is internal to itself. And yet, as

---

imperfect.) Given this, Baker suggests that the *teleia* virtue of the *Eudemian Ethics* is the single, new end-like virtue (namely, *kalok'agathia*) for the sake of which the other moral virtues exist as parts. 'And so, even though the *EE* does (in a way) identify *eudaimonia* as the exercise of all the virtues, that is not because *eudaimonia* is the exercise of all the virtues but rather because *eudaimonia* is the exercise of the *single teleion* virtue that arises out of the combination of all the other virtues' (190).

[4] I argue for this in Lear (2004), chs. 2–3.

[5] See Lear (2004), ch. 1 for detailed explanation of this point.

the perfect life requirement makes clear, not just any example of virtuous action counts as happiness. Activity rises to the level of *eudaimonia* only if it lasts for a long enough, perfect length of time. This is what I mean when I say that lasting for a perfect length of life makes a difference to the quality of virtuous action. Excellent activity achieves its internal end (*telos*) and good only when it endures for long enough.[6]

So, how much time do we need and why?

2. A Perfect Length of Life Is a Finite, Long-Enough Time

Before trying to answer these questions, we need to distinguish three ideas that may lie behind the intuition that happy lives are long lasting. First, there is the idea that the longer the happy person lives, the better. There are reasons to doubt Aristotle accepts this claim, but in any case this comparative point is not the one he is making when he says that *eudaimonia* requires a perfect length of life.[7] He is talking about the time needed to be happy to any degree at all. He is not saying that we will be happ*ier* with more time.

Second, there is the idea that a person must hold on to the good through to the end of life in order to qualify as happy. The *EE*'s emphasis on wholeness and its related appeal to Solon's dictum indicate that this is an idea Aristotle has in mind. And although it is unclear in the *EN* whether this is the point of the perfect life requirement in particular, it is a thought he endorses there, too:

What, then, prevents our calling that person happy who is active in accordance with perfect [*teleian*] virtue and adequately supplied with external goods, not for some chance time [*chronon*] but in a perfect life [*teleion bion*]? Or should we add [*prostheteon*] also 'keeping on living this way and dying accordingly'? For the future is unclear to us and we maintain that

---

[6] This is not the only place where Aristotle suggests that some virtuous actions are somehow more perfect than others, even when they are all activities of the very same virtue. (1) In the *EN* I 10 discussion of the relation between luck and happiness, Aristotle maintains that although a virtuous person is able to act virtuously in (make something *kalon* out of) extreme misfortune, such conditions make it impossible for him to perform the sort of virtuous action that rises to the level of happiness. I cannot discuss this fascinating and difficult idea here (see Cooper (1985)). However, an analogy Aristotle draws may clarify his intuition (1100b35–01a8): a good cobbler can make decent shoes—make artful products—no matter how poor the leather is with which he is provided. However, the leather needs to be of sufficiently fine quality if he is to make shoes that are beautiful and of a sort that he, as a craftsman, aims to make. Similarly, a virtuous person always has it in his power to act well—this is why he can never become wretched—but he needs adequate circumstances in order to act in the manner that constitutes the human ideal (cf. *Pol.* VII 13, 1332a1–28). (2) Aristotle distinguishes between leisurely and unleisurely exercises of virtue and insists that happiness is an activity of leisure (*EN* X 7, 1177b4–15; *Pol.* VII 15, 1334a10–40). It is likely, therefore, that in his view a brave person who spends his adult life at war is not happy. He acts courageously, but his whole life is devoted to actions that are teleologically subordinated to activities of leisure, whose good is entirely in themselves.

[7] Aristotle thinks that the good cannot in principle be improved. See Lear (2004), 202–4 for discussion.

happiness is an end [*telos*] and perfect [*teleion*, alt. end-like] in absolutely every way. (*EN* I 10, 1101a14–19)

I say that it is unclear whether this is the point of the perfect life requirement in the *EN* because, in this passage, Aristotle seems to treat the question of whether the happy person must hold on to happiness up to the point of death as additional to the question of whether he must have it for a perfect life ('should we add . . . ').[8] He seems in the *EN* to be trying to keep distinct two issues which, in the *EE*, he runs together: having the good through to the end of life and having the good for a long enough time. Also, in this chapter Aristotle seems to countenance the possibility that a happy person may lose his happiness (I 10, 1101a9–10). If this is indeed what he means, then he must believe it possible to achieve the perfect length of time necessary for happiness before one's death. True, Aristotle would not want to call the person who loses happiness 'happy' unless he regains his happiness later, something which will require (another) perfect time (I 10, 1100a4–9).[9] Even so, it is fairly clear that the perfect life requirement in the *Nicomachean Ethics* is not aimed primarily at the thought that happiness involves possessing the good up to the point of death.

Third, there is the idea that a person's good condition counts as happiness only if it persists for some long enough length of time. Aristotle seems to have this idea in mind when he requires that virtuous living last a long time and when he compares happiness to spring. To bring the distinction between the second and third ideas into view, imagine a person wrongly sentenced to life in prison who is exonerated after serving twenty years. He has a joyful reunion with his family and friends and then, a week later, has a heart attack and dies. This person's life certainly took a turn for the better and his friends will be glad that it did. They will also be glad that the good of freedom, once he got it, is one he kept to the end of his life. On the other hand, even though he regained his freedom, we would not celebrate him as someone who managed to regain well-being. He died before having enough time to flourish. Aristotle seems to be making a similar point when he says that a very unfortunate person could regain happiness, but only 'in some great and perfect time' (I 10, 1101a11–12).

It is this third intuition about the temporality of happiness that, I believe, lies behind Aristotle's perfect life requirement and that is my topic in this paper.

3. The Life-Projects Interpretation Considered

What counts as a long enough, 'perfect' length of time? Aristotle has most to say about this in the *Eudemian Ethics*, so I will begin with that formulation of the perfect

---

[8] By the way, this fact is also evidence that the perfect life requirement does not depend on the logic of 'more is better'.

[9] 'For as we said both perfect virtue and a perfect life are needed. For many reversals and all kinds of luck happen in life. And it is possible for the most flourishing person to fall into great misfortunes in old age, just as is told about Priam in the Trojan tales. No one would congratulate for his happiness someone who has experienced such misfortunes and died wretchedly.'

life requirement. There he evidently conceives of perfection—whether the perfection of life or the perfection of virtue—in terms of wholeness. To be perfect is to be complete, in possession of all one's proper parts. And in fact 'complete' is a common translation of *teleion/teleon*. We find this conception of perfection applied to time in *Metaphysics* V 16: 'the *teleios* time of each thing is that outside which it is not possible to take any time that is a proper part to it' (1021b13–14, Ross trans. emended).

It is very likely that Aristotle thinks of a perfect, complete time as the length of time corresponding to the beginning, middle, and end of some process. At least, in the *Nicomachean Ethics* he talks about the entire (*hapantos*) time in which, taken together, we find the perfection of a completed process and contrasts it with the parts of a given 'entire' time, each of which corresponds to a single stage of the relevant process (X 4, 1174a19–29). If this is correct, then a perfect length of time is the amount of time it takes for something to happen. It is the time of an event with developmental or narrative structure.

Now this interpretation of what counts as a perfect length of life raises perplexity because, famously, Aristotle insists that the highest human good, virtuous action, is not a process (*kinēsis*) but is instead an activity (*energeia*) that, by definition, is perfected at every moment in which it is engaged. If we can possess the perfection of the highest good in a single moment of time, what need is there to extend it?[10] There is no reason to *stop* engaging in this activity, of course. But since virtuous activity, qua *energeia*, is not an unfolding process, it seems that nothing essential to its value depends on how long it persists.

This problem is especially acute when we consider that, in the *Nicomachean Ethics*, Aristotle argues that perfect happiness is nothing other than the activity of theoretical contemplation. Not investigation; active contemplation of what one already knows. There is no plot in this.

However, in the *Nicomachean Ethics* Aristotle also maintains that there is another, secondary form of happiness: morally virtuous action. And in any case, in the *Eudemian Ethics*—the source of the interpretation of perfect life we are now considering—happiness is identified with the activity of all the virtues, including moral ones. This suggests an interpretation of the perfect life requirement that I will call the 'life projects' interpretation. Perhaps Aristotle's happy person requires a perfect, whole time because morally virtuous activity is the sort of activity (*energeia*) that occurs in a process (*kinēsis*).[11] The line of thought would be as follows: even though virtue is fully exercised at any given moment of action, the point of actions is to accomplish something, to make a change. It is therefore better for them not to be interrupted (perhaps the point of *EN* X 8, 1178a34–b3). In this way morally virtuous activity, fully actualized though it may be in every moment, is nevertheless perfected

---

[10] See Farwell (1995), 249–50 for more detailed explanation.
[11] Irwin (1985a), 306, *not. ad* 1098a18; (1985b), 105.

only over the course of a length of time long enough to bring to fruition the agent's virtuous projects.

Aristotle may seem to have something akin to the 'life projects' interpretation in mind when he argues in *EN* I 11 that the fate of our family and friends can affect our happiness even after our deaths.[12] The problem for this suggestion, however, is that the amount of time Aristotle seems to be requiring is longer than the time necessary to complete a virtuous action. Virtuous actions need not take very long at all. In the *EE*, however, Aristotle seems to be measuring by stages of life. There may perhaps be some virtuous actions that extend over such a long horizon, but it would be odd of Aristotle to think of these as typical or especially important manifestations of virtue such that a person could not count as happy without performing them. And in any case, it is doubtful whether Aristotle admits the possibility of life-long actions. In *Poetics* 8 he makes a point of saying that biological lives, and presumably their stages too, do not necessarily correspond to any single action; we should not confuse the story of heroic action with the recounting of a hero's life. In the *EN* he is clearer still that a perfect length of time does not correspond to the time needed for a single action. It is instead a time long enough to complete *many* glorious deeds:

From misfortunes of this sort [namely, severe ones] a person could not become happy again in a short time, but if at all, in some great and perfect time in which he is an achiever of fine and great things (I 10, 1101a11–13).

So the relationship of virtuous *energeia* to *kinēsis* does not explain why the virtuous person needs a perfect length of life in order to count as happy.

4. The Life-Stages Interpretation Considered

Let us consider another possibility, suggested by Aristotle's description in the *EE* of an *imperfect* life as missing one of its stages. Perhaps the complete length of living activity (*zōē*) he has in mind is not a particular action but rather the biological process from birth to death. (I do not mean to suggest that this process is only biological, since its stages will be divided in different ways depending on the culture one inhabits.) If this were the case, then when Aristotle says that virtuous activity (comprising many individual actions) must last a perfect length of life in order to

---

[12] The proposal is that the virtuous person aims to bring about the happiness of his children and friends, so that the success of his efforts may be realized (or thwarted) even after he dies (Irwin (1985a), 308, *not. ad* 1100a18). Such an interpretation would follow the mould of Bernard Williams' (1973) explanation of the badness of death, though grounding its disvalue in the ontological structure of action rather than (as Williams does) in the reason-giving power of desire. I should note, however, that I doubt this is quite Aristotle's thought here. His point seems to be that our well-being is affected by (because constituted by) the quality of 'our own' activities, including the activities of people who are 'our own'. Since some of these activities persist beyond our deaths, their quality can affect (though only slightly, Aristotle insists) the quality of our own lives. To the extent that extreme misfortune affects our own activities and happiness, so too does it affect the activities of our family and friends and, through them, our own, even after we are dead.

count as happiness, he would mean that it must persist through every stage of biological life, including especially the last one.[13] This may be the point of his approving here of the Solonic dictum to count no man happy until he's dead: 'For nothing imperfect (*ateles*) is happy, for it is not a whole' (*EE* II 1, 1219b7–8).

I will call this the 'life-stages' interpretation of the perfect life requirement. Although ultimately I do not think we should attribute it to Aristotle, it has a certainly plausibility. We treat the deaths of young adults and people in middle age as tragic—as stories ending in unhappiness—in a way that we do not normally treat the deaths of the elderly. A life that ends at an early stage is unfinished and while that need be no fault of the person himself, it seems that he dies with some potential for flourishing left unrealized.

A proponent of the life-stages interpretation of the perfect life requirement must explain why in Aristotle's view living through all the life stages typical of human life makes a difference to the quality of virtuous activity. He should try to explain why the virtuous person needs a full span of life in order to most perfectly actualize his perfect condition of soul such that, unless he does, he will not have the highest good, happiness. (Remember, the question is not whether it would be better to live through all the stages of life, but rather whether doing so is necessary in order to be happy at all.)

The relationship of happiness to human form might seem to provide just such an explanation. In both the *Eudemian* and *Nicomachean Ethics*, Aristotle argues that happiness, our ultimate end, is a matter of virtuous achievement of the characteristic human work (*ergon*). But, one might think, it is definitive of the human soul or form not simply to think and to perceive and to reproduce, but to do these things in specifically human ways. Going through the typical human life cycle is, in other words, the actualization of human form. Doing this virtuously and well would be happiness.

From this point of view, although we may act virtuously in some small stretch of time, we only fully actualize our virtue over a complete biological life. The thought would be that since it is essential to human nature to be, not just temporally extended, but temporally differentiated, so too human happiness—the virtuous activity of our human nature—consists of temporal stages. We may rightly admire a person for the virtue he exhibits in a single phase of life, the courage a young man shows on the battlefield, for example. But if his courage leads to an early death, then (according to the life-stages view) we would not rightly consider him to have been happy. He is not to blame for this of course. The point is just that, as explained above, even though virtuous activity alone is responsible for our happiness, there can be a gap between being virtuous and being happy. In order for a young man's battlefield courage to (partly) constitute happiness, it must be a moment in a life that also, at the

---

[13] Children cannot act virtuously, so strictly speaking childhood would not be a proper part of the happy life. On the other hand, the childhood of a virtuous, happy person is appropriately thought of as a time in which virtue was developing. From this point of view, we can include childhood as part of the happy life in a looser sense, not as a stage of possessing happiness but as a stage of promise (*EN* I 9, 1099b32–1100a5).

appropriate time, contains loving care for his family, just and wise political leadership, pious use of retirement, and resolute endurance of death. To lack any one of these kinds of virtuous action, even if through no fault of one's own, would be to lack a piece of the temporally differentiated whole that is excellent human life activity.

It is my sense that this is a view that would be favored by many modern-day Neo-Aristotelians (e.g. Philippa Foot, Michael Thompson), although so far as I know none of them has discussed the issue.[14] And it seems to me that this is an avenue Aristotle himself might well have taken in thinking about the relationship between happiness and time. To think of life in terms of stages is to focus on the cycle of different circumstances that predictably arise as we grow older and on the different kinds of life activities that typically engage us in these different circumstances and Aristotle is indeed interested in this. In the *Rhetoric*, for example, he argues that there are different standards of bodily beauty for different stages of life: a young man's body is beautiful when fit for athletic competition; a mature man's body is beautiful when it looks formidable and ready for war; an old man is beautiful so long as his body is free from painful deformity and strong enough for the necessities of daily life (I 5, 1361b7–14). In the ideal city of the *Politics*, the citizens are assigned to different tasks depending on their age: the young men are soldiers; older men fill positions of deliberative leadership; and the elderly men serve as priests (VII 9, 1329a13–34).

Even though the life-stages interpretation of the perfect life requirement is a possible Aristotelian position, however, it is unlikely to be Aristotle's. In the passage from the *Eudemian Ethics* we have been considering, he says that the activity of perfect virtue must persist through to the end of life, but he does not say that the end must come in old age. It would be odd if he did. Courage, in his view in the *Nicomachean Ethics* at least, is paradigmatically the virtue of risking death in battle (*EN* III 6). The central cases of courageous action are not the work of old men, therefore; they are the actions of people strong enough to go to war. And yet, Aristotle thinks of the brave person as willing to give up a life that is, in some sense, *already* happy—it is precisely for this reason that the prospect of death is painful to him (III 9, 1117b9–13). Indeed, Aristotle goes so far as to say that the virtuous person will give up his life from the motive of self-love on the grounds that a

---

[14] Irwin (1985b), 105 suggests a version of this view that is grounded in his inclusivist interpretation of *eudaimonia*. Neo-Aristotelians conceive of the virtues as excellences in managing the typical variety of human activity (e.g. justice is excellence in the human practice of cooperation; temperance is excellence in managing our desires for food and sex). They seem therefore to be thinking of the human *ergon* as composed of all the specifically human modes of living. For this reason, they reject Aristotle's attempt in the *EN* to isolate one supremely good human activity as constitutive of happiness. These tendencies in Neo-Aristotelianism originate, I suspect, from their drawing a closer connection between the concepts of *eudaimonia* and biological flourishing than Aristotle himself draws. Despite the fact that this is a common translation, *eudaimonia* does not mean flourishing, as we can tell from the fact that, according to Aristotle, human beings are the only mortal creatures capable of *eudaimonia* (*EN* I 9, 1099b32–1100a2; X 8, 1178b24; *EE* I 7, 1217a21–9). For Aristotle, the human *ergon* is not our typical life activity, but is rather the *best* activity of which, qua human beings, we are capable.

short, glorious life is preferable to a long life of humbler pleasures (IX 8, 1169a22–5). It is important to be clear about this: whatever we may think, Aristotle does not regard the soldier who risks his life for family and friends as caught between a rock and a hard place. To be sure, his situation is not ideal. But he acts from self-love and does not consider the happiness of his life to be contingent on surviving his ordeal. Aristotle wants to defend the rationality of giving up one's life for one's friends—not simply risking death, but acting bravely when death is almost certain (e.g. the Spartans at Thermopylae). And given his eudaemonism, that means he must regard virtuous self-sacrifice as consistent with the desire for happiness. None of this makes sense on the supposition that the relatively young man who dies on the battlefield is precluded from happiness on the grounds of having missed out on later stages of the normal human life span. So when Aristotle says in the *EE* that virtuous activity must last for a whole life, with all its parts, it is better to read him as saying that a person must live virtuously into his prime and through to the end, whenever that may come.

Of course, it is not possible to be virtuous *before* one's prime either. At least, it is not possible to be virtuous when one is a child. A perfect life, then, is not—as the life stages interpretation would have it—a life composed of all the seasons of human life. It is, rather, a life that reaches and lives into one season in particular. And so the question remains: once one has reached one's prime, how long is long enough?

5. It Takes Time to Be Good Fully

It will be helpful at this point to return to the *Nicomachean* introduction of the perfect life requirement:

The human good is activity of the soul in accordance with virtue, and if there are several virtues, in accordance with the best and most perfect (*teleiotatēn*). And further, in a perfect life (*en biōi teleiōi*). For one swallow does not make spring, and neither does one day. Likewise one day does not make someone blessed and happy, and neither does a short time. (*EN* I 7, 1098a16–20)

Notice that when it comes to spring, a perfect length of time is a time without kinetic differentiation. The reason we (in Chicago) hold off on rejoicing at the return of spring is not that we are waiting to see what *else* will happen; we are waiting to see whether the warm weather will *keep on* happening. How long is long enough to confidently declare that spring has arrived? That is hard to say. But the important thing for us to notice is that we do not measure by reference to an external goal towards which the days are progressing. That is to say, when it comes to spring, 'long enough' is not a time composed of beginning, middle, and end; it is not the time of a *kinēsis*.[15] This passage suggests, then, that there is nothing essentially developmental

---

[15] The time of spring is not a whole made of qualitatively distinct temporal parts, but it is still a time in which something achieves its end. The point is just that the end in question is immanent in the whole span

or narrative about the perfect life requirement. This impression is supported by Aristotle's discussion of how an unfortunate virtuous person may regain his happiness: he needs to perform glorious actions—many of them—for some lengthy, perfect time (I 10, 1101a11–13). Again, his point is not that the virtuous person needs to do a variety of things in order to be happy; it is rather that he needs to keep on doing the same kind of thing for long enough.

In the case of spring, it is easy to see why some long enough time is necessary. 'Spring' is the name of a season and a season just is a long stretch of time of similar weather. So no single warm day could possibly achieve the 'goal' or condition of being spring on its own, even if it should turn out to be a spring day. We cannot make such a straightforward case for *eudaimonia*, however. Aristotle seems to ground the need for a long, perfect amount of time in the fact that *eudaimonia* is the excellent performance of our characteristic work, as if we cannot fully achieve excellence in our *ergon* except over some long stretch of time.[16] His commitment to the idea that happiness is an unqualified end or goal (*telos*) motivates the perfect (*teleion*) life requirement (*EN* I 10, 1101a14–19; X 7, 1177b24–6). Yet, since virtuous action is an *energeia*, isn't the *telos* or goal achieved in a short stretch of time, indeed in a moment? In what way does a single pleasant, leisurely, well-equipped virtuous action fall short of perfection? How could it be better to do more of the same?

Here let me pause to suggest that many of us are strongly inclined to think of the relationship between virtue and virtuous action as the relation between psychological cause and effect. This is not wrong exactly, but it is a model that can mislead us when we ask ourselves the question: what is involved in *being* virtuous? Someone with the cause/effect model might be inclined to answer: to be virtuous just is to possess the psychological condition of virtue, as if there were nothing defective about this condition from the point of view of virtuous existence. But as Aristotle points out, you can be virtuous in this sense while sleeping throughout your life and never doing

---

of time, rather than an external result of it. So even if we give up the *EE* model of a perfect time (namely, a whole time made up of beginning, middle, and end), we can retain the idea—required by the text of *EN* I 10 and X 8—that the perfection of a length of time is tied to an activity's achieving its (immanent) end.

[16] He does not simply tack on an additional qualification to the definition of happiness established by the *ergon* argument. To see this, we must place the *ergon* argument in the larger context of *EN* I. The *ergon* argument fleshes out the teleological conception of the human good which Aristotle develops in *EN* I 1–7 by linking it to facts about human nature; a thing's *ergon* just is the ultimate end characteristic of it as the kind of thing it is. (So, the *ergon* argument is not a new tack, but is rather a new technique for pressing forward on the previous, teleological approach to the human good.) The argument establishes that the excellent achievement of our *ergon*—our defining ultimate end and good—is virtuous rational activity. Aristotle then makes two additions that clarify possible confusions about what sort of virtuous activity constitutes happiness. Unsurprisingly, since it is of a piece with the underlying motivation for the *ergon* argument, he resolves the confusions by appealing to the fact that the human good is a *teleion telos*, a perfect, end-like end. If there are many virtues (problem #1), happiness is activity of the most *teleion* one. And if virtuous action can last for different lengths of time (problem #2), happiness is activity that lasts a *teleion* length of time. Since *teleion* has been explained in terms of and consistently used to refer to teleological superiority, we should expect this meaning to be present here as well.

a thing (I 8, 1098b31–9a1). For Aristotle, virtuous action is not simply the effect of virtuous disposition of soul; it is its actualization. From this point of view, what is involved in *being* virtuous in the fullest sense is actually doing the sorts of things a virtuous person does.[17] If you want to know what it is to be virtuous, you should look not so much to disposition of soul as to virtuous choices and actions (as indeed Aristotle does in his detailed studies of the virtues), for it is these virtuous choices and actions that constitute the fullest actuality of excellent human being.

Why am I bringing up this familiar point? Aristotle insists that virtue is a stable disposition of soul (II 4, 1105a32–3). What I want to suggest is that the disposition must be stable *because*, in Aristotle's view, its actualization is *essentially* habitual. Indeed, Aristotle easily moves between ascribing stability to the disposition and to the activity. And although it is true that virtuous action is stable because the disposition is, Aristotle is as likely to attribute the stability of the disposition to the inherent stability of virtuous activity in itself:

For in no aspect of what human beings do is there such stability as there is in activities in accordance with virtue: they seem to be more firm-rooted even that the various kinds of knowledge we possess; and of these very kinds of knowledge, the most honorable are more firm-rooted because of the fact that those who are blessed spend their lives in them more than anything, and most continuously, for this is likely to be why forgetfulness does not occur in relation to them. (*EN* I 10, 1100b12–17, Rowe trans.)[18]

When we think of the virtuous action that is our human good, we should not think of one-off isolated acts; we should think of the rarely interrupted activity of living virtuously. Notice that according to my interpretation, unlike the others we have surveyed, the perfect life requirement applies just as much to theoretical virtuous activity as it does to morally virtuous activity. For Aristotle, to *be* a wise thinker in the fullest sense is to be continuously engaged (insofar as possible) in active contemplation. Returning to our earlier metaphor, a virtuous action (moral or theoretical) is like a spring day: to identify an action as virtuous is to connect it to a wider context of regularly acting in the same way.

Aristotle's perfect life requirement springs from his conceiving of our highest good as a virtuous, stable, fully actual way of being. A person may in principle possess the psychic condition that is virtue for only a short time (because he dies young) and so a good person may exercise that virtuous capacity for only a short time. But without a long time, he will not have the chance to be a virtuous person in the fullest sense, though this is in no way his fault, because that way of being essentially is a persistent, habitual mode of living.

---

[17] Cf. X 8, 1178b18–20: Aristotle assumes that since the gods have the most perfect form of life, they must be fully active, rather than asleep, presumably because sleeping would be a less perfect form of life.

[18] I follow Rowe in reading *toutōn autōn* in I 10, 1100b15 as referring to the kinds of knowledge.

An analogy may make this suggestion more plausible. Think about what it is to be a great basketball coach. It is habitual; it describes a way of life. A person may have an extraordinary ability to encourage and direct players and to determine strategy, but if for some reason he coaches only one game, then we will not say that he was a great coach. He *might* have been a great coach, but he was not in fact. I want to suggest that Aristotelian virtue is, in this way, like being a great coach. It is an active way of being. If a good person dies too young, then his virtuous activity will not have persisted long enough for us to say truly that he was virtuous—a great man—in the sense of having lived a virtuous life. Being virtuous in the fullest sense turns out to be more like a season than we might at first have expected; it comes into being only once it has lasted long enough.

6. Self-Knowing Activity Takes Time

My analogy between virtue and coaching is intended to make my suggested reading of the perfect life requirement seem worth exploring. But it does not itself illuminate why virtue (or for that matter the demi-virtue of the coach) has this temporal character or why Aristotle might have thought it did. How far can we justify Aristotle's conception of virtuous action as the stable actualization of a stable character beyond pointing out where it resonates with our intuitions? There may not be much to say to someone who views virtuous actions as the discrete effects of a virtuous mind in appropriate circumstances. Nevertheless, in this last section of my chapter I will try to push a bit further and to do so I will set out on what might at first seem like a new tack.[19]

There is another passage in the *Nicomachean Ethics* that refers to the notion of perfection in time, which we have not yet examined. In his discussion of virtue friendship, Aristotle remarks that it takes time for such friendships to develop:

Friendships of this sort need time and habitual association; for as the saying goes, it is not possible for people to know each other before savoring the proverbial salt together; and neither can they accept each other or be friends before each is seen to be (*phanēi*) loveable, and is trusted, by the other. Those who are quick to behave like friends towards each other wish to be friends, but are not unless they are also loveable, and know this [about each other]; for the wish for friendship is quick to come into being, but friendship is not. This kind of friendship, then, is perfect (*teleia*) both in respect of time and in the other respects. (VIII 3, 1156b25–34)[20]

---

[19] See Price (1980) for a quite different explanation, which depends on the assumption that wise choice is made with a view to something like a lifeplan. I share Broadie's (1991: 198–202) objections to this interpretation (despite my believing that other versions of the so-called 'Grand End View' can withstand her criticisms).

[20] Translation greatly influenced by Rowe. Irwin (1985a: 306, *not. ad* 1098a18) notes but does not discuss the relevance of this passage to the perfect life requirement.

Aristotle emphasizes here that time is necessary for mutual knowledge of virtue. In the first instance we see someone act well and admire her for it. We are attracted to her and wish to spend time together. But until we actually have spent sufficient time together, it will not be clearly apparent to us (*phanēi*) that this person is indeed good and loveable. (Interestingly, Aristotle also draws a connection between time and knowledge in *Poetics* 7. A beautiful tragedy should last however long it takes for the audience to grasp it as an ordered whole and remember it easily.)

When Aristotle says that friendship takes time, he is not, I think, sounding a note of caution, as if we need to make sure we were not deceived in our initial impression. At least, I hope he is not, because that would not be true to the phenomenology of needing time to become friends. When I meet someone I like, I assume that my initial judgment is correct. What happens over time—through spending and savoring the proverbial salt together—is that I learn something about the other person I *could not* have known in a short time: I learn that a good, decent, brave, generous person is who she is in the habitual, stable sense we were discussing before. I learn that she is more than someone whose heart is in the right place—that much was clear pretty much from the start. Over time I learn that she has achieved the more significant standard of being good over and again, of making her good intentions actual as a way of life. More important, it takes time for me to learn that her good will towards me in particular is firm. Only over time is it possible to know that, beyond being friendly towards me on this or that occasion, she is a true friend of mine. This is just another way of saying that friendship is a stable disposition of character (*EN* II 4, 1105a32–3). It is a sort of virtue shared by two (*EN* VIII 1, 1155a3–4).

Notice, Aristotle's point is not simply that it takes time to *know* that the person towards whom I feel friendly is, indeed, a friend. The point, rather, is that it takes time for us *to be* friends because it takes time for us to know that we are. Friendship, like all the human virtues, is a self-knowing form of life. Thinking about the distinction we draw between being a biological mother and being a 'real' mother (an instance of friendship in Aristotle's sense) may help make this point evident. Biological motherhood is a stable relation I hold to my child, but it is one that could hold without either of us knowing that it does. Considered as an aspect of my non-rational nature, motherhood does not require self-knowledge. Normative motherhood, by contrast, is a self-conscious activity of caring for another person as my child against the backdrop of my knowledge that it is in particular my place and my obligation to do so. Because motherhood in this sense is both a stable and a self-knowing form of life, it is not a condition one can acquire right away, simply by becoming a biological mother. Knowing my child as my child and myself as a mother in the relevant sense and, therefore, being a mother in the relevant sense is something that takes time.[21]

---

[21] Remember that mothers (and fathers, too) begin relating to and caring for their child before he is born. And for many people, the process of 'bonding' can take longer than we are comfortable admitting. Perhaps Aristotle's point that all friendship takes time would ease the anxiety of parents in this situation.

Notice that in discussing *philia* between mother and child, I have switched from talking about the time it takes to know the other as a friend to me to talking about the time it takes to know myself as a friend to her. I want to suggest that it takes time for us to know ourselves as stably virtuous and, therefore, that it takes time for us to be virtuous in the fullest sense. A person who has recently acquired virtue—a newly minted good human being—knows what she is doing. (The idea that there is a moment in which virtue is minted in the human soul is, of course, a fiction, but a useful one for our purposes.) She chooses her action and she chooses it for its own sake. She sees clearly what matters to her here and now; she knows that she is right so to care; and she knows that the course of action she chooses is correct. But what she cannot know from the beginning is whether she is, as a matter of habit, the sort of person who regularly sees what matters and what to do. Perhaps some great event will reveal to her that the values by which she steers her life are illusions or in some other way inadequate. (After all, some people think happiness is health when they are sick and then, when they become healthy but poor, think that it is wealth, *EN* I 4, 1095a22–5.) Or, if this is unlikely, more complex situations may still reveal to her that she is not, as she hoped she was, the sort of person who knows how to put her good values into action. This is, I think, a very real and reasonable concern. A person needs a relatively long time of acting well in order for it to be evident—to herself and also to her fellow citizens—that virtuous is what she *is*. (We may in a short time see that we have acted as a virtuous person would act; we may give ourselves credit for it and see in ourselves great promise of virtue; but we cannot see that virtue structures our entire way of life. Seeing that just takes time.) We need time to see how this action fits into a wider context, to see whether it is an instance of a habitual way of being or rather a piece of moral luck.

Self-knowledge is necessary for rational virtue. So if there is an epistemological requirement—an amount of time one must persist in virtue in order to know that one fully is a virtuous person—this is, in our case, an ontological requirement as well.

How long is long enough? There is unlikely to be any answer to this that is independent of the virtuous agent's own sense that he has in fact reached the fullness of virtuous living. But perhaps it is wrong to expect more. An analogy to theoretical rational activity may be fruitful. Aristotle distinguishes between valid and perfect (*teleion*) syllogisms. A perfect syllogism demonstrates its conclusion in a way that is apparent to intellect (*Prior Analytics* I 1, 24b23–4). It is not simply that the conclusion follows from the premises, but that we (or an excellent thinker?) can *see* that it does simply in virtue of the premises themselves. Whatever the details of his view may be, presumably Aristotle is trying to say that the activity of theoretical demonstration reaches its *telos* or goal (and therefore is *teleion*, perfect) when the mind's success in grasping the intelligible structure of the world is apparent to itself.[22] The

---

[22] I do not mean to suggest that, in Aristotle's view, a perfect syllogism is self-evident in the sense of being effortless. It may well take some intellectual effort to grasp. (I thank Ben Morison for helping me appreciate this point during discussion of his paper, 'What Makes a Syllogism Perfect?' presented to the

form of theoretical success is self-conscious. Whatever the criteria for perfect syllo-gisms turn out to be, they will be determined by reference to that goal.

I am suggesting something similar about the time needed for happiness, success in achieving the good of practical reason. We may not be able to say anything very determinate about how long a perfect length of life is, beyond saying that it reaches through to the end of life whenever that comes. Given the vagaries of the sphere of action, it may be that different people in different circumstances require more or less time. But whatever the details of a particular judgment may be, it will be determined by the fact that happiness, the highest human good, is something *kalon* (noble, beautiful); it is the self-conscious and habitual activity of virtue in conditions of moderate good fortune. However long it takes to achieve that will be long enough.

Let me conclude this section by clarifying what I take myself to have been doing. Aristotle certainly believes that virtuous activity—being virtuous in the fully actual sense—is a stable form of living, not a single virtuous deed. Indeed, the stability of this form of living is a mark of its constituting happiness. This explains why he compares an individual virtuous action to a spring day, something whose character as virtuous depends in part on its being a moment in a longer 'season' of good living. (An advantage of my interpretation is that it holds good for both forms of happiness, political and contemplative.) I offered the example of being a good coach in order to show that, at least to some degree, we share this intuition too. But since we may wonder whether to trust this intuition as a guide to moral theory, I have attempted to construct an Aristotelian rationale, based on a remark about the virtue of friendship, for his claim that virtuous action rises to the level of being happiness only if it persists for a long, 'perfect' amount of time. Admittedly, however, I have gone well beyond any explicit rationale Aristotle himself gives for the claim that happiness takes time.

7. A Perfect Length of Life Is Something We Might Wish for Too

We have looked at several reasons someone might think happiness depends on living a long time. We considered the view that happiness is composed of certain external goods, such as children and grandchildren, which can only be acquired later in life. We quickly rejected this as an interpretation of Aristotle, since in his view happiness is constituted by virtuous activity alone. Second, we considered the 'life projects' view, the view that happiness is composed of virtuous projects whose kinetic struc-ture takes time to unfold and reach fulfillment. Although Aristotle may indeed believe that happiness qua morally virtuous practice is necessarily temporally

University of Chicago's Ancient Greek and Roman Philosophy Workshop, January 2014, in which he presents a rather different view of perfect syllogisms than the one I describe here. See Morison (2015).) My point is simply that, according to Aristotle, perfected theoretical thinking takes the form of a syllogism in which everything necessary for grasping the truth of the conclusion is present immediately to the mind, e.g. without need for further premises or conversion.

extended for this reason, the amount of time needed for a single virtuous action is significantly shorter than the length specified by the perfect life requirement. Third, we considered the 'life stages' view, the view that excellent human activity consists in acting well in the ways typical of all the stages of human life. Though we conceded an Aristotelian spirit to this interpretation, it cannot do justice to Aristotle's own evident desire to count as happy courageous lives cut short on the battlefield. Finally, we considered the view that virtuous action is essentially a (self-knowing) moment in the broader activity of habit and thus that it takes time for virtuous action to be constituted as the self-knowing, stable, active way of *being* good and happy that it is. I think that something like this last view is what Aristotle intends by the perfect life requirement. But is my reading charitable? Aristotle tells us in the *EN* that practical philosophical inquiry is not finished until we bring theory back to the facts and see whether it fits with and illuminates our experience (X 8, 1179a16–22).

I know that reflection on death and the passage of time is the prerogative of old age. But the dawning of middle age (notice I still say 'dawning') brings with it a host of occasions to think about time. My parents have retired and are starting to seem old. I know that I, like the toddlers in the classic book, *More, More, More Said the Baby*, will never have enough time with them. But as I already said, this feeling that more is better is not the point of Aristotle's perfect life requirement.

Middle age brings another problem of time into view that is closer to his topic, however. It heightens one's awareness that reconciliation over the hurts of previous, more turbulent years takes time. We may have gone through the process (*kinēsis*) of reconciliation, but the full actuality of reconciliation does not come into being as soon as apologies are traded and a good party or vacation is shared. Will we have enough time together to *be* reconciled? Turning to the world of work, middle age involves moving into positions of authority—the University of Chicago will soon be run to a significant degree by the colleagues in my tenure cohort. Will we be able to do it well?

My worry here is not about whether we are virtuous. We probably are not, but let's assume we are decent enough. *Ex hypothesi*, the decent person is aware when she acts that her heart is in the right place and is reasonably confident that she has chosen correctly. But events may conspire to make the values that have guided her so far unequal to new circumstances (e.g. financial crises and the attendant changes in the structure of American higher education may make the value of a faculty-run university pieces of nostalgia). Or even if the values are still vital, circumstances may be so unusual or the stage of action so much bigger that she is not able to figure out how to make those values actual in action. What the decent person cannot know simply in one or two actions is whether she actually *is*, as a matter of a way of life, a fine and good person. But *that* is what she wants to be and she will not fully have achieved it until she knows that she has. She will need a long, perfect length of life.[23]

---

[23] Thanks to Agnes Callard, Anton Ford, Jonathan Lear, and participants at the University of Kentucky Workshop in Ancient Philosophy for comments on this paper. Thanks also to Jonathan Beere, whose objection to a much earlier version of this chapter caused me to rethink the issue afresh.

7

Why Is Aristotle's Vicious Person Miserable?

Gösta Grönroos

1. Introduction

By leading a life in accordance with the virtues, Aristotle's virtuous person brings her human nature to perfection, and is as happy as a human being can be. This may suggest that happiness (*eudaimonia*) amounts to being in this natural state, and that how the virtuous person experiences that state, by enjoying it or not, has no bearing on her happiness. But if this is how Aristotle conceives of happiness, then arguably, there is little overlap between his notion of *eudaimonia*, and any notion of happiness of which enjoyable experience is an integral part. Indeed, on the view that being happy amounts to being in a perfected natural state, it may seem that 'well-being', rather than 'happiness', is the apt rendering of *eudaimonia* in the first place.

But at least in one respect, the perfect natural state of the virtuous person may seem to bear on her experiential state. For the virtuous person is harmonious in the sense that her desires never clash with one another.[1] The virtuous person does what she finds out to be the good thing to do not only willingly, and for its own sake, but also wholeheartedly, and without distraction from any contrary impulse pulling her away from it. But even the harmonious condition of the virtuous person provides no straightforward reason for attributing an experiential notion of happiness to Aristotle. For the mental harmony may be what in part explains the success of the virtuous person in achieving her own fulfilment. That is, the absence of mental conflict enables her to realize her nature. But that does not imply that her happiness consists, even in part, in her experiencing that harmonious condition.

However, in his account of the contrary case to the virtuous person, namely, the vicious, or bad person, Aristotle implies that the experiential state matters for happiness.[2] For the bad person falls short of happiness not only on account of failing

---

[1] For an exception to the view that the virtuous person is entirely unconflicted, see Charles (1984), 169–73.

[2] For the view that vice is the contrary (*enantia*) to virtue, see *EN* VII 1, 1145a15–18.

to realize her human nature. In addition, the bad person is miserable precisely on account of what it feels like to be in that state. Arguing for the view that we should do our utmost to become good, and to avoid wickedness, Aristotle points out that the bad person is full of remorse, finds nothing lovable about herself, indeed hates herself, and even considers suicide (*EN* IX 4, 1166b11–13, 24–8).[3] By contrast, if the bad person's lack of happiness were merely a matter of not being in the perfect natural state, then arguably, she could even be enjoying herself in the less than perfect state.

The question I want to raise is why the bad person is in such a miserable state. One reason for the bad person's failure to realize her nature is that, in contrast to the virtuous person, she is not harmonious in her motivational states. For the bad person is conflicted between opposing impulses pulling her in different directions (*EN* IX 4, 1166b19–22). But without further qualifications, appeal to the bad person's conflicted state does not explain why she feels so bad about herself. Going for the fulfilment of one desire at the expense of competing desires may cause nuisance, but it does not in an obvious way lead to self-contempt, let alone to a suicidal condition.

The purpose of this chapter is to explain what the conflicted mental state of the bad person amounts to, and why she is so exceedingly miserable on account of it. In view of the fact that Aristotle pinpoints the conflicted vicious life as the most miserable one, understanding the condition of the bad person is instrumental in understanding its contrary, the happy condition of the virtuous person. I will argue that the bad person's mental conflict consists in a clash between two different kinds of desire, and that fulfilling one of the desires violates values that she also desires, and holds in esteem. More precisely, the bad person feels miserable not only on account of failing to fulfil her desire for the truly good life, but also on account of doing things that are degrading for her. The virtuous person, by contrast, fulfils her desire for the good life, and is pleased that she is good (*EN* IX 9, 1170b8–10), and even loves herself.[4]

It should be pointed out that there is no conflict between this understanding of happiness, and the claim that it takes a certain natural state to be happy. For it is precisely by fulfilling the desire for the good life that one comes to realize one's nature. For this reason, the distinction between an objectivist and a subjectivist notion of happiness is inapt to capture Aristotle's position, at least without further qualifications.[5] In fact, at least three different distinctions should be separated. The

---

[3] As for attributing self-hatred to the bad person, I go on the manuscript variant in L[b], or Parisiensis 1854, of *EN* IX 4, 1166b12, reading *misousi te* instead of *misountai*. So Irwin (2001), 90 note 28. Nothing in the context suggests that bad people flee from life because they are hated by other people, but rather because they hate their own life. Admittedly, hatred of one's own life is not equivalent to self-hatred, but the context strongly suggests that the bad person hates not just her life, but herself for her miserable character.

[4] A further reason for why the virtuous person enjoys her condition is the pleasure taken in virtuous activity (*EN* I 8, 1099a7–17; X 7, 1177a22–7). However, I shall leave the part played by pleasure in the virtuous life for another occasion.

[5] For discussion, see Kraut (1979), 180–6; Annas (1993), 43–6; Jost (2002), xiii–xxiv.

first concerns the question whether happiness is, or involves, an experiential state or not. The second concerns the question whether happiness is determined by the individual in the sense that what anyone thinks will make her happy, will do so. The third concerns the question whether happiness amounts to the same thing for all individuals. I opt for the view that Aristotelian happiness is an enjoyable experiential state brought about by the fulfilment of the specifically human desire, namely wish (*boulēsis*). Wish is a desire for what is truly good for a human being, and what is good for a human being is determined by facts about human nature, and not by what the individual happens to think is good for her.[6]

The attempt to explain the miserable state of the bad person faces a tough challenge. As mentioned, the fact that the bad person is conflicted in her motivational state does not suffice to explain her self-hatred. One option is that the bad person acts against what she thinks is good, and in fact does what she thinks is bad, and degrading for her. The problem, then, is that this construal of the mental conflict of the bad person seems to conflate her with the akratic one. But the bad person, in contrast to the akratic one, acts on what she believes to be good. A proper account of the bad person's conflict should still manage to explain why the bad person is remorseful, and even hates herself. Whereas the akratic condition does provide a straightforward explanation of these feelings, the nature of the bad person's conflict makes it harder to explain them.

2. The Mental Conflict

In order to understand why the bad person feels remorse, and even hates herself, we need to explain what it is about the bad person's mental set-up that prompts these feelings. More particularly, we need to understand what it is about the bad person's conflicted state that prompts them. I will argue that the mental conflict of the bad person consists in a particular kind of value clash between desires, such that by fulfilling one kind of desire, she violates other values, which she esteems. She is remorseful on account of doing things, which she finds degrading for herself.

But as mentioned, it is not obvious that the bad person even is conflicted. For the bad person pursues what she believes to be good, and acts on the reasoned view about how to achieve it (*EN* VII 8, 1151a5–7). The akratic agent, by contrast, acts against her own conception of what the good thing to do is (*EN* VII 4, 1148a4–11). Although the bad person may be wrong about what the good really is, no conflict need arise between her reasoned view of what to do, based on that erroneous conception of the good, and her other desires. In so far as the bad person succeeds in her pursuit of what she thinks is good, she should be as content as the

---

[6] For the purposes here, I set aside the important question whether it is the prospect of obtaining a certain state, or of experiencing that state, which ultimately *motivates* our pursuits. But for a balanced discussion, see Soll (1998), 23–6.

virtuous person, leaving no desire frustrated. Think of a bad person, who at the expense of virtues such as temperance and justice, successfully pursues a life of excessive wealth, power, and public praise. Whether or not a virtuous, and hence a morally appropriate, way to live, it does not suggest a conflicted life full of remorse.

But in *EN* IX 4 Aristotle indeed seems to portray the bad person as conflicted: 'the soul of [bad people] is at odds with itself, and the one part, because of its wickedness, grieves at holding back from some things, whereas the other part is pleased, the one part pulling in this direction, the other in that direction as if tearing it apart' (1166b19–22).[7] But if the bad person pursues what she takes to be good, it is not obvious why, and in what way, she is conflicted.[8]

In their commentary, Gauthier and Jolif even dispute that this characterization actually concerns the bad person. They argue that with the exception of lines 1166b11–14, the account of inferior people (*hoi phauloi*) at 1166b2–26 is concerned with the akratic person exclusively (Gauthier and Jolif (1970), 733–4). Of course, since lines 1166b11–14 depict bad people (*hoi mochthēroi*) particularly as shrinking from life, and destroying themselves, these lines are still testimony to the miserable condition of the bad person. But if Gauthier and Jolif are right, then there is no contradiction with the view of the bad person as unconflicted. For the miserable condition of the bad person may be due to other factors. For instance, Aristotle may follow Plato in portraying the bad person as being insatiable, because of her pursuit of bodily pleasures, which provide no lasting contentment (*Gorgias* 493e6–4a3).

However, it is more straightforward to take the short characterization of the akratic person on lines 8–11, rather than the discussion of the bad person on lines 11–14, to be the exception from the main topic. That is, Aristotle starts the account by referring to inferior people in general as being conflicted. He then, on line 5, specifies bad people as a particular kind of inferior people, namely as those that are entirely inferior (*hoi komidei phauloi*). He only then, on line 8, gives the case of the akratic person as a comparison (*hoion*), and fleshes out this case in the following three lines.[9] The akratic conflict consists in going against what one believes to be good for oneself, and instead going for what one believes to be harmful (8–10). But after this comparison, from line 11 onwards, he returns to his main concern, which is to elucidate what it is that makes the conflicted *bad* person miserable.

Still, the characterization of the bad person as conflicted between different desires does not by itself explain why she feels remorse, let alone self-hatred. Nevertheless, at *EN* IX 4, 1166b23–5 the bad person is portrayed not only as conflicted, but as

---

[7] στασιάζει γὰρ αὐτῶν ἡ ψυχή, καὶ τὸ μὲν διὰ μοχθηρίαν ἀλγεῖ ἀπεχόμενόν τινων, τὸ δ' ἥδεται, καὶ τὸ μὲν δεῦρο τὸ δ' ἐκεῖσε ἕλκει ὥσπερ διασπῶντα. The metaphor of tearing the soul apart features in Plato's soul/city analogy, see, e.g. *Republic* V, 462a8–b1, 464c7–8, and *Laws* IX, 875a5–b1.

[8] For discussion, see e.g. Annas (1977), 553–4; Irwin (2001), 89; Brickhouse (2003), 4. Sarah Broadie notices that Aristotle nowhere explicitly claims that the bad person is unconflicted (Broadie 1991, 177 note 41).

[9] For a parallel account, see *EE* VII 6, 1240b11–14.

remorseful as well: 'after a short while he grieves that he was pleased, and had wished that these things had not been pleasant to him. For bad people are full of remorse.'[10] This portrayal of the bad person as full of remorse is in flat contradiction with Aristotle's claim in book 7 of the *Nicomachean Ethics* that, in contrast to the akratic person, the bad person is not remorseful (*EN* VII 7, 1150a21–2; 8, 1150b29–36).[11] But I shall assume that the book IX account gives Aristotle's considered view. The purpose in book VII is to articulate the akratic person's condition, the bad person merely providing a contrast in certain respects. Lack of remorse on the part of the bad person is invoked as an explanation of why she cannot change her ways. In book IX, on the other hand, the issue concerns the self-love of the virtuous person, which is more closely related to the question what makes the virtuous person happy. In this context, the bad person's remorse does not imply that she can be reformed. Moreover, the account of the bad person's state is considerably longer, and detailed, than anything to be found in book VII.

But most importantly, in *EN* IX 4 Aristotle articulates what kind of mental conflict both the akratic and the bad person are susceptible to. It consists in having an appetite for one set of things (*heterōn men epithumousin*), but wishing for another set of things (*alla de boulontai*) (*EN* IX 4, 1166b7–8). So the conflict is put forward as a clash between two different kinds of desire, namely appetite (*epithumia*) and wish (*boulēsis*), respectively. The distinction between appetite and wish is well established in Aristotle's psychology, and they are distinguished by reference both to their domicile in the soul, and to their objects. The non-rational part of the soul harbours appetite, the object of which is pleasure (*DA* III 9, 432b6; *EE* II 7, 1223a34), whereas the rational, or reason possessing, part harbours wish, the object of which is the good (*DA* III 9, 432b5; *EE* II 10, 1227a28–9).[12]

In section 4, I shall elaborate on the relation between wish and the good, but for now, let me pinpoint that the object of wish is the ultimate end of specifically human pursuits, namely the good life, or happiness, and what is conducive to it. But in other works, and in the biological works most notably, the notion of the good is a stand-in for anything desired, and pursued (*DA* 7, 431a8–12; 10, 433b8–10; *MA*, 700b25–9), without in any way suggesting that these things appearing good to the agent are

---

[10] ἀλλὰ μετὰ μικρὸν γε λυπεῖται ὅτι ἥσθη, καὶ οὐκ ἂν ἐβούλετο ἡδέα ταῦτα γενέσθαι αὑτῷ· μεταμελείας γὰρ οἱ φαῦλοι γέμουσιν (*EN* IX 4, 1166b23–4).

[11] Cf. Annas (1977), 553–4; Irwin (2001), 73–4; Brickhouse (2003), 6. Broadie plays down the contradiction by distinguishing between remorse for particular actions, on the one hand, and remorse for what kind of person one has become, on the other (Broadie 2009, 164 note 18). In the end, I do not see how remorse for what kind of person one has become can be independent of the assessment of one's particular actions.

[12] Less directly in *Rhet.* I 10, 1368b37–9a7. This is not the place to defend the distribution of the different kinds of desire, but for considerations against locating wish in the reason-possessing part of the soul, see Price (1995), 111; Moss (2012), 161–2. To keep things manageable, I leave out the third kind of desire, namely spirited desire (*thumos*), which belongs to the non-rational part. But see, e.g. Cooper (1996), 102–14; Lear (2006), 128–9; Grönroos (2007), 260–4; Pearson (2012), 111–39.

conducive to her happiness. So in explaining animal and human pursuits, Aristotle employs the term 'the good' (*tagathon*) equivocally.[13] Hence, nothing implies that whatever appearing good is seen as (or, for that matter, is) pertinent to the ultimate end of human pursuits. A chocolate bar may appear good to a person on account of appearing delicious, without implying that she takes it to be pertinent to happiness. The chocolate bar may appear good even to the virtuous person, without implying that she takes it in any way to be conducive to the good life.[14]

But back to the kind of conflict Aristotle has in mind. It arises when the pursuit of pleasure violates values embraced by the rational part of the soul. This is why the bad person wishes that the things pursued had not been appealing to herself in the first place (*EN* IX 4, 1166b22–4). For instance, if a person values justice as a good, then a conflict of this kind arises when the person does something unjust. She may choose the unjust action under another description, such as being pleasant, or for the sake of some other value. But in either case, the conflict consists in the unjust action's violating a value embraced by the agent, and not just its blocking a just action from being performed. Indeed, in the particular situation, there might not even be room for doing something just, but merely for refraining from doing the unjust thing. So the conflict need not even be a matter of choosing between doing something just or doing something unjust.

To be clear about the kind of mental conflict at issue, let us distinguish between two cases. In the one case, an agent must choose one, and only one, of two options, X and Y say, both of which she wants. The conflict consists in the fact that whichever option she goes for will block the acquisition of the other. However, if it were possible to have both X and Y, no conflict would arise. But in the case, which concerns us here, if the agent chooses X, then the conflict at issue does not consist in the fact that the acquisition of X blocks the acquisition of Y, but in the fact that the very acquisition of X violates Y. So in this case, even if it were possible to have both X and Y, a conflict would still arise.

Of course, the mere presence of wish and appetite need not lead to a conflict. Even the virtuous person has appetites, and satisfying appetites like hunger and thirst, or sexual desires, is perfectly proper from the point of view of the virtuous life. A conflict between the desires of the non-rational part, and those of the rational part of the soul, may arise when the satisfaction of the one is at the expense of the other. But the kind of conflict the bad person suffers from arises when the satisfaction of desires of the non-rational part violates values embraced by the rational part. One case is that of satisfying an appetite in a way, which would be entirely proper unless the situation

---

[13] Cf. Pearson's distinction between a narrow notion of the good as the object of *boulēsis* specifically, and a broad notion of the good as the object of desire (*orexis*) generically (Pearson 2012, 70–2).

[14] Cf. also, *EE* VII 2, 1235b24–6a15. Katja Vogt (manuscript) argues that even if all pursuits aim at *some* good, not all particular actions aim at the ultimate good, albeit that the ultimate good, the good life, may *constrain* the particular pursuits.

demanded otherwise. For instance, a person may choose to finish her meal, although the virtues of justice and of courage demand of her to take immediate action to prevent a burglar from entering the neighbour's house. Finishing the meal is not in itself an improper thing to do, but becomes so when other concerns are overriding. Another case is that of satisfying an appetite in a way which in itself, regardless of the circumstances, violates virtue. For instance, finishing the meal in an improper manner, through excessive intake of food and drink, in itself violates the virtue of temperance.

The account of the conflict as arising from the pursuit of a value, which violates another value embraced by the agent, is a good starting point for explaining the bad person's remorse. A person may certainly grieve at having to refrain from something she regards as good, although she deems that what she opted for instead exceeds it in goodness. For she would have preferred to have it all, without having to choose one of them at the expense of the other. Choosing between going to a party or to a concert may not be difficult, but may still cause some nuisance in view of the missed event. But to feel remorse, and self-hatred, something more seems to be involved. The strong feelings of remorse and self-hatred suggest that she regards it as degrading, and as something she should not have chosen under any circumstances. It is not that she grieves at what she missed, but that she feels bad about what she did.

3. Two Options Dismissed

Understanding the mental conflict as a clash between different values is, I think, what provides the best starting point for explaining the bad person's feelings of remorse, and self-hatred. Nevertheless, there are other options that deserve consideration. One option is that the mental conflict of the bad person is instrumental in nature (Brickhouse 2003, 12–19). On this option, the bad person conceives of pleasure as the good, and acts on the reasoned view of what will maximize pleasure over time. However, even the bad person can be conflicted between the reasoned view of what will give most pleasure over time, and an intermittent urge to do something pleasant at odds with this reasoned view. Although the pleasure from having a doughnut right now in no way measures up to the lost pleasure from the gourmet dinner in half an hour, the bad person, due to her weakness for pleasure, may still irrationally go for the doughnut. On this account, the bad person suffers from diachronic akrasia, and cannot stick to the view of what will benefit her in the long run. But in contrast to the case in which the akrasia consists in a clash between conflicting values, this kind of diachronic case concerns the same value, such as pleasure.

To begin with, it is not obvious that all bad persons are susceptible to diachronic akrasia. On the instrumentalist reading, indulgence in pleasure, which is the goal of the bad person, in the end weakens the bad person's ability to stick to deliberated plans to maximize pleasure over time. But even if this may be the case of some bad people, the instrumentalist reading does not provide an argument that would rule out in principle that a bad person could successfully stick to long-term planning with a view to maximizing pleasure.

Furthermore, the suggestion fares poorly in explaining the remorse, and the self-hatred, of the bad person. According to the instrumentalist reading, the bad person regrets her akratic action on account of the failure to maximize pleasure. But feelings of remorse, and of self-hatred to the point of considering suicide, seem unlikely to follow.[15] Perhaps constant failure in achieving even a fair share of pleasure is reason for regret, and even for self-hatred in that regard. But it is more reasonable to think that these strong emotions of feeling contempt for oneself presuppose that the bad person considers the pursued value to be bad, indeed degrading, and not worth pursuing at all.

Another option is that Aristotle follows Plato in pointing out that the conflicted bad person is not only pursuing the wrong things, but that she is not even capable of any consistent, and successful, pursuit at all. Arguing against Thrasymachus's thesis that injustice is of more benefit to the individual than justice, Socrates points out that injustice in fact makes the individual incapable of achieving anything in a consistent way, because of inner conflict (*Republic* I, 351e10–2a9).

According to this Platonic reading, the source of the miserable condition of the bad person is her inclination to pursue what is appealing at the moment, without forming a reasoned, and stable, conception of the value pursued.[16] For that reason, the bad person cannot even conceive of an overall strategy for her life. There is simply no articulated value, and no conception of what it is to be a human being in the first place, which could bind that strategy together. Although the bad person is able to figure out what to do in the particular situation, and even to plan for the future, the lack of a unifying value deprives her of fully fledged practical knowledge. So according to this Platonic interpretation, the bad person's problem is not that she cannot stick to what she believes to be good, but that she does not even have a consistent, and lasting, conception of the good in the first place.

It is true that Aristotle occasionally portrays the bad person as having no stability, always changing, and not being the same (*EN* VIII 8, 1159b7–9). But on this Platonic reading, it is unclear what the mental conflict on the part of the bad person would come to. The bad person's alleged lack of systematic conception of the value she pursues does not explain the conflict. To the contrary, in fact. For to the extent that the objects of pursuit vary, it is even less clear what the conflict comes to. Perhaps the conflict consists in an impulse action's blocking the acquisition of something else. But in order to generate a conflict it seems that the bad person must cling to the value of the blocked action. If the person is to feel distressed, then she should hold the value

---

[15] For the same point, see Roochnik (2007), 213.

[16] See Irwin (2001), 87–9, 91–4. Irwin's view is more particularly that the bad person lacks not merely a stable conception of the good, but that she does not even have a clear idea of what she is, and that, hence, she has no real concern for herself in the first place.

of the blocked action in even higher esteem than that of the action actually performed. That suggests the kind of stability in the bad person's evaluative outlook that this Platonic reading denies to her.

But the main objection to the Platonic reading is that there are no compelling reasons for ruling out that Aristotle's bad person could have a thoroughly thought-out conception of the value pursued, such as bodily pleasure, which would make successful prudential reasoning possible. That is, to the extent that the bad person conceives of bodily pleasure as the ultimate good, that would seem to suffice in order for her to be able to form an overall plan. In that case, bodily pleasure is chosen for its own sake, and serves as the ultimate end for all actions. Indeed, Aristotle even claims that the self-indulgent person pursues pleasures 'because of decision, because of themselves, and because of nothing else resulting from them' (*EN* VII 7, 1150a19–21).[17]

What is more, Aristotle leaves it open that the bad person may successfully pursue whatever she values as good. More precisely, the bad person may deliberate correctly about what to do given a certain end (*EN* VI 9, 1142b18–20). This capacity to successfully achieve one's ends is labelled 'cleverness' (*deinotēs*), and it is found in the virtuous, as well as in the bad person (*EN* VI 12, 1144a23–36). Despite the fact that the bad person accomplishes something bad, her effort to achieve her ends need not be hampered by any inner conflict. It is true that excellence in deliberation (*euboulia*) requires that both the end and the deliberation towards that end are correct (*EN* VI 9, 1142b28–33), but that fact does not rule out successful reasoning concerning whatever end. So even if Aristotle attributes mental conflict to the bad person, it does not make her incapable of consistent, and successful, pursuit of a desired end.

It should be noticed that there is a common assumption in both the Platonic, or more precisely, in Irwin's Platonizing interpretation, and in the instrumentalist reading, respectively. On both interpretations, wish (*boulēsis*) is taken to be a desire for whatever the agent believes to be good. According to Irwin, the bad person's wish is a reasoned desire for whatever the agent figures out as good, although in fact it is not good (Irwin 2001, 78). But Irwin does not take into account the general description of the conflict of bad people, namely, that they wish for some things, but have appetites for other things. On his reading, it is not clear what the clash between wish and appetite comes to. In particular, since the object of the bad person's wish seems to be just as variable as that of her appetites, it is not even clear in what sense there is a clash between the values of wish and appetite, respectively.

On the instrumentalist reading, again, the bad person's wish is a reasoned desire of how to maximize pleasure over time (Brickhouse 2003, 5). The conflict consists in a clash between this desire, and the intermittent urge for immediate gratification of

---

[17] Irwin, it should be noticed, refers to this passage as evidence against his own view (Irwin 2001), 78.

whatever appetite. So on this reading, the conflict is between a reasoned, and an unreasoned, desire for pleasure. On the bad person's evaluative standards, satisfying the intermittent urge is not by itself a bad thing to do, but becomes so when it blocks the wish to maximize pleasure over time.

But as I have argued, the mental conflict of the bad person consists in a clash of values in the sense that the very value of wish is violated by the bad person's pursuits. For doing what the bad person chooses in fact violates the good. That is what the clash between appetite and wish comes to. But in order to see this, we need to qualify the assumption that wish is a desire for whatever the agent believes to be good. We need to distinguish between the good as the value which fulfils wish, and the conception of the good upon which a person acts. Since that conception may be erroneous, the action based thereupon may not fulfil what the reason possessing part of the soul desires.

4. Wish and the Apparent Good

The problem of attributing a conflict between appetite and wish to the bad person is that in her case, both desires seem to have the same object. For the bad person is typically described as pursuing pleasure as the ultimate good in life (*EN* III 4, 1113a33–b2; IX 8, 1168b15–23). The self-indulgent person (*akolastos*) is a particularly clear case (VII 3, 1146b19–24; 7, 1150a19–21; 14, 1154b9–15), but not all varieties of vice seem equally obviously related to the pursuit of pleasure. What about the coward, the boastful, or the stingy person?[18] Some of these cases may be explained by the pursuit of pleasure and the aversion of pain, but in other cases appeal to pleasure and pain may seem out of place. Be that as it may, for the purposes here, I will take my starting point in the bad person who acts on the view that pleasure is the ultimate good.[19]

Of course, it is not any kind of pleasure that the bad person conceives of as good. Pleasures related to virtuous activities are not at issue, but a certain range of base pleasures manifested in the cravings of the body, as well as in greed and hunger for power.[20] Nevertheless, on the assumption that the bad person conceives of pleasure as the ultimate good, and that her decisions to act are based on that conception, it seems that what she has an appetite for, and what she wishes for, come to the same

---

[18] Thanks to Hallvard Fossheim for bringing this to my attention. See, also, Irwin (2001), 86–9.

[19] Admittedly, the characterization of the bad person as acting on the considered view that pleasure is the overall good implies a hedonist. But whether she is a philosophically reflected hedonist or not turns on what demands we put on how articulate that view must be. Perhaps there are bad people pursuing pleasure without a particularly articulated view of pleasure as the good. For discussion, see Pearson (2012), 141–3.

[20] As far as base pleasures are concerned, Aristotle distinguishes between necessary ones related to bodily functions, such as those had from satisfying hunger, and unnecessary ones, for instance those had from amassing wealth, both of which may be excessive (*EN* VII 7, 1150a16–21).

thing. So the account of the bad person's conflict between appetite and wish should accommodate this feature.

My suggestion is that although the bad person pursues what she believes to be the ultimate good, and believes it to be what she really wants, nevertheless it is not what she wishes for. Hence, on pursuing pleasure as the good, the bad person does not wish it, despite the fact that she thinks so. In fact, she is oblivious of what she really wants. The strange-sounding idea that people may do what they do not want to do, although they think they want it, is anticipated in Plato's *Gorgias* (466c9–468e5). The challenge is to spell out this idea in more detail.

Aristotle makes it clear that the good for a human being is not whatever a person happens to think is good for her. For what really is good for a human being is to live virtuously. In other words, the good for a human being is an objective value in the sense that there is something which really is good regardless of what people happen to think is good for them. In fact, only the virtuous person pursues what by nature is good for human beings (*EN* III 4, 1113a15–33). So despite the fact that all people are said to pursue the good (I 1, 1094a1–3; X 2, 1172b35–6), they may go wrong, pursuing what in fact is not good but merely appearing to be so. In particular, however skilful in spotting ways to do what she believes to be good, the agent may go wrong in forming her conception of the good.

The reason why people tend to go wrong about what is their own good, is that the specifically human good does not belong to the obvious and apparent things, like pleasure and wealth (*EN* I 4, 1095a20–6). In fact, the assumption that it is obvious what the human good is, is an obstacle to obtaining it: 'While there are many other things about which it is not easy to judge correctly, this is even more the case with what most people think is the easiest, and what they think anyone knows, namely, what of the things in life should be chosen, and what would fulfil one's desire if obtained' (*EE* I 5, 1215b15–18).[21] So the difficulty in achieving the good is aggravated by oblivion of its demands.

A crucial source of error in forming the conception of the good is a mistaken conception of what it is to be a human being. For as Aristotle makes clear, the virtuous person pursuing the good, does not choose what she believes to be good for a different kind of nature, but what is good for what she actually is, which is to say a rational being (*EN* IX 4, 1166a19–23). As far as the bad person is concerned, in pursuing base pleasure, she does not pursue what is good for her true self, which is to say the reason possessing part of her soul. The anonymous paraphrast is even more explicit: 'For the reasoning part is what it is to be human, for the sake of which the good person does everything, and pursues everything good, but for the sake of which the bad man does nothing. For the bad person does not have thinking as the end of

---

[21] περὶ πολλῶν μὲν οὖν καὶ ἑτέρων οὐ ῥάδιον τὸ κρῖναι καλῶς, μάλιστα δὲ περὶ οὗ πᾶσι ῥᾷστον εἶναι δοκεῖ, καὶ παντὸς ἀνδρὸς τὸ γνῶναι, τί τῶν ἐν τῷ ζῆν αἱρετόν, καὶ λαβὼν ἄν τις ἔχοι πλήρη τὴν ἐπιθυμίαν.

his own activities, but base pleasure. For this reason, he does not wish what is good for himself for his own sake.'[22] So an important reason for the bad person's erroneous conception of the good is her ignorance of what she really is.

But despite the fact that the bad person pursues what merely appears to be good, Aristotle thinks that even the bad person has a desire for the real good. Evidence for this view can be gathered from *EN* X 2. He takes on Eudoxus's argument that pleasure is the good, pointing out that in so far is it is based on the assumption that every creature, rational and non-rational alike, seeks pleasure, there is room for doubt. For it is not obvious that what unintelligent creatures (*ta anoēta*) pursue is good. However, Aristotle is adamant that in so far as practically wise creatures (*ta phronima*) are concerned, what they seek is good (1173a2–4). But in order to block the objection that bad people pursue what merely appears good, but without being so, Aristotle argues that even bad people have a desire for the real good: 'but equally in bad people too there is something by nature good, which is greater than what they are in themselves [i.e. qua bad], and which aims at the proper good' (1173a4–5).[23] So the idea is that human beings, even if they are bad, and pursue what is not good, still have an element within them, which desires the real good.

But even if it is the case that the bad person desires the real good, we need to explain how it happens that the bad person nevertheless seems to desire, and to pursue, what merely appears to be good. The crucial discussion is in *EN* III 4, where Aristotle addresses the question of whether the object of wish is something determined by nature, or whether it comes to whatever is regarded as good. He disarms the dilemma whether wish (*boulēsis*) is for what in fact is good, or for whatever appears to be good, by distinguishing between two different senses of the expression 'the object of wish' (*to boulēton*). On the one hand, it may signify the natural object of wish, namely the truly good, but on the other hand, it may signify whatever appears good to a person, even if it is not.

One way of fleshing out this distinction is that when a person is said to wish for the good, there is an opaque reading, on which the person wishes for whatever she thinks is good. On this reading, the object of wish is what she represents as good. But there is also a transparent reading, on which the object of wish is the real good, or what is good by nature (*phusei*). So on pursuing an object on an erroneous conception of the good, the bad person, on the opaque reading, may be said to wish for what appears good to her, despite the fact that on the transparent reading her

---

[22] τὸ γὰρ διανοητικόν ἐστι τὸ ἀνθρώπινον εἶναι, οὗ ἕνεκα ὁ μὲν σπουδαῖος πάντα ποιεῖ καὶ τὰ ἀγαθὰ πάντα ζητεῖ, ὁ δὲ φαῦλος οὐδέν. οὐ γὰρ τὴν θεωρίαν ὁ φαῦλος ἔχει τέλος τῶν ἑαυτοῦ πράξεων ἀλλὰ τὴν ἡδονὴν τὴν φαύλην· ὅθεν οὐ βούλεται τὰ ἀγαθὰ ἑαυτῷ ἑαυτοῦ ἕνεκα. [Heliodor.] *In EN paraphr.* 193. 33–7 Heylbut.

[23] ἴσως δὲ καὶ ἐν τοῖς φαύλοις ἔστι τι φυσικὸν ἀγαθὸν κρεῖττον ἢ καθ' αὑτά, ὃ ἐφίεται τοῦ οἰκείου ἀγαθοῦ. So I here take the *phauloi* to refer only to inferior, or bad, rational animals, excluding non-rational animals. For the opposed view, see Michael of Ephesus, Mich. *In EN* 538. 2–4 Heylbut; Grant (1874), 318; Stewart (1892), 407.

wish is not for the merely apparent good, but for the real good, which is the only thing that can fulfil her wish.[24]

The view, then, is that on the transparent reading, the object of wish is what fulfils this desire, regardless of what the person happens to think is good. So even in the bad person, the merely apparent good does not fulfil her wish, although on the opaque reading, she may be said to wish it. Aristotle points out that the less-than-virtuous people tend to be deceived about the real good through pleasure, and to believe, erroneously, that pleasure is the good (*EN* III 4, 1113a33–b2). It is for this reason that in the bad person wish and appetite may seem to be for the same thing. But on the transparent notion of the object of wish, there is room for a conflict between the wish for the good and the desire for what the bad person believes to be good, or what appears good the her.[25]

Admittedly, this suggestion raises the question what it means to have a desire for the real good, although one pursues the merely apparent good based on an erroneous conception of the good. For the implication seems to be that the bad person's wish is an unarticulated, or even unconscious, desire. In other words, the agent would be able to possess a desire without any conception, or any representation, of its object. Indeed, wish would seem to be no intentional state in the first place.

Keeping in mind that wish is a desire for the good as the ultimate end of life, or for happiness, and that a person must form an action-guiding conception of the good in order to achieve it, it is conceivable that even though the person goes wrong in forming that conception, she still wishes for the real good. Imagine a person who thinks that wealth is the ultimate good thing, and that becoming rich will make her happy. But on becoming rich, she finds out that she is not content, and even feels that something important is missing in her life. She may then be inclined to revise her view of what the good comes to, and of what kind of life would make her happy. But in order to explain her motivation to probe her conception of what the good life comes to, an appeal to a desire for the truly good is called for. For if her wish were for whatever she thinks is good, then she should have no impetus to change her view.

So even though wish cannot prompt the agent to act without an action-guiding conception of the good, the object of wish is not determined by that conception.

In the present interpretation, then, the bad person pursues what is not good despite the fact that she desires the real good. For because of the erroneous conception of the good, the bad person's pursuit is directed towards the merely apparent good. The seeming contradiction that the bad person's wish both is, and is not, for the good, again, is dissolved by pointing out that the object of wish may come either

---

[24] Cf. also, *EE* II 10, 1227a18–31. For a transparent definition of *boulēsis*, see *Top.* VII 8, 146a36–b9, and discussion in Corcilius (2011), 119–21. I elaborate on the two senses of the object of wish in more detail in Grönroos (2015), 74–81.

[25] Note that even the truly good is an apparent good in so far as it appears good to the virtuous person. All pursuits of the good are based on a representation of the good. For further discussion, see Moss (2012), 4–8, 159–61; Pearson (2012), 79–83.

to whatever is conceived of as good, or to what actually fulfils the wish for the good. So the mental conflict of the bad person consists in wishing for the real good, but pursuing the merely apparent good.

5. Pleasure and Deception

It should not come as a surprise that a person may be mistaken about what the happy life amounts to, and that she pursues the wrong things on that erroneous conception. What is surprising is that the bad person insists on pursuing the wrong things, and that she is not prepared to abandon her erroneous conception of the good despite the fact that she does not manage to fulfil her wish. For although her pursuit of pleasure does not fulfil her wish, she sticks to her conception of pleasure as the good, and pursues more of it.

As mentioned, Aristotle points out that pleasure is a source of deception (*apatē*) concerning the good (*EN* III 4, 1113a33–b2). The task now is to spell out what this deception comes to. To begin with Aristotle repeatedly pinpoints the pleasant (*to hēdu*) as the apparent good (*EE* VII 2, 1235b26–7; *MA* 700b28–9). Of course, something's appearing to be good to someone may be veridical, and it may not even be related to the good life in the first place. But the kind of deception Aristotle has in mind concerns the conception of the good as the ultimate end of our pursuits. So in some sense we may be deceived by pleasure to believe that we should look for it as the ultimate good.

We may take our lead from Aristotle's distinction between two different kinds of ignorance put forward in his account of voluntary action. He distinguishes between ignorance about facts, which makes the action non-voluntary, and ignorance about the universal, which does not make it so (*EN* III 1, 1110b30–11a2). To begin with, a person may be ignorant about whether a particular thing is good. For instance, a glass of wine may seem good to a person, because she thinks it will be a source of gustatory pleasure.[26] But on having a sip of it, she realizes that it is corked, not pleasant at all, and, hence, no good. There is a whole range of different kinds of ignorance about facts, but what is important is that in most cases the mistake is detected by the agent herself. For in the above case, when the desire motivating the action is not fulfilled, to the frustration of the agent, she immediately realizes the source of the frustration, and no longer has any desire for the particular glass of wine.[27]

But the ignorance may even concern the very conception of what the good, or advantageous, is. The bad person typically conceives of bodily pleasure as the ultimate

---

[26] In this example, the wine's appearing good need not imply that it is seen as pertinent to happiness.

[27] A striking example of a factual mistake which goes unnoticed is Oedipus's having sex with his mother on the ignorance about the identity of Jocasta. Explaining this mistake crucially turns on how the action is described. But importantly, on the description Oedipus himself performed it, he presumably even enjoyed it.

good, although it is not. In this case, the mistake may be noticed, but importantly, it may also go unnoticed. But if bodily pleasure is not the good for a human being, and, hence, does not fulfil wish, then it may seem that the bad person should notice it, and be inclined to revise her conception of the good. However, the bad person's conception of the good as bodily pleasure not only motivates its pursuit, for on obtaining it, she will still think that it is good, and look for more pleasure in the future. Hence, in addition to an erroneous conception of the good, the mistake goes unnoticed even in experience. So in some sense her experience of pleasure as good is deceptive.

It sounds awkward to say that we may be deceived about what we experience as good. What else than the subjective criterion of experience could decide that? In particular, considering the fact that wish is a desire for the real good, even in the bad person wish is fulfilled only by what really is good. But since the bad person acts on what seems to be good without being so, the action will frustrate that desire. So why does she not notice the mistake, and why does she look for more pleasure? The explanation, I conjecture, is that the bad person may not be aware of the source of her frustration. In particular, since pleasure is the object of appetite, a desire of the non-rational part of the soul, it does satisfy a desire. So on successfully pursuing pleasure, the bad person is satisfied as far as appetite goes, regardless of the erroneous assumption that pleasure is good. But since pleasure is not the good, it does not fulfil wish, and the bad person will be left frustrated without being able to spot the source of the frustration.

Compare this case to a thirsty person, who has a craving for a soft drink, and believes it to be the best means to quench her thirst, whereas in fact the increase of blood sugar concentration will make her even thirstier. Hence, on having the soft drink, her desire to quench the thirst will be frustrated. But despite the fact that the thirst is not quenched, there is something enjoyable about the soft drink, which makes the thirsty person stick to the view that soft drink will quench her thirst, and go for more of it. Just as the thirsty person may be at a loss of why the thirst is not quenched, so the bad person, satisfying her appetites, may not be aware of the source of her frustration.

This piece of psychology provides the prerequisites for explaining the kind of deception the bad person suffers from. Since she feels satisfaction from pleasure, that is a sufficient reason both to believe that pleasure is good, and to pursue more of it. But even if satisfying appetite may bring some contentment, there is another desire, namely wish, which is left frustrated. Indeed, the satisfaction of appetite may even violate the values of wish. But in contrast to the akratic and the enkratic person, the bad person need not be aware of the conflict and may not understand the reason for her frustration. In particular, she may still stick to the view that pleasure is the good, and think that the remedy to the frustration is to have more pleasure.

In this way, sense can be made of the claim that the bad person is conflicted, and that the conflict consists in a clash between appetite and wish, albeit not in the instrumental way suggested by Brickhouse, nor in the same way as the akratic person is conflicted. Being conflicted between the short-term and the long-term supply of pleasure does not constitute a clash between values in which one value is violated by the pursuit of the other value. The akratic person, again, knows what the good thing to do is, and that yielding to pleasure is not good for her, but nevertheless, she cannot resist the temptation. Since the bad person, by contrast, does not know what the good is, she has no articulated understanding of the clash between values. But her wish for the good is nonetheless frustrated.

6. The Miserable Condition of the Bad Person

The above account of how the bad person's mental conflict makes her frustrated and discontent does not on its own explain her feelings of remorse and self-hatred, which make her prone even to consider suicide. Perhaps repeated failure to achieve contentment, and the constant frustration of the person's innermost desire for a good life, is reason in itself for remorse and self-hatred. So maybe these uncomfortable feelings need not presuppose that the person realizes that what she has done is in fact bad and degrading for her.

However, according to Aristotle, the bad person is distressed over the fact that she found the things pursued appealing in the first place (*EN* IX 4, 1166b22–4), and does not love herself because she has nothing lovable about her (1166b25–6). Moreover, the bad person is said to look for company with others in order to forget about her many odious deeds (*duscheron*) in the past (1166b13–17). Taken together, these remarks suggest that the bad person feels remorse because she is aware of the fact that what she has done is intrinsically bad and degrading. Her distress at the fact that she found these things appealing indicates that her remorse extends beyond the particular bad actions, and that she feels remorse for being such a bad person so as to be pleased by them.

The challenge now is to attribute to the bad person sufficient cognition of her doing bad things in order to explain her remorse, but without putting her on a par with the akratic person. A crucial difference between the bad and the akratic person, respectively, is that only the akratic person has a correct conception of the good, and even a sound, reasoned view of what to do in the particular situation. It is just that she cannot resist her desires to the contrary, to simplify it grossly. The bad person lacks at least this knowledge, since she has an erroneous conception of the good. But is there another sense in which the bad person may be said to pursue what she takes to be good, and still be aware of its badness?[28]

The puzzle at hand may be put as a dilemma. On the assumption that the bad person has some grasp of the fact that what she is doing is bad, the puzzle is why she does not attempt to replace her erroneous conception of the good. On the one hand,

---

[28] One suggestion is that the bad person has 'some residual recognition of what virtue is and what it requires, with enough psychological force, even, to impel him to commit suicide' (Pakaluk 1998), 177.

if the grasp is insufficient to impel the bad person to replace her conception of the good, then the question is whether it is sufficient to explain the remorse. On the other hand, if the grasp is sufficient to challenge that conception, and hence to explain the remorse, it is difficult to distinguish the bad person from the akratic person. For then it would seem that the bad person acts against her conception of the good.

As pointed out in section 4, even in bad people there is something by nature good, which longs for its own proper good (*EN* X 2, 1173a4–5). But I also argued that the bad person has no grasp of what his own proper good is. My conjecture now is that even the bad person has a sense, albeit an unarticulated one, of virtue, which is insufficient to guide actions, but which is sufficient for remorse.[29] I base my conjecture on Aristotle's remarks on the natural virtues in *EN* VI 13. For he claims that we are just, moderate, and courageous, right from birth, but that it takes reason to turn these dispositions for virtue into full (*kuria*) virtues (1144b1–17). What Aristotle seems to have in mind is that even small children have a sense of justice, say, perhaps in terms of having one's fair share of some good. This sense of justice is unsophisticated, and it would not suffice in the face of more complex cases, in which, for instance, unequal distribution is just. Through experience and reasoning the individual can develop this sense to a full virtue.

But in the bad person, the natural virtues are not developed to full virtues. Developing them to full virtues requires guided, repeated experience of them, turning them first into habituated virtues, which in turn serves as the basis for an articulated understanding of them, and recognition of virtue as good.[30] Lest one is fortunate enough to be easily turned into virtue, developing the natural virtue into a full one is a cumbersome process, giving little gratification in the short term, and requires that the person forms a successful action-guiding conception of virtue. Since only fully virtuous actions fulfil the desire for the real good, the exercise of mere natural virtues does not leave the person content. Instead, the more easily accessible value of pleasure takes over and becomes formative of her conception of the good. One reason for preferring pleasure over virtue is that it is easier to satisfy the desire for pleasure, and to form a successful action-guiding conception of it. The person turning bad may have a sense, but no real understanding, that her pursuit of pleasure is in conflict with the demands of virtue, but she brushes them aside as mere sentimental rubbish at best, or as coercive measures imposed by the community at worse.

On this suggestion, the bad person is attributed some cognition of virtue. But importantly, realizing that her pursuits of pleasure are at the expense, and even in violation, of virtue, does not imply a successful action-guiding conception of virtue as the good. In the state of frustration, the bad person starts to waver. She realizes that

---

[29] My suggestion is somewhat in line with Broadie's in Broadie (1991), 161.

[30] Cf. Burnyeat (1980), 73; Mele (1984), 142–3. I take full virtue to be distinct from both natural (φυσική) and habituated (ἐθιστή) virtue.

her pursuits provide no lasting contentment, and that violating values such as justice and temperance did not give the award she expected. At first, she may not even realize that it is an erroneous conception of goodness that impedes her in the quest for a good life, and that it should be replaced by a conception of goodness as virtue.

But even if the bad person has neither a conception of the real good, nor experience of fully virtuous action, the bad actions may still clash with her sense of the values attached to the natural virtues. For instance, in order to maximize pleasure, the bad person finds herself prudentially justified in violating justice precisely in terms of what she takes to be the ultimate end of her pursuits. But since she has some sense of justice acquired through the exercise of the natural virtue of justice, she may still be aware that she violates an important value, which, however, she has not taken the trouble to articulate and internalize through practice.

Admittedly my suggestion offers no conclusive explanation of the remorse and the suicidal condition of the bad person. Since remorse, and particularly the suicidal condition, seem to presuppose not only that the agent feels uneasy about her present condition and that she has a vague sense of violating important values, but that she realizes in some fuller sense that what she has done is bad, and even degrading, why does she not attempt to revise her conception of goodness or at least abandon it? Moreover, if the bad person is aware that she violates an important value, then she seems to be in the same situation as the akratic person who acts against her knowledge of the good.

The bad person still differs from the akratic one in having no articulated conception of the virtuous life as good, let alone a successful action-guiding conception of virtue. The bad person simply does not know what to do instead. She may, both from own experience and from comparison with the virtuous people's lives, come to realize that her conception of goodness is misguided, even perverted. But since her bad character has become deeply entrenched, which has made her a slave to appetite, she has difficulty forming an alternative conception, which could be conducive to the good life.[31] In particular, she can find no enjoyment in anything other than base pleasure. But even without a clue as to what to replace her erroneous conception of the good with, she can feel the remorse for being the kind of person doing odious things.[32]

---

[31] *EN* VII 7, 1150a19–22; 8, 1150b29–36 seems to have it that the bad person is beyond rescue, but for a more upbeat account, see *Cat.* 13a23–9.

[32] I wish to thank audiences in Uppsala and Rome for fruitful discussions, and Hallvard Fossheim and Miira Tuominen for comments on drafts of the chapter. I acknowledge a grant from the Swedish Research Council (2010–1399).

8

Epicurus on Pleasure, Desire, and Friendship

Panos Dimas

In the evidence available to us, Epicurus presents himself a hedonist, that is, one who claims that pleasure is not only the highest but also the only good. He is also a eudaemonist, who claims that the highest good for every human being is the happiness of that being. As a hedonist, he should be expected to believe that pleasure is the ingredient on which human happiness solely depends. Admittedly, however, there is little clarity as to what it is to which being a hedonist amounts for Epicurus, or even whether he is a fully committed hedonist. Part of the reason is that we lack a rigorous exposition of his views. Other than aphorisms and fragments, all we have by him is a very condensed summary in the *Letter to Menoeceus* (*Ep. Men.*). Scholarly work has been almost as fragmentary as the evidence. We need an overall characterization of his axiology and I attempt one here, as I see it emerging from the evidence we have. My focus is mainly on what Epicurus' axiology is and how the various statements concerning it hang together, not so much its plausibility. I sketch an interpretation of Epicurus' peculiar notions of pleasure, as well as his views on rational choice and desire. I conclude that he is an unwavering hedonist of the egoistic sort, and test this conclusion on what has seemed hardest to align with an interpretation of him as a hedonist, namely his view on friendship. This interpretation will consist basically of five claims that will become clear as they are made in the course of this chapter. It will be helpful to begin with an outline of what I take to be the theoretical framework of Epicurus' ethical thinking.

I

Two theses constitute the basis of this framework, or so I claim: psychological and ethical hedonism. The former is descriptive. It makes a psychological claim about motivation, and it is to be construed as an egoistic claim. It is this: only an agent's experiences of pleasure and pain have motivational significance for this agent. Hence, any agent is motivated to act in order to maintain himself in a state of pleasure and remove himself from a state of pain, or to pursue what he expects will be pleasant and avoid what he expects will be painful for him. So, agents are motivated by pleasure or pain as these states concern *them* and not as they concern others, and they are motivated by nothing else, except derivatively and ultimately by reference to pleasure or pain. 'Motivation' here is not a normative notion but merely a descriptive one; it designates a psychological tendency and the claim is that humans have this tendency as a matter of psychological fact.

Being a descriptive claim, psychological hedonism has, in and of itself, no normative force. What humans have a psychological tendency to want to do need not be good or, for that matter, bad for them. Ethical hedonism, of the egoistic type, makes the normative claim that it is good for the agent to maintain himself in a state of pleasure and remove himself from a state of pain, or to pursue what he expects will be pleasant and avoid what he expects will be painful for him. On this view, pleasure is the only intrinsic good, whereas pain is the only intrinsic bad, and whatever else is good or bad for an agent, it is that derivatively, by reference to pleasure or pain.

Psychological hedonism fits well with ethical hedonism, for it claims that it is good for agents to do what they have a psychological motivation to do. It may also be used as grounds for holding ethical hedonism, particularly among thinkers who are attracted to a naturalist approach to ethics, as is Epicurus. It makes sense for a thinker of such disposition to make the point that it is good to do what belongs to one's psychological nature to want to do. Few would doubt that Epicurus is an ethical hedonist. Still, Julia Annas in her *Morality of Happiness* and more forcefully John Cooper in his chapter entitled 'Pleasure and Desire in Epicurus' have argued that Epicurus is not an adherent of psychological hedonism.[1] Cooper's reason is that Epicurus 'believed a person could perfectly well learn to be motivated by other considerations than the pleasure or pain of an action or of its consequences'.[2] But notice first that this concedes that psychological hedonism must have played some part in Epicurus' thinking. That subjects can learn to be motivated by things other than pleasure would seem to concede that pleasure alone is what was motivating them at some point. Moreover, learning 'to be motivated by other considerations than the pleasure or pain of an action or of its consequences' does not, in itself, preclude that Epicurus is a psychological hedonist. For even though we may come to be motivated by things other than pleasure, it may still be true that the attraction these things have for us is owed ultimately to pleasure. If, however, we can learn to be motivated by things not through pleasure, things that do come to have value for us, though not because they are connected to pleasure, then, clearly, we come to appreciate

---

[1] Cooper (1999), 485. Annas (1993), 240–2 attributes to Epicurus the view that things other than pleasure, such as friendship, can have intrinsic value. This view is incompatible with psychological hedonism, because an agent holding that things other than pleasure have intrinsic value will not act with the sole aim of procuring pleasure, as psychological hedonism would require; instead, the source of value can be other than pleasure.

[2] Cooper (1999), 485.

as good things other than pleasure. If this is true about Epicurus, then Epicurus ends up abandoning also ethical hedonism.

Cooper claims further that the 'we' in the passages from the *Ep. Men.* that support psychological hedonism is to be taken in the sense of 'we Epicureans' and not 'we humans'.[3] In his view, these passages make claims about how Epicureans are motivated, not about human motivation in general. Still, if 'motivated' here is not used normatively, that is, if it means simply 'having a psychological tendency as a matter of psychological fact', which is what it means in psychological hedonism, then Epicurus thus interpreted would be saying that such motivation is a psychological fact only for Epicureans. If, on the other hand, 'motivation' is used normatively, we would need to know on what basis the Epicureans came to be convinced that they ought to be so motivated.

It is not true without qualification that Epicurus in the relevant passages makes a claim only about the Epicureans. In the *Ep. Men.* he says that we recognize pleasure as an innate good (*sungenikon agathon kai sumphuton, Ep. Men.* 129,1–5) and for this reason we refer every choice and avoidance to pleasure:

For we recognize pleasure as the good which is primary and congenital; from it we begin every choice and avoidance, and we come back to it, using the feeling as the yardstick for judging every good thing. Since pleasure is the good which is primary and congenital, for this reason we do not choose every pleasure either, but we sometimes pass over many pleasures in cases when their outcome for us is a greater quantity of discomfort. (*Ep. Men.* 129,1–7)[4]

When he speaks about referring all choice to pleasure, he may well be speaking and probably does speak about the Epicureans only. But he says they do so because they recognize it as an *innate* good. Of course, to say that they recognize pleasure as a good is to make a value claim about it, and it may be that this is a statement that concerns only Epicureans who are ethical hedonists. But he also says that these people recognize pleasure as an innate good too, and, unless we take Epicurus to be claiming that the Epicureans are already born with an innate ethical theory, we should take this to be a descriptive claim about psychology, and most likely not only about the psychology of a subset of people who end up becoming Epicureans.

In the *De Finibus* we read that, as soon as every animal is born, it seeks pleasure and receives it as good, while it avoids pain. This happens before the mind is sufficiently mature to hold beliefs. It is what animals, including humans, do naturally, on account of being the kind of beings that they are. No belief or argument is needed. The animal actually *senses* pleasure as good, in the same way it senses that fire is hot:

---

[3] Cooper (1999), 486–9.

[4] All translations are from Long and Sedley (1987). The Greek text: ταύτην γὰρ ἀγαθὸν πρῶτον καὶ συγγενικὸνἔγνωμεν, καὶ ἀπὸ ταύτης καταρχόμεθα πάσης αἱρέσεως καὶ φυγῆς, καὶ ἐπὶ ταύτην καταντῶμεν ὡς κανόνι τῷ πάθει πᾶν ἀγαθὸν κρίνοντες. Καὶ ἐπεὶ πρῶτον ἀγαθὸν τοῦτο καὶ σύμφυτον, διὰ τοῦτο καὶ οὐ πᾶσαν ἡδονὴν αἱρούμεθα, ἀλλ' ἔστιν ὅτε πολλὰς ἡδονὰς ὑπερβαίνομεν, ὅταν πλεῖον ἡμῖν τὸ δυσχερὲς ἐκ τούτων ἔπηται.

Hence he says there is no need to prove or discuss why pleasure should be pursued and pain avoided. He thinks these things are sensed just like the heat of fire, the whiteness of snow. (*De Fin.* 1.30)[5]

Torquatus appeals to intuition to offer an even stronger argument. If men were deprived of all sensation, he says, they would have nothing left on the basis of which to pursue or avoid anything:

What does it [nature] perceive or what does it judge except pleasure and pain as a basis for its pursuit or avoidance of anything? (*De Fin.* 1.30–1)[6]

I take this to mean that the removal of sensation eradicates motivation for the sole reason that it eliminates the possibility of feeling pleasure or pain. Eliminating this possibility renders non-functional whatever innate tendency the animal—including the human animal—may have for orienting itself toward, or away from, anything. Feelings of pleasure and pain are indispensable if such a tendency is to be active, and so they are what motivation, considered as an aspect of human psychology, is ultimately referred to.

It is clear that the validity of these statements concerning psychology is not confined to Epicureans; they are meant to be valid for all animals, and hence also the nature of the human psyche in general. What we have here is, first, a general claim about human psychology—as well as animal psychology in general. Humans are naturally attracted to pleasure and have a natural aversion toward pain. Torquatus' further deprivation-of-all-sensation argument makes the stronger claim that pleasure and pain are, as a matter of psychological fact, the only things to which humans respond motivationally. Then, we get an axiological claim and a justification for it. Pleasure is a good and human beings recognize it as such. The reason it is a good for humans is that they have a natural psychological tendency to move toward pleasure and away from pain. They recognize it as such as a consequence of precisely this psychological tendency. This is what Epicurus confirms when he says that all good and bad lies in sensation: *epei pan agathon kai kakon en aisthēsei* (*Ep. Men.* 124,7).

On the basis of this evidence we have a clear-cut case of ethical hedonism argued for on the basis of psychological hedonism. As a claim about psychology, the latter carries no normative weight. It says nothing about whether doing as we are psychologically inclined to do is good or bad. However, Epicurus interprets the fact that we are naturally inclined for pleasure and against pain as nature's sign that we ought to go for pleasure as good and shun pain as bad.[7] It is nature that reveals to humans the former as having value, and the latter as having disvalue. Moreover, since natural

---

[5] *Itaque negat opus esse ratione neque disputatione quamobrem voluptas expetenda, fugiendus dolor est. Sentiri haec putat, ut calere ignem, nivem esse albam.*

[6] *Ea [natura] quid percipit aut quid iudicat, quo aut petat aut fugiat aliquid, praeter voluptatem et dolorem?*

[7] Cf. *Ep. Men.* 129.1–7, cited on the previous page.

inclination is solely for pleasure and against pain, only pleasure is good and only pain is bad.

There can be little doubt, and it has hardly been doubted, that Epicurus is an ethical hedonist. But the only argument for ethical hedonism we find in the available evidence is that humans are naturally inclined for pleasure and against pain. Unless we credit Epicurus with psychological hedonism, we remain in the dark as to what may have convinced him of ethical hedonism.

II

As an ethical hedonist Epicurus claims that pleasure is the only good and pain the only bad. But he says less than many might have wished about what he takes pleasure or pain to be. He does say pleasure is a feeling (*pathos*, cf. *Ep. Men.* 129), and implies that pain is a feeling too. They are both feelings that come about as a result of, and thus depend on, sensation. Hence, Epicurus is able to say, as we have seen, that all good and bad lies in sensation: *epei pan agathon kai kakon en aisthēsei* (*Ep. Men.* 124,7). However, Epicurus does not offer a precise characterization of either pleasure or pain, most likely because he does not think he needs to do so. After all, he calls pleasure something *symphyton* and *syngeniton*, implying that it, in that way, is immediately recognizable to humans for the thing that it is. Therefore, no more detailed account of it is needed for his purposes. However, in the *De Finibus* we get useful information on what pleasure and pain range over: 'everything in which we rejoice is pleasure, just as everything which distresses us is pain.'[8]

Epicurus is a materialist who believes that feelings presuppose a suitable atomic arrangement on which they supervene. So pleasure and pain are not themselves that arrangement. Pleasure is an experiential state, an element of the subject's conscious life, and the same is also true of pain. Pleasure designates an experiential state of a subject that the subject who is in that state finds agreeable, and pain one he finds disagreeable.

When Epicurus says that all good and bad lies in sensation, we should take his point to be not that nothing else has value, but that only pleasure has intrinsic value and only pain has intrinsic disvalue. Characterizing the value or disvalue of some-thing as 'intrinsic' indicates that this something has value or disvalue in virtue of being what it is and nothing else. Other things, such as tasty meals or bitter medicines, can be good or bad derivatively.[9] I use 'derivatively' as a generic term for all kinds of value or disvalue constructed by reference to pleasure or pain.[10] So, for instance, we may say that the waiter approaching to take Paul's order is instrumen-tally related to the pleasure Paul expects to get from having his dinner, and so his

---

[8] *omne autem id, quo gaudemus, voluptas est, ut omne quo offendimur, dolor*; I.37.
[9] Cf. *Ep. Men.* 129; *De Fin.* I. 29–30.
[10] For a distinction between pleasure and its cause see also (Key Doctrines *KD*) 8.

value for Paul is instrumental, whereas Paul's actually having his dinner is constitutively related to the pleasure he gets from having it, and has, as such, constitutive
value.

There is an interesting complication in Epicurus' axiology that needs to be taken
into account. Not everything in which we take pleasure or because of which we feel
pain is good or bad—though of course the pleasure we take is good and the pain we
feel bad. So, for instance, Epicurus says that death is nothing to us, by which he
means that it has zero value. Now Epicurus knows that the prospect of one's own
death is, as a matter of fact, a cause of apprehension in some way or another for one.
At the same time, he broadly characterizes any negative feeling as pain. But if pain is
invariably bad,[11] it is unclear how it is that the disvalue of the pain caused by the
belief that one will inevitably die does not spill over to that which causes it, namely
the prospect of one's death. Here is where we need to have a look at a crucial notion
in Epicurus' axiology, namely the one that goes by the name 'empty' (*kenon*).

We may distinguish between two ways in which pleasure and pain are caused
according to Epicurus. For he holds that there exist physical and psychic pleasures,[12]
to which there correspond interestingly distinct, but unfortunately neglected, processes of causation.

Anything that causes the pleasures and pains referred to as physical does so
immediately, that is, as the subject actually makes contact with the things *themselves*
that are the causes of these feelings; when one enjoys a meal, it is the having itself of
the meal that causes pleasure, as one is having it, and it is the taking itself of the bitter
medicine that causes pain as one takes it. We may call the causes of such pleasures or
pains immediate. Psychic pleasures and pains, on the other hand, are caused by way
of beliefs, as past events are brought to awareness through memory beliefs, or future
events are anticipated through expectation beliefs. But also, and as importantly,
psychic pleasure or pain may be experienced as one makes perceptual contact with
something, though not by this something itself, but through an interpretative belief
the subject holds about it. We will say that pleasures and pains caused in this way are
caused *mediately*, and the things or events that these beliefs are about we will say are
mediate causes.

Epicurus holds that all immediate causes of pleasure or pain are good or bad
derivatively, depending on whether they cause pleasure or pain. Things, however,
become complicated with the mediate causes of pleasure or pain, as Epicurus does
not take all of them to be good or bad. Though all feelings of pain are bad, not all
mediate causes of this sort need be bad, despite the fact that they cause feelings of
pain, and similarly with pleasure. Whether they are or not depends on the truth-value
of the belief through which they cause these feelings. If they are true representations
of the world, the feelings they cause are properly caused, and they are proper causes

---

[11] Cf. Diogenes Laertius, x. 3.   [12] See Diogenes Laertius, x. 137.

of these feelings. If they are false, these feelings are not properly caused, and they are not proper causes of them. Only the proper mediate causes of pleasure or pain are (derivatively) bad.[13]

It is on this basis that Epicurus thinks he can argue that the fear of death is irrational. Nothing can be done about the fact that pain is bad, and that this fear too, as pain, is bad. What he does say is that this is an empty pain; death pains us emptily (*kenōs lypei*) because it is caused by a belief that misrepresents death. Epicurus believes that if the correct beliefs about death replace the mistaken ones people hold about it, they will not cause pain to those who come to hold them, and so people's fear of death will disappear.

We can have empty pains or pleasures only in the context of mediate causation of these feelings. Characterizing a feeling as *kenon* amounts simply to claiming that it is caused through false beliefs. Though scholars tend to take *kenon* as a straightforwardly normative notion, it is in fact a purely descriptive one. It also has the same sense when it is used in connection with desire, as we are going to see. However, as we saw briefly in Epicurus' statement about death, the notion does have normative implications, and, when we return to the notion in connection with desires, we shall have to understand how this is so.[14]

Epicurus is more famous for having drawn the following distinction between pleasures. According to Diogenes Laertius' report from the *Peri haireseōn kai phygōn*, we have a kind of pleasure referred to as kinetic and another one referred to as katastematic. Formally, both kinds of pleasure are characterized in terms of pain. Kinetic is the pleasure produced in an agent as pain is being removed. Katastematic is the pleasure the agent has in the state of absence of all pain, physical and mental.

This kind of distinction between two kinds of pleasure arguably finds support in the *Ep. Men.*:

For the steady observation of these things makes it possible to refer every choice and avoidance to the health of the body and the soul's freedom from disturbance, since this is the end belonging to the blessed life. For this is what we aim at in all our actions—to be free from pain and anxiety. Once we have got this, all the soul's tumult is released, since the creature cannot go as if in pursuit of something it needs and search for any second thing as the means of maximizing the good of the soul and the body. For the time when we need pleasure is when we are in pain from the absence of pleasure. [But when we are not in pain] we no longer need pleasure. This is why we say that pleasure is the beginning and end of the blessed life. (*Ep. Men.* 128,1–11)[15]

---

[13] All causes of pleasure apart from the non-proper mediate causes are axiologically good and all causes of pain apart from the non-proper mediate ones are axiologically bad. At the same time it is important to bear in mind that the importance Epicurus assigns to prudential considerations would make it true that also immediate and proper mediate causes of pleasure can be bad, prudentially, and immediate and proper mediate causes of pain good in the same way.

[14] For a fuller exposition of the distinction between immediate and mediate pleasures see Dimas (2014b), 57–62.

[15] τούτων γὰρ ἀπλανὴς θεωρία πᾶσαν αἵρεσιν καὶ φυγὴν ἐπανάγειν οἶδεν ἐπὶ τὴν τοῦ σώματος ὑγίειαν καὶ τὴν τῆς ψυχῆς ἀταραξίαν, ἐπεὶ τοῦτο τοῦ μακαρίως ζῆν ἐστι τέλος. τούτου γὰρ χάριν πάντα πράττομεν, ὅπως

The state that the soul is in when it is free from disturbance, the state of *ataraxia*, is one of calm. But Epicurus also says this is a pleasant state to be in.

> When we say that the end is in pleasure, we don't mean the pleasures of the profligate and those lying in enjoyment, as think some who are ignorant and do not agree with us, or do not understand, but the freedom from pain in the body and from disturbance in the soul.[16]

Following tradition, it is to this pleasure we shall be referring as katastematic, and we shall be referring to all the other pleasures that the subject experiences as the subject is released from pain as kinetic. And we shall follow Epicurus in referring to the state a subject is in when having katastematic pleasure as one of *ataraxia* or calm. It is clear from the passages above that, according to Epicurus, there is no time at which an agent in a conscious state does not experience pleasure or pain. We do not have a positive characterization by him of what it is like to be experiencing katastematic pleasure, as we do not have any characterization of what it is like to be experiencing any pleasure. But I strongly doubt he thinks of it as a sort of activity one engages in while in the state of *ataraxia*, as has been suggested.[17] I take Epicurus' view as regards katastematic pleasure to be that, when achieved, the state of *ataraxia* has itself experiential content, and that this content may be characterized as a deeply felt contentment permeating the conscious life of the agent. If asked, an agent in such a state would probably not have more to say than that he feels very well. But that would be a direct report on his experiential state, not a report on a reflection upon activities he engages in when being in that state.

There is an all-important and much-neglected difference between kinetic and katastematic pleasure of which it is crucial that we become aware. It may be that it has not been duly appreciated because of some obscure remarks in the *De Finibus*, where Torquatus speaks about the final and ultimate end (*extremum et ultimum*) as being pleasure, without qualification. Torquatus says: 'this [the ultimate end] Epicurus situates in pleasure, which he wants to be the greatest good, with pain as the greatest bad.'[18] But in the passage from the *Ep. Men.* above, Epicurus points to an axiological difference between kinetic and katastematic pleasure. Now Epicurus is clear that every pleasure is an intrinsic good. However, his view, I propose, is that katastematic

μήτε ἀλγῶμεν μήτε ταρβῶμεν. ὅταν δὲ ἅπαξ τοῦτο περὶ ἡμᾶς γένηται, λύεται πᾶς ὁ τῆς ψυχῆς χειμών, οὐκ ἔχοντος τοῦ ζῴου βαδίζειν ὡς πρὸς ἐνδέον τι καὶ ζητεῖν ἕτερον ᾧ τὸ τῆς ψυχῆς καὶ τοῦ σώματος ἀγαθὸν συμπληρώσεται. τότε γὰρ ἡδονῆς χρείαν ἔχομεν, ὅταν ἐκ τοῦ μὴ παρεῖναι τὴν ἡδονὴν ἀλγῶμεν· <ὅταν δὲ μὴ ἀλγῶμεν> οὐκέτι τῆς ἡδονῆς δεόμεθα. Καὶ διὰ τοῦτο τὴν ἡδονὴν ἀρχὴν καὶ τέλος λέγομεν εἶναι τοῦ μακαρίως ζῆν.

[16] Ὅταν οὖν λέγωμεν ἡδονὴν τέλος ὑπάρχειν, οὐ τὰς τῶν ἀσώτων ἡδονὰς καὶ τὰς ἐν ἀπολαύσει κειμένας λέγομεν, ὥς τινες ἀγνοοῦντες καὶ οὐχ ὁμολογοῦντες ἢ κακῶς ἐκδεχόμενοι νομίζουσιν, ἀλλὰ τὸ μήτε ἀλγεῖν κατὰ σῶμα μήτε ταράττεσθαι κατὰ ψυχήν (*Ep. Men.* 131, 8–12).

[17] As claims Cooper (1999), 498.

[18] *Hoc Epicurus in voluptate ponit, quod summum bonum esse vult, summumque malum dolorem* (*De Fin* 1.29).

pleasure, and only it, is also the final good.[19] There is no other end for which this is a means. And, most importantly, no other pleasure than the katastematic one is sought only for its own sake and not for the sake of anything else. Hence Epicurus' eudaemonist ethics declares katastematic pleasure the greatest good (*summum bonum*). As eudaemonist, it claims that happiness is the end at which all humans aim in their actions; they want it for what it is and for the sake of nothing else, and katastematic pleasure is the constituent of their happiness.

We should now be able to make sense of some poorly understood statements Epicurus makes about pleasures, simply by deducing them from his claim about the final end.[20] First, he says that katastematic pleasure never increases. There is a good formal reason for this, obviously, since it is the greatest good. For if the pleasure of a certain state of *ataraxia* were greater than the pleasure of another such state, we would have to admit to the absurd claim that something which is greatest could be greater than something else which is also greatest.

Second, since katastematic pleasure is the greatest good, kinetic pleasures must be lesser goods. There is no formal reason, therefore, that would prevent them from varying in magnitude. So Epicurus also says that kinetic pleasures can increase in intensity, but they reach a limit when the state of katastematic pleasure is achieved:

> The pleasure in the flesh does not increase when once the pain of need has been removed, but it is only varied. And the limit of pleasure in the mind is produced by rationalizing those very things and their congeners which used to present the mind with its greatest fears. (*KD* 18)[21]

There is a further crucial consequence, the point of which may be easily missed. Since only katastematic pleasure is the final end, no kinetic pleasure can be a final end. As pleasures, they are, of course, good, and this is a reason for which they are being procured. But this is not the only reason they are being procured, because if it were, they would also be final ends. Since all actions ultimately aim at the final end, procuring kinetic pleasures is bound to be highlighting additional motivation, aside from the fact that they are intrinsic goods. Indeed, apart from being intrinsically good, kinetic pleasures are also good because they are instruments for achieving the ultimate good.

This is confirmed in *Ep. Men.* 128,1–11.[22] There, Epicurus remarks that rational choice presupposes the right understanding of the final good. Clearly the choice referred to here cannot concern the final good. Being final, this is not chosen; it is only aimed at. The choice in question can only concern the goods that are not final, including

---

[19] Cf. Annas (1993), 238, 335.

[20] A number of difficulties in interpreting how Epicurus understands pleasure are discussed in Nikolsky (2001).

[21] Οὐκ ἐπαύξεται ἐν τῇ σαρκὶ ἡ ἡδονή, ἐπειδὰν ἅπαξ τὸ κατ᾽ ἔνδειαν ἀλγοῦν ἐξαιρεθῇ, ἀλλὰ μόνον ποικίλλεται. τῆς δὲ διανοίας τὸ πέρας τὸ κατὰ τὴν ἡδονὴν ἀπεγέννησεν ἥ τε τούτων αὐτῶν ἐκλόγισις καὶ τῶν ὁμογενῶν τούτοις, ὅσα τοὺς μεγίστους φόβους παρεσκεύαζε τῇ διανοίᾳ.

[22] See p. 170, this volume, where the passage is cited in full.

kinetic pleasures. This marks a departure from classical hedonism, which is typically thought not to leave room for the ranking of pleasures. If pleasure is simply the good, nothing outside the subject's preference can support claims that some pleasures are better. Not so with Epicurus. For his axiology is two-dimensional. All pleasures are choice-worthy as intrinsic goods but, since only katastematic pleasure is the final good, kinetic pleasures are also chosen for their instrumental value. Though their intrinsic value provides no basis for ranking them, their instrumental value does.

Also prudential versions of classical hedonism allow that pleasures be treated as instrumental goods. Indeed instrumental value can often override intrinsic value, which all pleasures have in classical hedonism, in decisions pertaining to maximizing a specific pleasure. But classical hedonism, even of the prudential sort, has no advice to offer as to what pleasure the agent ought to maximize. Epicurus' characterization of the final end offers a firm objective basis for ranking kinetic pleasures according to their instrumental value. Depending on the circumstances in which an agent finds himself, some kinetic pleasures can have more value than others to the extent that they enable the agent more efficiently to attain the final end.

At this point I want to clear up what I believe is a confusion regarding the distinction between kinetic and katastematic pleasure. It is often thought that the kinetic–katastematic distinction is between pleasures that are motions and a pleasure that is not a motion but, rather, static. This characterization of the difference is obscure and, if it has stood for so long, it is because it draws on the plausible intuition that the katastematic–kinetic distinction somehow must signify a distinction between motion and rest. If some pleasure is to be associated with rest, it must be katastematic pleasure. Hence, it becomes all too easy to infer that all other pleasures, that is, the kinetic ones, are motions. But this understanding is fundamentally wrong.

To begin with, it is unclear what it would mean for any pleasure to be a motion. Any pleasure, regardless of whether it is kinetic or katastematic, is an *aisthēsis*. All perceptions, of course, supervene on motions of atoms, but that does not make *them* motions. However, let us suppose that pleasure turns out on some account to be itself a motion. If this is to be an essential property of pleasure *as* pleasure, it must be true of all pleasures, which would also include the katastematic ones. And we would not be able to say that, really, even though pleasure is a motion, katastematic pleasure is not, without implying that Epicurus uses the term 'pleasure' homonymously. But there is no evidence anywhere that the term is used in this way among the Epicureans, while there is clear evidence to the contrary. In the *De Finibus* we read:

The pleasure we pursue is not just that which moves our actual nature with some gratification and is perceived by the senses in company with a certain delight; *we hold that to be the greatest pleasure which is perceived once all pain has been removed.* (*De Fin.* 1.37)[23]

---

[23] *enim hanc solam sequimur quae suavitate aliqua naturam ipsam movet et cum iucunditate quadam percipitur sensibus,* sed maximam voluptatem illam habemus quae percipitur omni dolore detracto.

There is zero indication here that 'pleasure' is used homonymously. And there is testimony that Epicurus himself uses the term *chara* to characterize both kinetic and katastematic pleasure. As Diogenes reports, this same term is used for kinetic pleasure in the passage from *Peri hairēseōn kai phugōn* that actually coins the terms 'kinetic' and 'katastematic.' It is also used for katastematic pleasure in a passage from the *Peri telous* quoted by Plutarch, where it is also said to be *akrotatē chara*:

The stable condition of the well-being in the body and the sure hope of its continuance holds the most extreme and certain joy for those who can correctly calculate it. (Us 68, Fr. B 11)[24]

At the same time it seems reasonable that 'kinetic' in kinetic pleasures, as opposed to 'katastematic' in the katastematic ones, should be indicative of some kind of motion. What kind this is is explained in the passage from the *De Finibus* (1.37) discussed above, where pleasure is said to be a motion in our nature (*naturam ipsam*). Notice that this passage distinguishes this motion from what is referred to as a perception of it, and it is the latter but not the former that is said to be pleasure. The motion to which the term 'kinetic' alludes, then, is quite clearly a physiological one. It is the motion during which the body moves, as it were, from a state of need to a state of balance.

Kinetic are said to be only these pleasures that are felt while pain is at the same time being eliminated, and are felt only as long as pain is being eliminated. It is the pleasures felt when—though not whenever—a physiological lack is replenished in the organism, and while it is being replenished. However, physiological lack is registered in the human psyche through perception of pain, whereas the process of replenishment is registered as a perception, which is nothing other than the pleasure felt.

On the view I propose here, an agent can have no kinetic pleasures while he is in the state of katastematic pleasure. This is precisely the point I take *KD* 3 and 18 to be making.

The pleasure in the flesh does not increase when once the pain of need has been removed, but it is only varied. And the limit of pleasure in the mind is produced by rationalizing those very things and their congeners which used to present the mind with its greatest fears. (*KD* 18)[25]

If kinetic pleasures could be had also in the state of katastematic pleasure, it is unclear why they (kinetic pleasures) could not vary in magnitude. Epicurus is categorical that they cannot. The above passage states unequivocally that the pleasures of the flesh do not increase when pain is removed, but only vary. Moreover, kinetic pleasures are felt only for as long as they alleviate pain, and they are no longer felt when pain is removed. On the other hand, katastematic pleasure is felt when the pain is removed. The same is true of kinetic pleasures that are of the mind. Once the mind rationalizes all those things that fill it with fear, the kinetic pleasure in the mind reaches its limit. Once, for

---

[24] Τὸ γὰρ εὐσταθὲς σαρκὸς κατάστημα καὶ τὸ περὶ ταύτης πιστὸν ἔλπισμα τὴν ἀκροτάτην χαρὰν καὶ βεβαιοτάτην ἔχει τοῖς ἐπιλογίζεσθαι δυναμένοις (Plutarch, *contra Ep. beat.* 1089d).

[25] Οὐκ ἐπαύξεται ἐν τῇ σαρκὶ ἡ ἡδονή, ἐπειδὰν ἅπαξ τὸ κατ' ἔνδειαν ἀλγοῦν ἐξαιρεθῇ, ἀλλὰ μόνον ποικίλλεται. τῆς δὲ διανοίας τὸ πέρας τὸ κατὰ τὴν ἡδονὴν ἀπεγέννησεν ἥ τε τούτων αὐτῶν ἐκλόγισις καὶ τῶν ὁμογενῶν τούτοις, ὅσα τοὺς μεγίστους φόβους παρεσκεύαζε τῇ διανοίᾳ.

instance, Epicurus has convinced those of us who attach disvalue to our forthcoming death that it has none, relief, that is, pleasure, replaces the negative painful feeling that accompanied the thought of our death before we were so convinced.

Of course different pleasures may be and are being felt while in the state of *ataraxia*. We are pleased in the knowledge that death is nothing to us, but this pleasure is other than the relief we feel as we become convinced that our fear of death is groundless. These, I suggest, constitute different modes of katastematic pleasure, ways in which the latter gives itself to perception representing different hues in which it becomes manifest to the agent. Reading a book, listening to music, or enjoying a drink in the state of *ataraxia* are not kinetic pleasures on top of, or on the side of, katastematic pleasure. They are not preceded by pain and in no way function as pain removers. They are simply different expressions of katastematic pleasure. Not only is the experience of katastematic pleasure a deeply felt contentment, then; it is also one that may be seasoned, and is in that way articulated, through distinct pleasurable experiential states of the subject.[26]

We can now make sense of a remark in the *Letter to Menoeceus* that has proved resistive to interpretation: 'we say that pleasure is both the beginning and end of the blessed life' (128,11–129, 1). Commentators are puzzled that Epicurus calls pleasure both *archē* and *telos*. They have opted to take this formulation as an exaggerated manner of speaking, in which both terms (*archē* and *telos*) have the same reference. I suggest that *archē* and *telos* pick up different things. The pleasure to which Epicurus refers as the beginning is kinetic, whereas the one he refers to as the end is katastematic. The beginning is the pleasure needed to remove pain, thereby contributing toward moving the subject to a katastematic state; the pleasure of this latter state, in all the varied ways it becomes manifest to the agent who is in that state, is the end. It is a pleasure the subject may lose, but not one he may use as a stepping stone to another pleasure.

III

This interpretation throws light on some difficult remarks Epicurus makes about desires that we should look at here. We do not have an analysis by him of desire. However, the way he speaks about it has a clearly recognizable affinity to Plato's view from the central passages of the *Philebus*.[27] According to Plato's schema, desire is the psychic counterpart of a physical need, one that arises because the body is disturbed from its original state of equilibrium. Desire satisfaction aims at the restoration of equilibrium in the body, and desire satisfaction is achieved as restoration takes place. The feeling corresponding to the disturbed bodily state is pain, whereas the one signaling the process of bodily restoration is pleasure.

---

[26] So I take it that, for Epicurus, katastematic pleasure cannot coexist with kinetic. But see Woolf (2009), among others, who argues that, for example, luxury may increase *kinetic* pleasure when one is already in a state of katastematic pleasure (or happiness); see esp. 171, 177.

[27] See esp. *Philebus* 34eff.

Epicurus adopts this schema for bodily desires and a suitable version of it for non-bodily desires. For he thinks there are also desires conditional upon the need for restoring calm in a soul that is disturbed. The feeling corresponding to the presence of unease in the soul, as for instance fear about the future, is pain. The feeling corresponding to restoring calm is pleasure. Hence, as these desires become satisfied, the subject experiences kinetic pleasure.

We have learned to think of desire as being quite generally for pleasure, which could suggest the view that Epicurus believes that there are desires for both kinds of pleasure. This is not the case. We do not have any evidence where Epicurus speaks about desires aiming at katastematic pleasure. In the evidence we have he only speaks of desires for kinetic pleasures, the satisfaction of which functions as a facilitator for reaching katastematic pleasure (*Ep. Men.* 127,10–1).

Repeatedly he speaks of desire as something which arises when the organism feels pain. In the section on desires in the *Letter to Menoeceus* he says that, once the state of calm is reached, that is, the state of no pain or fear, the animal need not go about looking for pleasure, the implication being clear that the cause generating desires is absent and therefore so are also the desires. Epicurus concludes: 'only then do we need pleasure, when we are in pain due to absence of pleasure. But when we are not in pain we do not need pleasure' (128, 10–11).

I take the pleasure, the absence of which is said to be causing the pain that then pushes for pleasure, to be katastematic pleasure. I take the pleasure that the pain thus caused pushes for to be kinetic. The process described here is the one generating desires as Epicurus understands them, and is set in motion by antecedent causes, not ends sought. Falling out of the state of calm, the experiential equivalent of which is katastematic pleasure, is what causes the pain referred to here. That in turn pushes for kinetic pleasure, the limit of which is reached when the state of calm is restored.

Epicurus' overall view on desire is, I suggest, non-teleological. He does not believe, as maybe did the Cyrenaics, that it is the pleasure expected that is pulling the agent; desire is not a general aiming at the end which is katastematic pleasure. Desire does of course have an end; it is to alleviate a need in order to bring the human being to a state of balance, physiological or psychological. For Epicurus, then, desires are caused by antecedent needs. Their function is to move the subject to take measures so as to remove pain, and in particular the pain that has disturbed the subject's state of calm. Removing this pain will restore the state of calm. But the desire did not come about for restoring the state of calm. It came about in order to remove the annoyance of pain. There are desires only for kinetic pleasures.

To be sure, the talk about needed pleasures does not preclude the possibility that Epicurus may also allow end-directed wishes. Presumably, he would allow for subjects gradually to be able to develop a general wish to maintain themselves in a state of katastematic pleasure. But it is significant that in his account of desire he speaks about pleasures needed in order to alleviate pain. The desires he speaks about are only for kinetic pleasures; they are kinetic desires, as we may call them, and his account for them is non-teleological. If we now couple this with the result from our discussion on pleasure, we get that in the state of katastematic pleasure subjects do not have desires for pleasures, though they do enjoy a variety of pleasures.

Of the desires Epicurus speaks about, some are said to be natural (*phusikai*) and can be necessary or non-necessary:

We must reckon that some desires are natural and others empty, and of the natural some are necessary, others natural only; and of the necessary some are necessary for happiness, others for the body's freedom from stress, and others for life itself. (*Ep. Men.* 127, 8–11)[28]

Natural are the desires Epicurus believes it is in the nature of human beings to have. They are tied to basic physiological, bodily, and psychological needs such as nutrition, protection of the body, and peace of mind. In addition there are the so-called empty desires (*kenai*). These may be about things for which there are also natural but non-necessary desires. The notion of 'empty', as applied to desires, bears similarities to its application to pleasures. Subjects get empty pleasures or pains, we recall, through beliefs that misrepresent the world. Desires as Epicurus speaks of them come about as a result of disturbance of the state of calm, and they are ultimately for restoring the subject to that state. Empty are the desires that are based on a mistaken view of the way in which this is to be achieved. Herein lies the important dividing line between necessary and non-necessary desires.

Maintaining oneself in a state of katastematic pleasure, the final end, requires a plan for obtaining the pleasures necessary for avoiding pain. Though the mechanism controlling desires is non-teleological, teleology enters the system via prudence, which declares self-sufficiency (*autarkeia*) a great good (*agathon mega*, 130, 5). But it too is good because it has instrumental value: it minimizes the agent's external dependence in securing the final end. Prudence requires that the subject has the correct view of the way in which this goal is to be achieved.

The *Letter to Menoeceus* identifies three types of necessary desires: necessary for '*eudaimonia*', for the repose of the body, and for living. These are natural because they serve needs that belong to human beings given their nature. They are necessary because they are the absolute minimum a human subject has to satisfy to stay alive, avoid bodily pain and maintain mental peace. They are for the things that relieve, or secure against, pains threatening an overall state of calm, and, as importantly, they do so at the lowest possible cost for the subject in terms of resources needed and personal energy spent. Compatibly with Epicurus' non-teleological leanings they are not characterized positively, for this or that kind of thing in particular, but solely as building the agent's defence against pain.

As regards the necessary facilities for bodily recreation and protection from adverse weather, say, a cabin may be as good in providing them as a mansion. But the cabin is easier to obtain, and therefore a desire for the pleasures it provides would

---

[28] Ἀναλογιστέον δὲ ὡς τῶν ἐπιθυμιῶν αἱ μέν εἰσι φυσικαί, αἱ δὲ κεναί, καὶ τῶν φυσικῶν αἱ μὲν ἀναγκαῖαι, αἱ δὲ φυσικαὶ μόνον· τῶν δὲ ἀναγκαίων αἱ μὲν πρὸς εὐδαιμονίαν εἰσὶν ἀναγκαῖαι, αἱ δὲ πρὸς τὴν τοῦ σώματος ἀοχλησίαν, αἱ δὲ πρὸς αὐτὸ τὸ ζῆν.

be more effectively managed. It points to a shorter path to the final end. But the distinction between necessary and non-necessary is only a functional one. In special, maybe, but possible circumstances where a mansion would be easier to obtain, the necessary would have been the desire for the mansion.

Even in normal circumstances such a desire would be natural, for it originates in the need for bodily recreation and protection. That it is not necessary even though it is natural implies that being unable to acquire, or even having to vacate, a mansion does not lead to pain so long as a cabin can be obtained. However, were the focus of the desire to be not on the mansion as satisfying basic needs but on it *as* mansion, it would no longer be natural, but the result of empty belief (*kenodoxia*); it would be an empty desire. Empty belief is a mistaken belief, one whose content does not corres-pond to anything in the actual world. There are all sorts of reasons why a belief can be mistaken, but the cause of empty beliefs in this context is a blurred view of the final end, a lack of proper understanding of it, as Epicurus says. The fact that kinetic pleasures have intrinsic as well as instrumental value may easily confuse the subject. The intrinsic value of the pleasures of a mansion may blind him to the fact that, more importantly, these are instrumental to the even more valuable intrinsic and final value of the katastematic pleasure. Or he may mistakenly think that living in a mansion is an unavoidable means for reaching katastematic pleasure. Finally, he may even come to think that such pleasures constitute the final end. All these can be reasons for which the subject may develop unjustifiably strong desires for kinetic pleasures.

Notice that when Epicurus recommends that empty desires or, for that matter, feelings of pleasure or pain, need to be expunged, it is not because he thinks that the falsity of the beliefs on which they rest is bad in itself. He could not do that, for he would then have to explain how untruth is bad in itself, when he has already said that the only thing that is bad is pain. His recommendation is functional. It only addresses the fact that false beliefs are a poor compass for orienting oneself in the world and, as such, more likely to be harmful than beneficial as instruments for securing the final end. Epicurus is explicit about this (*KD* 10).

All the evidence we have presents desires as based in a need-mechanism. Desires are for pleasures necessary for the need to eliminate, or protect against, pain. Indeed, the only desires discussed in the evidence that are strictly speaking non-need-based are the empty desires (*kenai epithumiai*). But notice that what makes them empty is that they are *thought* to be necessary, even though they *are* not. These too are treated as need-based, though mistakenly. As already anticipated, desires are only for kinetic pleasures. On Epicurus' view, therefore, subjects in katastematic pleasure have no desires. They merely wish to maintain themselves in that state. If they do have desires, this is evidence that they are not in a state of katastematic pleasure.[29]

---

[29] Cf. Rosenbaum (1990), 24.

IV

The same non-teleological need-based approach governing Epicurus' view on desire governs also his view on virtue. There is ample evidence that he takes justice and other virtues to have merely instrumental value. He does, however, make claims suggesting to many, as discussed more specifically below, that he is only a pseudo-hedonist who deep down thinks of virtue as an end in itself. Indeed, in the *Letter to Menoeceus* he declares prudence (*phronēsis*) the greatest good (132, 7), and makes also this statement:

> It [prudence (*phronēsis*)] teaches the impossibility of living pleasurably without living pru-
> dently, honorably, and justly, and the impossibility of living prudently, honorably, and justly
> without living pleasurably. (*Ep. Men.* 132, 9–11)[30]

Both legs of this claim have seemed incompatible with hedonism. According to Julia Annas, the notion of pleasure is here extended to that of living pleasurably in a way that clearly does not derive from any obvious thoughts about pleasure.[31] Annas understands the first leg as saying that prudence, honor, and justice are ends in themselves and that a life in accordance with them is pleasurable, as a consequence of being honorable and just. The explanation for this she finds in the second leg. Prudence, honor, and justice are sources of pleasure on account of being what they are, and a life of prudence, honor, and justice is pleasurable simply in virtue of being that kind of life. So pleasure must include living virtuously as something we seek for its own sake.[32]

Such an interpretation goes against the spirit of the interpretation I defend. More importantly, it goes against the letter of the relevant passages. Now, Epicurus is clear that prudence furnishes all the other virtues with value. But, for him, prudence gets its own value from its ability to recommend plans for securing the final end. He is also clear that, though philosophy provides the theoretical framework for this advice, it is ranked under prudence. Clearly, then, prudence derives its value from the final end by being a tool for securing it. If the other virtues derive their value from prudence, then it follows that they too must be deriving it from the final end through a similar mechanism as prudence.

The two-legged claim from the *Letter to Menoeceus*, therefore, demands an entirely different reading. It will be helpful to begin with the second leg, since the claim it makes is quite straightforward. If living virtuously threatens living a pleasurable life, subjects will be inclined to sacrifice virtue for pleasure. Therefore the only way to secure that one leads a virtuous life is if such a life is compatible with living pleasurably.

---

[30] φρόνησις ... διδάσκουσα ὡς οὐκ ἔστιν ἡδέως ζῆν ἄνευ τοῦ φρονίμως καὶ καλῶς καὶ δικαίως, <οὐδὲ φρονίμως καὶ καλῶς καὶ δικαίως> ἄνευ τοῦ ἡδέως. συμπεφύκασι γὰρ αἱ ἀρεταὶ τῷ ζῆν ἡδέως καὶ τὸ ζῆν ἡδέως τούτων ἐστὶν ἀχώριστον.

[31] Annas (1993), 340–3.   [32] Annas (1993), 340–3.

To make sense of this passage we need to understand the first leg compatibly with the second, or so I claim. The following, I suggest, is the correct way to understand it. Prudence is indispensable because it is the prime instrument in the service of a pleasurable life. It is for this reason that it is valuable. Moreover, the other virtues get whatever value they have from prudence. If that is so, then their value also consists in their being instruments for living a pleasurable life. They, as prudence, are indispensable purely for their instrumental value. They are indispensable for living a pleasurable life not because they are goods in their own right, possessing which supplies the agent with pleasure; they secure a pleasurable life because they are indispensable instruments for it.

Finally, I would like to turn to Epicurus' position on friendship because this is the point at which a hedonistic interpretation of Epicurus seems to have come under strong pressure. It has been said that he is of two minds about it.[33] We find remarks in the *De Finibus* on the Epicurean view to the effect that one ought to love the friend as much as one loves oneself:

Friendships are not only the most loyal aides to pleasures but also their producers both for friends and ourselves, who enjoy them in the present and are inspired with hope for the near and distant future. Thus it is not possible to secure uninterrupted gratification in life without friendship nor yet to preserve true friendship unless we love our friends as much as we love ourselves. Hence this is a fact brought about in friendship and friendship is connected with pleasure. (*De Fin.* 1.67)[34]

Either such remarks are a sign that Epicurus abandons hedonism, realizing that people can learn to be motivated by things other than pleasure, or his position is inherently unstable, aiming at a hedonistic account of friendship, while at the same time succumbing to the idea that friends have intrinsic value.[35]

In reading this passage from the *De Finibus*, it is important to bear in mind that Torquatus structures his exposition as a response to objections by opponents to Epicureanism that, if pleasure is the greatest good, friendship will cease to exist (*De Fin.* 1. 66). Torquatus aims to show that Epicurean hedonistic axiology allows for as genuine a friendship as one would wish. The core claim of this exposition is, clearly, that friendship is inseparable from pleasure. He offers two reasons for this claim. First, life without friends would be full of dangers, entailing an overwhelming risk of unease. In addition to being effective as means to the final end, friendship is itself a

[33] Annas (1993), 342.

[34] *amicitiae non modo fautrices fidelissimae sed etiam effectrices sunt voluptatum tam amicis quam sibi, quibus non solum praesentibus fruuntur, sed etiam spe eriguntur consequentis ac posteri temporis. quod quia nullo modo sine amicitia firmam et perpetuam iucunditatem vitae tenere possumus neque vero ipsam amicitiam tueri, nisi aeque amicos et nosmet ipsos diligamus, idcirco et hoc ipsum efficitur in amicitia, et amicitia cum voluptate conectitur.*

[35] Such an interpretation of the Epicurean view is presented, for example, by Rist (1980): although the bulk of his argument stresses the contractual nature of Epicurean friendship as bringing security and other advantages to the friends, he still maintains that it is 'valuable per se' (124).

producer of pleasure.[36] What we have here, then, is the same justificatory principle as we do for the virtues. Friendship is instrumental both in reaching and in contributing to secure katastematic pleasure.

The passage then goes on to a second phase of argument containing the seemingly contra-hedonistic advice that one ought to love one's friends as much as one loves oneself. Now notice that Torquatus does not simply assert this. He offers it as the inference of an argument, which we shall do well to try and identify if we want to understand the claim this inference makes. Friendship is indispensable for pleasure, and the only way to protect friendship is if one comes to love the friend as one loves oneself. That friendship is indispensable for pleasure is the consideration that assumes precedence. Then comes the premise that in order to secure friendship one needs to love the friend as one loves oneself. Here too, then, the justification for the feelings one needs to develop toward the friend is referred to pleasure.

On this account of the Epicurean position on friendship there is no sign that Epicurus departs from hedonism. But this forces the second question. Is the Epicurean position on friendship unstable, caught between accepting the need to assign intrinsic value to friendship and a strict adherence to hedonism?

In trying to answer this question, we may start by noting that Epicurus' position is unequivocally egoistic. It is the love I have for myself that moves me to have you as my friend. But to make you my friend, I need to make myself attractive to you. So, what do I do? I start with the reasonable assumption that you love yourself as I love myself. To make myself attractive to you I need to tend to the love you have for yourself. It is impossible for me to love you as you love yourself, but I can do the second best thing: I can bring myself to love you as I love myself. So one can come to love the friend as one loves oneself, then, and one's motivation for doing so need be nothing other than the love one has for oneself.

A reason why one might not be satisfied with this answer is that the love for the friend must somehow be unselfish. I believe Epicurus has a rejoinder that does not violate the common intuitions about friendship. If you love me as much as you love yourself, would I care that this is because of your love for yourself? I think not, and more importantly, I don't see why I should. If it really is the love for yourself that makes you love me as much as you love yourself, then this is decisive evidence that you consider me extremely important, indeed as important as you consider yourself. What this is a sign of is not only that you consider me as valuable as you do yourself, but, even more importantly, that you cannot properly value yourself unless you also value me as much.

Defending Epicurus against objections regarding selfishness is no defense of his hedonist account of friendship. Egoism does not by itself commit anyone to hedonism. It might seem that, Epicurus' egoistic leanings notwithstanding, loving the other

---

[36] Cf. *De Fin.* 1.67, cited on the previous page.

as one loves oneself presupposes treating the other as one treats oneself, namely as an end. But this need not follow. Loving the other as one loves oneself does not imply doing so for the same reason one loves oneself. All it implies is that the strength and commitment of the feeling one has for the other is the same as the strength and commitment of the feeling one has for oneself. On some views one's selfish motivation for loving the friend is the desire to become oneself virtuous. In the case of Epicurus, the motivation for loving another is that the other is seen as the greatest source of pleasure for one.

However, we have not yet answered the charge that Epicurus' treatment of friendship is a sign that he abandons hedonism, or that, if he does not, his position is unstable in that it is forced to allow that things other that pleasure have intrinsic value. The above interpretation of his account of friendship leaves wide open the possibility that humans treat themselves as ends in themselves, and hence they ought also so to treat their friends. If this is so, more things than just pleasure are ends, namely ourselves and our friends. Inadvertently, and largely due to the difficulty of harmonizing friendship with hedonism, Epicurus would then seem forced to abandon hedonism or be an inconsistent hedonist.

The motivation for such an objection is likely to be the overwhelmingly influential Aristotelian idea that we are somehow ends, and friends are to be treated in the same way, as ends. Though this is not the place for a full exposition, it would be useful to reflect shortly on reasons why this idea would sound very strange to Epicurus. If, as I claim, he holds that the only thing having intrinsic value is pleasure, then nothing can be ascribed value without reference to pleasure. The *Letter to Menoeceus* is emphatic that every good and bad lies in sensation; the passage from the *De Finibus* is clear that value disappears if sensation is removed. There are many more. Therefore, there is no room, if Epicurus is to be consistent, for the self or one's own self, to have intrinsic value. In fact, I want to claim, in Epicurus' view it does not. The Epicurean notion of the 'self' is confined to the physical arrangement comprising one's body, as well as one's psychological set-up, which is comprised of sensations and one's set of beliefs. The body provides for the capacity to feel and perceive, and though it is valuable for this reason, its value is derived, in that it is causally involved in the production of pleasure, and as being what feels pleasure. Precisely of this kind is also the value of beliefs. This is what *De Finibus* 1.68, discussed above, confirms by cashing out the proper feeling to have toward the friend—which is the proper feeling one ought to have toward oneself—in terms of working for the friend's pleasure as one works for one's own. Loving oneself, therefore, amounts to tending to oneself as a vehicle for perceiving pleasure, and that is precisely what loving the friend amounts to, namely making oneself a vehicle for the pleasure of the friend.

Epicurus' claims on friendship do not signal a rejection of hedonism; nor do they destabilize his hedonism. His hedonism may account for the fundamental intuitions on friendship, while at the same time being able to point to plausible conditions for the termination of friendship.

9

How Feasible Is the Stoic Conception of *Eudaimonia*?

Katerina Ierodiakonou

I. Introduction: Human Beings Can in Principle Have a Happy Life

Therefore, the goal becomes 'to live consistently with nature', i.e. according to one's own nature and that of the universe, doing nothing which is forbidden by the common law, which is right reason, penetrating all things, being the same as Zeus who is the leader of the administration of things. And this itself is the virtue of the happy man and a smooth flow of life, whenever all things are done according to the harmony of the daimon in each of us with the will of the administrator of the universe. (Diogenes Laertius 7.88;[1] trans. B. Inwood and L. Gerson)

Terence Irwin (2006, 345–6) summarizes the three fundamental doctrines of the Stoic ethical theory in the following way: (i) Eudaemonism: the ultimate end for rational action is the agent's own happiness. (ii) Naturalism: happiness and virtue consist in living in accordance with nature. (iii) Moralism: moral virtue is to be chosen for its own sake and is to be preferred above any combination of items with non-moral value. The Stoics, he further adds, took these three doctrines to be inseparable: The correct grasp of human happiness shows that it consists in living according with nature, which requires living according with virtue in preference to any other aim. Following Aristotle, the Stoics claimed that the human good consists in the fulfilment of human nature, understood as the nature of a rational agent. The things that accord with this rational nature include health, safety, wealth, and the other things that Aristotle regarded as external goods and the Stoics called 'preferred

---

[1] διόπερ τέλος γίνεται τὸ ἀκολούθως τῇ φύσει ζῆν, ὅπερ ἐστὶ κατά τε τὴν αὐτοῦ καὶ κατὰ τὴν τῶν ὅλων, οὐδὲν ἐνεργοῦντας ὧν ἀπαγορεύειν εἴωθεν ὁ νόμος ὁ κοινός, ὅσπερ ἐστὶν ὁ ὀρθὸς λόγος, διὰ πάντων ἐρχόμενος, ὁ αὐτὸς ὢν τῷ Διί, καθηγεμόνι τούτῳ τῆς τῶν ὄντων διοικήσεως ὄντι· εἶναι δ' αὐτὸ τοῦτο τὴν τοῦ εὐδαίμονος ἀρετὴν καὶ εὔροιαν βίου, ὅταν πάντα πράττηται κατὰ τὴν συμφωνίαν τοῦ παρ' ἑκάστῳ δαίμονος πρὸς τὴν τοῦ τῶν ὅλων διοικητοῦ βούλησιν.

indifferents' (*proēgmena adiaphora*); but they mainly include the exercise of rational nature in rational efforts, and this exercise of rational nature is virtue.

So, the Stoics seem to have been optimists concerning the attainability of human *eudaimonia*, or happiness. Divine reason rules the cosmos and gives structure to the best possible world. Human nature, too, is rational, so that it can perfectly apprehend and adjust to the order of the universe. There is no irrational part in the human soul that poses insurmountable obstacles for ultimately achieving a fine-tuning of the human life with the cosmic realm. This life according to nature ensures for human beings the enduring tranquillity that defines, in Stoic ethics, *eudaimonia*. For human happiness presupposes a virtuous life, and human virtue depends on the excellence and exercise of our rational capacities. To put it briefly, the Stoics believed that only those of us who are wise are virtuous, and therefore happy. But is this optimism justifiable, realistic, feasible? If, according to the Stoics, human beings can in principle be happy, does this imply that they actually attain happiness, at least to some degree?

II. Do Human Beings actually Attain Happiness, at least to some Degree?

The Stoics often repeated that, with very few notable exceptions, there are no wise men, that the Stoic philosophers themselves were not wise, that wise men are as rare as the Ethiopian phoenix.[2] Ordinary people are in their majority fools, since it is extremely difficult to possess knowledge and act virtuously. Indeed, although ordinary people may acquire over time a better understanding of certain things, as long as they do not realize in full their rational nature, they cannot be said to be virtuous and reach happiness. That is to say, the Stoics insisted that human beings are either wise or fools, and thus either virtuous or vicious; there are no degrees of virtue and vice, or in other words, virtue and vice do not admit of intensification (*epitasis*) and relaxation (*anesis*):[3]

> They [i.e. the Stoics] think that all goods are equal and that every good is worth choosing in the highest degree and does not admit of being more or less intense. They say that of existing things, some are good, some bad, and some neither. The virtues—prudence, justice, courage, temperance, and others—are good; and their opposites—imprudence, injustice, and the others—are bad; neither good nor bad are those things which neither benefit nor harm, such as life, health, pleasure, beauty, strength, wealth, good reputation, noble birth, and their

---

[2] e.g. Plutarch, *De Stoic. rep.* 1048E; Sextus Empiricus, *M* 7.432; 11.181; *PH* 1.91; Alexander, *De fato* 199.14–22. For Socrates', Diogenes', and Zeno's portraits as Stoic paradigms of wise men, see for instance Epictetus, *Diss.* 3.21.18–19; 4.8.31.

[3] According to Ammonius (*in Isag.* 98.3–7), the philosophical use of the terms 'ἐπίτασις' and 'ἄνεσις' has its origin in music. They are often used as opposites in connection with the chords of a musical instrument, and also in characterizing the produced sounds; that is, increasing the tension of a chord produces a higher sound, whereas reducing its tension produces a lower sound, and so 'ἄνεσις' is connected with low sounds and 'ἐπίτασις' with high sounds. Cf. Ierodiakonou (1999), 155–6.

opposites death, disease, pain, ugliness, weakness, poverty, bad reputation, low birth, and such things... For these things are not good, but things indifferent in the category of preferred things. (Diogenes Laertius 7.101–2;[4] trans. B. Inwood and L. Gerson. Cf. also: Plutarch, *De virt. mor.* 449F–450A)

The analogies which the Stoics employed to stress that there is nothing between the virtuous wise men and the vicious ordinary people are illuminating:

(i)   A stick is either straight or crooked (Diogenes Laertius 7.127; Simplicius, *in Cat.* 237.29–238.1).

(ii) A man drowns in the sea whether he is an arm's length from the surface or five hundred fathoms (Plutarch, *De comm. not.* 1063A–B).

(iii) The blind are blind, even if they are going to recover their sight a little later (Plutarch, *De comm. not.* 1063A–B; Cicero, *De fin.* 3.48; 4.64).

(iv) However close people come to their destinations, they are not yet there (Diogenes Laertius 7.120).[5]

In addition to these notorious Stoic analogies, there are three texts by Porphyry, Simplicius, and Boethius, which also refer to the Stoics' view that there are no degrees of virtue, though these texts are less frequently quoted in the context of Stoic ethics. In their commentaries of Aristotle's *Categories*, and in particular in their comments about whether the Aristotelian category of quality admits of the more and the less, Porphyry (*in Cat.* 137.23–8.32), Simplicius (*in Cat.* 284.12–5.8), and Boethius (*in Cat.* 257B–C) all discuss the intensification (*epitasis/intentio*) and relaxation (*anesis/ relaxatio, diminutio*) of qualities (*poiotētes*) as well as of the corresponding qualified things, their qualia (*poia*). According to these commentators, there are at least three different views expressed in antiquity on this issue:

(i)   The first view, which Porphyry and Boethius attribute to some unidentified Platonists, while Simplicius attributes it to Plotinus himself, advocates that all qualities of material things, as well as their qualia, admit of intensification and relaxation, because matter itself admits of the more and the less.

(ii) The second view, which they all attribute to Aristotle, distinguishes between the qualities themselves, which do not admit of intensification and relaxation, and their qualia, which on the contrary may admit of the more and the less; for

---

[4] δοκεῖ δὲ πάντα τὰ ἀγαθὰ ἴσα εἶναι καὶ πᾶν ἀγαθὸν ἐπ' ἄκρον εἶναι αἱρετὸν καὶ μήτ' ἄνεσιν μήτ' ἐπίτασιν ἐπιδέχεσθαι. τῶν δ' ὄντων φασὶ τὰ μὲν ἀγαθὰ εἶναι, τὰ δὲ κακά, τὰ δ' οὐδέτερα. Ἀγαθὰ μὲν οὖν τάς τ' ἀρετάς, φρόνησιν, δικαιοσύνην, ἀνδρείαν, σωφροσύνην καὶ τὰ λοιπά· κακὰ δὲ τὰ ἐναντία, ἀφροσύνην, ἀδικίαν καὶ τὰ λοιπά. οὐδέτερα δὲ ὅσα μήτ' ὠφελεῖ μήτε βλάπτει, οἷον ζωή, ὑγίεια, ἡδονή, κάλλος, ἰσχύς, πλοῦτος, εὐδοξία, εὐγένεια· καὶ τὰ τούτοις ἐναντία, θάνατος, νόσος, πόνος, αἶσχος, ἀσθένεια, πενία, ἀδοξία, δυσγένεια καὶ τὰ παραπλήσια... μὴ γὰρ εἶναι ταῦτ' ἀγαθά, ἀλλ' ἀδιάφορα κατ' εἶδος προηγμένα.

[5] The last two analogies can also be found in a papyrus fragment (*PMilVogl.* 1241); for its date, its controversial attribution to Chrysippus, and its reconstruction, see Decleva Caizzi and Funghi (1988); Roskam (2005), 25–7.

instance, health itself does not admit of intensification and relaxation, but a person may be more or less healthy than another.

(iii) The third view, which they all attribute to the Stoics, argues that some qualities, namely those which the Stoics called 'dispositions' (*diatheseis*), for instance the virtues and their qualia, do not admit of intensification and relaxation; on the other hand, some other qualities, namely those which the Stoics called 'states' (*hexeis*), for instance the 'intermediate qualities' (*mesai poiotētes*) of the 'intermediate arts' (*mesai technai*) and all that is qualified by them,[6] admit of the more and the less.

Finally, Porphyry and Simplicius report a fourth view, according to which all 'enmattered' (*enhyloi*) qualities and their qualia admit of the more and the less, whereas qualities which are 'immaterial' (*ahyloi*), that is, those corresponding to the Platonic Ideas, do not admit of intensification and relaxation. Porphyry rejects this view as wrongly positing immaterial qualities that are actually substances, and for this reason cannot be said to admit of degrees.

Among these three commentaries that discuss the degrees of qualities and of the corresponding qualia, it is only in Simplicius' commentary that we find further evidence of the Stoic doctrine that virtues do not admit of intensification and relaxation. In an earlier passage in which he undertakes to clarify why the Stoics defended the reverse thesis from that of Aristotle (*Cat.* 8b27–9a13), namely that virtues are dispositions rather than states, Simplicius (*in Cat.* 237.29–8.1) claims that, according to the Stoics, virtues are dispositions, because dispositions do not admit of intensification and relaxation, and virtues, too, do not admit of intensification and relaxation (*anepitatous einai kai ananetous*). Interestingly enough, Simplicius also attempts to offer an explanation of why the Stoics thought that virtues do not admit of intensification and relaxation, by referring to their theory that virtue is knowledge:

In reply to the Stoics who claim that the virtuous type is stable and that the intermediate admits intensification and relaxation, it is worth raising the difficulty whether the man who possesses virtue, but who fails either because of his training or because of his nature, is not less virtuous. They will perhaps say that because virtue is knowledge it has of itself stability; for because it contemplates its own *logoi* and aims at doing everything according to itself, its activity is stable since it abides in the unchanging form of knowledge. (Simplicius, *in Cat.* 286.35–287.5;[7] trans. B. Fleet with modifications)

Indeed, the Stoic doctrine that virtue and vice admit of no degrees is firmly grounded on Stoic epistemology: Since virtue is knowledge, and there is no cognitive state

---

[6] For examples of intermediate arts, see for instance Stobaeus, *Ecl.* 2, 113.24–14.3.

[7] πρὸς μὲν γὰρ τοὺς ἀπὸ τῆς Στοᾶς τὸ μὲν σπουδαῖον γένος βέβαιον λέγοντας, τὸ δὲ μέσον ἐπίτασιν καὶ ἄνεσιν ἐπιδέχεσθαι, ἀπορῆσαι ἄξιον, εἰ μὴ ὁ ἔχων τὴν ἀρετήν, ἐλλείπων δὲ κατὰ συνάσκησιν ἢ τὴν φύσιν ἧττον ἂν εἴη σπουδαῖος. ἴσως δὲ ἐροῦσι τὴν ἀρετὴν ἐπιστήμην οὖσαν ἐξ ἑαυτῆς ἔχειν τὸ πάγιον· τῶν γὰρ οἰκείων λόγων οὖσα θεωρητικὴ καὶ στοχαζομένη ἀεὶ τοῦ καθ' ἑαυτὴν πάντα ποιεῖν ἐνεργεῖ βεβαίως ἑστῶσα ἐν τῷ ἀμεταπτώτῳ εἴδει τῆς ἐπιστήμης.

between knowledge and ignorance, those who are not wise and virtuous are fools and vicious. For both the wise men and the ordinary people are said to have 'cognition' (*katalēpsis*), but only in the case of the wise does this constitute 'knowledge' (*epistēmē*); in the case of ordinary people, their judgements, even though they may be true, or for that matter both true and such as could not be false, are nevertheless grouped by the Stoics together with the false and accidentally true judgements, treating them all as mere opinions (*doxai*). And in Stoic ethics, too, something similar applies: The actions that ordinary people perform in accordance with nature, the so-called 'appropriate actions or duties' (*kathēkonta*), are grouped together with those that are contrary to what is appropriate and treated as 'mistakes' (*hamartēmata*); so, everything that ordinary people do is a mistake, even when it is exactly what the wise would have done in parallel circumstances, the so-called 'perfectly appropriate or correct actions' (*katorthōmata*).

In this way, the Stoics made a sharp distinction between the wise and virtuous men, who are completely incapable of error, and the ordinary and vicious, who are capable of error because of the inconsistency and irrationality of their judgements. The fact that a particular judgement happens to be true, or a particular action happens to be in conformity with what is appropriate, is less important than the fact that it is done by someone who, on some other occasion, could make a false judgement or could perform an action contrary to what is appropriate. What ordinary people lack, according to Chrysippus, is the special sort of fixity or firmness of the judgements and actions characterizing exclusively those of the wise men; that is to say, only those who are wise have a stable and reliable disposition, so that their judgements and actions are consistent, secure, and impregnable to any reasoning that might be used to change their mind:[8]

> Chrysippus says: 'he who makes progress to the highest degree performs all the appropriate actions in all circumstances and omits none.' And he says that his life is not yet happy, but that happiness supervenes on him when these intermediate actions become secure and conditioned and acquire a special sort of fixity. (Stobaeus, *Ecl.* 5, 906.18–7.5;[9] trans. B. Inwood and L. Gerson. Cf. also: Sextus Empiricus, *M* 11.200–1)

But even this special sort of fixity or firmness of those who are wise should not necessarily be understood as a guarantee that their virtuous disposition remains irreversible. There was a disagreement among the Stoics on this topic: Chrysippus claimed that in certain situations, for example, owing to drunkenness, even the wise men may become again vicious, while Cleanthes said that virtue cannot be lost under any circumstances, for it consists in secure intellectual grasps (Diogenes Laertius 7.127).

---

[8] On this topic, see for instance Inwood (1985), 208–9; Brennan (2005), 176–80.

[9] <Χρυσίππου. Ὁ δ' ἐπ' ἄκρον, φησί, προκόπτων ἅπαντα πάντως ἀποδίδωσι τὰ καθήκοντα καὶ οὐδὲν παραλείπει. Τὸν δὲ τούτου βίον οὐκ εἶναί πω φησὶν εὐδαίμονα, ἀλλ' ἐπιγίγνεσθαι αὐτῷ τὴν εὐδαιμονίαν ὅταν αἱ μέσαι πράξεις αὗται προσλάβωσι τὸ βέβαιον καὶ ἑκτικὸν καὶ ἰδίαν πῆξιν τινὰ λάβωσι>.

III. Ancient Critics: Cicero, Plutarch, Alexander of Aphrodisias.

According to Stoic ethics, therefore, human beings can in principle be happy, but it is extremely difficult, even for the wise men, to actually attain and maintain a happy life. For it seems that in Stoicism there is no such thing, strictly speaking, as moral progress (*prokopē*); ordinary people cannot become more or less virtuous, or for that matter more or less vicious, that is, they cannot progress within morality. This is in any case how Cicero, Plutarch, and Alexander of Aphrodisias understand the Stoic doctrine, and this is why they severely criticize it by raising three main objections.

First objection: Isn't it counter-intuitive to think that all virtues are equal and all vices on a par?

What, then, are your conclusions? That all who are not wise are equally miserable; that all who are wise are supremely happy; that all right acts equally right and all wrongdoing is equally wrong. These maxims sound wonderful on first acquaintance, but become less convincing on mature reflection. Common sense, the facts of nature, and truth herself proclaimed the impossibility of being persuaded that there was really no difference between all the things which Zeno made equal. (Cicero, *De fin.* 4.55;[10] trans. R. Woolf)

For instance, isn't it counter-intuitive to think that someone like Plato was a fool just like any other ordinary man (Cicero, *De fin.* 4.21)? And conversely, isn't it astonishing to claim that wise men can in principle be as happy as gods are (Plutarch, *De comm. not.* 1076A–B)?

Second objection: Is it possible to suddenly change from being absolutely vicious to being perfectly virtuous?

So in philosophy we should assume neither progress nor any perception of progress, if the soul discards and purges itself of none of its stupidity, but deals in absolute badness right up to its acquisition of the absolute and perfect good. In that case, the wise man has changed in a moment from the greatest possible worthlessness to an unsurpassable virtuous character, and has suddenly shed all the vice of which he failed to remove even a part over a considerable time. (Plutarch, *De prof. in virt.* 75C;[11] trans. A. Long and D. Sedley)

Third objection: If there is actually no sign of human happiness, in what sense is the world order rational?

---

[10] *Quae sequuntur igitur? Omnes qui non sint sapientes aeque miseros esse; sapientes omnes summe beatos; recte facta omnia aequalia, omnia peccata paria; quae cum magnifice primo dici viderentur, conidersts minus probabantur. Sensus enim cuiusque et natura rerum atque ipsa veritas clamabat quodam modo non posse adduci ut inter eas res quas Zeno exaequaret nihil interesset.*

[11] οὕτως ἐν τῷ φιλοσοφεῖν οὔτε προκοπὴν οὔτε τινὰ προκοπῆς αἴσθησιν ὑποληπτέον, εἰ μηδὲν ἡ ψυχὴ μεθίησι μηδ᾽ ἀποκαθαίρεται τῆς ἀβελτερίας, ἄχρι δὲ τοῦ λαβεῖν ἄκρατον τὸ ἀγαθὸν καὶ τέλειον ἀκράτῳ τῷ κακῷ χρῆται. Καὶ γὰρ <ἀκαρεῖ χρόνου καὶ ὥρας ἐκ τῆς ὡς ἔνι μάλιστα φαυλότητος εἰς οὐκ ἔχουσαν ὑπερβολὴν ἀρετῆς διάθεσιν μεταβαλὼν ὁ σοφός, ἧς οὐδ᾽ ἐν χρόνῳ πολλῷ μέρος ἀφεῖλε κακίας ἅμα πᾶσαν ἐξαίφνης ἐκπέφευγε>.

If virtue and vice alone, in their [the Stoics'] opinion, are good and bad respectively, and no other creatures are capable of receiving either of them; and if the majority of men are bad, or rather, if there have been just one or two good men, as their fables maintain, like some absurd and unnatural creature rarer than the Ethiopians' phoenix; and if all bad men are as bad as each other, without any differentiation, and all who are not wise are all alike mad, how could man not be the most miserable of all creatures in having vice and madness ingrown in him and allotted? (Alexander, *De fato* 199.14–22;[12] trans. A. Long and D. Sedley)

Similarly, if there is actually no sign of human happiness, how can we accept that there is providence?

What is more, Chrysippus does not represent as a good man either himself or any of his own acquaintances or teachers. What, then, do they think of the rest of mankind? Or do they think just what they say, that all are madmen and fools, impious and lawless, at the extremity of misfortune and utter unhappiness? And yet that our state, thus wretched as it is, is ordered by the providence of the gods? (Plutarch, *De Stoic. rep.* 1048E;[13] trans. H. Cherniss)

It is also quite telling that Cicero replaces the analogies which the Stoics employed, in order to show that there are no degrees of virtue and vice, with other analogies which are meant to indicate the exact opposite, namely that virtue and vice admit of intensification and relaxation. That is to say, the Stoic analogies of the drowning and blind man are criticized by Cicero as ill-chosen, and he suggests in their place the analogy of the recovery one makes with the help of medication in cases of poor eyesight or bad health, which he considers as more suitable to be compared with the progress towards the attainment of virtue:

These are cases in which, however much one progresses, one remains in the same state that one is trying to get out of until one finally emerges. But they are not good analogies for virtue. The swimmer cannot breathe before breaking the surface; the puppies are as blind just before opening their eyes as they would be if they were to remain always in that condition. Here are some better analogies: one person has blurred eyesight, another a weak body. By applying a remedy they improve day by day. Every day, one gets stronger, the other sees better. It is like this for every keen seeker after virtue. Their faults and their errors are gradually cured. (Cicero, *De fin.* 4.65;[14] trans. R. Woolf)

---

[12] εἰ γὰρ ἥ μὲν ἀρετή τε καὶ ἥ κακία μόναι κατ' αὐτοὺς ἥ μὲν ἀγαθόν, ἥ δὲ κακόν, καὶ οὐδὲν τῶν ἄλλων ζῴων οὐδετέρου τούτων ἐστὶν ἐπιδεκτικόν, τῶν δὲ ἀνθρώπων οἱ πλεῖστοι κακοί, μᾶλλον δὲ ἀγαθὸς μὲν εἷς ἢ δεύτερος ὑπ' αὐτῶν γεγονέναι μυθεύεται, ὥσπερ τι παράδοξον ζῷον καὶ παρὰ φύσιν σπανιώτερον τοῦ φοίνικος τοῦ παρ' Αἰθίοψιν, <οἱ δὲ πάντες κακοὶ καὶ ἐπίσης ἀλλήλοις τοιοῦτοι, ὡς μηδὲν διαφέρειν ἄλλον ἄλλου, μαίνεσθαι δὲ ὁμοίως πάντας ὅσοι μὴ σοφοί>, πῶς οὐκ ἂν ἀθλιώτατον ζῷον ἁπάντων ὁ ἄνθρωπος εἴη, ἔχων τήν τε κακίαν καὶ τὸ μαίνεσθαι σύμφυτα αὐτῷ καὶ συγκεκληρωμένα.

[13] καὶ μὴν οὔθ' αὐτὸν ὁ Χρύσιππος ἀποφαίνει σπουδαῖον οὔτε τινὰ τῶν αὐτοῦ γνωρίμων ἢ καθηγεμόνων. τί οὖν περὶ τῶν ἄλλων φρονοῦσιν; ἢ ταῦτα ἅπερ λέγουσι; μαίνεσθαι πάντας, ἀφραίνειν, ἀνοσίους εἶναι, παρανόμους, ἐπ' ἄκρον ἥκειν δυστυχίας, κακοδαιμονίας ἀπάσης· εἶτα προνοίᾳ θεῶν διοικεῖσθαι τὰ καθ' ἡμᾶς οὕτως ἀθλίως πράττοντας.

[14] Ista similia non sunt, Cato, in quibus quamvis multum processeris, tamen illud in eadem causa est a quo abesse velis, donec evaseris. Nec enim ille respirat antequam emersit, et catuli aeque caeci, priusquam dispexerunt ac si ita futuri semper essent. Illa sunt similia: hebes acies est cuipiam oculorum, corpore alius

The Stoics' ancient critics fail, I think, to understand the Stoic doctrine on virtues and vices. For some of the Stoic analogies clearly imply that, even though there are no degrees of virtue and vice, it is perfectly possible for ordinary people to be closer to or farther away from being virtuous and happy, just like they can be closer to or farther away from their destinations. In other words, it is absolutely consistent with the Stoic moral principles to hold that human beings may go through a gradual transition from being fools and vicious to becoming wise and virtuous, but during this transition they cannot be said to be more virtuous or less vicious.[15] The Stoics insisted on this point, because they considered it important to stress that it makes no sense to think of a virtuous person as being more virtuous than another, since it makes no sense to think of a wise man as being wiser than another. Analogously, in the case of the Stoic account of vices: The Stoics claimed that all vices are equal, but this does not entail that they are therefore the same or equally tolerable. On the contrary, they made it clear that some vices are absolutely unacceptable, whereas others are easier to endure, depending on the nature of the transgressions as well as on whether or not they derive from an incurable character. Zeno, for instance, is reported to have maintained that Plato could at least have hoped to become wise, whereas the tyrant Dionysius' only hope could have been nothing more than to die (Cicero, *De fin.* 4.56; Stobaeus, *Ecl.* 2, 113.18–23).

The Stoic opponents' critical stance is due, I believe, to the fact that they operate with a different notion of virtue and vice, though it is not clear whether they actually adhere to it or they adopt it merely for dialectical purposes. For their objections make sense only in so far as they think of virtue and vice as extremes in a continuum, just like hot and cold, for instance, in which case something can be hotter or colder than something else and the less cold something becomes the more hot it is. However, on the Stoic account there is a gap between virtue and vice; virtue is a perfect disposition and vice is its opposite, with nothing in between. Perhaps a more apt analogy to the Stoic conception of being virtuous or vicious would be that of being alive or dead, and not that of being more or less healthy, as Cicero suggests; for human beings are born, so to speak, at a certain moment, and also they die at a certain moment. It is true that we may claim that someone's unhealthy addictions lead closer to his or her death; but even in such cases nobody can be described, at least not strictly speaking, as being more or less alive or dead. Hence, the Stoics believed that, although virtues are equal and vices are on a par, progress towards a virtuous and happy life is feasible. There is no paradox in the claim that in making progress towards virtue a fool does not become less vicious, and cannot be said to be more virtuous than another.

---

languescit; hi curatione adhibita levantur in dies; valet alter plus cotidie, alter videt; his similes sunt omnes, qui virtuti student; levantur vitiis, levantur erroribus.

[15] Cf. Donini and Inwood (1999), 724–7; Cooper (2005), 199–200; Roskam (2005), 27–30; Graver (2007), 135–8.

IV. Admittedly a Demanding Theory, but not Unrealistic.

Nevertheless, even if moral progress is possible in Stoicism, there should be no doubt that the Stoics advocated a demanding theory. For not only are there no degrees of virtue and vice, in the sense that someone cannot be more or less virtuous than someone else with regard to a particular virtue, the virtuous person cannot be said to possess certain virtues and lack others. In other words, the Stoics seem to have followed the Socratic ideal of the unity of virtues:

> They [the Stoics] say that the virtues are inter-entailing, not only because he who has one has them all but also because he who does any action in accordance with one does so in accordance with them all. For they say that a man is not perfect unless he possesses all the virtues nor an action either, unless it is performed in accordance with all the virtues. (Plutarch, *De Stoic. repugn.* 1046E–F;[16] trans. A. Long and D. Sedley. Cf. also: Stobaeus, *Ecl.* 2, 63.6–10)

There was in fact an argument among Stoic philosophers about how to understand the plurality and at the same time the inseparability of virtues: Aristo of Chios disagreed with Zeno in positing a plurality of virtues, but followed the generally accepted Stoic view that virtue is unitary and the virtuous person acts in accordance with all virtues (Plutarch, *De virt. mor.* 440F–1A).[17]

Furthermore, the Stoics have been severely criticized for expounding an inhuman, and thus unattainable, moral theory that forces us to renounce human emotions in our pursuit of a virtuous and happy life. Passages from Stoic sources like the following have often drawn the attention and caused the disapproval of both ancient and modern critics:

> Whenever you are getting attached to someone, don't let it be as though they're something undetachable—but more as if you had a jar or a crystal goblet, so that when it breaks, you'll remember that it's that sort of thing and not be upset.... In the same way, remind yourself that the person you love is mortal, not one of your own possessions, something given to you for the present, not undetachably nor forever, like a fig or a cluster of grapes, in the due season of the year—and if you hanker for that in winter, you're a fool. If you long for your son or your friend like this, at a time when that has not been given to you, rest assured: you are hankering for a fig in winter. (Epictetus, *Diss.* 3.24.84–7;[18] trans. M. Schofield. Cf. also: Epictetus, *Diss.* 4.1.111–13; *Ench.* 3, 7, 11, 15, 26; Marcus Aurelius, 11.34)

---

[16] Τὰς ἀρετάς φησιν ἀντακολουθεῖν ἀλλήλαις, οὐ μόνον τῷ τὸν μίαν ἔχοντα πάσας ἔχειν, ἀλλὰ καὶ τῷ τὸν κατὰ μίαν ὁτιοῦν ἐνεργοῦντα κατὰ πάσας ἐνεργεῖν· οὔτε γὰρ ἄνδρα φησὶ τέλειον εἶναι τὸν μὴ πάσας ἔχοντα τὰς ἀρετάς, οὔτε πρᾶξιν τελείαν, ἥτις οὐ κατὰ πάσας πράττεται τὰς ἀρετάς.

[17] On the Stoic views concerning the unity of virtue, see for instance Schofield (1984); Cooper (1998), 253–61; Alesse (2000), 293–309; Gill (2006), 150–7.

[18] ὅταν τινὶ προσπάσχῃς, οὐδενὶ τῶν ἀναφαιρέτων, ἀλλά τινι τοιούτῳ γένει, οἷόν ἐστι χύτρα, οἷον ὑάλινον ποτήριον, ἵν' ὅταν καταγῇ, μεμνημένος [μὴν] μὴ ταραχθῇς... τοιοῦτόν τι καὶ σὺ ὑπομίμνῃσκε σεαυτόν, ὅτι θνητὸν φιλεῖς, οὐδὲν τῶν σεαυτοῦ φιλεῖς· ἐπὶ τοῦ παρόντος σοι δέδοται, οὐκ ἀναφαίρετον οὐδ' εἰς ἅπαν, ἀλλ'

Bernard Williams, for instance, finds this detachment from our individual concern for family unintelligible and intolerable to the extent that Stoicism turns out to be, according to him, a philosophy that we cannot believe:

If the chilling ritual of reminding oneself, when embracing one's loved ones, that they are mortal beings is somehow supposed to cheer one up, this can only be because there is a conception at hand, which one would supposedly accept if one were introduced to it, that loved ones are, as mortal creatures, not ultimately valuable to the wise person. We can scarcely find such an outlook either intelligible or tolerable. (Williams (1997), 213)

Admittedly, Stoic passages like the above sound shocking in isolation. However, modern scholars have tried to defend them, by reading them in the context of the Stoics' overall moral theory. They have argued that the Stoic inflexible demands were supposed to simply make clear what the Stoics should have been ready for; or, that they did not entail the complete eradication of human emotions as fundamental aspects of our natures; or again, that they made perfect sense for the Stoics who were not willing to jeopardize what they valued as our human freedom and autonomy.[19] Whether such interpretations are convincing or not, the question remains: Did the Stoics offer concrete advice to help us progress morally and come closer to reaching *eudaimonia*?

As it has already been said, the Stoics thought that in principle everyone can improve morally. They also thought that the way someone behaves in a given situation depends entirely on that person's cognitive disposition at the time. Hence, moral progress depends on the development of one's reason, so that he or she comes to act in a morally appropriate manner. This is, of course, the result of a long process in consecutive stages that ends, according to the Stoics, with the wise man's secure and fixed judgements and moral actions (Cicero, *De fin.* 3.20).[20] To this end, the Stoics claimed, concrete advice is needed, moral advice that may guide ordinary people in their challenging, if not close to impossible, quest for virtue and happiness:

Furthermore, that which you mention is the mark of an already perfect man, of one who has attained the height of human happiness. But the approach to these qualities is slow, and in the meantime, in practical matters, the path should be pointed out for the benefit of one who is still short of perfection, but is making progress. (Seneca, *Epist.* 94.50;[21] trans. R. Gummere)

The concrete moral advice in Stoicism took the form of certain rules or precepts, the *praecepta,* which are practical instructions and guidelines focusing on individual

ὡς σῦκον, ὡς σταφυλή, τῇ τεταγμένῃ ὥρᾳ τοῦ ἔτους· ἂν δὲ χειμῶνος ἐπιποθῇς, μωρὸς εἶ. οὕτως κἂν τὸν υἱὸν ἢ τὸν φίλον τότε ποθῇς, ὅτε οὐ δέδοταί σοι, ἴσθι, ὅτι χειμῶνος σῦκον ἐπιποθεῖς.

[19] Cf. Annas (2002b), 118–20; Cooper (2005); (2012), 158–66; Russell, unpublished article.

[20] On the Stoic theory of οἰκείωσις as the general background of this process and on its consecutive stages, see for instance Roskam (2005), 24–5.

[21] *Deinde istud, quod dicis, iam perfecti viri est ac summam consecuti felicitatis humanae. Ad haec autem tarde pervenitur; interim etiam inperfecto sed proficienti demonstranda est in rebus agendis via.*

cases. These precepts were placed alongside the general doctrines of Stoic ethics, the *decreta*, that constitute the abstract principles on which the precepts are based.[22] The question that was raised, understandably, concerned the issue of whether the introduction of concrete precepts was consistent with the Stoic system:

> To one who knows, it is superfluous to give precepts; to one who does not know, it is insufficient. For he must be told not only what he is being instructed to do, but also why. (Seneca, *Epist.* 94.11;[23] trans. R. Gummere)

Seneca's letter 94 is written against those who insisted that there is no need for rules of contact concerning specific situations in human life. Moral progress, these philosophers claimed, may rest entirely upon the knowledge of the basic doctrines of Stoic ethics, which provide sufficient help for every situation. On the other hand, letter 95 criticizes those who rejected every kind of dogmatic knowledge and limited moral guidance to the recommendation of precepts. It has been suggested that the first group is represented by the Stoic Aristo, who strongly disapproved of precepts, whereas in letter 95 Seneca may be thinking of his own teacher Sotion and some Sceptics who made abundant use of moral rules.[24] But although it seems that there were philosophers before Posidonius who believed that precepts could be useful and important, it was probably the later Stoics, and in particular Panaetius, who emphasized practical instructions over abstract principles and stressed the continuity between the virtuous tendencies of ordinary people and the perfect virtue of wise men.[25]

Seneca himself adopts a favourable, though cautious, stance towards the use of practical guidelines in moral education:

> I admit that precepts alone are not effective in overthrowing the mind's mistaken beliefs; but they do not on that account fail to be of service when they accompany other measures also. In the first place, they refresh the memory; in the second place, when sorted into proper classes, the matters which showed themselves in a jumbled mass when considered as a whole, can be considered in this way with greater care. (Seneca, *Epist.* 94.21;[26] trans. R. Gummere)

---

[22] On the Stoic views about *praecepta* and *decreta*, see for instance Kidd (1978); Mitsis (1993); Inwood (1999).

[23] *Praecepta dare scienti supervacuum est, nescienti parum. Audire enim debet non tantum, quid sibi praecipiatur, sed etiam quare.*

[24] Dihle (1973). For a different interpretation of these letters, see Schafer (2009); according to him, the distinction between *praecepta* and *decreta* is not 'between rules and the general principles that produce rules, but rather between non-technical instructions and other techniques of moral guidance on the one hand, and the teaching of philosophical doctrine on the other' (Schafer (2009), 11).

[25] Sedley (2003, esp. note 35) and Tieleman (2007, esp. 135) question the degree to which Panaetius actually broke new ground in the development of Stoicism, and in particular his traditional reputation as the Stoic who was sympathetic to human frailty and shifted the focus from the sage to the non-sage.

[26] *Concedo per se efficacia praecepta non esse ad evertendam pravam animi persuasionem; sed non ideo nihil ne aliis quidem adiecta proficiunt. Primum memoriam renovant; deinde quae in universo confusius videbantur, in partes divisa diligentius considerantur.*

After all, the educational value of precepts seems indisputable in consideration of the fact that it is not possible to become virtuous without going through a long process of moral reform; for virtue is teachable, according to standard Stoic dogma, and ordinary people become, if at all, virtuous and wise from first being vicious and fools:

Posidonius (in book one of his *Ethical Discourse*) says that a sign that virtue exists is the fact that the followers of Socrates, Diogenes, and Antisthenes were making progress; and vice exists because it is the opposite of virtue. And that it is teachable (virtue, I mean) Chrysippus says in book one of his *On the Goal*, and so do Cleanthes and Posidonius in their *Protreptics* and Hecaton too. It is clear that it is teachable because base men become good. (Diogenes Laertius 7.91;[27] trans. B. Inwood and L. Gerson)

Indeed, it was the aim of the Stoic school to educate ordinary people in such a way that they become virtuous, and thus happy. For the Stoics defined philosophy not merely as a body of knowledge, but as a certain practice (*askēsis*) whose purpose is virtue:

The Stoics said that wisdom is scientific knowledge of the divine and the human, and that philosophy is the practice of expertise in utility. Virtue singly and at its highest is utility, and virtues, at their most generic, are triple—the physical one, the ethical one, and the logical one. (Aëtius I, Pref. 2 = [Plutarch], *Plac.* 874 E;[28] trans. A. Long and D. Sedley)

And there are plenty of passages, especially in the writings of Epictetus and Marcus Aurelius, which testify to the Stoic claim that wisdom and virtue is a matter of action as well as words, that the philosopher's deeds should match and harmonize with his doctrines.[29] So, modern scholars have recently been particularly interested in highlighting those aspects of Stoic philosophy that reveal its character not only as a theoretical system and an intellectual activity, but as a way or as an art of life. Michael Frede, for instance, draws our attention and comments on the case of Euphrates of Tyre, a Stoic philosopher of the second century AD, who had no original philosophical views of his own and wrote no theoretical treatises, but wanted to be known as a philosopher by what he did; thus, he ate properly, drank properly, walked decently, and looked at others decently:

Human life is a matter of banal things, getting up, eating, doing one's work, getting married, having children, looking after one's family... This is what life is about. If there is something non-banal about it, it is the wisdom with which these banal things are done, the understanding and the spirit from which they are done. (Frede (1997), 6)

---

[27] τεκμήριον δὲ τοῦ ὑπαρκτὴν εἶναι τὴν ἀρετήν φησιν ὁ Ποσειδώνιος ἐν τῷ πρώτῳ τοῦ Ἠθικοῦ λόγου τὸ γενέσθαι ἐν προκοπῇ τοὺς περὶ Σωκράτην, Διογένην, Ἀντισθένην. εἶναι δὲ καὶ τὴν κακίαν ὑπαρκτὴν διὰ τὸ ἀντικεῖσθαι τῇ ἀρετῇ. διδακτήν τ' εἶναι αὐτήν, λέγω δὲ τὴν ἀρετήν, καὶ Χρύσιππος ἐν τῷ πρώτῳ Περὶ τέλους φησὶ καὶ Κλεάνθης καὶ Ποσειδώνιος ἐν τοῖς Προτρεπτικοῖς καὶ Ἑκάτων· ὅτι δὲ διδακτή ἐστι, δῆλον ἐκ τοῦ γίνεσθαι ἀγαθοὺς ἐκ φαύλων.

[28] οἱ μὲν οὖν Στωικοὶ ἔφασαν τὴν μὲν σοφίαν εἶναι θείων τε καὶ ἀνθρωπίνων ἐπιστήμην, τὴν δὲ φιλοσοφίαν ἄσκησιν ἐπιτηδείου τέχνης, ἐπιτήδειον δ' εἶναι μίαν καὶ ἀνωτάτω τὴν ἀρετήν, ἀρετὰς δὲ τὰς γενικωτάτας τρεῖς, φυσικὴν ἠθικὴν λογικήν.

[29] e.g. Epictetus, *Diss.* 3.15.10–13; 3.22.45–6; 3.24.110; 4.8.22–4; *Ench.* 46; 49.

Other scholars have insisted on the therapeutic methods of Stoic philosophy, that is to say both on the doctrinal positions which tried to cure human beings from their irrationality as well as on the practical instructions which aimed at guiding ordinary people to a virtuous life. They have claimed that in Stoicism the connection between theory and practice is seamless, that Stoic moral theory was meant above all to be lived, not just systematized and elaborated to meet criticism and challenge. It has even been suggested that Stoic philosophy is itself a form of cognitive psychotherapy and stands behind modern forms of cognitive psychotherapy.[30]

In this respect, Stoicism has been acclaimed as a living philosophy, and Stoic ethics has been regarded as a paradigm of how to bridge theory and practice, of how in general ethics should be done. At the same time, though, it has often been remarked that it is not easy to arrive at the wisdom and virtuous disposition Stoic philosophers required from ordinary people, and so very few human beings, if any, could actually aspire to reach *eudaimonia*. But is it really unusual for an ethical system to posit an ideal which is difficult, if not impossible, to attain?

V. Conclusion: Designing, Building, and Driving a Ferrari.

There is no ancient ethical theory that explicitly talks about degrees of virtue and vice; nothing relevant in Plato's dialogues or in Aristotle's treatises. On the contrary, the Aristotelian commentators point out and elaborate on the fact that Aristotle's notion of virtue in the strict sense does not admit intensification and relaxation; it is only the so-called 'imperfect' (*ateleis*) or 'physical' (*physikai*) virtues, that is, our good natural dispositions, which can be of different degrees.[31] As to the Neoplatonists' scales of virtues, from Plotinus' and Porphyry's to the more complicated versions in later Neoplatonism, and especially in Iamblichus' work, they do not come down to different degrees of virtue but to a hierarchy of virtues; that is to say, the Neoplatonists' scales constitute different stages in a progressive divinization of the human soul, which begins with the so-called 'political' (*politikai*) virtues and leads up to the 'purificatory' ones (*katharseis*).[32] Hence, in the whole tradition of ancient ethics,

---

[30] e.g. Hadot (1995), 264–76; Sorabji (1997), 209; Schofield (2003), 253–6; Gourinat (2009), 507–11; Cooper (2012), 144–225; Robertson (2010); Sellars, unpublished article.

[31] On the Peripatetic views about the intensification and relaxation of imperfect virtues, see Ierodiakonou (1999). The distinction between perfect (τελεία) and imperfect virtues as well as the distinction between virtue in the strict sense (κυρίως) and natural virtues are found in Aristotle (e.g. *EN* I 13, 1102a5–6; 7, 1098a17–18; 9, 1100a4; VI 13, 1144b1–9; *EE* II 1, 1219a35–9), but they do not imply degrees of virtue.

[32] On the Neoplatonists' scales of virtue, see for instance O'Meara (2005), 40–9; Brisson (2006). The Neoplatonic distinctions go back to aspects of Plato's dialogues, especially in the *Republic* (e.g. 500d5–9; 518d9–519b5), where Plato seems to distinguish between the virtue of being wise and the virtues of the body or the political virtues that are instilled into the citizens' souls by training (cf. Sedley (2013), 82–8); however, presenting different types or levels of virtue is not the same as recognizing degrees of virtue.

there was really no discussion of what it would mean to say that someone is more or less virtuous than someone else, or more or less virtuous in one occasion than in another.

In general, ancient moral theories posited an ideal of the virtuous man that was rather demanding and hard to attain. It may be thought that the Stoics' demands were more stringent than those made by other ancient philosophers, but it seems that it is in the nature of a moral theory to build aspirations that are difficult for human beings to reach, or even beyond our reach. As Julia Annas remarks:

No classical virtue theory takes seriously the idea that virtue could be achieved by conforming to your society's conventions; this would leave out what ethics is all about—aspiration to an ideal, trying to live better. (Annas (2006), 525. Cf. also: Annas (2002b), 121)

Let's say, it is like building a Ferrari car; its engine is designed with a top speed of 310 km/h, but in driving it one does not actually reach this speed. Ethical systems design ideal models that we strive towards, though it is clear that very few of us, if any, are able to follow them in everyday life. Stoic ethics is no exception. The Stoics' insistence on rigidly distinguishing between the wise and virtuous men and the ordinary people who are fools and vicious has reasonably been interpreted as having a protreptic, rhetorical, and pedagogical significance; it should be taken as an invitation to ordinary people to persevere in their efforts and seek to improve themselves further, without ever lapsing into complacency over results already achieved.[33]

But isn't it intimidating and demoralizing for human beings to keep on trying to become virtuous and constantly be told that they have not achieved their goal? This is one of the reasons why modern ethicists have found the Stoic position awkward, to say the least.[34] They have introduced instead a developmental account of virtue, which recognizes a clear difference between the mediocre non-virtuous and the horrendously vicious. For if it is impossible to be perfectly virtuous, they have claimed, we can still be virtuous in a less than full way that takes into consideration our limitations as well as the structures of the societies we live in. In other words, even if the ultimate goal is not attainable, there are still alternatives which are worth pursuing and perfectly realistic. This is the concession the Stoics were not willing to make. They believed in the importance of an aspiration towards an ideal, and designed their theory as a demanding model that we should keep on striving for. Still, it is important to realize and bear in mind that, even if we never manage to achieve it, the Stoic conception of *eudaimonia* is no less attainable or feasible than that of any other ancient ethical theory.[35]

---

[33] Cf. Donini and Inwood (1999), 726–7.   [34] Cf. Annas (2011), 65.

[35] I would like to thank Christopher Gill for his incisive and helpful comments on an earlier draft of this chapter.

10

The Pyrrhonian Idea of a Good Life

Svavar Hrafn Svavarsson

Pyrrho of Elis advocated a nihilist attitude towards reality and knowledge, according to which a thing is neither decidable as something specific nor is it really anything specific. This attitude should deprive its holder of all beliefs (save this insight) and above all furnish him with tranquillity. Neo-Pyrrhonists interpreted Pyrrho's philosophy as radical scepticism to be opposed to Academic scepticism. They also appropriated Pyrrho's promise of tranquillity. Of our Neo-Pyrrhonist sources, Sextus Empiricus makes the most of sceptical tranquillity, in a complex and perplexing attempt to explain that the sceptic aims at tranquillity but attains it by chance.

Pyrrhonian Tranquillity

Happiness as tranquillity emerged as a philosophical conception in the works of Democritus, a while before the teleological conception of happiness as a unified and ultimate goal of desire and action took shape in the works of Plato.[1] Conceiving happiness as tranquillity or some kind of mental contentment, Democritus thought that its conditions were the possession of the excellences. These were internal to the agent, rendering him self-sufficient and protected against the vicissitudes of fortune. For Democritus, they consisted above all in the wisdom that enables the agent to find peace of mind.[2] This rational capacity consists in the management of desires, the unruliness of which perturbs the mind. According to Democritus moderation should prevail, and in its wake tranquillity. This ideal is more modest than that developed by Plato, according to whom reason was the gateway to godlikeness, although this godlikeness no doubt included tranquillity.

Tranquillity is not an obvious candidate for happiness within teleological conceptions of happiness as the objective well-being that is advocated by Plato and Aristotle. It is a state of mind which constitutes at most the subjective side of happiness. We

---

[1] For a general account of tranquillity in Democritus, Epicurus, the Stoics, and the Pyrrhonists, see Striker (1990).

[2] For an account of Democritus' moral psychology, see Kahn (1985), 25–9.

should bear in mind the difference between the two kinds of conception and resist the temptation to measure the Pyrrhonian idea of subjective tranquillity by the standards of teleological ideas of happiness as objective well-being, even if such ideas do include the notion that there is a subjective side to happiness. Tranquillity was neither objective well-being nor was meant to be. It follows that an explanation of tranquillity even as happiness need not refer to a theory of human nature, let alone a teleological theory. Nevertheless those who propose that happiness is tranquillity do assume that as a matter of fact some people do want to be happy in the sense of being tranquil. Most philosophers would agree with them, but add that for most people, and certainly for the philosophers themselves, everything depended on the source of the tranquillity.

Within the Pyrrhonist tradition, we can discern two closely connected explanations of tranquillity. Both explanations connect tranquillity (*ataraxia*) with the absence of the anxiety (*tarachē*) that supposedly inheres in or entails having beliefs. One explanation is that people become tranquil if they rid themselves of beliefs. Thus beliefs are causally connected with anxiety; shed beliefs and you shed anxiety. The other explanation limits the scope of beliefs so that people become tranquil if they rid themselves of positive beliefs about good and bad; shed positive beliefs about these ethical values and you shed anxiety. A further characteristic of Pyrrhonist explanations of tranquillity is of a different kind: Living without beliefs—and therefore being tranquil—the Pyrrhonist acts on what appears to him to be the case. But leading a life based on appearances does not in itself contribute to the Pyrrhonist's tranquillity. In all our testimonies for the Pyrrhonist idea of tranquillity, the promise of tranquillity is independent of the identification of motivational sources as appearances. Insofar as the Pyrrhonist suffers appearances, he may be anxious. It is only in virtue of his not having beliefs that the Pyrrhonist is tranquil; his tranquillity is qualified.

I shall address the explanation of tranquillity but not the claim that the Pyrrhonist lives following appearances. Why would the fact that one had beliefs entail that one was anxious? Would one not expect the contrary? May having beliefs not be likelier to ensure contentment, while the absence of beliefs, or one's inability to form a belief, entailed anxiety? That is how David Hume famously saw the matter (*A Treatise of Human Nature* 1.4.7.8–10 = SBN 268–9). The Pyrrhonist insight is that having beliefs entails a commitment which gives rise to strong attachment to supposed truths. This strong attachment, then, is identical with or entails anxiety. And insofar as these beliefs concern ethical values, they give rise to an intensity of pursuit and avoidance that inevitably betrays anxiety. Although we hardly need to agree with it, I think we can appreciate this insight if we consider the idea of the *fanatic*, fixated on the truth of his own beliefs. For us, the fanatic stands at the extreme end of a spectrum, at the other end of which stands the Pyrrhonist, disavowing beliefs altogether. One may suggest that, for the Pyrrhonist, all dogmatists (committed as they are to the truth of their beliefs) are fanatics.

Texts and testimonies we have for Pyrrhonist notions of tranquillity fall into four kinds. The first kind is limited to the views of Pyrrho of Elis, most importantly as expounded by his disciple Timon of Phlius. The second is Aenesidemus' first-century BC revolutionary interpretation of Pyrrhonism as radical scepticism to be opposed to the mitigated Academic scepticism of Philo of Larissa. The third kind is the Pyrrhonism of Sextus Empiricus, probably at work around 200 AD, indebted to Aenesidemus and other unknown sceptics. Finally, we have the account recorded by Diogenes Laertius, written after Sextus, undoubtedly sharing many of his sources, but nevertheless different from his.[3] In fact, Diogenes is conspicuously different from Sextus exactly in his treatment of tranquillity. In all cases we find Pyrrhonists making claims about their tranquillity and promises to those who would follow them. But these claims are different from each other. Other possible sources of information fail to mention this aspect of Pyrrhonism.

I submit that it was a challenge for the Neo-Pyrrhonists to integrate the idea of tranquillity, although integral to Pyrrho's philosophy, into their radical scepticism. It requires a deft touch from a radical sceptic to claim that he and those of his ilk are tranquil in virtue of their scepticism. The most sustained attempt to elicit tranquillity from radical scepticism, or perhaps rather import into radical scepticism, namely that of Sextus Empiricus, is beset with difficulties. I shall suggest that he looked for help to the Pyrrhonists' medical counterparts, the Empiricists. But first consider Pyrrho and Timon on the tranquil life.

The Original Pyrrhonist on Tranquillity

The most important testimony preserved concerning Pyrrho's philosophy is Timon's explication, quoted by Aristocles of Messene, preserved in Eusebius of Caesarea (*PE* 14.18.1–5 = DC[4] 53). It contains two remarks about happiness and tranquillity, italicized below:

It is above all necessary to investigate our own knowledge; for if we by our nature know nothing, then there is no need to inquire into other matters. There have also been some among the ancients who made this pronouncement, against whom Aristotle has argued. Pyrrho of Elis was also a powerful advocate of such a position; but he himself has left nothing in writing, while his disciple Timon says that *whoever wants to be happy should consider these three questions*. First, how things are by their nature; second, in what way we should be disposed towards these things, and lastly, what will happen to those so disposed. He says that he [Pyrrho] declared that things are equally indifferentiable and unmeasurable and undecidable [or: indifferent and unstable and indeterminate]; because of this neither our perceptions nor opinions tell the truth or lie. Because of this, then, we must not trust them, but we must be without opinions and lean to neither side and remain unwavering, saying concerning each

---

[3] See Barnes (1992), 4241–301.   [4] DC refers to Decleva Caizzi (1981).

individual thing that it no more is than is not or both is and is not or neither is nor is not. *What happens to those so disposed, according to Timon, is first non-assertion, and then tranquillity, while Aenesidemus says pleasure.* These, then, are the main points of what they say.

While this passage has been interpreted in conflicting ways, the interpretative focus has usually been on the metaphysical and epistemological rather than on the ethical message. Although I shall leave aside these debates and concentrate on the ethical part, it is necessary to explain Pyrrho's views on reality and knowledge cursorily. Pyrrho has an insight into the nature of things. Insofar as he does, he is dogmatic and apparently unaware of (or at least unconcerned by) possible allegations of self-refutation, of which later Pyrrhonists were well aware. There are broadly two interpretations of his insight. According to Pyrrho, statements about things are neither true nor false, (1) because things are undecidable, or (2) because things are indeterminate. At all events, since there can be neither true nor false beliefs about things, according to Pyrrho, one should avoid beliefs altogether. Timon offers this insight into the nature of things to those who want to be happy. He suggests that having realized the truth of the insight one will refrain from asserting anything (which is a characteristic of those who hold beliefs). Such non-assertion then entails tranquillity. The passage offers no further explanation of this capture of tranquillity. Apparently it is sufficient for one to become tranquil if one realizes (on whatever grounds) universal undecidability and indeterminacy and therefore stops making any positive claims about anything.

We can seek further elucidations of this tranquillity in three kinds of testimonies about Pyrrho. First, the biographical accounts of Pyrrho emphasize his admirable state of mind, which is called indifference, impassivity, and tranquillity. Anaxarchus of Abdera, possibly a follower of Democritus, is said to have admired Pyrrho's indifference (DL 9.63); the latter performed menial tasks with total indifference, including that of washing pigs (DL 9.66). According to another story, Pyrrho remained calm on board a ship during a vicious storm, pointed to an equally calm pig saying: 'in such tranquillity should a wise man keep himself' (DL 9.68). Plutarch, relating the same account, talks of Pyrrho's impassivity (*On Moral Progress* 82F = DC 17B). Pyrrho's tranquillity is presented in terms of impassivity and indifference; he is untroubled in that he is unaffected and indifferent. At all events, Pyrrho is tranquil because of his wisdom.

Secondly, we have Timon's questions directed towards Pyrrho concerning the source of this state of mind. He suggests that Pyrrho has overcome what vanquishes all others, 'affections, belief, and pointless legislation' (Eusebius, *PE* 14.18.19 = DC 58). Timon also asks him how he rid himself of the beliefs of sophists and all persuasion, implying that such are the sources of his tranquillity (DL 9.65). Further, Plutarch suggests that Pyrrho's reason and philosophy enabled him to attain impassivity, while Diogenes also emphasizes the role of reason in acquiring the perfect attitude (Plutarch, *On Moral Progress* 82F; DL 9.66). Assuming that the Aristocles passage presents Pyrrho's philosophy, one infers that his state of mind comes about as a result of his realizing that one should not have beliefs of any kind because of the undecidability and indeterminacy of reality. One of the things he realizes is that he should not have the belief that some things are good or bad, for he held that 'nothing is good or bad, just or unjust, and equally in all cases that nothing is in truth, but that people do everything by law and custom, for each thing is no more this than that' (DL 9.61). This testimony may imply a tendency to demarcate the general indeterminacy of reality and apply it especially to ethical values, as is evident from the biographical accounts.

Thirdly, there are Timon's elegiac couplets about the nature of the good (SE, *M* 11.20 = DC 62). These couplets have been translated and interpreted in various ways. I offer the following translation, according to which the Pyrrhonist expresses a view consistent with the negative view that there are no ethical values: 'Having a correct yardstick of truth, I will relate a fiction, as it evidently is to me, that the nature of the divine and the good is forever, from which life becomes most equable for man.'[5]

The speaker promises to relate what is evidently to him a fiction. It is so evidently to him, because he possesses the correct yardstick of truth. He claims to know that it is false that there is a nature of the divine and good which serves as the foundation of the best life; there are no natural goods. Again, this crucial insight is emphasized. We are invited to infer that believing that there are natural goods actually precludes tranquillity.

Alas, none of these testimonies satisfactorily explains the reason why those who share the Pyrrhonist insight are free from anxiety. They do not explain why having beliefs, especially about good and evil, inevitably entails anxiety. Yet this is the crux of the Pyrrhonist claim that accepting Pyrrho's insight leads to tranquillity. Is the thesis just this: since having beliefs is never warranted—there being neither true nor false beliefs—not having any beliefs secures the absence of anxiety? This thesis looks uninformative; we lack a middle term—so to speak—that explains the connection between beliefs and anxiety. As far as I can see there is only one testimony that comes close to hinting at the reason, namely Timon's remarks that 'desire is absolutely the first of all bad things' (Athenaeus 8.337A = DC 65). One may infer that by shedding beliefs, one sheds desires—at least certain kinds of desires—and in that sense avoids anxiety. The idea would then be that beliefs, in particular beliefs about what is good and what bad, what should be chosen and what avoided, ground desire and aversion. Here we may have a middle term. We actually find this idea both in Democritus and Sextus Empiricus.[6]

---

[5] For a detailed argument, see Svavarsson (2002).

[6] For an elaboration of Pyrrho's idea and in particular the Democritean background of this idea, see Svavarsson (2013).

Aenesidemus on Tranquillity

Deserting the cause of the Academics Aenesidemus rebelled against Philo of Larissa and offered a new scepticism, appropriating the name of Pyrrho. Between Timon and Aenesidemus, Pyrrho's philosophy does seem to have become little more than a curiosity. Even after the emergence of Aenesidemus, Cicero's references to Pyrrhonism are to the Pyrrho of the indifferent disposition but not to a sceptic of any kind. In fact, Pyrrho is rarely associated with scepticism until after the time of Aenesidemus.[7] After that time, it becomes a difficult question what the difference is between Pyrrhonian and Academic scepticism.[8] On Pyrrhonian accounts, Academic sceptics, at least from Carneades onwards, and certainly during the time of Philo of Larissa, are negative dogmatists.

In Aenesidemus' view the Academy had fallen prey to dogmatism and inconsistency. He may have believed that Arcesilaus was a genuine sceptic who made no claims *in propria persona*. Such a view is at least discernible in Sextus Empiricus.[9] And perhaps Aenesidemus thought that Arcesilaus was a sceptic precisely because of Pyrrho's influence; therefore Pyrrho was the father of genuine scepticism, and not Arcesilaus.[10] At any rate Aenesidemus offered Pyrrhonism as a radical alternative to Academic scepticism. It is likely that he had access to some testimonies for the views of Pyrrho, and that he genuinely (if erroneously) found them indicative of radical scepticism. Little is known about what texts he may have had. At all events, given the scant information about Pyrrho's views, he very probably had considerable interpretative leeway that enabled him to present Pyrrho's as an essentially Academic philosophy: He makes no affirmations about the reality of things, but only states how things appear to him; he suspends belief on all issues because of undecidable dispute between contrary accounts of reality; without subscribing to their conclusions he advances arguments against dogmatic theses in order to destroy objects of dogmatic beliefs; like parallel arguments within the Academy, such arguments are dialectical. When Pyrrho's stance is thus viewed within the framework of Academic scepticism, he can pass off as a genuine sceptic.

There is, nevertheless, one fundamental difference between the Academic stance and that of Aenesidemus. The latter states that the Pyrrhonist is happy in the sense of being tranquil. This difference is evident to Sextus (*PH* 1.232): 'And he [Arcesilaus] says that the aim is suspension of belief about everything, which, we said, is

---

[7] According to Sextus (*PH* 1.234), Aristo associates the Academic sceptic Arcesilaus with, among others, Pyrrho.

[8] See especially Aulus Gellius, *Attic Nights* 11.5.5.

[9] *PH* 1.232: 'Arcesilaus...certainly seems to me to have something in common with what the Pyrrhonists say—indeed his persuasion and ours are virtually the same.'

[10] See SE, *PH* 1.234: '[Aristo] called him "Plato in front, Pyrrho behind, Diodorus in the middle".' The same is said in DL 4.33 and Eusebius, *PE* 14.5.13.

accompanied by tranquillity.' Aenesidemus' main reason for retaining this part of Pyrrho's philosophy may have been his desire to offer his audience something comparable with what the Stoics and Epicureans of the day offered as happiness. Additionally, he was surely aware of the role tranquillity played in the philosophy of Pyrrho himself, given Cicero's testimony and the anecdotes about Pyrrho's life. Glossing over it was hardly an option if one wanted to name one's stance after Pyrrho, as Aenesidemus certainly did. And perhaps he acknowledged the centrality of the Pyrrhonian promise of tranquillity. But by making the tranquillity proposition part of his description of the Pyrrhonist, Aenesidemus takes on board a problematic thesis: how can a genuine sceptic maintain that sceptics—to the exclusion of others— attain happiness as tranquillity?

Aenesidemus suggests that the Pyrrhonist is happy in that he is tranquil while the dogmatist is perturbed. Our most important testimony for Aenesidemus' views comes from Photius' *Library* (169b21–30):

Neither the Pyrrhonists nor the others know the truth in the things that are; but the philosophers of other persuasions are ignorant in general, *wearing themselves out uselessly and expending themselves in ceaseless torments*, and especially ignorant of this very thing, that they have cognition of nothing of which they believe they have cognition. But he who philosophizes according to Pyrrho is happy in other ways and especially in the wisdom of knowing above all that he has firm cognition of nothing. And with regard to what he might know, he has the breeding to assent no more to its affirmation than its negation.

While the torments of dogmatists are clearly contrasted with the happiness of Pyrrhonists, it is not clear why dogmatists are tormented. Aenesidemus seems to imply that they are tormented because of their ignorance, in particular their failure to realize that they have no knowledge (i.e. their ignorance of their ignorance), since the Pyrrhonists seem to secure their happiness exactly by realizing their own ignorance. If this is his claim, then according to Aenesidemus erroneously believing that one has knowledge entails 'expending oneself in ceaseless torments'. This stance brings to mind Socrates' avowed ignorance, and his charge against his interlocutors that he is wiser than they are in that he knows that he does not know. It is not as radical as that attributed to Arcesilaus (Cic., *Acad.* 1.44), who didn't even pretend to know that he didn't know. At all events Aenesidemus, unlike Pyrrho, is wary of allegations of self-refutation. He qualifies his assertion that the Pyrrhonist knows that he does not know with the observation that, 'with regard to what he might know', for example (or perhaps in particular) that he does not know, he assents 'no more to its affirmation than its negation'. So, after all, he does not affirm that he does not know, thus forestalling immediate charges of self-refutation.

We are not told how it happens that one's admission of ignorance leads to happiness, although Diogenes preserves an indication, which is not overly helpful (9.107): 'The sceptics say the end is suspension of belief, which is followed by tranquillity *like a shadow*, as the followers of Timon and Aenesidemus say.'

We now know, first, that Aenesideman happiness is tranquillity, or the absence of anxiety associated with pretensions to knowledge, and secondly, that it follows suspension of belief like a shadow. The first claim is evidently derived from Pyrrho himself and has no other precedent in the history of philosophy. It is the most conspicuous thread connecting Pyrrho and Aenesidemus, as well as Sextus. Aenesidemus affords us no further elaboration. So, according to Aenesidemus, (i) dogmatists are anxious because they believe they have knowledge, (ii) Pyrrhonists are happy because they do not think they have knowledge and suspend belief, and (iii) tranquillity follows suspension of belief like a shadow.

We shall encounter kindred claims in Sextus. And we shall also see that Sextus is confronted with severe problems in explaining both why the Pyrrhonist is tranquil and why he can claim to be tranquil. The claims pose a problem for Sextus because they look dogmatic. He should not assert that the Pyrrhonist is tranquil, but rather suspend belief. Instead, Sextus offers tranquillity as the sceptic's end.

Returning to Aenesidemus, he does not pose tranquillity, or even happiness, as a Pyrrhonist end. That much is clear from Photius' account, according to which he argued that there simply is no end (170b30–5): 'The eighth and last argument attacks the end, allowing that neither happiness, pleasure, prudence nor anything else is the end, which any philosophical persuasion might believe, but rather that there is altogether no end lauded by all.' Assuming the dialectical context of this argument, he would then suspend belief on whether there is an end or not. The only way he can claim that the Pyrrhonist is tranquil is by reporting it as what appears to him, and this holds good for other claims as well.

There is one testimony which poses a curious problem. At the end of the Aristocles passage, in which Timon recounts Pyrrho's views, Aristocles adds that, whereas Pyrrho promises tranquillity to his followers, Aenesidemus promises *pleasure*. This remark could be interpreted as a vague reference to a mental state similar to tranquillity, especially in the light of the closeness of the two terms in Epicurean philosophy. Another interpretation is possible. Discussing different conceptions of the good, Sextus mentions Aenesidemus' remark, 'that while all people think good that which attracts them (*to hairoun autous*), whatever it may be, the specific judgments which they have about it are in conflict' (*M* 11.42). This remark does not entail that, according to Aenesidemus, whatever one likes is the good. As we have seen, Aenesidemus advanced arguments against there being ends (and indeed about there being natural goods). Rather, his remark entails that what one chooses as one's good depends on what one likes. In that sense, pleasure might play a part in Aenesidemus' account of the sceptic's state of mind. This is a tentative attempt to solve a persistent problem.[11]

---

[11] There is also the possibility of *HΔONHN* being a corruption of *EΠOXHN*; for a discussion of that suggestion, see Polito (2014), 291.

Before we go on to consider Pyrrhonian tranquillity in Diogenes and Sextus, it should be mentioned that Pyrrhonism was closely connected with medical Empiricism.[12] No details about this connection emerge from our knowledge of Aenesidemus' views, except that Diogenes (9.116) reports that one Heraclides was Aenesidemus' teacher. This Heraclides may have been the Empiricist doctor from Tarentum.[13] At all events the fact that the two groups of thinkers were close in outlook invites the thought that, in a manner similar to that of Empiricism, Pyrrhonism aimed at curing people of anxiety by creating tranquillity. I shall return to the connection of Pyrrhonism and Empiricism in the section on Sextus' version of Pyrrhonian tranquillity.

Diogenes on Sceptical Tranquillity

In light of Aenesidemus' distancing himself from an endorsement of a Pyrrhonian end, we should bear in mind what both Sextus and Diogenes have to say about the divergent views of sceptics about the end of the sceptic, and the fact that they actually do so. Diogenes nowhere offers an account of the sceptic's end as tranquillity identical to that offered by Sextus, as we shall see when we consider Sextus' account. What Diogenes says is this (9.107): 'The sceptics say that the end is suspension of belief, which tranquillity follows in the manner of a shadow, as Timon and Aenesidemus say.' There is no mention of the end as tranquillity. It is difficult to see in what way suspension of belief can be an end on a par with human happiness; it is likelier that Aenesidemus' suggestion reflects an attempt to disassociate scepticism from ethical claims. But Diogenes adds (9.108): 'Some also say that the sceptics declare that the end is impassivity, others say calmness.' Here, Diogenes refers to a stance very close to what we do find in Sextus, who repeatedly offers tranquillity as the end, and offers an explanation which we shall consider below.[14] One apparently disingenuous part of Sextus' explanation is that the sceptic finds tranquillity *fortuitously* (*tuchikōs*) after he has suspended belief. Yet Sextus actually elaborates this point by offering Aenesidemus' shadow simile (*PH* 1.29): 'But when they [the sceptics] suspended belief, tranquillity followed as it were fortuitously, as a shadow follows a body.'

Further, Sextus offers the end of tranquillity as the usual suggestion of sceptics, while suspension of belief is presented almost as an afterthought (*PH* 1.30): 'Some eminent sceptics have further added to these ends [i.e. tranquillity and moderate affection] suspension of belief in investigations.' In this manner Sextus has turned around the order we find in Diogenes. This is understandable, since Sextus offers an elaborate explanation of the sceptic's acquisition of tranquillity, which is unique to

---

[12] For a general discussion of the connection, with references, see Allen (2010).
[13] Cf. Polito (2014), 57.
[14] At one point in *PH* 3.235, Sextus uses the term 'impassive', when referring to the sceptics' prized state of mind, preferring that term to 'tranquillity'.

him. In light of the differences between Diogenes and Sextus on the end of scepticism, it appears safe to infer that Pyrrhonists gave differing accounts of sceptical
tranquillity.

The Tranquillity of Sextus

Sextus offers an intricate explanation of the tranquillity of sceptics in *PH* 1.25–30.
That explanation is offered in terms of the sceptic's end (*telos*). In view of Aenesidemus' account it is surprising that Sextus utilizes the term *telos* at all. But surely
Sextus is not committing himself to a teleological account of an ultimate object of
pursuit in a dogmatic manner. Prior to this account in terms of *telos* we find an
explanation of 'the causal principle of scepticism' (*PH* 1.12), in which Sextus refers to
an original anxiety prompted by the conflict of appearances and in turn prompting
the process that eventually leads to suspension of belief and tranquillity. He says:

The causal principle of scepticism is *the hope of becoming tranquil*. Men of noble nature,
anxious because of the anomalies of things, and at a loss as to which of them they should rather
assent to, came to seek what in things is true and what false, thinking that by deciding among
them they would become tranquil.

This passage is helpful for elucidating the status of tranquillity for Sextus. Those
noble people that eventually end up as Pyrrhonists have in common that they start by
seeking to rid themselves of the anxiety that attends the inability to assent to someone
of various conflicting appearances. It may be that the sceptic's *telos* is tranquillity just
in the sense that he hopes and tries to find truth in order to alleviate the anxiety he
feels because of the unresolved conflict of appearances. This account of the sceptics'
starting point does not commit Sextus to any teleological views. It is a description of
an original motivation characteristic of those who happen to end up as sceptics.

Consider now the explanation of tranquillity in terms of the sceptic's *telos* (*PH* 1.25):

Now an end is that for the sake of which everything is done or considered, while it is not itself
done or considered for the sake of anything else. Or: an end is the final object of desire. Up to
now we say that the end of the sceptic is tranquillity (*ataraxia*) in matters of belief and
moderate affection (*metriopatheia*) in matters forced upon us.

Here Sextus distinguishes between two ends, or perhaps two aspects of one end. We
are familiar with the first end, namely tranquillity or the absence of anxiety caused by
the sceptic's inability to assent to some appearances rather than others, that is, his
inability to commit himself to beliefs. The latter end is different. The sceptic hopes to
avoid anxiety and be moderately affected by things that necessarily happen to him.

We immediately get an explanation of the first aim, tranquillity in matters of belief
(*PH* 1.26):

For the sceptics began to do philosophy in order to decide among appearances and to
apprehend which are true and which false, so as to become tranquil; but they came upon

equipollent dispute, and being unable to decide this they suspended belief. And when they suspended belief, tranquillity in matters of belief followed fortuitously (*tuchikōs*).

This explanation refers back to the hope of the noble people (in *PH* 1.12); instead of straightforwardly explaining the aim of a sceptic qua sceptic it refers to the original motivational source of someone who has yet to become a sceptic. Further, the hope does not motivate scepticism as much as philosophizing with a view to gaining knowledge. The pre-sceptic's anxiety, arising as it does out of the conflict of appearances, is topic-neutral. It arises because the person is puzzled as to the truth of the various conflicting appearances; call it epistemic anxiety. This epistemic anxiety could have led the novice philosopher anywhere. As it turned out some novice philosophers found it impossible to decide between appearances and therefore they suspended belief, thereby turning into sceptics. This suspension of belief is quite general and not confined to any specific topic. It is at this point, when the person suspended belief as a sceptic, that tranquillity followed his suspension of belief. The immediate explanation of why tranquillity followed suspension of belief is this: it did so by chance (*tuchikōs*).

At first sight, this explanation is bizarre. But perhaps Sextus does not wish to be convincing but rather offer a description of what happens. He will nevertheless attempt to add to this explanation of the connection between suspension of belief and tranquillity. Before we turn to that attempt, consider *whose* end Sextus is discussing, the novice philosopher's or the mature sceptic's. If by this account Sextus intends to explain tranquillity as the end of the mature sceptic (as opposed to the motivational source of the novice philosopher), he would seem to be saying that by suspending belief in the manner of the sceptic one actually aims for (and reaches) tranquillity in matters of belief. For the sceptic has realized that this does work, albeit fortuitously. He has found that suspending belief brings tranquillity. Alternatively, Sextus could be taken to intend only to explain the reason why the person who became a sceptic started to philosophize in the first place. It is in favour of the latter interpretation that Sextus here offers his account of 'the causal principle of scepticism' (*PH* 1.12) as an explanation of the sceptic's end: the person who turned out a sceptic aims at tranquillity in the sense that this is how he started on the road that led him to scepticism. But it tells against this interpretation that Sextus also says that the sceptic aims at moderate affection in matters of necessity. And this end is not specifically presented as part of the causal principle of scepticism, but as an end that is introduced after the person turns sceptic. And, to be sure, Sextus states (*PH* 1.25): '*Up to now* we say that the end of the sceptic is tranquillity in matters of belief and moderate affection in matters forced upon us.' It is not entirely clear what force this qualification is supposed to have. It appears to refer to the—so far—successful acquisition of tranquillity through suspension of belief.[15] All in all it therefore seems

---

[15] Cf. Janáček (1972), 54–5.

likelier that Sextus' description is not only of what the noble novice hopes to achieve through finding the truth, but also of what the mature sceptic hopes to achieve through suspending belief, namely tranquillity and moderate affection.

As yet Sextus has not explained why suspending belief would lead to tranquillity. He has only suggested that it does so fortuitously or by chance. But in what sense can one hope to gain something by chance? Tranquillity is the intended result of suspending belief, but it only comes about fortuitously? Let us leave this paradox aside for just a moment and consider another strange side to Sextus' account. Even if tranquillity follows suspension of belief by chance, the fact that it follows can nevertheless be explained. Or so Sextus would have us think, since he does offer an explanation of the relation between suspension of belief and tranquillity (*PH* 1.27–8).

Granting that this fortuitous relationship can be explained, one would have thought that somehow tranquillity followed suspension of belief in general. But it turns out that it is not by suspending belief on any and all issues that you become tranquil, but rather just on one specific issue, namely whether things are good or bad by nature: 'For those who believe that things are good or bad by nature suffer perpetual anxiety.'[16] Having beliefs about natural values entails anxiety. Sextus elaborates: (i) When one lacks a supposed natural good, one believes that one suffers a natural evil (and is on that account anxious); in order to remedy this state, one pursues with intensity the supposed natural good. (ii) When one has acquired this supposed natural good (the possibility of which Sextus grants), one becomes even more anxious, since (a) one is elated 'beyond reason and measure' (*PH* 1.27) and (b) one fears the loss of the supposed natural good (because of which fear one is ready to do anything). Obviously, if one does not have the belief that anything is good or bad by nature, then one is free both of the intense pursuit of supposed natural goods (and avoidance of supposed natural evils) and the unreasonable elation and fear that accompanies the acquisition of the supposed natural goods.

This tranquillity in matters of beliefs about natural values is supplemented by moderate affection in matters of necessity. As yet Sextus has not explained this latter part of the sceptic's goal, moderate affection. He admits that the sceptic suffers affections.[17] In that way the sceptic can indeed be disturbed 'by things that are forced upon him' (*PH* 1.29). But Sextus' point is that, again, if one believes that what one suffers is by nature bad, one is worse off than if one has no such belief. He points to ordinary people as the likeliest to harbour such beliefs. It is clear that this can only be the aim of the sceptic qua sceptic, who expects moderate affection in the absence of

---

[16] For a detailed argument concerning the options Sextus has in explaining how general suspension of belief leads to tranquillity, and in general on the difference between the two kinds of tranquillity, and the sources of Sextus' argument, involving Sextus' special arguments against ethicists in *PH* 3 and *M* 11, see Svavarsson 2011.

[17] What he means is open to interpretation; the scope of affections is extremely wide. He says (*PH* 1.29): 'We agree that at times they shiver and are thirsty and have other affections of this kind.' In *PH* 3.236, the sceptics are 'affected by way of their senses'. Often, affections are almost identical to appearances.

beliefs about natural values; it cannot refer to the beginner philosopher who aims at relieving his epistemic anxiety.

So far—Sextus claims—the sceptic has attained his end: he is tranquil, and it turns out that this is because he suspends belief. In order to explain the sceptic's aiming at tranquillity, Sextus tells a story of the painter Apelles, who gave up trying to paint foam frothing from a horse's mouth and throwing the sponge at the painting created a perfect picture of the sought-for foam (*PH* 1.28–9). Sponge-throwing looks like a risky method for creating images of difficult subjects. But the moral of the story seems to be this: suspend belief and you will find that you become tranquil in matters of belief.[18] In fact, Sextus uses the imagery found in Diogenes Laertius (9.107), who refers it to Aenesidemus and Timon, when he says (*PH* 1.29): 'But when they suspended belief, tranquillity followed as it were fortuitously (*hoion tuchikōs*), as a shadow follows a body.'

Sextus' references to tranquillity following suspension of belief fortuitously or by chance can be considered strange for various reasons. First, he offers an intricate explanation of the causes of the tranquillity of sceptics which seems to rule out the element of chance. Secondly, he suggests that one may hope for tranquillity if one suspends belief, even if its advent is by chance. Thirdly he suggests that shadows follow bodies (admittedly) *as if* by chance.

Sextus' account therefore seems to be faulty. One could attempt to save it. The adverb *tuchikōs* is not common. In Sextus the word only occurs in his description of sceptical tranquillity. The earliest writer to employ it is Polybius, who may have had in mind the meaning 'fortunately', 'luckily', even 'conveniently', rather than 'by chance' or 'fortuitously'.[19] It would not be surprising if that were the case. *Tuchē* itself straddles the semantic divide between 'chance' and 'good fortune', 'fortuitously' and 'fortunately'. Perhaps charity recommends that we translate Sextus' *tuchikōs* in the latter manner. He cannot be faulted on any count for claiming that it is fortunate and convenient for the sceptic that tranquillity follows suspension of belief.

But I suggest that there is a more reasonable way to understand Sextus' explanation of the sceptic's tranquillity and his reference to chance. Recall a point mentioned at the end of the section on Aenesidemus, namely that Pyrrhonism was closely connected with medical Empiricism. I suggested that tranquillity, on the Pyrrhonist account, might be analogous to health on the Empiricist account. Indeed, in a passage at the very end of the *Outlines* Sextus encourages such a thought, when he compares the sceptic, 'who wants to heal by argument (*logōi*) the conceit and rashness of dogmatists' (*PH* 3.280), to a doctor fighting bodily afflictions. Galen supplies us with

---

[18] See Striker (1990), 105–6.

[19] The earliest occurrences are, apart from Sextus: Polybius 28.7.1 (who also uses the adjective *tuchikos* in 9.6.5); Diodorus Siculus 2.19.5; 16.35.5; Ps.-Plutarch, *Placita philosophorum* 906E4 = Ps.-Galen, *De historia philosophica* 116.2.

some information about Empiricism.[20] At the very outset of his *On the Sects for Beginners* he says about medicine and doctors in general (1.64 [Kühn] = 1.1 [Helmreich]):

The aim of the art of medicine is health, but its end is the possession of health. Doctors have to know by which means to bring about health, when it is absent, and by which means to preserve it, when it is present.

In the second chapter he starts explaining the Empiricists (1.66 [Kühn] = 2.2 [Helmreich]):

The empiricists claim that the art comes about in the following way. One has observed many affections in people. Of these, some occur spontaneously (*apo tautomatou*), both in the sick and the healthy, e.g., nosebleeding, or sweat, or diarrhea, or something else of the kind which brings harm or advantage, though one cannot see what it is that produced the effect. In the case of other affections, the cause is manifest, but they, too, occur not due to some choice of ours (*ek proaieseōs*), but somehow by chance (*kata tina suntuchian*). Thus it just so happened that somebody fell or was hit or wounded in some other manner and that, hence, there was a flow of blood, or that somebody who was ill gratified his appetites and drank cold water or wine or something else of the kind, each of which had a harmful or beneficial effect. The first kind of beneficial or harmful event they called natural, the second, chance (*tuchikon*). But, in both cases, they called the first observation of such cases an incidence (*periptōsin*), choosing this name because one happens upon these things not on purpose (*aboulētōs*).

Here, then, we have an Empiricist take on the chance origins of successful treatments of diseases.[21] The explanation of the origins is in terms of chance. This seems to be the same point as Sextus makes. The explanation Galen offers in *An Outline of Empiricism* is slightly more picturesque (p. 44: 2.36.19–23 [Deichgräber]):

Those cases of knowledge are said to come about spontaneously which come about by chance or by nature; by chance, as when somebody who has a pain in the back of his head happens to fall, cuts the right vein on his forehead, loses blood, and gets better.

This story is presumably not intended to show that one should let oneself fall when one has a headache in the hope of losing just enough blood, but rather that one has come to expect, from this experience, that a headache may be alleviated by taking blood. In the same way, I suggest, Sextus is at pains to explain the advent of tranquillity as the result of suspending belief in the face of equipollence. His point is that it was a remedy that the sceptics came upon by chance.

---

[20] See Walzer and Frede (1985). This collection contains *On the Sects for Beginners* (*De sectis ingredientisbus*), *An Outline of Empiricism* (*Subfiguratio empirica*—only preserved in a Latin translation), and *On Medical Experience* (only preserved in Arabic). Translations cited are Frede's. See also Deichgräber (1965).

[21] For an account of such chance discoveries of remedies, see Frede (1988), 84–5. See further *On the Therapeutic Method* (*De methodo medendi*) 10.163.14 [Kühn], where Galen complains about the Empiricists' explanations of the origins of treatments.

It is reasonable to ask about Sextus' explanation of tranquillity in terms of the absence of value beliefs. He claimed that what accounted for the fact that suspension of belief leads to tranquillity was the suspension of value beliefs. Is this explanation consistent with the claim that the sceptic came upon tranquillity by chance? I see no reason to think the two propositions inconsistent. The sceptic could have found out, in particular, still by chance, that there was one kind of belief the suspension of which was accompanied by tranquillity, namely positive beliefs about natural values. Further, that does not entail that the sceptic stops suspending beliefs in other domains. Indeed, his suspension of belief, based on comparing contrary accounts and appearances and reaching equipollence, remains topic neutral, even if suspension of belief regarding one topic is found to be attended by tranquillity.[22]

We have attempted to explain Sextus' claim that the sceptic is free of his original anxiety caused by the conflict of appearances. The reason for this tranquillity is that he no longer harbours beliefs about things being by nature good or bad. The thought is inviting that originally the novice believed that this conflict was bad; hence his anxiety. But the sceptic no longer believes this. Hence the conflict is no longer troubling, or at least only moderately so, as is the case with what he suffers but does not depend on his having beliefs. This seems to me to be a reasonable way of explaining the difference between the epistemic tranquillity that the novice hoped for and the tranquillity that he actually finds.

---

[22] It should also be borne in mind that according to Galen some of the Empiricists, and certainly ones predating Sextus, allowed for the use of reason in analysing treatments. This kind of reasoning was termed *epilogismos*. Similarly, Sextus can reason about the sources of the sceptic's tranquillity, so long as the conclusion of his reasoning is couched in terms of appearances. See Galen, *On the Sects* 5.11.8–5 [Helmreich]. For the Empiricist use of reason, see Frede (1988), 87–9. For Sextus on the use of reason, cf. Allen (2010), who discusses Sextus' criticism of (some) Empiricists' disavowal of the use of reasoning, and Svavarsson (2014).

11

Plotinus' Way of Defining *'Eudaimonia'* in *Ennead* I 4 [46] 1–3

Alexandrine Schniewind

1. Introduction

Plotinus is not the philosopher one first thinks of when mentioning ancient Greek theories on happiness.[1] An important reason for this neglect is that over a long period of time Plotinus was not considered to have a consistent ethical theory. At best, he was attributed an elitist ethic, reserved, as it stands, for the sages.[2] Over the decades, a recurrent critique of Plotinus' ethics has been that it does not give sufficient practical indications to the ordinary man of how to become good. This opinion has been revised within the past decade.[3] For instance, it has been accepted that Plotinus had developed thoughts on happiness. He even wrote a whole treatise, *Ennead* I 4 [46],[4] entitled *On Happiness (Peri Eudaimonias)*, dedicated to the topic. In this treatise, Plotinus gives a detailed description of the sage, who is presented as being perfectly happy. While this treatise offers Plotinus' longest sustained presentation of what it is like to be happy, its theoretical part on happiness falls much shorter. In fact, only the first three chapters (counting altogether sixteen chapters) explicitly deal with theoretical aspects; the remaining thirteen chapters brush the picture of the happy wise man through the example of the various aspects of a happy life, as envisaged by Plotinus. Plotinus' ethics is more descriptive than prescriptive,[5] but this does not mean that his descriptions lack theoretical background. It means,

---

[1] In the following I will use 'happiness' and 'well-being' synonymously with the Greek word *eudaimonia*.

[2] Dillon (1996).   [3] Cf. Schniewind (2003).

[4] The references indicate the place of the treatise within Plotinus' *Enneads*, as well as, between square brackets, the chronological order of the treatise. In the following, I will quote the passages of the *Enneads* according to the classical English edition established by Armstrong.

[5] Cf. Schniewind (2003).

rather, that Plotinus uses the descriptive format in order to indicate how a wise man lives in accordance with important conceptual guidelines. Plotinus builds his definition of happiness on a strong metaphysical ground that then legitimates the mental state attained by the happy wise man.

The aim of the present chapter is to look more closely at the first three chapters of the treatise *On Happiness* in order to show how Plotinus deals with what we can consider to be the theoretical exposition of his conception of happiness. Particularly noteworthy are the first two chapters of the treatise. They are dedicated to a lengthy and rather polemic presentation of various approaches and definitions of *eudaimonia* as given by some of Plotinus' predecessors, namely, as it seems, Peripatetics, Stoics, Epicureans, and probably also Sceptics. The Platonic position is not presented, as Plotinus certainly takes it for granted that his own view coincide with Plato's.

Plotinus' aim is obviously to show, in a first step, what he takes to be the risks and even absurdities inhering in these definitions of happiness, so that he can then, in a second step, which takes place in chapter 3, come up with his own definition of *eudaimonia*. The advantage of this strategy of preceding his own definition by a rather eclectic and polemic discussion of other definitions is to indicate to his readers that his definition is exempt of those apparently incoherent elements.

Such openings of treatises are not an exception in Plotinus. Similarly to Aristotle, who often gives a detailed account of the *status quaestionis* of a specific philosophical topic, Plotinus often starts his treatises by evoking a polemical and controversial question, enumerating a series of approaches linked to the question and then showing that they weren't treated in the right way. The usual pattern, as in *Ennead* I 4, is to introduce afterwards a solution to the problem. However, the way Plotinus proceeds in the opening chapters of *Ennead* I 4 [46] is striking. In most cases he does not clearly attribute the positions mentioned to a specific philosopher or philosophical school, and mostly his account seems to be more an unfair caricature than a thorough discussion. This makes reading these chapters irritating, as the intended strategy is not immediately evident to the reader. Also, the first two chapters of *Ennead* I 4 [46] evoke several aspects which do not immediately insert themselves in a coherent *status quaestionis* of *eudaimonia*. In fact, it seems that Plotinus does not really intend to give a full overview of the discussions on *eudaimonia*. Much more, his aim seems to be to prepare the ground for his own account of it.

It is useful, therefore, to examine in detail the opening chapters of *Ennead* I 4 in order to show the strategies used by Plotinus to implement his own definition of *eudaimonia*. Such a focus on the rhetorical and dialectical strategies has not yet been placed, and even the recent English translation with commentary of *Ennead* I 4 by McGroarty[6] is disappointing on this point. I would like to start with a first glance at Plotinus' own definition of *eudaimonia*, as given in *Ennead* I 4, chapter 3, as it makes

---

[6] McGroarty (2006).

the understanding of the two first chapters so much easier. For instance, it helps to put the whole discussion of chapters 1–2 in a frame that then makes much more sense. Plotinus establishes in chapter 3 his own definition of well-being with two terms: 'life' (*zoē*) and 'the good' (*to eu*). Happiness consists in a fulfilled and perfect life that becomes identical with the life of Intellect (*nous*), one of the three Plotinian principles:[7]

> Well-being will belong only to the being which lives superabundantly: this will have the best, if the best among realities is being really alive, is perfect life. So its good will not be something brought in from outside, nor will the basis of its goodness come from somewhere else.[8]

This aimed definition of happiness is the reason why Plotinus focuses on mistaken uses of these terms and other related notions in the first two chapters of his treatise. This raises the question of whether the two first chapters gain a clearer meaning once read retrospectively. In that sense it seems that the function of the first two chapters is mainly to serve Plotinus dialectically, perhaps because he fears that his approach might seem too counter-intuitive if it were presented as such immediately to his readers. One might wonder if Plotinus' strategy is successful or not. This is a question, among others, which we shall examine in the present chapter.[9]

2. Good Life and Well-being

Plotinus opens his treatise by assuming that 'good life' (*to eu zēn*) and 'well-being' (*to eudaimonein*) are synonymous: 'Suppose we assume the good life (*to eu zēn*) and well-being (*to eudaimonein*) to be one and the same.'[10] This first sentence of the treatise addresses the main question straight away: what are the consequences of such an identification? Plotinus quickly indicates that other schools make such an equivalence of the terms and he seeks to show that this might be the reason why their definitions of happiness are too wide and include too many living beings, as they are not restricted to humans. Plotinus' aim is to show that putting *to eu zēn* and *to eudaimonein* as being synonyms may on the face of it be problematic.

This assumption, as it turns out, is part of a discursive strategy: Plotinus asks, at every stage, what *would* happen *if* he were to proceed as other schools do. In this

---

[7] Plotinus establishes three principles through which he outlines the metaphysical and ontological framework of his philosophy. The principles are: the One (*to hen*), Intellect (*nous*), and Soul (*psuchē*). For a general outline of these principles, cf. O'Meara (1995).

[8] *Enn.* I 4, 3, 26–30.

[9] Another striking element in the first two chapters is Plotinus' way of using the expression '*to eu*': it is not quite clear if Plotinus uses this expression as a synonym of '*to eu zēn*' or if it is rather meant to be a synonym for '*to agathon*'. Needless to say, both ways of interpreting his use of such a term have far-reaching implications.

[10] *Enn.* I 4, 1, 1–3. Note the grammatical form of verbal substantives. According to Schwyzer (1951), 515, this form allows to indicate a movement of *becoming something*. This confers to the terms a more active connotation.

context, he uses the grammatical optative mood, a hypothetical style, denoting a potentiality, and avoids a direct or frontal critique. This allows Plotinus to give the impression that he is slowly working himself into the terminology. Within this context of asking whether this equivalence is adequate or not, he makes use of a range of technical terms which mainly evoke specific Hellenistic doctrines. He handles these terms in his own rather eclectic way, pointing out, for instance, relations between them which are far from being evident to us, as they don't follow the usual doctrinal framework in which those terms are traditionally used. Examples of this are the use of the terms *pathos*, *eupatheia*, and *kataphysin*: all of them draw heavily on Stoic philosophy, but the manner in which Plotinus refers to them is somehow unusual. What is more, the way in which Plotinus infers relations between these terms and other philosophical terms is also far from being obvious. In this context, Plotinus does not explicitly say to whom he refers, neither does he quote, be it even loosely, any precise passages, which would allow us to place the discussion in a certain context. It quickly appears that he is referring not only to a single definition of happiness, but rather to a whole series of definitions and to some of the problematic elements they contain.

The way of assimilating *eu zēn* and *eudaimonein*, seems to refer to Aristotle. In *Nicomachean Ethics* and *Eudemian Ethics* Aristotle indeed uses those two expressions synonymously.[11] But as indicated by Graeser, this is simply a way to give a *consensus communis*.[12] Plotinus' criticism is directed toward the fact that Aristotle uses the notion of 'life' (*zoē*) too widely, since plants and animals take part in it and that therefore they could also be called 'happy'.

However, the Stoics and Epicureans could just as well be targeted, as a testimony of Michael of Ephesus allows us to guess that they too made use of this kind of equivalence.[13] Furthermore, the continuation of the chapter makes clear that the Stoics are Plotinus' main target. Their way of using the previously mentioned equivalence of *to eu zēn* and *to eudaimonein* is what Plotinus attacks heavily. In doing so, he takes up technical terms which are directly linked to the Stoic doctrine, for instance the terms *eupatheia* and *ergon oikeion*.[14] Plotinus suggests that if *eu zēn* includes all the non-human living beings, one would have to say that happiness consists in *eupatheiai*, 'good feelings', or else to be an *ergon okeion*, an 'accomplishment of one's proper work', since both these terms designate, according to Plotinus' report of the philosophical use of the terms, states which are not limited to human beings only.[15] For instance, birds whose *ergon okeion* is the activity of singing and who might feel *eupatheiōs* while doing so, would have to be called 'happy'.[16] In the following section of this chapter, I will focus on the term of *eupatheia*.

---

[11] *EN* I 8, 1098b 20–1; *EE* II 1, 1219b 1–3.   [12] Graeser (1972), 38.

[13] Michael of Ephesus, *SVF* III 17. Cf. McGroarty (2006), 43.

[14] These terms are not limited to the Stoics, though; they are used just as well by Aristotle and Plato.

[15] *Enn.* I 4, 1, 5–10.

[16] *Enn.* I 4, 1, 8–10. It might be noteworthy that Zeno, in his discussion of the passions, uses an ornithological metaphor, saying that they are volatile and 'fluttering' (*SVF* 1.206); cf. Long and Sedley (1987), i: 422.

3. Good Feelings

Good feelings, *eupatheiai*, are a central aspect of Stoic ethics. They are the kind of mental state that characterizes a happy person, whereas *pathos* as such, passion, is on the contrary a source of unhappiness and unsatisfactory experience. Traditionally, the Stoics count three primary good feelings as a counterpart to the four 'primary passions' that are appetite, pleasure, fear, and distress.[17] *Eupatheia* is joy (*chara*), opposed to pleasure; carefulness (*eulabeia*) is opposed to fear; will (*boulēsis*) is opposed to desire.[18] These good feelings are side effects (*epigennēmata*) of the right use of reason and virtue.[19] Other good feelings fall under these three primary ones, as recorded by Diogenes Laertius:

- joy subsumes the secondary good feelings of: delight (*terpsis*), sociability (*euphrosunē*), cheerfulness (*euthumia*);
- carefulness subsumes the feelings of: respect (*aidōs*) and cleanliness (*agneia*);
- wishing subsumes the feelings of: kindness (*eunoia*), generosity (*eumeneia*), warmth (*aspasmos*) and content (*agapēsis*).

Long and Sedley stress that these good feelings, as they include a wide spectrum of attractive human characteristics, temper the austerity of the Stoic sage, so strongly emphasized in many ancient sources.[20] Interestingly enough, Plotinus himself stresses similar characteristics of his own wise man later on in the very same treatise I 4. In chapter 12 for instance, the *spoudaios* is said to be always joyful (*hileōs*), calm (*hesuchōs*), and contented (*agapētē*).[21] Interestingly, he does not say here that these characteristics are *eupatheiai*; he instead considers them to be part of what he calls elsewhere 'noble emotions' (*ta asteia*).[22]

These noble emotions and good feelings clearly show that the wise person is not exempt of emotions; this person is able to make a proper use of them, always guided by reason. As stressed by van Riel, the feeling of joy (*chara*) must not only be understood as 'good'; it is explicitly also described as a positive excitement, with a physiological reaction quite near to that of pleasure, with the difference, however, that joy is based on a right judgement, as opposed to pleasure.[23] As shown by van Riel, pleasure, in the Platonic approach, needs external criteria to be determined in its quality. Only such pleasures that are clearly identified as being measured and guided by the knowledge of what is good, are admitted as part of the good life.[24]

In Plotinus, joy is linked to the experience one makes of the Good, as an object of desire,[25] but it is also, contrary to the Stoic use of the term, used by Plotinus in a

---

[17] As stressed by van Riel (2000), 90, the *pathos* of pain has no positive counterpart.
[18] DL 7.116, SVF 3.431. Cf. Long and Sedley (1987), i: 407.
[19] Cf. van Riel (2000), 90.   [20] Long and Sedley (1987), i: 420.   [21] *Enn.* I 4, 12.
[22] *Enn.* IV 3 [27], 32, 1–6. For a detailed account of Plotinus' conception of these 'noble emotions', cf. Schniewind (2014).
[23] Cf. van Riel (2000), 91.   [24] Cf. van Riel (2000), 11–12.
[25] Cf. van Riel (2000), 101; and also *Enn.* VI 7, 24, 4–9 and 25, 16–32.

larger sense that does not imply rationality, including then all *pathēmata* of the soul, be they rational or irrational.[26] This happens for instance in *Ennead* VI 7 [38], a treatise that is chronologically quite near to the treatise I 4 'On Happiness'. In *Ennead* VI 7, entitled 'How the Multitude of the Forms Came into Being, and on the Good', Plotinus uses the term *eupatheia* in a way that is of great interest to us, as it contrasts with the critique of the notion expressed by Plotinus in *Ennead* I 4. In *Ennead* VI 7, soul is described as being in a state of *eupatheia* while ascending through the stages of the intelligible principle that is Intellect and contemplating the Good: 'if all the other things about it perished, it would even be pleased, that it might be alone with this: so great a pleasant feeling (*eupatheia*) has it reached.'[27]

In that same context, Intellect too is said to be in a state of *eupatheia*. It is presented as having two aspects, the 'thinking intellect' (*nous emphrōn*) and the 'loving intellect' (*nous erōn*).[28] The state of *eupatheia* corresponds to the stage of the loving intellect.[29] The Stoic use of *eupatheia* is thus considerably changed by Plotinus, as it is present at the various stages of the intelligible realm (on the level of Soul and Intellect) and expresses the emotion due to the unification with the First Principle, the One.[30] This use of *eupatheia* is very close to the use Plato makes of it in *Phaedrus* 247d, where souls are said to have good feelings (*eupatheia*) when contemplating the Forms, just in the same way as Gods do. In other words, souls experience good feelings before even entering a body:[31]

Now the divine intelligence, since it is nurtured on mind and pure knowledge, and the intelligence of every soul which is capable of receiving that which befits it, rejoices (*agapa*) in seeing reality for a space of time and by gazing upon truth is nourished and made happy (*eupathei*) until the revolution brings it again to the same place.[32]

Why, then, is Plotinus so hostile to *eupatheia* in I 4? Apparently, the context of treatise I 4 calls for a strong exclusion of *eupatheia*, whereas in other contexts, as for example in treatise VI 7, Plotinus sees no objection to making use of the term. Rist mentions this paradox: 'As so often, Plotinus goes back on his own language and reintroduces terms—with new meanings—which he has rigorously excluded before.'[33]

4. Perception and Well-being

Having thus considered good feelings and having aimed at excluding animals from the definition of happiness, Plotinus examines in *Ennead* I 4, chapter 2, the status of perception (*aisthēsis*). He asks if one might get rid of plants in the definition of happiness in saying that a happy living being would at least need to have access to

---

[26] *Enn.* VI 7, 30, 17–18 and *Enn.* II 2, 3, 12–15. Cf. van Riel (2000), 113 and 119.
[27] *Enn.* VI 7, 34, 36–8, translation by Armstrong, modified for '*eupatheia*'.
[28] *Enn.* VI 7, 35, 20–9.   [29] *Enn.* VI 7, 35, 24–6.   [30] Cf. van Riel (2000), 114.
[31] Cf. Hadot (1987), 338.   [32] *Phaedrus* 247d; translation by H. N. Fowler (1925).
[33] Rist (1967), 150.

aisthēsis?[34] Taken as an emotion (*pathos*), perception is linked by Plotinus to the question of awareness and consciousness: is perception an affection (*pathos*) and is it to be considered as meaning 'being aware of one's experience (*to pathos mē lanthanein*)?[35] If this is the case, then one needs to say that this affection (*pathos*) must be good (*agathon*) in itself even before one becomes aware of it.[36] But this is only one alternative among three others, the three being guided by considerations about the temporal consecution between the terms of affection (*pathos*), awareness of it (*mē lanthanein*), and perception (*aisthēsis*), as well as the status of the good. The three alternatives are the following:

(1) The affection (*pathos*) is in itself good; it is followed by an awareness of it and only then it comes to perception.[37] Plotinus gives, as an example, the fact that being in a natural state (*to kata physin*) is good, even if one is not aware of it.
(2) The good is attributed to perception and knowledge (*gnōsis*) of an actual affection (*pathos*), so that it is linked to awareness of something.[38] This option implies that 'good' would have to be taken as being synonymous with 'perceived as good'.
(3) The third alternative consists in a combination of both *pathos* and *aisthēsis*: the good is the result of both.[39] It seems that Plotinus aims at leading the whole argument *ad absurdum* through this third option.

Plotinus wants to show that without awareness of something and, furthermore, without knowledge (*gnōsis*) of that thing, it is not possible to say of something that it is good. And as soon as knowledge is involved, one needs something on a higher ontological level than *sense-perception*. In Plotinus' words: the question is if one is in a state of *eu zēn because* one knows that this is a good state and feels happy *because* it procures pleasure, or if one must know that this state procures pleasure and that this pleasure is the good.[40] Plotinus' idea is to direct the attention to the notion of judgement (*to krinein*) involved in saying that pleasure is the good, and insists that it is more valuable than mere affection (*pathos*). His conclusion is that the good life will not belong to those who only feel pleasure, but only to those who are capable of knowing that pleasure is the good.[41] And here Plotinus attains the conclusion he was aiming at: the capacity of judgement comes from *logos* and *nous* and obviously never from *sense-perception*.[42]

What are we to think of these three alternatives which are far from being easy to spell out neatly? Why does Plotinus use so much space on them? What is gained for the discussion? This gives Plotinus the opportunity to comment on the notion of *pathos*, which is not only important for the Stoics and Epicureans, but also for the Sceptics (especially the expression *kata pathos* which is used in chapter 2; for the

[34] *Enn.* I 4, 2, 1–2. [35] *Enn.* I 4, 2, 4. [36] *Enn.* I 4, 2, 4–5. [37] *Enn.* I 4, 2, 3–6.
[38] *Enn.* I 4, 2, 8–13. [39] *Enn.* I 4, 2, 13–15. [40] *Enn.* I 4, 2, 15–19.
[41] *Enn.* I 4, 2, 21–3. [42] *Enn.* I 4, 2, 26.

Sceptics this means to live in accordance with one's affections). A major difficulty is to tie these alternatives to known philosophical positions and one is tempted to say that this isn't really Plotinus' goal. He obviously is perfectly content with giving a rather sketchy view of the three options, without going into detail, his aim being to step quickly to a conclusion which shows that it is by far too complicated and risky to rely on notions such as *pathos*, *kata pathos*, *sense-perception*, and, of course, also *pleasure*, when one wants to approach a sound definition of *eudaimonia*.

At this stage of the two opening chapters of *Ennead* I 4, Plotinus makes a shift from his initial discussion of the notion of 'life' (*zoē*, chapter 1) to the more complex notion of 'good' (*to eu, to agathon*, chapter 2). In asking what can be considered as being good (*agathon*), Plotinus starts with the lowest ontological level, namely with perception (*aisthēsis*) and the affections (*pathos*), to which he adds the notion of pleasure (*hēdonē*). He shows that these notions need to be completed by epistemic notions such as awareness and judgement (*krinein*), which are linked to *logos* and *nous*. The end of chapter 2 ends thus in a climax, which is followed by a kind of general critique of those who give tribute to rationality but then do not manage to live up to those high-level criteria they themself posed within their theory.[43] Plotinus' point is to say that the whole argument crashes if rationality is not the sole criterion of happiness. If we diminish rationality to a mere natural state (*kata physin*), it becomes a simple means to an end:

Do you add the rational because the reason is more ingenious and can easily investigate the primary things according to nature, or [would you require reason] even if it was neither capable to trace them out [i.e. the primary things according to nature], nor to obtain them? But if you [require reason] because it is better capable to discover them [the primary things according to nature], *eudaimonia* will also belong to those without reason, if without reason by their nature they can reach the primary natural needs. And then reason would be a servant and would not be chosen for itself nor in turn the perfection of it, which we say is virtue.[44]

Reading this passage, as well as the others mentioned so far, raises the question of why Plotinus thinks it necessary to come up with such a critique: does he really believe his own position to be so counter-intuitive that it has to be prefaced by all this criticism? Chapter 1 was quite easy to follow and one could quickly see what its point was: revealing that the notion of life runs the risk of including all living beings. So it becomes clear that Plotinus will have to come up with his own definition of life that would avoid these problems or else reject life as a constituent in the definition of happiness. Chapter 2, on the contrary, is much trickier, as many things are mingled in a very sketchy way. It is clear, however, that it aims at saying that the notion of

---

[43] Cf. *Enn.* V 9 [5], 1. Plotinus comes up with the same critique and the same way of proceeding, but with a better structure.

[44] *Enn.* I 4, 2, 35–43; my translation.

good (*agathon*) needs to be linked to rationality and cannot be located at the lower ontological levels, namely within perception and affection.

These are, I believe, Plotinus' two main points and we'll see that these are precisely those he'll pick up in his own definition of happiness.

5. Plotinus' Own Definition of Happiness

Plotinus' own definition of happiness is grounded in the two terms previously discussed by him in the first two chapters: 'life' (*zoē*) and 'the good' (*to eu, to agathon*). The arguments he has been advancing so far have made clear that both terms need to be treated with caution and even require redefining. So the expression '*to eu zēn*' remains at the centre of the discussion and Plotinus shows that one might indeed say that '*to eu zēn*' is equivalent to '*to eudaimonein*', but only if one gives the right definition of '*to eu zēn*'. What is more, Plotinus puts '*zoē*' and '*to eu*' together and says that the perfect life (*teleios zēn*) is the true '*agathon*'. This was obviously his aim, right from the beginning, that is, to show that one might very well keep the equivalence of *to eu zēn* and *to eudaimonein*, if only one bothers to redefine the terms. His redefinition is quite radical: the notion of 'life' gets a completely new meaning. It is said to be homonymous: 'The term "life" is used in many different senses (*pollachōs legomenon*),[45] distinguished according to the rank of the things to which it is applied, first, second and so on.'[46]

According to Plotinus, the homonymous sense of 'life' means that it has many different ontological levels. The life which is meant in the definition of happiness as being *to eudaimonein*, is a very specific kind (*eidos*) of life: it is the highest level of fulfilled life, the First Life, the Perfect Life from which all the other lives come.[47] And that's why 'life' taken in a homonymous way means that there are differences in clarity of lives: some are clearer (*tranotēs*), others are darker (*amudrotēs*).[48] Happiness belongs thus to the person who possesses that First and Perfect Life in its full intensity (*agan zēn*).[49] This has a strong meaning, since this life bears no deficiency at all and is in fact the life of Intellect (*nous*):

Often it has been said that the perfect life and the true life and the real life is in that noetic nature, and that the other lives are imperfect and are only reflections of life, existing imperfectly and impurely, and no more lives than their opposite.[50]

As for the notion of the good, it too has to be taken homonymously, since for it too only the first and perfect good can be part of the definition of happiness.[51]

To conclude, let us come back to our initial question. Why does Plotinus choose to formulate his first two chapters as he does? Isn't there something peculiar about his

---

[45] As defined by Aristotle, *DA* 413a.   [46] *Enn.* I 4, 3, 18–20.   [47] *Enn.* I 4, 3, 33–4.
[48] *Enn.* I 4, 18–23.   [49] *Enn.* I 4, 3, 24–8.
[50] *Enn.* I 4, 3, 33–7. Translation by McGroarty (2006).   [51] *Enn.* I 4, 22–30.

scatty way of presenting them, staying in a hypothetical mood and adding to it a polemical attitude? Does it help us if we take him to be in a defensive mode, thinking that his upcoming definition might be rejected at first sight? Is his approach involving different ontological levels of life and good considered to be too bold to be accepted without preparation? Or, on the contrary, does he believe that his approach is precious and needs to be saved from sloppy readers who will unknowingly mingle his approach with other uses of the same terms? In this case Plotinus' approach should rather be taken as a necessary preparation, perhaps even with the chosen effect of leaving the readers at the end of chapter 2 in a kind of *aporia*, which is then solved by the very clear outline of Plotinus' own account in chapter 3.

It seems certain that Plotinus does not intend to address precise pieces of theory in his two opening chapters. His sole aim is to throw in the technical terms, showing how one should deal with them and alerting his audience about some inherent risks to using those terms. Plotinus' main aim is thus to proceed, in a first step, in a negative way, eliminating all the elements that might disturb the definition of happiness he intends to give.

12

On Happiness and Time

Eyjólfur K. Emilsson

I

It is well known that happiness (*eudaimonia, eu zēn*) and virtue were the central notions of ancient ethics. The question can be raised, however, whether the ancient notion of *eudaimonia* is the same as the modern notion of happiness. Isn't it misleading, it may be asked, or even quite wrong, to talk about happiness in relation to the ancients? The Greek term would be more accurately translated as 'human flourishing', 'having a good life' or 'well-being' maybe but definitely not by 'happiness'. Indeed many translators and scholars of ancient philosophy avoid the words 'happiness' and 'happy' as a rendering the Greeks terms *eudaimonia* and *eudaimōn*. I shall not quarrel with this, but I shall stick to the word 'happiness' nevertheless, well knowing that there are differences between this and the Greek *eudaimonia*. The differences should, however, not obscure the fact that there may well be an important common core. In an interesting recent article, Mark Chekola (2007, 53) writes that there is 'a logical or conceptual core of the concept of happiness that goes back at least to the ancient Greeks and still forms our general understanding of the concept of happiness.' Among the features of this logical core, Chekola mentions that (a) happiness has to do with one's life as a whole, (b) happiness is relatively long-lasting, not just a day but a significant period, (c) happiness makes life worthwhile, (d) happiness is something all people desire.

Chekola may be right in holding that these ideas are central to our notion of happiness. Something close to his core is what remains, when perfunctory, light-hearted uses of 'happiness' and 'happy' have been cleansed away. Such special uses are especially common in the case of the adjective: think of the use of 'happy' in phrases like 'Are you happy with that verdict?' where 'happy' appears as a synonym of 'content'. This use and sense is only minimally connected with happiness in the important sense of the word in virtue of which happiness is of great concern for most people and of interest to philosophers. Even if this is so, it is legitimate to raise the question to what extent Chekola's core ideas are a deeply ingrained commonplace going back to the ancient Greeks.

II

I shall in this chapter address this question with respect to the two first-mentioned ideas in Chekola's core: is the view that happiness is necessarily an enduring condition and that it has to do with one's life as a whole a part of the heritage from ancient Greece and Rome?

One reason why one may think that this is indeed the classical view is that there are two celebrated texts, both arguably taken as archetypically and representatively ancient Greek, that seem to assert this: I am thinking of the account of the meeting between Solon and Croesus given by Herodotus in book one of his *Histories* and of Aristotle's account of happiness in book I of his *Nicomachean Ethics*.[1] The latter text actually alludes to the former. Both texts assert that one has to wait with the judgement about a person's happiness till the person's life is completed, and at least Aristotle explicitly holds that happiness is no ephemeral affair.

Let us recall some of the points Solon made in his conversation with Croesus in the treasure chamber in Sardis on the fourth day of Solon's visit. Croesus inquired who was the happiest man that the wise widely travelled Solon ever had met.[2] Croesus thought it must be he himself, and he was quite disappointed when Solon mentioned in the first and the second place some insignificant people by Croesus' light. He asked Solon then if he didn't at all appreciate his, that is, Croesus' happiness. In responding to this, Solon says: 'Consider the end; call no man happy till he is dead'. He then goes on to expound the number of days there are, on the average, in a human life and to enlist the dangers and calamities each of these days may bring. Predictably, Croesus had to learn his lesson the hard way.

There are several interesting things to note about the exchange between Solon and Croesus. For one thing it is remarkable how both Croesus and Solon seem to take a totally objective view on happiness in the sense that both assume that there are objective, public criteria for happiness: Croesus, for his part, does not express any doubt that Solon can provide him with an objectively correct answer to his question who is the happiest person Solon has met. Though disappointed, Croesus does question the correctness of Solon's placing the Athenian Tellus number one. According to most contemporary accounts of happiness, even by philosophers, happiness is a certain kind of feeling and as such subjective. From this point of view we would suppose that Solon would have said something about his favourite candidates' inner life, something about how they felt about life and things. But he didn't. Not a word about anything of the kind. As ancient views developed, we indeed see a trend

---

[1] Kitto (1951: 110–11) relates the story in his popular book *The Greeks* noting that 'it throws such light on the Greek mind'.

[2] See Herodotus, I, 30–2. It should be noted that the adjective for 'happy' in this exchange is *olbios*, not *eudaimōn*, which is the standard term in Plato, Aristotle, and the subsequent tradition. The substantive Herodotus uses and apparently intending to convey the same notion is, however, *eudaimoniē* (Ionian for *eudaimonia*).

towards an internalization of happiness: the Epicureans take happiness to consist in pleasure and a certain tranquillity of mind which also is pleasant, while Aristotle, the Stoics, and the Neoplatonists all identify happiness with the activity of reason, though their respective accounts how this is so differ significantly. If Solon and Croesus had been, say, Epicureans, Croesus would hardly have bothered asking Solon who was the happiest; if he, however, had bothered, Solon, considering Croesus as a candidate, would have inquired about his state of mind with respect to pleasure and pain.

Today it is commonly assumed, I believe, that happiness is subjective in two ways: First, it is thought to be an internal feeling of each person's soul or mind and secondly, which is not a necessary consequence of the first, it is believed to be up to each person to judge if he or she is happy. It is presumed to be a personal, internal affair where each one is the final authority about him- or herself. Even if happiness was made internal in the ancient philosophical tradition, it was never subjective in this latter sense of infallible individual authority: it was always presumed that certain courses of life, pursuits, and avoidances were objectively valid with respect to happiness, others not.

Interesting as these comparisons may be, I primarily wish to direct our attention to another aspect of Solon's remarks: Why does Solon say that one should not call anyone happy till he is dead? The reason he gives is that there are so many days in a human life each one of which can bring many surprises and disasters. But why does it follow from this that we have to wait till the last day to judge if a person is happy? If Solon were a latter day utilitarian, he could have said that we have to wait because if we want to know who is the happiest person in the world we just have to count the happy hours each has had and the winner will emerge. Perhaps a subtle utilitarian would insist on also measuring the intensity of the pleasant happy feeling but I shall ignore such subtleties here: they do not affect the main point. In any case, for the utilitarian, it would make good sense to wait till the lives compared have come to an end because normally there seems to the possibility of some more happiness while a person is alive. So we should not count anyone out of the competition till there is no hope of more happiness.

The rhetoric of Solon's little speech to Croesus does not indicate that he thought about human happiness along these utilitarian lines. Rather, Solon's emphasis on the number of days in a life and the danger each of them may bring suggest that he (or rather Herodotus) regarded the human good as something very fragile and contingent; powers and events beyond the individual's control can easily ruin it. Furthermore, his words suggest one dreadful day may ruin one's luck forever; a great number of good days in early life does little to alleviate the damage done by a devastating blow late in life. A late catastrophe can ruin the happiness of a whole life.

All this suggests that according to Solon the place on the temporal arrow is quite significant when it comes to judging a person's happiness: he did not think like a modern utilitarian according to whom we merely count the good times disregarding in which part of life they occurred. Perhaps a comparison with a sports game is not out of place: according to Solon happiness is like a football match: two goals and an impressive performance in the first half becomes quite insignificant if the team collapses in the second half and loses 2:4. Similarly: splendour and prosperity in early and mid-life followed by a calamity, humiliation, and, finally, a disgraceful death makes the whole life a bad one, unhappy.

I shall now turn to Aristotle's *Nicomachean Ethics*. As we shall see, Aristotle shares certain insights with Solon, for example, about the relevance of a good end of life. Nevertheless, his thought about these matters also takes a different direction. Aristotle's definition of happiness given in chapter I 7 of his *Nicomachean Ethics* is that happiness is activity, *energeia*, of soul in accordance with virtue. By 'in accordance with virtue' he means 'in accordance with excellence of reason': he has established the virtue or excellence of each thing consists in doing well what is the nature of the thing in question to do, and human nature consists in reason. He leaves it open at this stage which kind of virtue is at stake, whether it is practical virtue or theoretical or both. Right after this general statement he adds 'in a complete life. For one swallow does not make a summer, nor does one day; and so too one day, or a short time, does not make a man blessed and happy' *(EN* I 8, 1098b18–20).

In the following chapters of *Nicomachean Ethics* I, Aristotle raises some questions his definition gives rise to. In particular he is concerned with testing it against received opinions about happiness—the opinions of most people and of the wise. In the course of this Aristotle says:

For there is required [for happiness], as we said, not only complete virtue but also complete life, since many changes occur in life, and all manner of chances, and the most prosperous may fall into great misfortunes in old age, as is told of Priam in the Trojan Cycle; and one who has experienced such chances and has ended wretchedly no one calls happy. *(EN* I 9, 1100a4–9)[3]

In a direct continuation of this, he turns his attention to Solon's famous words, 'consider the end', 'call no man happy till he is dead'. He notes that there is an apparent contradiction between Solon's view and his own: if happiness is essentially an activity, one should think that happiness is there when the activity is going on and only then, while the dead are presumably quite inactive. Aristotle, however, takes Solon's meaning to be that the reason why we shouldn't call anyone alive happy is that we cannot be quite sure whether great misfortunes will befall a person in the future. He points out that virtue is extremely stable and, consequently, so is activity in accordance with it. So a virtuous person can take quite a few blows and still act virtuously, and, hence, be happy. Many great misfortunes may, however, ruin a person's happiness. Aristotle concludes this discussion thus:

---

[3] This and other translations of Aristotle here are those of *The Complete Works of Aristotle, Revised Oxford Translation,* edited by Jonathan Barnes (Princeton: Princeton University Press, 1984), sometimes slightly modified.

Why should we not say that he is happy who is active in conformity with complete virtue and is sufficiently equipped with external goods, and not for some chance period but throughout a complete life? Or must we add 'and who is destined to live thus and die as befits his life'? Certainly the future is obscure to us, while happiness, we claim, is an end and something in every way final. If so, we shall call blessed those among living men in whom these conditions are, and are to be, fulfilled—but blessed *men*. (*EN* I 10, 1101a14–21)

Aristotle clearly shares Solon's view that external events beyond the agent's control can have an effect on happiness. There is a difference, however, in that Aristotle thinks virtue, and hence happiness, is an extremely stable condition. Happiness, we have been told, is the activity or exercise of virtue. Once virtuous, the successful exercise of virtue is fairly easy to come by: it does not require great means—on this Solon explicitly agrees (Hdt. I, 32, 5). Aristotle, however, strongly emphasizes that only very great misfortunes can deprive the happy man of his happiness (*EN* I 10, 1101a9–13). As suggested by Dewald (2011), according to Herodotus happiness significantly depends on good fortune and that human beings are very much subject to the whims of fortune and control little themselves. If this impression is correct, Aristotle disagrees on this point: he clearly thinks that happiness mostly depends on virtue; virtue, which in turn depends on one's reason.

In this insistence on the crucial role of reason in securing a good life, Aristotle follows Plato and Socrates who initiated the startling view that the cultivation and right use of reason is a guarantee of a good life: according to them, no matter what happens, a man of reason cannot really be harmed.[4] Aristotle, of course, does not follow them all the way and makes a number of concessions to Solon's line of thought, which presumably represents the traditional, more common-sense view than that adopted by Socrates and Plato. So Aristotle's position is somewhere in between the extreme view which may have been that of Herodotus that so far as happiness is concerned human beings are at the mercy of powers beyond their control, and the Socratic–Platonic view that a man of reason will remain happy or at least unharmed in any circumstances. Aristotle actually goes a long way towards agreement with his philosophical predecessors but makes a concession to the traditional view in extreme cases.

Though with certain modifications, Aristotle famously also agrees with Solon that ending life well, or at least not badly, is a precondition of calling someone happy. This is shown especially by Aristotle's remark that nobody who suffers great misfortunes and ends badly, like Priam, is called happy. Aristotle's point is not merely the trivial one that Priam did not die happy but rather that the fact that he should have such a sad end affects the judgement that he ever was a happy man. This understanding is confirmed by the second quote above where Aristotle expresses his final view: 'happy' can be truly predicated of virtuous people of some means in the middle of their lives

---

[4] On the important role given to reason for the happy life from Socrates on, see Frede (1996).

but only on condition that their external fortune does not drastically turn against them. Thanks to the stability and resourcefulness of virtue, this rarely happens but it may.

These two aspects in which Aristotle follows Solon, that happiness depends on favourable external conditions and that it cannot be pronounced till the life has come to an end, are connected: as we have seen, Aristotle explicitly says that the reason why one has to suspend judgement about this while the person is alive is that the future is uncertain and something disastrous may still happen so long as the person lives. Aristotle clearly thinks that since virtue is a stable condition, if it weren't for the sinister possibility of a great misfortune which incapacitates the ability to exercise virtue, it would be quite safe to pronounce living people engaged in the kind of activity Aristotle takes happiness to consist in to be happy.

This is, however, not all there is to the matter so far as Aristotle is concerned. He reveals a certain interesting inconsistency in his account of happiness in relation to time: on the one hand, he insists that we cannot say whether someone is happy till he is dead; on the other, in the same breath, he praises people as happy who are not at all dead. He says for instance:

Nor, again, is [the happy person] many-coloured and changeable; for neither will he be moved from his happy state easily or by any ordinary misadventures, but only by many and great ones, nor, if he has had many great misadventures, will he recover his happiness in a short time, but if at all, only in a long and complete one in which he has attained many splendid successes. (*EN* I 10, 1101a9–13)

As we see here, Aristotle speaks of such a person as *regaining his happiness*. This presupposes that the person was happy already long before he died and that he or she is yet to suffer some great misadventures, which he or she may recover from so as to regain happiness. He is presuming that this person was happy but lost his or her happiness. Yet, at this stage in his discourse, Aristotle is about to tell us that at most we can call someone who is alive happy only if the person is actually doing well and will continue so till the end. How could we have judged correctly that the person who lost his or her happiness and regained it was happy before the loss, if we only can judge this of someone who is engaged in virtuous activity and is destined to do so till the end?

Perhaps this is an easily forgivable little inconsistency that does not much affect Aristotle's account in the end. I find it probable, however, that this discrepancy is a sign of a real tension in his view on happiness. Let us pursue this.

Aristotle, as we have seen, defines happiness as an activity (*energeia*). According to his *Metaphysics* IX 6, 1048b23–8 activities are complete at every instant (cf. *Phys.* III 2, 201b31–2; *Met.* XI 9, 1066a20–1; *DA* III 7, 431a6–7; *EN* X 4, 1174a14–23): they do not need time to be brought to completion. Activities are thus contrasted with what he calls processes or motions (*kinēseis*). This does not mean that Aristotle is saying that activities are something mysterious, taking place in some dimension that is totally outside the realm of time. As Ackrill (1997: 150) notes, it is rather the simple point that once activities are going on they are fully going on and do not require more time to be completely there. Other examples he gives of activities are 'to live', 'to live well', 'to be happy' (*eudaimonein*), 'to see', and 'to think'. All these are supposed to be such that if it is truly said of somebody that she lives or lives well or sees or thinks, then the perfect tense also holds true: if I am living it is *eo ipso* true that I have lived; if I am living well, have lived well; if I am seeing, I have already seen; if I am thinking, I have already thought. Aristotle wants to maintain that being happy, *eudaimonein*, belongs to this class: thus if I am happy now, I have been happy in the sense that I have already achieved happiness. Thus, activities, contrary to processes such as building a house, are supposed to be complete, to have reached their end if they occur at all.

Admittedly, Aristotle actually sometimes uses the term 'activity' more broadly so that it covers both activities in the narrow sense sketched above and what he calls processes or motions (*kinēseis*), which in such contexts are labelled incomplete (*ateleis*) activities. For example, he says in *De Anima* that 'a process (*kinēsis*) is a kind of activity but an incomplete one.' (*DA* II 5, 417a17–18; cf. also *Phys.* III 2, 201b31; VIII 5, 257b8). Might the preceding account of happiness as a complete activity not be questioned with reference to such passages? Might Aristotle not simply be using 'activity' in the broader sense when he defines happiness as activity of soul in accordance with virtue? If so, there is no presumption that the activity in which happiness is said to consist should be completed at the time at which it occurs—no more so than the activity of building a house is completed when the builder is in the midst of building it. Several other passages make it clear, however, that when calling happiness an activity he intends activity in the narrower sense. For instance, in the *Metaphysics*, Aristotle says in the context of the difference between processes and activities, taking 'living well' and 'being happy' as examples of activities narrowly speaking: 'We are living well and have lived well, we are happy and have been happy, at the same time' (IX 6, 1048b26). This makes it quite clear that he thinks of happiness as activity in the narrow sense. By putting happiness and being happy in this group—a group to which also belongs the thinking activity of God—Aristotle is indicating the perfection of happiness and the happy life: happiness is not the sort of thing that, like a building being built still has to achieve something in order to be what it is. According to this we should suppose that anyone engaged in activity of soul in accordance with virtue is already happy.

The account of happiness as 'activity in accordance with virtue' can be rendered more or less consistent with the addition 'in a complete life': a person is happy if he or she is engaged in activity in accordance with virtue from the time the person acquired virtue till the end of life. There is no inconsistency involved here: Aristotle is simply putting a further restraint on happiness by insisting that the virtuous activity must continue throughout life. His allowance for losing and regaining happiness should be taken as a simple but understandable slip. Nevertheless, there are two strains in his thought that do not coexist altogether happily: On the one hand, there is the emphasis on happiness as self-sufficient, self-contained activity. This is something one should think was fully realized at any time the activity is taking place. On the other hand, there are the considerations of time and the insistence that happiness is something that applies to a whole lifetime.[5]

It is tempting to think that according to Aristotle's conception of happiness that insists on considering the whole lifetime, the term 'happy' is taken to apply primarily to the life, only secondarily to the person. That is to say, we first ask: is this a happy life? If the answer is 'yes, it is', we say that the person, whose life it is, is happy. (There need not be any real inference in this: arguably, according to Aristotle, the human being is his or her life; the life, however, is the primary notion.) It was mentioned above, that according to Aristotle, 'to live' counts as an activity as opposed to a process. It is something complete in the sense that if you live you also have already lived. Aristotle, however, also has a different conception of life according to which life is essentially something that unwinds itself in time and with a certain temporal structure. Organisms by nature go through a maturing period, blossom and decay. I do not wish to suggest that such biological facts directly inform Aristotle's views on human happiness, which surely is to be evaluated by other criteria than strictly biological ones. Still, these biological facts may provide a background for his views on human happiness. Aristotle surely belongs to the class of thinkers for whom the narrative structure of life matters for the evaluation of happiness.[6] The judgement about the goodness of a life has to take the whole of his or her life into account and, moreover, it has to consider the way it is going, whether for example something blemishes it towards the end.

III

Let us now turn our attention to post-Aristotelian ancient philosophers. It strikes me as quite remarkable that most, if not all, major schools after Aristotle disagree with him on the points that he has in common with Solon, that is, the points that Chekola takes to belong to the core of the notion of happiness, that is, that it is (necessarily) an enduring condition and that it pertains to life as a whole. These later ancient thinkers—Epicureans, Stoics, and Platonists, share the view that a happy life, if it is there at all, is there fully in the now. They all also agree that a life, once happy, does not become any happier by lasting longer. This is a view that rejects the narrative aspect of happiness on which Aristotle insists. Epicurus and his followers, the Stoics and Plotinus all insist on this. And they do so despite in other respects holding quite different views on what happiness actually consists in. For the Epicureans it is sheer

---

[5] Cf. *Eudemian Ethics* II 1, 1219a37, where Aristotle says that the activity of anything less than a full life is an incomplete activity.

[6] Such a view is lucidly defended by Velleman (1991). See also MacIntyre (1981), 203–4; Taylor (1989), 51–2.

pleasure, for the Stoics it is the easy flow of life which results from a disposition to always aim for what is right/in accordance with nature. For Plotinus happiness is a state of intuitive thought that is really outside time.

The Epicureans, who thought that the sole goal in life is pleasure and that happiness hence consists in a life in pleasure, believed that the length of a person's life is irrelevant to the person's happiness. Epicurus says in his *Key Doctrines* 19: 'Infinite time and finite time contain equal pleasure, if one measures the limits of pleasure by reasoning.' This statement is obscure for several reasons. For instance, it is not at all clear what Epicurus means by the qualification 'if one measures the limits of pleasure by reasoning.' In the continuation, which seems to be meant as an explication or justification of this, he says:

> The flesh places the limits of pleasure at infinity, and needs an infinite time to bring it about. But the intellect, by making a rational calculation of the end and the limit which govern the flesh, and by dispelling the fears about eternity, brings about the complete life, so that we no longer need an infinite time. (*Key Doctrines* 20)

This is of course quite obscure too. Presumably the point is that a person who has realized (with the aid of reason) that happiness is the pleasure that exists in the moment and reached a state of freedom from mental disorder, that is, freed himself or herself of the fear of death, is completely content and does not need or desire any more time to be completely happy. This is a state of pleasure according to Epicurus, indeed 'the limit' of pleasure beyond which pleasure cannot be increased (cf. Epicurus, *Key Doctrines* 3; Cicero, *De fin.* I, 33–47). So Epicurus is probably saying that a person who through the use of right reasoning concerning the nature of pleasure and of death could rightly say 'I am completely happy; nothing can increase my happiness now. It would not become greater if it lasted longer or lesser if it should turn out to be short-lived.' This understanding seems to be confirmed by the Epicurean spokesman in Cicero's *De Finibus bonorum et malorum* (Cicero, *De fin.* I, 19).

Is Epicurus saying then that time has no bearing on happiness? Well, that depends on what we mean by 'time has no bearing'. If I understand Long and Sedley I (1987, 154) correctly in their commentary on this passage, they suggest that indeed time has a bearing for Epicurus and that by this remark he is not excluding that happiness grows with time; Epicurus' point here, Long and Sedley suggest, is merely that once the fear of death is removed all rational, hedonistic motivation for desiring immortality is removed.

It seems to me, however, that even if Epicurus held this view and it may follow from what he says here, he wants to make a stronger point. Taking for granted the interpretation we gave of the difficult phrase, 'if we measure the limits of time by reasoning', Epicurus indeed says that for the person who has reached the pleasure of tranquillity a finite time contains just as much pleasure as an infinite one. Since nothing is specified about the length of the finite time of tranquillity needed to equal an infinite time, the claim must be that any finite time of tranquillity equals any other finite time. In other words, once a person has reached this state, he or she gains no more pleasure by being in it longer. As we shall see, the Stoics and Plotinus held essentially the same view.

According to the Stoics happiness and virtue are so closely tied that it is impossible to have the one without the other. In Diogenes Laertius we find the following account of virtue and happiness:

Virtue is a consistent character, choiceworthy for its own sake and not from fear or hope or anything external. Happiness consists in virtue since virtue is a soul which has been fashioned to achieve consistency (*homologia*) in the whole of life. (Diogenes Laertius, VII, 89=*L & S* 61 A)

In calling virtue a character (*diathesis*), the Stoics imply that it does not admit of degrees: one is either fully virtuous and happy or not at all (cf. Simpl., *In Cat.*, 237, 25–238, 29=*L & S* 47 S). The consistency in question is the perfection of reason: the virtuous person is internally consistent and consistent with nature at large. Such a person masters the art of living: he or she possesses the skill to consistently select what is right. In this connection it is worth emphasizing that virtue itself, which is the only thing choice-worthy for its own sake, does not depend on the success of the choices it makes: though being the skill of making right choices, the value of virtue lies in the correctness of the aiming, not in the success of the shot: a sudden wind can sway the arrow off its intended, right course. That does not affect the goodness of the marksman.

The sources are not too clear on the exact relationship between virtue and happiness in Stoicism. The two are evidently coextensive: if you are virtuous, you are happy and vice versa. As Long and Sedley (1987, 398–400) note, the two are, however, different concepts. Virtue is mostly characterized as a disposition, as a kind of knowledge or expertise. It is evident from Epictetus that this expertise is in constant application: it is after all the art of living and that is what we are doing all the time. The Stoic wise man even goes to bed and sleeps artfully (cf. Epictetus, *Discourses* III, 2; 10). The original Stoic, Zeno of Citium, defined happiness as 'the good flow of life' and others used the same or similar formulations (Stob., II, 77=*L & S* 63 A). Perhaps the reference to flow suggests that happiness is meant to be virtue in act: the art which is constantly being applied makes life flow smoothly and well. Seneca speaks of 'peacefulness and constant tranquillity' (Ep. 92, 3), which presumably reflects his understanding of this 'good flow'.

Plutarch describes the Stoic position on happiness and time as follows:

The Stoics say a good is not increased by the addition of time, but even if someone becomes prudent only for a moment, in respect of happiness he will in no way fall short of someone who employs virtue forever and lives his life blissfully in virtue. (Plutarch, *On common conceptions* 1061 F=SVF III, 55)

Plutarch does not mean that someone who is happy for just a short moment is during that time, just as happy as someone else who has been happy for years but on the whole the latter is happier because he has been happy longer. He means something stronger and in fact rather striking, namely that if happy at all, even for just a moment, one becomes just as happy *tout court* as someone who has been happy for a long time. Actually, the textual evidence suggests this latter interpretation: For Plutarch says that 'a good is not increased by the addition of time' and since he in the context equates good and happiness, the claim is that one doesn't become any happier by being happy for a longer time. Actually, the Stoic claim that happiness is not a matter of degree, if interpreted strictly, implies that happiness does not increase by lasting longer: for the Stoics the word for happy has no comparative or superlative.

This reading is supported by other ancient reports on Stoicism. Cicero has Cato, the Stoic spokesman in *De Finibus* say: 'For these reasons we do not think happiness ('*beata vita*') is more choice-worthy ('*optabilior*') or desirable ('*expetanda*') if it is long-lasting than if it is brief' (*De fin.* III, 46; cf. also Seneca, Ep. 132). He then goes on to support this with some unlikely comparisons: 'Just as, provided that the merit of a shoe is to fit the foot, many shoes or smaller or larger shoes are no better than few ones, so in the case of things whose goodness consists in propriety and opportune-ness, more and longer are not to be preferred to few and brief.'

Cato continues to discuss some objections to the Stoic position. He is unimpressed by the argument claiming that if good health is more valuable when lasting longer, the exercise of wisdom, i.e. virtue, i.e. happiness, is more valuable when lasting longer. Those who make use of this argument fail to realize that the value of health is estimated by duration, that of virtue is measured by opportuneness. These people might then just as well say that an easy death or an easy childbirth would be better if protracted. They fail to see that some things are better short than long and vice versa in other cases. (*De fin.* III, 47).

What does Cicero's Cato mean by 'measured by opportuneness'? He has explained in the preceding that he uses this term, '*opportunitas*' to render what in Greek is *eukairia*, which means something like appropriateness. How can happiness be measured by appropriateness? The idea is presumably that the happy person, that is, the wise, that is, the one who masters the art of living, is one who always aims at what is appropriate in the circumstances he or she is in. In evaluating whether someone is happy the proper question to ask is not whether the person has been in this state for a long time but whether the person is aiming in the right way at what is appropriate in the circumstances. This state of aiming well is not additive in the sense that one has more of it by being in it longer.

As regards the irrelevance of duration, we find the same intuition as we have seen in Epicurus and the Stoics in Plotinus. Moreover, though not particularly extensive, he is the ancient thinker who gives the fullest extant account of such a position. Let us consider what he has to offer.

Plotinus starts his little treatise, 'On whether happiness increases with time', *Ennead* I. 5, by asking 'whether happiness increases with time, though it is understood always to refer to our present state...And a state is something present, and so is the activity of life' (I. 5. 1).[7] It is not so clear at whom this question is directed. Beierwaltes (1967, 73) suggests that it is directed at 'unphilosophical' and uncritical views, the views of ordinary people, presumably. Linguiti (2007. 79–81), however, persuasively argues that Plotinus throughout this treatise has Aristotle and his followers in mind. Indeed, the very occurrence of 'actuality of life' (*energeia tēs zōēs*) here (and of other phrases reminiscent of Aristotle's ethical doctrines) supports this, even if Aristotle is nowhere mentioned by name and his views not explicitly engaged with.

Aristotle defines happiness as an 'activity of soul in conformity with virtue' (*EN* I 7, 1098a16–17; cf. X 7, 1177a12); and as already noted, he generally insists that activities are complete at any instant in the sense that if they are occurring they do not need (more) time to be complete (cf. *EN* X 4, 1174a19). He, however, famously insists that even if happiness is rational activity of soul, one must add 'in a complete life'. Plotinus is evidently questioning this addition. Admittedly, Aristotle nowhere says or implies that happiness increases proportionally, that happy twice as long implies twice as happy. The view Plotinus is concerned to reject is not, however, or is not necessarily, this strong view: it seems that his target is any view that takes a person's present happiness as being in any way determined by the person's happiness or lack thereof at other times.

In chapter 5 of I. 5, Plotinus expresses the doubts someone might have about his own position, that is, doubts about the position that happiness does not increase with time. He has an imaginary opponent say:

> Well then, if one man has been happy from beginning to end, and another in the latter part of his life, and yet another has been well off at first and then changed his state, do they have equal shares? (I. 5. 5, 1–3)

I take it that the sceptic is suggesting that the one who has been happy throughout has a larger share of happiness than do the two others because he has been happy longer. (I do not know why Plotinus has his sceptic bring in *two* others who differ in their allotted periods of happiness. It seems that one such person would suffice for his argument. Perhaps he is inviting the reader to think of both late-losers and early bloomers, and early losers and late bloomers, assuming we would reach the same conclusion in both cases, even if there may be a certain presumption in favour of the late bloomer when compared with the early loser, when we compare such persons with someone happy throughout his or her life. He does not follow up this possibility.) In any case, Plotinus responds:

---

[7] Here and elsewhere in this chapter I make free use, but often with some modifications, of A. H. Armstrong's Loeb translation of Plotinus.

Here the comparison is being made between people who are not happy, with a man who is happy. So if this latter has anything more, he has just what the man in a state of happiness has in comparison with those who are not; and that means that his advantage is by something that is present. (I. 5. 5, 4–8)

I take it that with this response Plotinus is saying: You may think that the person who has been happy his or her entire life has a larger share in happiness and, hence, is happier than those who have been happy only for a part of their lives. But note that when you compare the one who is always happy with the one who was happy only in, say, the first part of life but not in the latter half and come to the conclusion that the former is happier, you will agree that in the first part of their lives there was no difference between the two: they are both happy. When comparing the latter halves of their lives, you see that the one is happy, the other not happy, and of course you judge that the happy one is happier than one who is not happy at all. In any case, in so judging we are not comparing accumulated happiness over time but only judging on the basis of something that is present.

This response does not at all address the intuitions of someone like Aristotle who thinks one must consider a long period in order to judge someone's happiness. Such intuitions see happiness as essentially involving a person's history; it is linked to the temporal structure of life, and successes and failures of intentions and wishes presumably enter crucially into the evaluation. Plotinus does not address such concerns at all. What his response to the sceptic brings out, however, is that there is no necessary inference from 'longer' to 'more'. He succeeds, I think, in explaining why we may hold the one who is happy throughout to be best off of the three, without assuming that his or her happiness accumulates over time.

Plotinus then turns to the case of unhappiness.

Isn't a person more unhappy the longer he is unhappy? And do not all other troubles make the misfortune worse the longer they last, long-lasting pains and griefs for instance, and other things of that stamp? But if these troubles in this way make the evil increase with the passage of time, why do not their opposites in the same way cause an increase in happiness? (I. 5. 6, 1–7)

First, let us note that Plotinus presumably rejects the presuppositions of the last question. At any rate, in his other treatise on happiness he explicitly denies that physical suffering has a bearing on happiness at all (I. 4. 5–6). This also seems to follow from the concise statement of Plotinus's own view in chapter 7 of this treatise, which we shall come to shortly. The questions here, however, presuppose that pain and illness have a bearing on happiness, and Plotinus accepts this, no doubt for the sake of argument.

By way of responding to these questions, he notes that 'that which lasts longer in the same state is not all present at once' (I. 5. 6, 16–18). Actually, if the misfortune has increased by its persistence, it is because of the added grief and pain at the moment, not because of the long duration as such: past pain does not exist any longer and is irrelevant to present unhappiness. So Plotinus sticks to his previous strategy also on this question. It is noteworthy, however, that he seems to endorse the view that it may happen that the 'evil will grow worse the longer it lasts since the badness of the state will be increased by its persistence' (I. 5. 6, 13–14). Thus he seems to admit that there may be a causal connection between past and present suffering, that the persistence of suffering may in itself aggravate the present condition. He remarks but does not expand on the point that 'as regards happiness, it has a boundary and a limit and is always the same' (I. 5. 6, 18–19). As we saw, that happiness has a limit above which it will not increase plays a role in the Stoic and Epicurean grounds for holding that happiness does not increase with time. That he should bring this up suggests that he regarded happiness differently from the negative states: the latter admit of degrees. However that may be, he insists that the degree of present suffering and present unhappiness are to be judged solely on the basis of what they are now, at the present time; the duration in the past is, as such, irrelevant.

The point of discussing suffering, grief, and unhappiness was that here duration counts, or so a hypothetical objector maintained. And the objector's point was that if it does count, why not say the same about happiness? Plotinus has responded to this in the way we have just seen, but one may wonder if he has not, in his response, trivialized his main point. He insists that it is indeed the state of a person at the present time alone that matters for the judgement of the person's happiness. But if he allows that past unhappiness may cause present unhappiness, has he not compromised his point about the irrelevance of the past? Would not someone who thinks that a person's whole history enters into the judgement of present happiness agree that indeed, trivially, we are judging the person's happiness presently, but as a matter of fact the person's state at other times is part of the basis for this judgement? Well, no: there is a crucial difference between Plotinus's view and that of somebody thinking along such lines. The latter takes the past (and even the future (cf. Aristotle, *EN* I 10, 1101a20–1) to be constitutive of the judgement about the present state in the sense that we evaluate how happy persons are in part from facts about how happy they were or will be. Plotinus does not do so, even if he may allow for a certain causal connection between the past and the present unhappiness.

In chapter 7 of our treatise Plotinus considers another objection against his own view: we divide time into past, present, and future, and we have no problem counting and measuring past time. The same can be said about things and events of the past, deceased people for instance: we have no problem counting them. So—and here comes the question—why could not happiness be just like that, why is there not as much happiness as there is happy time gone by? This hypothetical objector may be thinking that past time and future time are in a sense quite real and hence relevant in the present. At least we can count the past and past things. And we can count past time and hence past happy time. Why not say that a person is happy in proportion to the amount of happy time lived, an amount which we can measure? Plotinus does not have his objector specify whether he is assuming that the person who has been happy longest is necessarily happy at the time of judgement, or whether he is thinking that even if the person is not happy now, at the time of judgement, he still counts as the happiest if he has been happy for the longest total time. Presumably, someone who thinks, as Plotinus' imaginary objector does, that one can count and measure past happiness, would not want to privilege the state at the moment of judgement. The objector's judgement is on a par with 'Pelé is the greatest soccer player ever', even if Pelé no longer plays soccer and, for example, Messi is much better than him at the time of judgement. For the objector, the judgement 'the happiest' is a judgement concerning the achievement in a lifetime. This may or may not be judged on the basis of the length of time. Pelé is for instance not the best soccer player because he played longer than anyone else. He is the best because he consistently played so well over many years. Others played reasonably well for a still longer time. But we may count Pelé as the best soccer player because he consistently played extremely well for a quite considerable time, not just one spring but for two decades or so. The case of happiness may be slightly different: an objector of the sort Plotinus envisages may for instance think that the state of a person at the end of life has a special weight as, for example, Aristotle seems to think (the objector Plotinus brings up does, however, not make this point). However this may be, this kind of objector does not privilege the present time of judgement so as to insist that this overall happy person is necessarily in a good state now at the present moment of judgement.

Plotinus responds to this objector thus: 'It would be absurd to say that happiness that no longer is present is greater than the happiness that is present. For being happy has to be taking place, but time over and above the present cannot any longer exist.'[8] This translation is meant to reflect the delivered Greek text.[9] Plotinus' main modern editors, Henry and Schwyzer, conjecture συμμεμενηκέναι, 'to persist', 'to endure' instead of the MSS. συμβεβηκέναι. Given the context, this conjecture, however, does not yield a very good sense: so far, Plotinus has been insisting that the happiness there is, is in what is present. The persistence of happiness, by contrast, has not played any role in his reasoning. On the other hand, συμβεβηκέναι can mean 'to occur', 'take place', 'exist', which gives reasonably good sense here: the happiness attributed to a person must be occurring happiness.

Plotinus is so far quite in agreement with what we have seen in the Hellenistic philosophers. He, however, has a different story to tell about happiness in the end. According to him happiness, which he identifies with the best life, is the life of intellect and this is outside time (I.5.7; I.4.3). The best life is the life of intellect because its life is life in the fullest sense; hence, the best. A major difficulty, noted by Rist (1967, 148) is that in Plotinus' positive account of happiness in his later and

---

[8] Henry and Schwyzer Paris edition (1951) emends συμβεβηκέναι to συμμεμενηκέναι. The Henry and Schwyzer Oxford edition (1964), gives συμβεβηκέναι, whereas in their *addenda ad textum* in vol. iii (1982) the editors revert to συμμεμενηκέναι. As pointed out by Igál (1982, note *ad. loc.*) and Linguiti (2007, note *ad loc.*), there is no reason to change the text. I, however, do not agree with Igál's translation: '*La felicidad exige estar junta*', nor with Linguiti's, who follows him. 'Take place' seems to do the job.

[9] Τὸ μὲν γὰρ εὐδαιμονεῖν συμβεβηκέναι ἀξιοῖ, ὁ δὲ χρόνος ὁ πλείων παρὰ τὸν παρόντα τὸ μηκέτι εἶναι (I. 5. 7, 12–13).

longer treatise on happiness, *Ennead* I.4, he clearly wishes to say that only the sage is happy while also asserting that every normal human being has a counterpart in intellect, leading a happy life there. So how can Plotinus avoid admitting that everybody is happy, if happiness consists in living the life of intellect? I argued in Emilsson (2011) that the sage has come into touch with the intelligible realm, his own noetic self, in such a way that he leads intellect's life in a much fuller sense than other human beings. This makes him immune to worldly adversity.

IV

Let us, finally, consider some common features shared by Epicureans, Stoics, and Plotinus.

1. It is common to all three to hold that happiness does not essentially depend on external goods or the absence of so-called external misfortunes. Even if the Epicureans identify evil with pain and distress, they hold that bodily pain will not make a happy person unhappy (cf. Epicurus, *Key Doctrines* 4). Moreover, the external goods necessary for a good life are easily procured (Epicurus, *Ep. Men.* 25 ff.).

2. All three hold that happiness, as each of them understands it, is an enduring state. Someone who has mastered the Epicurean way of life and adopted Epicurean fearlessness, will, according to the theory, not be easily deprived of the ability to remain happy. We already noted about the Stoics that in calling virtue/happiness a 'character' (*diathesis*), it is implied that this is a lasting state of the soul. So having once mastered the art of living, a person will remain virtuous and happy. Similarly, though this may not be said explicitly, a Plotinian happy sage will certainly not become unhappy. Nothing external will make him so and since he is a sage nothing internal would do so. However, even if the happy Epicurean, Stoic, and Plotinian sage can be pretty sure about being happy in the future as well, their present happiness is not conditioned on this knowledge.

3. The latter day ancients we are considering all believed that happiness has a limit. Once that limit is reached there can be no increase.

4. It is worth noting also that all three hold that happiness is an undisturbed state of mind. Even if Plotinus would not adopt any of the Hellenistic terminology of peace of mind to describe his own position, the happy life for him is the undisturbed intellectual life. Moreover, according to all three, this peace of mind is gained through a certain transformation: in order to become happy we have to change our views and habits of thought and action. This is of course connected with the view on external goods in (1) and with the view in (2) that once happy the happy will remain in that state: the transformation of character needed for happiness is irreversible.

5. For both Epicureans and Stoics happiness is very much in the present moment (cf. Hadot (1995) and Goldschmidt (1979), 168–86). This is admittedly quite vague but let me try to explain. First, let us note that all negative attitudes and feelings regarding the past and the future are excluded: no fears, no worries, no regrets. For the Epicureans pleasant memories of past pleasures and anticipations of future ones admittedly play a role (cf. Diog. Laert., II, 89). This has, however, nothing essentially to do with the past-ness of the original pleasures remembered. The pleasant memories are present pleasures. Seneca asks in one of his letters: 'O when shall you see the time when you shall know that time means nothing to you, when you shall be peaceful and calm, careless of the morrow, because you are enjoying your life to the full?' (Ep. 32, 4). This suggests that he conceives of happiness as living in the moment, as enjoying the now to the full. Plotinus, on the other hand, insisting that happiness is in the timeless, would of course not pin happiness to the present moment. I believe, however, that he would hold that someone who is happy in the sense of living the timeless life of intellect is indeed happy at each moment (see Emilsson (2011), 357–8). Another way in which happiness may be said to be in the present according the Epicureans and the Stoics, has to do with the fact that a person's history, the structure of life so far or in the future, has no bearing on the judgment that she is happy. One is happy or not on account of one's present state alone and this present state doesn't have anything essential to do with the past or the future. This does, however, not exclude that some aspects of our present state are past- or future-directed, for example, memories or intentions.

6. We may still find the view that a longer life in happiness is no happier than a shorter one counter-intuitive. One reason for the apparent counter-intuitiveness is presumably the following: everyone given the choice would prefer the longer happy life. This may be true. But it does not follow that in selecting the longer life, for example, by eating more healthy food and less unhealthy food, one is selecting more happiness. Just as likely one is just selecting a longer life. Nor is longer happiness necessarily in any real sense more happiness. If a cup is white it does not become whiter by staying white longer. Leaving out the Epicureans, let us consider how the Stoics would look at the matter. Someone might object to the Stoics as follows: 'Even a Stoic wise man, who by definition is virtuous and happy, will make prudential choices like anyone else. In so doing the wise Stoic will select the things that are appropriate. Often this may involve selecting a longer-lasting good (which the Stoic refuses to call a good preferring to describe it as a preferable) rather than the short-lived one, *ceteris paribus*. Given the choice between two light bulbs, price and everything else being equal, the wise man will normally go for the longer-lasting bulb. This shows, the critic maintains, that the Stoic's choices and actions betray his theory: she too plans for future happiness. This objection, however, fails entirely for at least two reasons. First of all, even in

selecting a longer lasting good or preferable, the wise man is not selecting longer happiness. To think that happiness comes to one as a consequence of the things selected is a fundamental error according to Stoicism. Rather, happiness consists in the internal activity of selecting rightly, as already has been noted. Secondly, as we also noted, the good Stoic selects what is appropriate. The appropriate thing may be the longer lasting or it may not. That depends. There may well be a specific reason for preferring the more short-lived bulb. Sometimes of two good things the shorter one is preferable everything else being equal, for example, a short visit to the dentist rather than a long one.

The post-Aristotelian philosophers we have been considering all deny that happiness is accumulative: you cannot become any happier by being happy for a long time. They would deny that past happiness and even future happiness has any weight in judging how happy you are now at the present moment. Happiness is a state which is solely to be evaluated from what is presently. Many people no doubt find this deeply counter-intuitive. They think the claim is refuted by the fact that everyone, including the post-Aristotelian thinkers in question, would prefer a longer happy life to a short one. That there is such a preference is indeed probably true but, as we have seen, it does not follow that this necessarily betrays the belief that by choosing the longer happy life one is choosing to become happier or thinking one will be happier that way. The Stoics, for instance, would no doubt remind the critic that quite generally the 'longer' or 'more' of something in itself preferable is not necessarily more choice-worthy. Moreover, the Stoics might say, and Plotinus and the Epicureans may essentially agree, that if the sage prefers the longer happy life, given the choice between this and a shorter one, this is simply a function of what happened to be the most rational options for the sage in the circumstances. They are not made most rational by having a longer happy life as a consequence. There may, however, be a reason why the most rational option would normally have this as a result. The Stoic sage finds an optimally rational alternative in almost every situation. In exercising her rationality in this way she is, as we have seen, wise and happy. Now, *life* as such will in most situations be preferable to death and, hence, in most situations be the rational choice. Since the sage in selecting life is, so long as she is a sage, guaranteed a happy life, she will normally select the longer life which in fact is going to be happy. That does not mean that she has preferred a longer happy life over a short happy life, so described. Still less does it follow that she preferred this thinking that the longer happy life must be the rational choice.

We saw in connection with Aristotle that he took a different view. Admittedly, Aristotle nowhere says or implies that happiness accumulates like savings you have regularly put into your bank account over the years. He does hold, however, that past and future states matter crucially for judging whether a person is happy now. When he, as we saw, says that we can indeed ascribe happiness to a living person who is doing well on condition that he will stay so till the end and nothing disastrous happens to him in the future, he is clearly implying that future misfortune and unhappiness may affect the judgement whether the person is presently happy.

What really is at issue here between Solon and Aristotle on the one hand, and the Hellenistic philosophers and Plotinus on the other, is two rather different conceptions of happiness: the difference concerning happiness's relations to time really amount to different conceptions of what happiness is. If we go along with the post-Aristotelians, we would say that happiness is a totally self-contained state and does not concern life as a whole, if by that is meant the total temporal stretch of life. Moreover, it is worth pointing out that there is clearly a strand in Aristotle that goes in the same direction. I have in mind, of course, his categorization of happiness as an activity, which in principle also is something self-contained. It is just that Aristotle also brings in other considerations in his account of happiness. If we were to generalize about Greek philosophical thought concerning happiness and time, we would not come to the conclusion with Chekola that happiness is something that pertains to life as whole in the temporal sense of that phrase and that it is an essentially enduring condition. It is of course not that the post-Aristotelian philosophers thought that happiness is just a momentary bliss. As we have seen, they believed that those able to achieve this state are also in general able to remain in it. This does not change the fact, however, that the state as such does not refer to the past or the future.

13

Why Do We Need Other People to Be Happy?

Happiness and Concern for Others in Aspasius and Porphyry

Miira Tuominen

1. Introduction

1.1 Happiness, virtue, morality

Why we need other people in order to be happy might, prima facie, seem like a silly question. Of course we need other people. Life is no fun without them. On reflection, one might consider that human beings naturally have social needs and if those needs are not satisfied, life cannot be happy. All this is perhaps true, but, as is well known, ancient conceptions of a good life were based on different kinds of considerations. It was generally supposed that virtue is necessary for happiness (*eudaimonia*), even though opinions diverged as to whether it is also sufficient. If the good life requires morality, it might seem obvious that other people are needed for a good life as well since other people are vital in the exercise of morality. However, a well-known and from the modern perspective puzzling feature of ancient ethics is that it focuses on the virtues of an individual human being conceived in a context of general suppositions concerning human nature. And yet, the exercise of virtue—at least those virtues that Aristotle conceives as virtues of character and the late ancient Platonists as social or political[1]—requires other people. Surely, one cannot be just without being just towards someone (even though in the context of Plato's *Republic* book IV, for example, this is not altogether obvious), generous without being generous to someone, and so on. Therefore, it seems that, in the context of ancient ethics, other people

---

[1] For a discussion on the connection between the Aristotelian and Plotinian distinctions of virtues, see O'Meara (2013).

are needed in a good life because they are necessary for social or political virtues or virtues of character and virtues are necessary for good life.

Does this, then, make other people instrumental to virtue and ultimately to the agent's happiness? This would seem like an overtly egoistic point of view and ancient ethics has indeed been accused of egoism.[2] I shall return to the question of egoism later on in this essay. For now, it is important to note that even though other people are required for virtue and happiness, the role of virtue is not instrumental to an individual's quest for happiness. It has been argued that even though virtues are necessary for happiness in the ancient theories, they are not mere means for individual flourishing or attaining personal fulfilment or satisfaction. The role of virtues in a good life is *constitutive* rather than instrumental.[3] Being virtuous (as for the Stoics) or acting virtuously (as for Aristotle) is what essentially constitutes a good life—although from an Aristotelian perspective not even virtue guarantees happiness. By contrast, for the Stoics and the Platonists virtue is not only necessary but also sufficient for happiness. External goods depending on circumstance, such as health and wealth, are not necessary for virtue. Virtue depends on the person's inner condition alone and happiness depends on inner virtue and nothing else.

In the following, I shall argue that, in particular in the commentary of Aspasius on the *Nicomachean Ethics* and Porphyry's treatise *On Abstinence from Killing Animals* (*De abstinentia*), we find important developments both in the formulations concerning human sociability (especially in Aspasius) and in the formulations of justice (especially in Porphyry's *On abstinence*) that define the relevant human tendencies and the relevant virtues in other-regarding terms. Even though it would be exaggerated to claim that the definitions and developments ascribe other people a constitutive role in a good life and in the definition of virtue, Aspasius to some extent develops the notion of sociability and Porphyry the one of justice in other-regarding terms.

I shall discuss Aspasius and Porphyry together in this contribution even though Aspasius is a relatively early Aristotelian and Porphyry is a post-Plotinian Platonist (and a proponent of 'the harmony thesis' between Plato and Aristotle) who did not belong to the tradition of understanding the human being as a political or sociable animal. However, the systematic question of the role of other-regard in the virtuous life concerns both of them and both have interesting things to say about it. Especially Porphyry's *On abstinence* is a relatively neglected text despite its highly interesting and carefully developed argument against harming non-human animals[4]

---

[2] Some scholars also concede that ancient ethics is formally egoistic even though not egoistic in content; see note 3 below for Annas (1993); and Irwin (2007), ch. 9.

[3] See, e.g. Annas (1993).

[4] I articulate the general argument of the treatise in terms of not harming non-human animals, even though the traditional descriptions concern eating or killing animals. However, the notion of not injuring or harming (Greek βλάβη and derivatives) living creatures is so central in the treatise that I find it a much more accurate reference to what one needs to abstain from than killing or eating.

and, I think, the argument should become better integrated to the discussion of Neoplatonic ethics.[5]

1.2 Egoism and altruism, self-interest and morality

Since happiness or flourishing (*eudaimonia*) is so central in ancient ethics, it has been criticized for egoism of some sort. However, many scholars have pointed out that even though ancient ethics is formally self-centred, it has very little to do with ethical egoism based on the claim that it is both necessary and sufficient for an action to be ethically right that it maximizes the agent's self-interest. Julia Annas, for example, has argued that even though ancient ethics is formally self-centred, it is not egoistic in content.[6] All in all, she claims, the opposition between egoism and altruism is not a pertinent tool for analysing ancient ethics because, in ancient ethics in general, there is no structural gap between self-interest and morality.[7] Annas has a strong point here: even though it is possible to find ancient discussions of a conflict between morality and self-interest, these notions do not form the axis around which the ethical discussions centre. In other words, the strong connection between virtue and happiness does not cancel the ethical value of virtuous action merely because virtue or virtuous action is analysed as constitutive of happiness and because happiness clearly seems to be in the agent's interest.

Some scholars have even suggested that ancient ethics is superior to modern ethics *precisely because* it does not depart from an initial opposition between self-interest and other-regard.[8] According to Pauline Chazán, the moral status of a person's actions and the state of her self are interdependent. Rather than accepting the requirement of impersonality central to modern moral theories, Chazán argues that in order for a person to develop a characteristically moral outlook, it is necessary that she values herself. Consequently, she argues that a person can act morally well without being motivated by 'what is widely regarded to be a specifically "moral" (as opposed to a self-interested) motive'.[9] Chazán claims that the ethics of Plato and Aristotle are superior to most of modern ethics because they preserve the connection between what is the best possible life for the agent and what in fact is morally good. However, she rightly emphasizes that virtues are not, for authors like Plato and Aristotle, means to achieve a good life. The ethics of Plato or Aristotle, Chazán continues, 'has no room for the rigid division into the "moral" and the "self-interested" of which contemporary moral philosophy is so fond'.[10] Even though this is perhaps an accurate generalization of Aristotle in particular who, in turn, is fond of comparing moral excellences or virtues (*aretai*) to non-moral excellences like skills, there is evidence that the Stoics in particular did recognize moral reasons as a

---

[5] Fay Edwards's work on the treatise, however, is forthcoming in the near future.
[6] Annas (1993), 127.   [7] Annas (1993), 323.   [8] Pauline Chazán (1998).
[9] Chazán (1998), 3.   [10] Chazán (1998), 4.

special category. Annas articulates this point in the way that, for the Stoics, moral reasons (i.e. considerations of virtue) *override* all other kinds of reasons.[11]

I tend to share with Chazán the intuition that concern for oneself is not in a necessary fundamental opposition with concern for others or with morality. More generally and more importantly, the distinction between egoism and altruism seems too thin in content to provide us with sufficient standards for evaluating the ethical value of human action. However, it is also true that an act that at first sight appears other-regarding might turn out not to be such if it is done from certain kinds of motives. Helping the poor, for example, certainly can be done from a more altruistic motives or reasons ('because I care for the well-being of others') and from more egoistic ones ('because caring for the well-being of others gives me a sense of moral superiority')—and the latter can be taken to cancel or at least diminish the genuinely other-regarding value of the action.

However, as to the question of whether the distinction between self-interest and other-regard offers us tools for deciding on the moral quality of an action, consider the following example taken from Michael Stocker.[12] Person A has a friend who is in hospital, let us call him B. A goes to visit him and B is happy to see her. However, suppose that A discloses to B that she came out of duty. Even if this duty would then be conceived of in other-regarding terms, it is questionable to what extent this would have lifted B's spirits and whether it would have been a good motivation or reason for coming. Similarly, if A said 'I came here because I value you as an end rather than as a means', B could perhaps deduce that A is taking a class in moral philosophy but whether the action became any better is dubious. By contrast, if A simply said 'I wanted to see you'—a claim that surely appears self-interested—this seems quite natural and does not in any obvious way cancel the other-concerned value of the action, even though the reason or motive is perhaps not explicitly other-regarding.

About Aristotelian ethics in particular, scholars have argued that there is an inbuilt element of other-concern in it. Martha Nussbaum's version of the argument underlines that, given that justice is the highest excellence or virtue (*aretē*) in Aristotelian ethics, all excellences have an other-concerned aspect, even when their definitions centre on describing the quality or state of the virtuous agent.[13] Others, such as Terence Irwin,[14] have argued more reservedly that even though Aristotelian ethics is not egoistic, it can be characterized as being self-centred.

According to Chazán, ancient and modern ethics also differ because in the latter 'a focal point of much moral theorizing has been the task of justifying morality to the

---

[11] Annas (1993), 121.

[12] Stocker (1976). One of Stocker's central points is that modern ethical theories are schizophrenic because they entail a sharp divide between reasons and motives, whereas the hedonists are better off in explaining cases like visiting a friend at the hospital exactly because they do not write themselves off from the explanation. This is an important point, I find, even though the distinction between reasons and motives is not central for my analysis.

[13] Nussbaum (1986/2001), 351.   [14] Irwin (2007), ch. 9.

rational egoist',[15] whereas this is not central in ancient ethics. However, it is important to note that we find arguments from both Plato and Aristotle, for example, in which they are responding to a very similar challenge when arguing that justice is beneficial to the just agent. One only needs to think about the requests of Glaucon and Adeimantus in Plato's *Republic* book II and Thrasymachus in book I, and the arguments directed at them.[16] In Aristotle's case, we can think of the hedonistic person he talks about in the *Nicomachean Ethics*. Simplifying a little, it is specifically in the opponents of these authors that we find forms of ethical egoism. Plato and Aristotle themselves, by contrast, rather tend to assume that there is no conflict between self-interest and morality, or, rather, *even for ethical egoists* like Thrasymachus or the hedonist in the *Nicomachean Ethics*, virtue is the only way to their supposed goal. Aristotle's discussion of hedonism in the *Eudemian Ethics* is built on the point, reminiscent of Plato's *Philebus*, that internal goods, that is the goods of the soul, are prior to the external ones and that even pleasure is an internal good in this sense. However, the argument to the effect that virtuous life is efficient for reaching the goals that the egoist hopes for does not entail that Plato and Aristotle would see virtue as subordinated to self-interest—that is, that the constitutive ethical power of virtue should be derived from pleasure or self-interest.

The charges of not being sufficiently concerned with other people's well-being seem all the more pressing when we consider Neoplatonic ethics. In the Neoplatonic framework, a person's ultimate end is to merge with the One, the highest principle of all being and unity in an experience that is, in a sense, fully private. Such an experience cannot be adequately communicated because all attempts to express what happens in this unification would introduce diversity and difference, which are not found in the One. In another sense, however, the experience is not private at all: this is because, when merging with the One, a person loses all individuality and becomes united with the absolute unity of everything there is. Since such an experience transcends thought and language, it is difficult to describe. In any case, such an experience is not social either in the ordinary sense of the word; the unification with the One is not described in terms of relations to other people.

Scholars often argue that Neoplatonic ethics is not as detached from social life and from concern for other people as it might initially seem. One reason is that Plotinus also endorses from Plato's metaphor of the cave the idea that the person who has progressed to understand the highest Good, needs to return to the cave and share this understanding with others.[17] In the following discussion, the Neoplatonic framework is relevant to Porphyry.

---

[15] Chazán (1998), 2.

[16] It is far less clear how exactly one should understand the *Protagoras* in this respect. I shall not consider this question in the present context.

[17] For an account of the return of the philosopher kings to the cave in Plato and inspired by Plotinus, see Caluori (2011). For a study emphasizing the role of political philosophy in late ancient Platonism, see O'Meara (2003). Alexandrine Schniewind, for her part (2003), has underlined the role of the Plotinian

It obviously falls outside the scope of this brief essay to argue for a specific claim about how we in fact should understand the relation between self-interest and concern for others or self-interest and morality. In general, I tend to see these as yet open questions. This means that I do not think that modern ethics has quite solved these issues either. Consequently, I do not think that the moral value of ancient ethics should ultimately be derived from the extent to which it can match modern expectations. Rather, ancient ethics is different from the modern one, and we need to respect these differences while looking for other-concerned considerations. In this chapter, I focus on discussing whether we can find evidence of other-concerned considerations in Aspasius' and Porphyry's accounts of happiness and what role those considerations play in their respective accounts. I shall argue that we can find, from both Aspasius and from Porphyry, noteworthy developments that suggest that both of them suppose concern for others vital for the pursuit of happiness.

2. Sociability: Human Being as a Political Animal

In general, the idea that human happiness requires other people might be taken to derive from the fact or alleged fact that human nature requires that we live in a community of some sort. The claim that a community (koinōnia) is important for human life occurs in the myth of Plato's Statesman in which the statesman's skill is considered in terms of 'voluntary care of voluntary bipeds' (276e10–12). Even though some doubt is cast on the analysis almost immediately in the dialogue (in 277a), the claim occurs there. Further, in the Republic happiness seems to belong to the whole of the city rather than to any part of it specifically, and this also seems to indicate the centrality of a structured community in some of Plato's reflections on happiness.

It is of course in Aristotle that we find a more programmatic statement of the necessity of a structured political community for a good human life. In the *Nicoma-chean Ethics*, as is well known, the role of sharing the life in a community is more complex because the happy life is required to be self-sufficient (*autarkeia*, EN I 7, 1097b5–8). However, as Aristotle immediately adds, this does not mean a solitary life but family, friends, and other citizens are necessary for a happy life because the human being is, by nature, a political animal (*EN* I 7, 1097b8–11).[18] Finally, however,

---

sage as an exemplary figure and thus profoundly connected to the life of the society. Andrew Smith (2005) bases his claim on the evidence we find in Porphyry's *Vita Plotini* and argues that we should not regard Plotinian ethics as self-centred because, as Porphyry described him, Plotinus was a very other-regarding man. I find the kind of evidence pointing to Porphyry's conception of Plotinus' conduct precarious: Porphyry's description surely reflects his own conception of ideal action—which reflects Plotinus' ideal of ideal action—and the conception of ideal action most probably reflects the authors' conceptions of the role of other-regard in an ethical life. However, I rather focus on the ethical statements of these two authors and the role of other-regard in their outspoken theory.

[18] I shall use 'political' as a translation of πολιτικός to capture Aristotle's emphasis on the necessity of a structured community with practices of justice for the human life. However, when talking about the

when he moves to consider the most perfect happiness of *theōria*, Aristotle concedes that, contrary to the virtues of character, the highest theoretical virtue can be exercised in solitude.

In the *Politics*, Aristotle's emphasis is on the claim that living in a *polis* is necessary for the human nature in the sense that someone who lives outside such a structured community by nature and not by chance, is not even a human being but inferior or superior to one. 'A human being is by nature a political animal, and one who is by nature and not by chance without a city is either base or superior to human beings' (*Politics* I 2, 1253a2–5).[19] He claims that living in a structured political community (a *polis*) is natural to human beings because they have a natural capacity for being aware of justice and injustice, good and bad, and for expressing the beneficial and the harmful in speech. This, according to Aristotle, makes the human being more political than other political or gregarious animals, such as bees (*Politics* I 2, 1253a7–8).[20]

In the *Nicomachean Ethics* (IX 9, 1169b13–22), by contrast, Aristotle points out that happiness or *eudaimonia* requires friendships, since it belongs to the human nature to live with others. As mentioned, in book X (chapter 7) he famously seems to contradict the claim that other people are necessary for happiness when describing the theoretical virtue as completely self-sufficient. He concedes that other people are necessary for the theoretically virtuous to *live* but that, contrary to the virtues of character, the theoretically virtuous does not need other people to exercise the virtue. He immediately adds, however, that it is perhaps *better* for the theoretically virtuous to have colleagues but, in any case, the wise person is the most self-sufficient:

But the wise person can theorize just being by himself, and the more he is wise, the more he can do this; perhaps he can do this [i.e. theorize] better if he has colleagues, but, all the same, he is the most self-sufficient. (*EN* X 7, 1177a32–b1)[21]

In what follows, I shall not be concerned with what exactly Aristotle means by his various statements of human sociability but only focus on the following points.

First, Aristotle's claim of human sociability in the *Politics* operates with the notion of a structured city-state in which different individuals have different social roles as well as specifically political functions, duties, and what we nowadays call 'rights'. He explicitly states that there is a contrast between human beings and gregarious animals that live in non-structured flocks or herds: a by nature *apolis* or non-political human being would be a beast if living in herds or a god if living alone.

---

property thus ascribed to the human species, I shall use 'sociability' because I have not been able to think of a better alternative (an abstract noun) derived from 'political'.

[19] ὅτι ὁ ἄνθρωπος φύσει πολιτικὸν ζῷον, καὶ ὁ ἄπολις διὰ φύσιν καὶ οὐ διὰ τύχην ἤτοι φαῦλός ἐστιν, ἢ κρείττων ἢ ἄνθρωπος.

[20] πολιτικὸν ὁ ἄνθρωπος ζῷον πάσης μελίττης καὶ παντὸς ἀγελαίου ζῴου μᾶλλον.

[21] ὁ δὲ σοφὸς καὶ καθ’ αὑτὸν ὢν δύναται θεωρεῖν, καὶ ὅσῳ ἂν σοφώτερος ᾖ, μᾶλλον· βέλτιον δ’ ἴσως συνεργοὺς ἔχων, ἀλλ’ ὅμως αὐταρκέστατος.

Secondly, in addition to being structured by social roles, living in a *polis* involves awareness of the good and the bad as well as the just and the unjust, and this is peculiar to human beings alone. Other animals are incapable of such moral cognition. The two points together imply that the kind of sociability Aristotle is talking about does not boil down to a need, willingness, or tendency to hang out with other human beings, nor does it mean simply that it would be beneficial for human beings to act in groups. As we shall see, in *On abstinence* Porphyry disagrees with such an opposition between human beings and other animals implying a confinement of justice to human beings.

A third aspect that needs to be mentioned at this point is that, in the passage from the *Politics*, Aristotle seems to be making the claim that living in a *polis* is necessary for the human essence but he says nothing specific about the good life. Since a good human life must be a human life and the latter is only possible in a structured community, the claim implies that the good life is possible only in a structured community. By contrast, the passage from the *Nicomachean Ethics* relates living in a community with friends to good life: friends are necessary for a happy person (1169b22). As mentioned, however, this claim is not unproblematic considering the self-sufficiency of theoretical virtue—which, in fact, in a sense transcends our strictly human nature.

All in all, Aristotle's statement of human sociability does not collapse with the kind of position that derives the relevance of other people to the good life from such claims about nature or human nature that are completely devoid of ethical relevance. His point is *not* that, because we have a natural need to be with other people and because happiness involves the satisfaction of needs, other people are necessary for happiness. By contrast, as we saw, the *polis* is necessary for the realization and communication of justice and injustice, of good and bad, and thus it is required for the realization of morality rather than simple need-satisfaction.[22] However, his position also differs from the kind of view that derives morality from sociability supposing that human beings have a natural tendency to be good to other people or to have natural other-regarding tendencies. Rather, Aristotle supposes that a properly human life and morality require political structures and functions and that the proper expression of morality is possible only within a political community. Moral virtue in Aristotle's framework is a disposition or state (*hexis*) of a citizen who acts within a structure of power and authority, not just a random bunch of other people. Therefore, as is well known, Aristotle's appeal to human nature differs radically from the kind of claims (typical of early modernity in particular) that distinguish a natural human condition from a political setting. This sits well with his statement in the *Politics* according to which a *polis* is a natural entity, a natural perfection of human communities.[23]

---

[22] For further differences between Aristotle's claims of human nature and modern meta-ethical naturalism, see Annas (1993), ch. II.4.

[23] See also Annas (1993), 146–54.

3. Aspasius' Re-interpretation of Sociability

3.1 'Doing good things also to others'

We know little of Aspasius' life. Galen mentions (*Affections of the Soul*, chapter 8) that one of his fellow citizens had studied abroad with Aspasius the Peripatetic, and it seems rather safe to identify this Aspasius with the commentator on the *Nicomachean Ethics*.[24] Thus Aspasius most probably flourished in the early second century CE[25] and he has written the earliest commentary on any work of Aristotle that has been preserved to a significant degree. Aspasius' commentary was much used by Alexander[26] and there are quite a few ancient references to commentaries that Aspasius is said to have written,[27] but only the commentary on the *Nicomachean Ethics* has been preserved. It covers books I–IV and VII–VIII, the commentary on book VII being only partial.

Even though we do not have Aspasius' comments directly on Aristotle's claim of the necessity of friends for the happy person in book IX, he refers to the human being as a political animal (*in Eth. Nic.* 19.9)[28] in his discussion of Aristotle's claim in book I chapter 7 that happiness requires a complete life (1098a18–20). What Aspasius says in his commentary is rather different from what we find in Aristotle. Most importantly, he brings the issue of sociability to a context where Aristotle makes no mention of it. When he goes on to articulate the claim of what sociability consists in, the formulation is quite different from Aristotle's.

Aspasius argues for the necessity of a complete life for happiness as follows:

And if a human being is a political animal in the sense of doing good things [also][29] to his [/her?] fellow human beings, for this a complete life is needed as well, in order for him [/her?] to do as much good as possible (19.8–10).[30]

The first important move that Aspasius makes is to give a new or at least very different interpretation of human sociability compared to the one we find in Aristotle. He is transforming an essential necessity of a structured community for human life and the realization of virtue, together with the claim that friendships are necessary for happiness, into a claim about good things done to others.[31] In addition, Aspasius is not just saying that human sociability involves doing *some* good things to

---

[24] For a discussion concerning this reference, see Barnes (1999), 1–4.

[25] Cf., however, Becchi (1994), 5365–6.   [26] Barnes (1999), 9–11.

[27] On Aristotle's *Categories, de Interpretatione, Physics, de Caelo, de Sensu,* and *Metaphysics*. For the references and the nature of these works, see Barnes (1999), 8–13.

[28] πολιτικὸν ζῷον ὁ ἄνθρωπος.

[29] καί deleted by Heylbut (1889) in his edition.

[30] εἰ δὲ καὶ ἐν τῷ εὖ ποιεῖν [καὶ] τοὺς κοινωνοὺς πολιτικὸν ζῷον ὁ ἄνθρωπος, δέοι ἂν καὶ πρὸς τοῦτο τελείου βίου, ἵν᾽ ὡς πλεῖστον εὖ ποιήσειεν.

[31] εὖ ποιεῖν [καὶ] τοὺς κοινωνούς; I shall discuss the καί later in the text.

others, he requires that, to express our natural sociability, one needs a complete life in order to do *as much good as possible*[32] also to one's fellow human beings.

In his edition of Aspasius' commentary in the *Commentaria in Aristotelem Graeca*, Heylbut has deleted the 'also' (*kai*) in the phrase 'doing good things also to others' (19.8–9).[33] Since the deletion does not have manuscript support and there seems to be no grammatical problem in having the 'also' in the sentence, I see no conclusive argument for removing it. This implies that we need to take Aspasius as saying, not that human sociability consists in doing good things to others. Rather, he is saying that it requires doing good things *also* to others. This entails that it is not just the good things done to others that make the complete life necessary; it is that only in a complete life can one do as much good as possible also to others. In fact, the same implication is already contained in the first 'and' (*kai*) in the sentence, and thus the second one could be taken as pleonastic. In any case, the meaning that one needs to do good things *also to others* is conveyed in both readings.

It is worth pointing out that I take Aspasius' expression 'as much good as possible'[34] as a quantitative rather than a qualitative claim. In other words, I think it is important to stress that Aspasius is talking about doing *as much good* or *as many good things* as possible also to others. The qualitative reading, by contrast, would make him say that one needs to do *as well as possible*. This qualitative reading, however, could not make sense of the addition 'also to others': How could one be doing as well as possible, also to others? Further, from the point of view of the Greek, it is the quantitative ('as much good as possible, also to others') that we need to adopt. This is because Aspasius is using *pleiston*, the superlative of *polu* (much), whereas the qualitative reading would require a superlative of the 'good' (*eu*). This also strengthens the impression that Aspasius' interpretation of 'doing good' (*eu poiein*) in this context is quite different from the 'acting well' (*eu prattein*) that we find in Plato and Aristotle referring to doing well and flourishing, in a word, being happy. Instead of saying that happiness or *eudaimonia* requires a complete life because only such a life allows one to *be* as good as possible and to do as well as possible, Aspasius employs, as it were, a different conceptual syntax for the notion of the good. He talks about doing good things also to other people and about maximizing these good things. Because one needs to do as much good as possible, also to others in order to be happy, happiness requires a complete life.

However, there is no indication that Aspasius' reference of doing good things also to others would entail a conflict or a contradiction with the person's doing well or being happy. Quite the contrary. It is precisely such maximal doing of good things also to others that is supposed to constitute happiness or *eudaimonia* in Aspasius' brief comment. Aspasius thus seems to recognize that the pursuit of

---

[32] ἵν᾽ ὡς πλεῖστον εὖ ποιήσειεν.   [33] εὖ ποιεῖν καὶ τοὺς κοινωνούς.
[34] ὡς πλεῖστον εὖ ποιήσειεν.

happiness is not in conflict with concern for other people (doing good things also to others) but rather requires it.

What I have called 'the conceptual syntax of the notion of the good' we find in Aspasius' comment—that is, analysing the good in terms of something one does to someone, also to others—is certainly not unprecedented in Aspasius' time. A well-known example of a similar 'conceptual syntax' is found in the traditional notion of justice as doing good to friends and bad to enemies[35] as it is formulated by Aristotle in the *Topics* I 10 (104a22; 30). A similar notion of justice is of course also discussed in Plato's *Republic* book I as Simonides' conception brought to the discussion by Cephalus.[36] Even though Plato and Aristotle surely discuss many of the virtues in terms of what one does to others (Aristotle, for example, formulates justice as an 'other-concerned' virtue in terms of it being 'towards another'),[37] the notion of the good as such for Plato as the explanatory or structural principle of the whole reality and the good as the human good, for example for Aristotle, seems more central in these authors.

Yet even though Aspasius' formulation of sociability underlines the action towards other people in a way not found in the passage that he comments on, it would be an exaggeration to call it 'an altruistic interpretation of human sociability'. The first reason for this is the 'also' (*kai*) just discussed. It is not only doing good things to others that amount to 'doing good things' (*eu poiein*) in the passage; this is what it is *as well*. Further, when specifying the objects of one's supposed good deeds, Aspasius is talking about one's fellow human beings (*koinōnoi*). Therefore, his formulation does not necessarily introduce an impartial concern for all human beings that is typically required of modern forms of altruism. Rather, the scope of other-concern that Aspasius' expression introduces seems relatively limited, one's fellow citizens. In Aristotle this would mean the free men living in the same city, the same group that is the widest application of Aristotle's notion of friendship (*philia*). However, given that Aspasius is living in a very different political environment, the Roman Empire, the scope of fellow human beings might be much larger in his case. However, there is no positive evidence that Aspasius would understand fellow human beings as covering the whole humanity, that is, that he would in this sense replace the Aristotelian limited sphere of other-regard by a Stoic impartial perspective of humanity.[38]

---

[35] δεῖ τοὺς φίλους εὖ ποιεῖν; τοὺς ἐχθροὺς δεῖ κακῶς. See also *Eudemian Ethics* 1241a35–6 in which εὖ ποιεῖν, 'doing good' is connected with εὖ πάσχειν 'having good done to [oneself]'. I thank Christian Tornau for drawing my attention to this passage of the *Eudemian Ethics*.

[36] See, e.g. τοῖς γὰρ φίλοις οἴεται ὀφείλειν τοὺς φίλους ἀγαθὸν μέν τι δρᾶν, κακὸν δὲ μηδέν in 332a9–10; see also ἐπ' ὠφελίᾳ μέντοι τῶν φίλων καὶ ἐπὶ βλάβῃ τῶν ἐχθρῶν in 334b5. For a discussion of this initial notion of the good in the *Republic*, see also Julia Annas, this volume, ch. 2.

[37] πρὸς ἕτερον (*EN* V 1, 1129b26–7; 30–3).

[38] For this difference between Aristotle and the Stoics, see also Annas (1993), 184.

3.2 Tendency to virtue and need to be with others

Despite these reservations, Aspasius makes several remarkable moves with respect to human sociability and his general formulation of virtues. Perhaps the most important of them are the following. Aristotle's formulation of the human being as a political animal does *not* claim either (i) that a certain tendency to be virtuous towards other people follows from natural sociability or (ii) that there is a need in human beings to be with others, the satisfaction of which belongs to a happy life. By contrast, Aspasius makes both these two claims. Or, rather, he makes the first claim and comes very close to articulating the second one as well.

As to the first point (i), Aspasius also formulates the claim of human sociability as follows:

The human being is a political and communal animal and loves the good, so that he delights if he does good things to his fellow human and, similarly, if he in general is aware that he has performed some good act (23.7–9).[39]

This passage shows that Aspasius, at least in some cases, takes human sociability to entail a tendency to love the good, to do good things to others, and to delight in doing these good things as well as to delight in worthy action in general. Since the pleasure related to virtuous action is one of the central characteristics of an Aristotelian virtuous person that Aspasius also seems to endorse, this formulation implies that Aspasius understands human sociability and political nature as including a tendency to virtue. Further, and in this respect he goes beyond Aristotle, Aspasius interprets the human sociable and political nature as containing the tendency to enjoy *doing good things to others*.

The last claim can mean either that the tendency to virtue that follows from the human being's social and political nature implies a tendency to do good things to others but that virtue is still to some extent distinguishable from what one does to others. Or, it can mean that virtue (that amounts to loving the good) must be interpreted precisely in terms of good things that one does to others. The latter, more radical claim would imply an even stronger other-concerned dimension in Aspasius' commentary than we found above but there is some evidence that the former is more likely to be true. Consider, for instance, a passage in which Aspasius prioritizes the other-concerned dimension of virtues but says that all of them, with the important exception of justice, can also be exercised towards oneself:

The activities of the rest of the virtues, except for justice, also occur with respect to the virtuous person himself, for example the temperate person not only uses temperance in relation to

---

[39] πολιτικὸν γὰρ ζῷον ὁ ἄνθρωπος καὶ κοινωνικὸν καὶ φιλόκαλον, ὥστε ἐάν τε τοὺς κοινωνοὺς εὖ ποιῇ ἥδεται, ἐάν τε ὅλως συνειδῇ ἑαυτῷ καλόν τι ἐργαζομένῳ.

others but also does this with respect to himself in his regimen, clothing, and other things related to life (53.26–30).[40]

The main upshot of this passage is that, with the exception of justice that can only be exercised towards others (and that Aristotle also takes to be other-concerned),[41] all other virtues can be exercised both in relation to other people and with respect to oneself. Therefore, all virtues cannot be identified as 'doing good to others' in Aspasius.

Before I move to discuss other implications of Aspasius' formulation, it is important to note two things. First, even though I only consider Aspasius' commentary on the last-mentioned point, that is, the formulation of virtues of character in other-concerned means, my point is not to deny that Aristotle was of the same or similar view. Aspasius' commentary, as a commentary, is surely dependent on the text it comments on—in this case Aristotle's discussion of the mean with respect to various virtues of character and a certain *aporia* that arises from it, namely whether all virtues are about the 'communication of words and actions' (*EN* II 7, 1108a11). Therefore, my discussion on this should not be taken to imply that Aspasius is more other-concerned than Aristotle; they are both discussing essentially the same point. Further, the discussion concerns only the virtues of character and the theoretical virtue is outside the scope of the present consideration. Thus Aspasius' discussion does not introduce a more other-concerned interpretation on the level of theoretical virtue.

The second point concerns terminology. When Aspasius says that human beings are political and communal, he uses the adjective *koinōnikos* that was common in Stoic texts, especially in Marcus Aurelius. Since the Stoics proposed an impartial concern to the whole humanity as rational beings, one might easily be tempted to conclude that Aspasius' other-concerned formulations of sociability are due to Stoic influence. However, such a conclusion cannot be drawn on the basis of this one term alone. As Jonathan Barnes has pointed out,[42] by the time of Aspasius, words that were introduced by one school or another as a technical term had been detached from the originating school and become common property. Therefore, we should not jump to the conclusion that the term alone reveals a Stoic tendency or Stoic influence on Aspasius.

As mentioned, Aspasius also comes close to interpreting human sociability as a need to be with others (ii) the satisfaction of which is necessary for happiness. He points out (171.27–32) that, as opposed to simply solitary animals such as lions and wolves and other animals that can live alone,[43] human beings are political and

---

[40] ἢ τῶν λοιπῶν ἀρετῶν αἱ ἐνέργειαι πλὴν τῆς δικαιοσύνης γίνοιντ' ἂν καὶ καθ' ἑαυτὸν τῷ ἐναρέτῳ, οἷον ὁ σώφρων οὐ μόνον ἐν τῇ πρὸς ἄλλον κοινωνίᾳ χρῆται τῷ σωφρονεῖν ἀλλὰ καὶ πρὸς αὑτὸν ἐν διαίτῃ ἐν ἀμπεχόνῃ τοῖς ἄλλοις τοῖς κατὰ τὸν βίον.

[41] See note 37 above.   [42] Barnes (1999), 5.

[43] καθ' αὑτὸ ζῆν; these animals are of course nowadays known not to be solitary.

communal and *need* someone to spend their days with and to live with.[44] According to Aspasius, a friend is best suited for this and even a virtuous and happy person needs friends and would not choose to live alone—even if he could otherwise have all the other goods except the friend (171.31–2).[45] Therefore, Aspasius indicates that human sociability involves a concrete need to be with and to share one's life with others, and that the satisfaction of this need is necessary for happiness.

3.3 The scope of other-regard and the role of others

Let me now return to the question of how we should understand the scope of other-regard in Aspasius' re-definition or re-interpretation of human sociability just discussed. His overall use of 'community' (*koinōnia*) and derivatives (*koinōnos, koinōnikos*) indicates that he means a political whole or a smaller community and the members thereof (e.g. 175.19 and 21, 181.16, 183.26–8), even though he also uses 'community' (*koinōnia*) for all kinds of relations (177.20), especially those involving communication (121.4 and 6). The last-mentioned connotation is so strong that at one point he needs to point out that interaction in accordance with justice is possible *even without speaking* (53.34–54.1). The way in which Aspasius talks about communities seems to indicate that he means a smaller community than the whole of humanity, thus following Aristotle rather than the Stoics on the scope of other-concern that justice requires.

However, it is also worth noting that, when discussing communal friendship (*koinōnikē philia*), Aspasius notes—as Aristotle also does (*EN* VIII 12, 1161b14–16)[46]— although very briefly, that someone could classify friendships based on hospitality under communal friendship (184.13).[47] A communal friendship is, according to Aspasius, based on some kind of agreement[48] but he does not explain the nature of this agreement. In any case, the suggested classification of hospitality friendship in the same category contains the potential for enlarging the scope of one's concern for others in Aspasius' (and Aristotle's) interpretation of human sociability. If this is the case, all strangers that one encounters become members of the same community provided that they satisfy the conditions for hospitality. This would not introduce an entirely impartial perspective of other-concern in Aspasius' interpretation of the human community in which the requirements of friendship (or *philia*) and justice are in place. However, the

---

[44] δεῖται τοῦ συνδιημερεύοντος καὶ συζῶντος (171.30). This claim has precedents both in Aristotle (as the claim that for the theoretically virtuous person it is better to have colleagues, *EN* X 7, 1177a34) and in Stoicism (Cicero, *de Officiis* 1.153). I am grateful to Christian Tornau for bringing the parallel in Cicero to my attention.

[45] ὥστε καὶ ὁ σπουδαῖος καὶ ὁ εὐδαίμων φίλου δεῖται καὶ οὐκ ἂν ἕλοιτο ζῆν καθ' αὑτόν, οὐδ' εἰ μέλλοι πάντα τὰ ἄλλα ἀγαθὰ ἕξειν.

[46] In VIII 3, 1156a28–31 Aristotle classifies hospitality friendship or φιλία under friendship of benefit.

[47] εἰς τὰς κοινωνικὰς δὲ τὴν ξενικήν τις τάξειε.

[48] ὁμολογία τις 184.1–2; cf. Aristotle's reference that friendships seem to exist in accordance with some kind of agreement (καθ' ὁμολογίαν τινὰ φαίνονται εἶναι in *EN* VIII 12, 1161b15).

extension of one's community to relations to strangers governed by hospitality excludes the most parochial restrictions of other-concern into the free men of one's own city-state.

With respect to the requirements of justice in friendships (or relationships governed by *philia*), Aspasius makes clear that all communities imply ethical treatment of others: 'where there is community, there is friendship and justice' (183.27–8).[49] This remark strengthens the impression that Aspasius at least to some extent connects the communal nature of human beings (human being as *koinōnikos*) to the requirement that one should act justly towards the other members of one's community. Perhaps Aspasius supposes that the agreement that according to him forms the basis of community friendship implies a tacit consent to treat other members of the community justly. Further, as indicated, given his remark that hospitality friendship might be taken to fall under community friendship, the implication seems to be that strangers will need to be treated justly as well. All in all, even though Aspasius does not make the point that one's community reaches the whole humanity, he does not restrict the requirements of justice merely to one's immediate vicinity in the sense that only those that already are members of one's community require just treatment. One's community extends to those strangers whom one encounters through the practice of hospitality.

Finally, Aspasius' commentary leaves the impression that the recipients of one's good deeds, good deeds that one needs to maximize in order to live a happy life, are not only the members of a very narrow community (i.e. merely one's fellow citizens). Rather, the requirements of justice extend to strangers who, as it were, become the members of our community when they come into contact with us in the confines of hospitality. Further, he understands the virtues of character as primarily other-concerning and only secondarily pertaining to oneself. However, he inherits from Aristotle (*EN* I 9, 1099a33–b2)[50] the disquieting thought that friends can be used as if as instruments in one's pursuits. Aspasius refers to his most cherished example, overthrowing a tyrant (that also was a common topos in those times) and points out that 'undoings of tyrannies have occurred through friends' (24.10) and 'if someone is in need of [money for] expenses, his friends confer it' (24.10–11, quoting from Konstan's (2006) translation). If, then, friends are used as if as instruments, does this not seriously weaken the ethical implications of concern for other people in Aspasius' commentary? All the more so when Aspasius seems to accept Aristotle's assimilation of friends to other external goods such as money that are used in virtuous action.

Concerning as this seems, it needs to be stressed that neither Aspasius nor Aristotle in fact claims that friends should be used *as* instruments but *as if as* (*kathaper*) instruments, and we should not jump to the conclusion that other people should be *mere* instruments for virtuous action in Aspasius. Yet, on the one hand,

---

[49] ὅπου δὲ κοινωνία ἔνεστι καὶ φιλία τις καὶ δίκαιον.

[50] πολλὰ μὲν γὰρ πράττεται, καθάπερ δι' ὀργάνων, διὰ φίλων καὶ πλούτου καὶ πολιτικῆς δυνάμεως, quoted by Aspasius in 24.9.

one cannot help having the impression that, at least at times, Aspasius conceives other people as necessary requirements and perhaps also the objects of one's virtue, and thus they are not the ultimate aims or goals of virtuous action. On the other hand, I am not quite convinced that performing good actions towards others for the sake of virtue necessarily cancels the other-regarding value of the action in a similar way as perhaps some other self-interested concerns do.

4. Porphyry's Reformulation of Justice: Concern for Other Creatures

4.1 The context of Porphyry's discussion

The narrowness of the scope of other-concern is certainly not a problem in Porphyry's *On Abstinence from Killing Animals (De abstinentia)*.[51] The discussion of justice in the treatise differs sharply from the majority of late ancient discussions on the topic. Porphyry's central concern in book 3 is to argue that justice does not merely regulate human relations but should be conceived as comprising non-human animals as well. The important point, however, is not only that we should extend the scope of justice and thus the scope of our concern for others to comprise non-human animals (and, in fact, ultimately plants). Porphyry also argues that it is exactly by enlarging the scope of our concern for others that we, at the same time or precisely because of doing so, promote the acquisition of our own goal, assimilation to god (*On Abstinence*, 3.26–7). Therefore, our concern for others means concern for ourselves, provided that we understand what or who we truly are.

In *On Abstinence*, Porphyry addresses a friend, Firmus Castricius, who, as Porphyry's informants have reported, has resumed his habit of consuming flesh (*On Abstinence* 1.1,1–13, Nauck). The open letter to Firmus is an attempt to make the friend return to abstinence from the living. Porphyry's arguments are mainly directed at those ancient schools and traditions that allowed meat eating (or that he took to allow meat eating) and the arguments about animal ethics are central but the treatise is not restricted to this topic. Rather, Porphyry expands his discussion to outline a more comprehensive programme of treating human beings, non-human animals, and ultimately plants (i.e. all living things) justly. He even suggests that we should not only refrain from injuring harmless living things that, in the context of *On Abstinence*, amounts to justice. We should also be beneficial towards and care for all living things in order to attain the greatest possible godlikeness:

[51] *On Abstinence from Killing Animals* is Clarke's translation of the title of the treatise, and in antiquity discussions of the same theme often had a name referring to eating meat (e.g. Plutarch's *De esu carnium*). However, because the titles do not originate from the authors and because Porphyry is concerned with not injuring animals (not only killing them even though killing is a central case of injury), a better title would perhaps be *On Abstinence from Injuring Animals*. I am grateful to Tua Korhonen for a discussion on this point. For a general discussion of ancient debates about vegetarianism, see Sorabji (1993).

That which is in the whole of being altogether superior [i.e. god] refrains from doing harm, and it is through its power also protective of all, beneficent towards all, and in need of nothing, whereas we become harmless towards all through justice, but because of our mortal [nature] we are in need of the necessities (3.26, 59–63).[52]

Porphyry thus suggests that whereas it is the virtue of justice that makes us harmless towards harmless living creatures, we should also assimilate ourselves to god as far as possible and care for living things as well. He is painfully aware that we are not completely self-sufficient but need nourishment to survive. However, he argues that there is a way of doing this with justice and care provided that we stop injuring harmless animals and use plants considerately.

The more specific context of Porphyry's discussion is his polemic against the Stoics for restricting the scope of justice to humanity. This is remarkable because, as mentioned, the Stoics are usually known for a larger scope of other-concern than is usual in the ancient context. However, Porphyry argues that the Stoics do not have sufficient grounds for restricting justice to humanity. According to Porphyry, the Stoics maintain that '[justice] only needs to be extended to [creatures] that are similar [to human beings] . . . and this is why they exclude non-rational animals [from the scope of justice]' (3.1, 20–2).[53]

From Porphyry's point of view, the Stoic reason for excluding non-human animals from the scope of justice is that they are dissimilar to human beings, the relevant dissimilarity being that they are not rational.[54] Porphyry launches a whole arsenal of arguments against the Stoic claim that animals lack rationality, and one of his key strategies is to show that the Stoic view is inconsistent with their own definition of rationality. First, Porphyry argues that animals have expressive *logos* as significant speech and then proceeds to argue that they have internal rationality conceived in Stoic terms as well. In this context, I cannot go into the details of Porphyry's argument.[55] However, it is important to note that even though in much of his polemic Porphyry argues against the Stoics that *on their conception of reason* animals are rational, his argument is not merely ad hominem. This is because at the opening of book 3 he says that 'we put forward' the conception that is both true and

---

[52] τὸ δὲ ἐν τῷ παντὶ κρεῖττον πάντως ἦν ἀβλαβές, καὶ αὐτὸ μὲν διὰ δύναμιν καὶ σωστικὸν πάντων καὶ εὐποιητικὸν πάντων καὶ ἀπροσδεὲς πάντων· ἡμεῖς δὲ διὰ μὲν δικαιοσύνην ἀβλαβεῖς πάντων, διὰ δὲ τὸ θνητὸν ἐνδεεῖς τῶν ἀναγκαίων. For the point that the good only does good, i.e. is entirely beneficial, whereas it is in the nature of the bad to cause harm and to injure, see Plato, *Republic* X 608e3–4: The good is protective and beneficent, whereas the bad [is said to] ruin and destroy (τὸ μὲν ἀπολλύον καὶ διαφθεῖρον πᾶν τὸ κακὸν εἶναι, τὸ δὲ σῷζον καὶ ὠφελοῦν τὸ ἀγαθόν).

[53] ταύτην [i.e. δικαιοσύνην] πρὸς τὰ ὅμοια δεῖν μόνα παρατείνειν εἰρήκασιν οἱ ἀντιλέγοντες, καὶ διὰ τοῦτο τὰ ἄλογα διαγράφουσι τῶν ζῴων.

[54] For a text for this as the Stoic view, see Diogenes Laertius, *Lives of Eminent Philosophers* (7.129, 6–8) where Chrysippus and Posidonius are said to maintain such a view.

[55] I devote a chapter to this theme in a study in progress on concern for ourselves and others in Porphyry's ethics of *On Abstinence*.

Pythagorean and according to which 'all soul that partakes in sensation and memory also is rational' (3.1, 22–5).[56]

However, the hinge point of Porphyry's argument that non-human animals must be included in the scope of justice is not rationality. Rather, he is clear that it is not permissible to take the life of a living thing because the life or soul belongs to the creature whose soul it is and it is not permissible for us to take it from them.[57] If it were necessary for our survival to eat meat, the injustice involved in taking the life of another living creature could be justified (3.18, 16–30).[58] However, as the consumption of flesh is neither necessary for survival (as mere living) nor for living well, it is simply unjust to take the lives of animals.

4.2 Justice as restraint from injuring harmless creatures

In addition to arguing against the Stoics on rationality, Porphyry also criticizes their definition of justice for being mere love for the human species (3.26, 47–8).[59] And such love, he also points out, ultimately boils down to self-love or selfishness (*philautia*). He does not elaborate on this remark but it suggests a remarkable line of argument. From the point of view of Porphyry's remark, any theory that only extends the requirements of justice to those creatures that are similar to us is merely a form of self-love. By contrast, genuine concern for others requires extending just treatment to creatures that are in some important sense different from us.

Rather than the Stoic justice in the realm of what is similar to us, Porphyry claims, justice must be defined as:

(JH) refraining and harmlessness towards everything that is not harmful (3.26, 48–50).[60]

The qualification 'everything that does not do harm' is important in Porphyry's argument against the claim that we can kill and eat animals because some animals are dangerous to human beings. Porphyry argues that even though it might be necessary

---

[56] φέρε ἡμεῖς τὴν ἀληθῆ τε ὁμοῦ καὶ Πυθαγόρειον δόξαν παραστήσωμεν, πᾶσαν ψυχήν, ᾗ μέτεστιν αἰσθήσεως καὶ μνήμης, λογικὴν ἐπιδεικνύντες. At any rate, any view that takes Porphyry's argument to be merely ad hominem needs to explain or explain away this declaration. I am grateful to Fay Edwards for a discussion on this point.

[57] See, e.g. arguments from Theophrastus (*de abst.*, 2.12, 16–2.13, 1). By contrast, some claim that the crux of Porphyry's argument is animal capacity to feel pain; see Dombrowski (1987), 774–91. However, this move, I take it, is an argument against those who claim that because we need to eat plants anyway there is no reason not to eat animals. Borrowing an argument from Plutarch, Porphyry counters this objection by saying that animals differ from plants because they can feel pain (3.19, 7–10). However, because Porphyry ultimately recommends extending justice to plants as well (e.g. 3.26.12–13), the requirement of justice cannot be dependent on the animal capacity to feel pain.

[58] This argument is quoted from Plutarch. For references, see Bouffartigue and Patillon (1977/1995) ii: 138 and 144–5.

[59] αὕτη μὲν γὰρ φιλανθρωπία τις ἂν εἴη.

[60] ἡ δὲ δικαιοσύνη ἐν τῷ ἀφεκτικῷ καὶ ἀβλαβεῖ κεῖται παντὸς ὅτου οὖν τοῦ μὴ βλάπτοντος. Porphyry's definition can be taken to have a precedent in Plutarch (*Septem sapientium convivium* 16, 159B) but his development of the definition is original. See Bouffartigue and Patillon (1977/1995), 138 and 188 for the parallel. I am grateful to Christian Tornau for drawing my attention to this issue.

to kill or injure some animals because of their savagery, this does not entail that domesticated animals should be killed (see, e.g. 2.2, 1–16). He also suggests that animals only harm us when it is necessary for their survival. If an animal has a sufficient amount of food, it will not attack human beings—a point that Porphyry in fact ascribes to Aristotle (3.12, 14–17). In terms of savagery, anger, and aggression he takes many humans to far surpass even the most terrifying animals: 'they murder their children and kill their fathers' (3.19, 17–18; trans. Clark)—most probably referring to Medea and Oedipus.

One intuition in Porphyry's argument that injuring animals that do not constitute a threat to our own lives is unjust is borrowed from Theophrastus: taking the life of another living creature would be like stealing something from another, that is, taking something that belongs to another against its will. In book 2 (chapter 13) quoted from Theophrastus Porphyry discusses the case with respect to plants. Instead of pointing out that plants do not have a will, he (or Theophrastus) claims that there is a way of using plants that does not mean stealing from them. From Porphyry's (and Theophrastus') perspective, plants can be used considerately (and justice observed towards them) if we only take fruit that they drop or if we only use some leaves while leaving the rest of the organism alive. Therefore, whether or not a living creature has reason and sensation, we can observe justice with respect to it. Doing so requires that we do not injure it or take its life—unless the creature itself poses an imminent threat to us.

Early on in book 3 when Porphyry opens his polemic against the Stoics on animal justice and rationality, he comes close to formulating a claim according to which human beings have a natural tendency to justice. He says:

> But we, even though all wolves and vultures approve of meat eating, we shall not agree that they are stating what is just. For, the human being is naturally harmless and refrains from injuring others to acquire pleasures. (3.1, 14–18)[61]

Considering that, as we saw, later on in the book Porphyry formulates justice as restraint from injuring harmless creatures (JH), this passage can be taken to point to the idea that we as a species are in fact inclined to justice rather than injustice. However, given that Porphyry also underlines human savagery in his reference to people murdering children and killing fathers quoted above, it is evident that the naturalness of such a tendency cannot derive from its universality among actual (and mythical or fictional) individuals. Rather, it is perhaps natural in some ideal sense, human being as perfected or uncontaminated. Such contamination, he assumes in book 3, is especially caused by the pursuit of pleasure that he takes to be the major reason for the human desire to eat meat and thus injure animals.

---

[61] ἡμεῖς δέ, οὐδ' ἂν πάντες λύκοι ἢ γῦπες τὴν κρεοφαγίαν δοκιμάζωσιν, οὐ συγχωρήσομεν τούτοις δίκαια λέγειν, ἔστ' ἂν. ὁ ἄνθρωπος ἀβλαβὲς ᾖ φύσει καὶ ἀφεκτικὸν τοῦ διὰ τῆς ἄλλων βλάβης αὑτῷ τὰς ἡδονὰς πορίζεσθαι.

4.3 Concern for others

Porphyry's definition of justice as restraint from injuring harmless creatures (JH) is of course at least formally concerned with others in the sense that it is formulated in terms of what we do or, rather, should refrain from doing to other creatures. However, one might criticize it for being rather thin. Porphyry was aware of one such objection, or a possible objection, and responded to it both at the opening of book 3 and in the final sections 3.26–7 of the treatise.[62]

The objection is that extending the requirements of justice to non-human animals might lessen our concern or justice towards human beings. Early on in the third book, Porphyry points out that justice finds its most beautiful expression in the reverence for gods (*eusebeia*), which for its part is promoted rather than hindered by abstinence from injuring animals. Thus there is no risk that observing abstinence from injuring animals would conflict with our quest for being just towards human beings (3.1, 5–10). He does not articulate the steps of his argument but rather seems to suppose that there is a whole cluster of virtues (justice, moderation, and plainness or simplicity to which he refers in 3.1, 1–2) that are benefited by the practice of abstinence. Towards the end of book 3, Porphyry addresses this objection again, first by pointing out—somewhat ad hominem—that a person who claims that extending justice to non-human animals destroys it does not himself secure justice towards human beings. Rather, denying that animals are subject to the requirement of just treatment shows that a person maintaining such a claim merely increases his own pleasure which is the enemy of justice (3.26, 22–5).

Porphyry's own position is that, quite contrary to the objection, our justice towards human beings is increased rather than decreased by extending justice to non-human animals:

The person who abstains from consuming all ensouled beings, even those that do not belong to the same community with them, will abstain even more from injuring those that belong to the same kind. For the one who loves the genus will not hate the species but, rather, the larger is the justice they save for that part[63] [of the genus] which is of their kin. (3.26, 27–33)[64]

---

[62] These are in fact the sections of book 3 that contain material that is mostly penned by Porphyry himself, whereas many of the chapters in the middle of the book contain large quotations or adaptations from other authors, especially from Plutarch (3.18.3–20.6; 3.20.7–24.5) and, to a lesser extent, from Theophrastus (3.25). Therefore, I consider the sections that I discuss in the body text as especially important for Porphyry's own position.

[63] Reading, with Bouffartigue and Patillon ταύτην as referring to δικαιοσύνη rather than to οἰκείωσις as Nauck does.

[64] ὁ γὰρ ἀπεχόμενος παντὸς ἐμψύχου, κἂν μὴ τῶν συμβαλλόντων αὐτῷ εἰς κοινωνίαν, πολλῷ μᾶλλον πρὸς τὸ ὁμογενὲς τῆς βλάβης ἀφέξεται. οὐ γὰρ ὁ τὸ γένος φιλῶν τὸ εἶδος μισήσει, ἀλλὰ μᾶλλον ὅσῳ μεῖζον τὸ γένος τὸ τῶν ζῴων, τοσούτῳ καὶ πρὸς τὸ μέρος καὶ τὸ οἰκεῖον ταύτην διασώσει. Bouffartigue and Patillon refer (vol. 2, note 4 on p. 252) to a parallel in Plutarch (*De esu carnium* I 7, 996a).

Therefore, for Porphyry, justice is not a limited good or a scarce resource in the sense that it would be exhausted or diminished when extended further. Quite the contrary: justice is something we can strengthen by practicing it more widely.

Porphyry also connects justice as restraint from injuring harmless creatures (JH) to Plato's discussion in book IV of the *Republic* and claims that treating animals justly belongs to a person whose reason leads the baser parts of the soul. By contrast, eating meat or otherwise injuring animals is a sign that the baser parts of the soul, especially the desire for pleasure, is leading the soul, which is, of course, unjust. From Porphyry's point of view (3.27, 9–18), extending one's concern merely to the human beings that belong to one's closest circles is by no means a thicker expression of justice. Rather, it is an indication that one is led by passions and especially by the desire for pleasure rather than by reason. Conversely, Porphyry suggests, if we are led by reason, we naturally extend our concern for others to the whole of humanity and, ultimately, to animals and plants.

We have now seen that Porphyry argues that rather than diminishing our justice towards human beings, extending it to non-human animals increases our justice towards (all) human beings. One reason for this, Porphyry suggests, is because we only treat animals justly if reason leads our souls and our desires follow reason's rule. Therefore, from Porphyry's point of view, justice as restraint from injuring harmless creatures is compatible with Plato's discussion of justice defined as *oikeiopragia* in *Republic* IV. Abstaining from injuring animals is only possible if each of the parts of the soul are minding their own business and not interfering in that of the others, in particular when reason is ruling over desire.

One might also object that if justice defined as refraining from injuring harmless creatures is the only other-concerned aspect of Porphyry's discussion, this entails merely a thin concern for others. In this context, I cannot consider this question at length.[65] However, it needs to be noted that our concern for others is not reduced to justice in the sense of abstinence from injuring harmless creatures. Further, even though this requirement seems thin, it is also rather difficult to follow especially in today's food trade. In any case, Porphyry claims—as any good Platonist around that time would do[66]—that our goal is to assimilate ourselves to god to the extent that it is possible in the human life. How, then, does he describe this god that we should assimilate ourselves to? As mentioned in the passage I quoted (3.26, 59–63), one of the key properties is that god is beneficent rather than harmful to creatures.

Therefore, when striving for assimilation, we should not only aim at abstaining from injuring harmless creatures. We should also be beneficent and care for other living creatures as god does. However, due to our mortal nature we cannot

---

[65] I discuss the objection and Porphyry's position in more detail in a chapter on justice in book 3 in my study in progress on concern for oneself and for others in Porphyry's ethics of *On Abstinence*.

[66] Following Plato's *Theaetetus* 176a–b that also constitutes Plotinus' starting point for his reflection on virtue in *Ennead* I.2.

completely assimilate to god's self-sufficiency but we need nourishment. Porphyry is clear (2.47) that we should definitely not starve ourselves to death; this would involve an injustice towards ourselves and would not even liberate our soul from the body. Our task is, on the one hand, to be as just as we can when nourishing ourselves: refraining from eating meat and using plants considerately. Further, to the extent that we aim at being happy and assimilating ourselves to god, we must also be good. The more we succeed in being good, the more good we do to others also in the sense of beneficence and care.

4.4 Concern for oneself

Given that Porphyry maintains that we must extend justice to non-human animals and ultimately to plants and that we must be beneficent towards all living creatures, does this mean that we neglect concern for ourselves? In other words, is our concern for others somehow detrimental towards ourselves? Porphyry recognizes such a challenge and the crux of his response is that such an objection can only arise if we seriously misunderstand who we truly are. It might very well be that our body diminishes if we abstain from injuring animals and consuming their flesh but because we are not identical to our body this does not mean that we overlook ourselves:

For this reason, the just person comes out as diminishing himself with respect to the body but he does no injustice towards himself; for through its [presumably the body's] education and mastery the inner good grows, and that is the assimilation to god. (3.26,69–3.27, 1)[67]

Therefore, through abstinence from injuring harmless creatures we promote what in fact is good for us, or what is in our own true self-interest provided that we understand what our true self is.[68]

Porphyry also suggests that understanding our true self is the key to true flourishing. We cannot be completely self-sufficient because we are mortal creatures and our 'becoming is located in lack', as Porphyry puts it (3.27, 27). However, in so far as we understand our true self (3.27, 40–4), we manage, in a sense, to transcend the lack of quality in our being and rather identify ourselves with resourcefulness. By doing so, we stop desiring external things and stop trying to fill an emptiness inside. Such futile desire for external things can be transcended and transformed when we cognize our true self (3.27, 43–4). When we understand our true self we also start promoting the inner good that does not require acquisitions from the outside. With this transformation, we also understand that abstaining from injuring other living creatures promotes our ascent towards (the assimilation to) god and thus brings us happiness rather than the misery that is characteristic of desiring external objects

---

[67] διὸ προσπίπτει ὁ δίκαιος οἷον ἐλαττωτικὸς ἑαυτοῦ τῶν κατὰ σῶμα, οὐκ ἀδικεῖ δὲ ἑαυτόν· αὔξεται γὰρ τῇ τούτου παιδαγωγίᾳ καὶ ἐγκρατείᾳ τὸ ἐντὸς ἀγαθόν, τοῦτ᾽ ἔστιν ἡ πρὸς θεὸν ὁμοίωσις. I take τούτου to refer to the body.

[68] For the importance of understanding our true self, see 3.27, 40–4.

(cf. 3.27, 37–40 with reference to Plato's discussion of the tyrannical person in *Republic* IX 580a1–7).

Porphyry's discussion is important because it explicitly recognizes the possibility that concern for others and concern for ourselves can conflict. As we have seen, he responds to this possibility by pointing out that if we understand the nature of our true self, no such conflict arises. Rather, practicing justice in ever-widening circles and aiming at assimilation to god in beneficence ultimately means the best possible concern we can extend to ourselves. This is because assimilation to god is where we, as philosophers, derive our happiness (*de abst.* 2.3, 3–5).

In fact, it is not only that we promote assimilation to god by being just to others. It is by extending our concern for others further and further that we become more and more assimilated to divinity. According to Porphyry, a person who acts on the basis of reason and restrains from injuring other citizens, people from other cities, and finally all human beings, guards the irrational element in him and is more reasonable and thus more divine—presumably more divine than a person who is only extending justice to human beings close to himself. Similarly, the one who abstains from injuring animals is more similar to god. Finally, the one who is capable of extending justice even to plants preserves the resemblance to an even greater extent. (3.27, 14–21) Therefore, whereas divinity to some extent belongs to those who are just towards all human beings, assimilation to god is only acquired when one is just towards animals as well. Finally, the greatest likeness to god is achieved when even plants are treated considerately, taking fruit they drop and leaves that allow the organism to live on.

5. Concluding remarks

In this essay, I have argued that we find important developments of the theme of other-concern in late ancient ethics. With respect to Aspasius, I have argued that he transforms Aristotle's account of the human being as a political animal in two important respects. First, he interprets the claim of human sociability (or human being as a political animal) as a natural tendency to virtue, a move that Aristotle himself does not make. Secondly, Aspasius also introduces other-regarding concerns into a discussion in which Aristotle makes no reference to such considerations. In his comments on Aristotle's claim that happiness requires a complete life in *Nicomachean Ethics* I 7, Aspasius explains Aristotle's remark by reference to human sociability as a tendency to do good things, also to other people. This does not quite amount to an altruistic formulation of human sociability: the scope of other-regard is not impartial but only covers one's fellow citizens with the extension to those strangers whom one encounters, and it is not merely to other people that the good things are done according to Aspasius' clarification. However, it is striking that Aspasius considers such things at all in this context. Further, in addition to indicating that in order to be happy one needs to do good thing also to others, Aspasius indicates that one needs to maximize doing good, also to others. Therefore, other-regarding good deeds have a constitutive rather than limiting role in one's happiness according to Aspasius.

With respect to Porphyry, I have argued, first, that he introduces an other-concerned definition of justice in *On Abstinence* 3 according to which justice must be understood as restraint from injuring harmless creatures. Further, he argues that the scope of justice must be considerably widened even from the Stoic extension of justice to the whole of humanity. According to Porphyry, such justice amounts to mere love for our species and, ultimately, to self-love. By contrast, true justice requires that one refrains from injuring other living creatures, especially that one refrains from taking their lives. By doing so, one promotes his or her true self-interest because, from Porphyry's perspective, treating animals justly amounts to the assimilation to god which is our goal and from which our happiness derives. Therefore, rather than being in conflict, concern for others and concern for oneself amount to the same practice of justice and beneficence that also constitutes our assimilation to god.

14

Happiness in this Life?

Augustine on the Principle that Virtue Is Self-sufficient for Happiness

Christian Tornau

Augustine's thinking about happiness is firmly rooted in ancient eudaemonism.[1] Like his philosophical predecessors, he takes it as immediately evident that all men want to be happy;[2] he also shares their assumption that happiness is reached and guaranteed through the stable possession of the supreme good (*summum bonum*). Augustine also agrees with the tradition that the *summum bonum* must meet certain formal requirements: It is the ultimate object of desire, for the sake of which everything else is chosen but which itself is not pursued for the sake of anything else;[3] it is complete insofar as through its possession every desire is satisfied;[4] and 'it must be such that one cannot lose it against one's will',[5] that is, it must be independent from bodily or external circumstances. These conditions, Augustine argues, are only fulfilled by the supreme unchangeable Being or God himself; therefore, happiness can only be achieved through the possession of God: 'Happy is he who has God.'[6] This definition from the early dialogue *De beata vita* basically remains the same throughout

---

[1] The basic study remains Holte (1962), esp. 221–31. For recent discussion see Müller (2010); Buddensiek (2009). See also Brechtken (1975), 11–84; Beierwaltes (1981); Wetzel (1992), 45–55; Rist (1994), 48–53; 148–202; Horn (1999). For an overview, which also informs about the biblical background (especially the *beatitudines* from the Sermon on the Mount), see de Noronha Galvao (1986–1994). Doignon (1987) is a useful collection of texts.

[2] Cic. *Hort.* fr. 58 Grilli = fr. 69 Straume-Zimmermann = Aug. *trin.* 13. 7: *Beati certe omnes esse volumus*. Augustine quotes this axiom approvingly from the first (*beata v.* 10, written in 386 AD) to the last of his writings (*c. Iul. imp.* 6. 11, written between 428 and 430).

[3] *civ.* 8. 8; 10. 3; *mor.* 1. 24 etc. For the classical eudaemonist background cf. e.g. Cic. *fin.* 1. 29. For the basic assumptions of ancient eudaemonist ethics cf. Annas (1993: 27–46). Their importance for Augustine is emphasized e.g. by Müller (2010), 19–24.

[4] Cf. *beata v.* 23–9; *mor.* 1. 5.

[5] *mor.* 1. 5: *tale esse debet quod non amittat invitus*. Cf. *beata v.* 11; *civ.* 11. 13.

[6] *beata v.* 11: *deum igitur... qui habet, beatus est.* Cf. *mor.* 1. 10; 1. 24. Discussions of happiness in Augustine often closely follow the eudaemonistic pattern: *mor.* 1. 4–61; *trin.* 13. 6–25; *civ.* 10. 1–3. For an analysis of Augustine's *deum habere* cf. Beierwaltes (1981), 43–55.

Augustine's work, even though the wording varies considerably. Alternative formulations for 'having God' are for instance 'enjoyment of God' (*frui deo*),[7] 'contemplation of God', 'enjoyment of truth',[8] or (taking up an expression from the Psalms) 'clinging to God' (*adhaerere deo*).[9]

There can, however, be no reasonable doubt that in Augustine ancient eudaemonism is thoroughly Christianized. This does not so much concern his 'ontologizing' identification of the ultimate object of desire with God, the Supreme Being. The idea that 'wisdom' or knowledge of the supreme entity is essential for the good life is of course not foreign to the ancient philosophical tradition, and Augustine himself felt that he was on common ground with the Platonists on this account.[10] In two other respects, however, he clearly and consciously deviates from classical eudaemonism. First, he firmly denied the possibility of happiness in this life and limited it to the life of the blessed after the resurrection, thus giving happiness a decidedly eschatological character.[11] 1 Cor 13. 12 ('For now we see through a glass darkly, but then we will see face to face') is often quoted to this effect.[12] Second, especially in his later years, he came to regard happiness exclusively as a gift of divine grace. For the mature and late Augustine, it is not possible for man to attain happiness through his own power; nor is man saved because of his own merits, for otherwise grace would cease to be grace.[13] Even virtue itself must be considered as a gift of God rather than a human achievement, if we are to avoid vainglory and pride (*superbia*, the root of all sins).[14] These modifications are, of course, intimately connected. One of Augustine's standard criticisms of 'the philosophers' is that their pride led them into thinking that they could achieve happiness by themselves in this life. This proud self-assertion made them unable and unwilling to grasp the importance of divine grace that manifests itself most compellingly in the incarnation of Christ.[15]

---

[7] e.g. *civ.* 8. 8; *trin.* 13. 10.

[8] *lib. arb.* 2. 35. Cf. Beierwaltes (1981), 44.

[9] Ps 72. 28: *mihi autem adhaerere* (or: *inhaerere*) *deo bonum est.* There are more than 50 quotations of this verse in Augustine, the earliest of which is *mor.* 1. 26 (388 AD). The different formulae may also be combined; cf. *mor.* 1. 35: 'If we *enjoy* his *contemplation* and completely *cling* to him, we are beyond doubt happy' (*cuius contemplatione perfruentes eique penitus adhaerentes procul dubio beati sumus*).

[10] Cf. *civ.* 8. 8. Among Platonist sources, one might cite Alcin. *Did.* 180. 41–2 Whittaker. The most noteworthy antecedent of the idea that happiness consists in contemplation is, of course, Aristotle.

[11] Cf. e.g. *civ.* 19. 4; *trin.* 13. 10 and, for a full discussion that takes into account the importance of grace for man's liberation from evil, *civ.* 22. 22–30. Some passages in the early work seem to endorse the classical notion that the wise man is happy because of his independence and inner tranquillity; they are duly retracted in the *Retractationes* (cf. *retr.* 1. 2 on *De beata vita*; *retr.* 1. 4. 3 on *sol.* 1. 14; *retr.* 1. 7. 4 on *mor.* 1. 53). For Augustine's development on this account, cf. Müller (2010), 50–9.

[12] e.g. *conf.* 10. 7; *civ.* 22. 29.

[13] Cf. e.g. *civ.* 14. 1: 'unless the undeserved grace of God (*indebita dei gratia*) liberated some [from their deserved punishment]'; *en. Ps.* 31. 1. 1. Already in *beata v.* 5 happiness is called a 'gift of God' (*dei donum*). Cf. van Geest (2004), 541.

[14] Ecli 10. 13, quoted e.g. in *civ.* 12. 6. Cf. *ep.* 155. 9 (discussed in the Conclusion of this chapter).

[15] *civ.* 10. 29; 19. 4; *ep.* 155. 2; cf. *conf.* 7. 26. A striking example of this way of reasoning is the argument of *trin.* 13, which starts from the usual eudaemonist assumptions but then turns to a detailed discussion of the 'mechanics' of man's salvation through Christ.

Now it was agreed among ancient ethicists that virtue was at least relevant, if not essential, for happiness. A maximal position was adopted by the Stoics, who condensed their view in the seemingly counter-intuitive formula that 'virtue alone was sufficient for happiness'.[16] Together with its equivalent, the equally famous paradox that 'only the moral good is of value',[17] it expresses the Stoic conviction that moral goodness or virtue or right reason is, as Cicero puts it, not only the *summum bonum* but even the *solum bonum*, the only good.[18] In the Hellenistic period the Stoic view had been heavily attacked by rival schools, especially the Peripatetics who, while granting the pre-eminence of virtue, nevertheless defended the natural intuition that bodily well-being and some external goods, such as social standing and friendship, could not be completely irrelevant for the good life.[19] In imperial times, however, its influence seems to have grown steadily. The principle that virtue is self-sufficient for happiness is quoted with approval—and, as a rule, without reference to its Stoic origin—by pagan and Christian writers alike and by adherents of various philosophical schools;[20] instead of being regarded as merely counter-intuitive or paradoxical, it was apparently taken to prove the high aspirations of a true philosopher and, accordingly, as a kind of default position any ethicist who wanted to be taken seriously had to adopt. As far as the Latin-speaking world is concerned, the triumph of the Stoic ideal is partly explained by the fact that it had been vigorously defended and claimed for philosophy as such by Cicero in the fifth book of his *Tusculan disputations*. As a school text, the *Tusculans* exerted an enormous influence which is also palpable in the work of Augustine, who was an assiduous reader of the *Tusculans* throughout his life[21] and whose basic ethical concerns and assumptions are clearly shaped by Cicero's account of the Hellenistic debate and of Stoic ethics in particular.[22]

However, in the framework of Augustine's eudaemonism as outlined above, the principle of virtue's self-sufficiency is far from being unproblematic. If the only way of attaining happiness is divine grace, and if happiness is strictly confined to the future life, will the importance of virtue not be radically reduced or even

---

[16] Zeno, SVF I. 187: ὅτι ἡ ἀρετὴ αὐτάρκης πρὸς εὐδαιμονίαν. For further evidence cf. SVF III. 49–67. In Latin e.g. *virtutem ad beate vivendum se ipsa esse contentam* (Cic. *Tusc.* 5. 1). Cf. Annas (1993), 388–411.

[17] SVF III. 29–45: ὅτι μόνον τὸ καλὸν ἀγαθόν.

[18] Cic. *fin.* 3. 12.

[19] Cf. Alexander of Aphrodisias' essay 'that virtue is not self-sufficient for happiness' (Alex. Aphr. *de an. mant.* 159–68 Bruns: ὅτι ἡ ἀρετὴ οὐκ αὐτάρκης πρὸς εὐδαιμονίαν).

[20] Cf. e.g. Ph. *Ebr.* 200; Clem. Al. *strom.* 4. 52. 1–3 (quoting Pl. *R.* 2. 361e); ibid. 5. 96. 5; Greg. Naz. *ep.* 32 = SVF III. 586. For the Platonists cf. Alcin. *Did.* 180. 39–41 Whittaker; Attic. fr. 2. 9–17 des Places; Plot. I 4. 4. 23–5. See Tornau (2013a), 143–4.

[21] For the evidence, see Hagendahl (1967), 138–56; 510–16. For the presence of the *Tusculans* especially in the *De beata vita* cf. Doignon (1987), 341–3.

[22] In this sense, Wetzel (1992), 45–55 has termed the position of the early dialogues, especially the *De beata vita*, 'Augustine's Stoicism'. I agree with Wetzel that 'Augustine's sensibilities in ethics are fundamentally Stoic' insofar as he 'refuses to accept the intrusion of fortune into the ideal of beatitude' (Wetzel (1992), 50).

annihilated, given that, whatever its exact definition, virtue is undoubtedly related to human dispositions and activities and concerns our attitudes and actions in this life? Theoretically, two solutions are possible.

(1) Augustine might dissolve the traditional nexus of virtue and happiness altogether and claim that happiness or eternal bliss is granted to those who have been elected or predestined by God for reasons that, though certainly just, are nevertheless unintelligible to humankind. He might, in other words, reject the ideal of self-sufficiency as a mere pretension of 'the philosophers' and claim that virtue is in fact totally dependent on grace which may or may not reward it with happiness. Critics from Julian of Aeclanum to Kurt Flasch have indeed reconstructed Augustine's mature and late doctrine of grace along these lines and objected that it transformed God into a tyrannical ruler who does not even allow inquiry into the reasons for his arbitrary decisions.[23] Yet this is obviously not Augustine's view. Until the end of his life, he wrestled with the problem of the compatibility of freedom and grace,[24] and his insistence (especially, but not exclusively in the sermons) on the importance of human virtue and the rewards God has promised for it can hardly be dismissed as mere lip service.

(2) Augustine might redefine virtue in exclusively Christian terms, equating it with faith, true worship, love of God and the neighbour, etc. There are indeed quite a number of passages where he does so,[25] and his view that human virtue itself is a gift of God's grace strongly points into this direction as well. By limiting both virtue and happiness to the adherents of the true religion and worshippers of the true God Augustine would have safeguarded the traditional nexus of virtue and happiness while making both—the whole system of moral values, as it were—depend on God and his grace. There are however difficulties with this reconstruction too. If it is true that Augustine understands happiness purely eschatologically, it would seem to follow that during his earthly life the virtuous Christian is as miserable as everybody else, his happiness being no more than a hope for the future. Moreover, since it is not clear whether and how specifically Christian virtues like faith and hope persist in eternal bliss, it might be suspected that virtue and happiness never actually coexist (after having been virtuous in this life, we are going to be happy in the next). On this 'retributionist' interpretation, as we may call it, virtue would clearly tend to become a means to an end. This would be very different from the original inspiration of the principle of self-sufficiency, even if its words were preserved.

[23] Julian of Aeclanum, *Ad Florum* = Aug. *c. Iul. imp.* 3. 76–7; Flasch (1994), 203–4; cf. Flasch (1995), 89; 115–16; 290–1. Augustine might indeed have insisted on God's absolute freedom concerning the election of the saved by pointing to Romans 9, and he sometimes did so; but as G. Aubry points out to me, it matters to him to read this text not only as a statement of God's power (which is most prominent in Paul) but also of his goodness.
[24] See especially the late treatises *De gratia et libero arbitrio* and *De correptione et gratia*.
[25] Cf. e.g. *ep.* 155. 5; ibid. 13–14.

In this chapter, I shall investigate more closely in what sense Augustine accepts the principle that virtue is self-sufficient for happiness and in what sense he does not.[26] As we shall see, his real answer comes closer to option (2) outlined above but contains elements of option (1) as well. After analysing Augustine's—negative—response to the Ciceronian version of the principle, I shall go on to argue that his innovative definition of virtue as love enables him to make virtue an integral part of his *telos* formula or description of the supreme good. I shall then focus on the different roles of virtue in this life and in the future one and argue that Augustine introduces a second or provisional form of happiness to correspond to virtue on this side of the *eschaton*. I am aware that it is at variance with the standard reading of Augustine as well as with his own official position to claim that he allows for such a thing as happiness in this life.[27] But I hope to show that his actual theory is more nuanced than his frequent grim opposition of earthly misery and celestial bliss suggests. I shall conclude with a—perhaps desperate—attempt to make sense of the Augustinian paradox that human virtue is a gift of divine grace.

1. Self-sufficiency According to 'the Philosophers': Augustine against Cicero

There is certainly one sense in which Augustine does not accept the claim that virtue is self-sufficient for happiness: the strong Stoic position that virtue is itself the supreme good and hence not just sufficient for, but identical with happiness. Let us consider the following text, which comes very close to an Augustinian *telos* formula:

Indeed, his wholly veracious prophet says: 'But for me it is good to cling to God' (Ps 72. 28). Now among the philosophers there is argument about the supreme good, to the attainment of which all our appropriate actions (*officia*)[28] are to be referred. The psalmist did not say: 'For me it is good to have riches in abundance', nor 'to wear imperial purple and have sceptre and diadem to mark my superiority', nor, as some even of the philosophers have not blushed to say: 'For me the pleasure of the body is good', nor, as the nobler philosophers, it is thought, have said more nobly: 'For me the virtue of my mind is good.' No, he said: 'For me it is good to cling to God.' (*civ.* 10. 18)[29]

---

[26] There are some important insights concerning this issue in Horn (1999), 176–8; 180–2. Horn has convincingly shown that in Augustine virtue remains a necessary condition for happiness; he does however not give a clear answer to the question whether it is also a sufficient one. At one point he seems to be envisaging a negative answer, citing *civ.* 19. 4 (Horn (1999), 181). For virtue in Augustine see also Rist (1994), 159–73 and, for an overview, Lavere (2000).

[27] Cf. e.g. Pizzolato (1987), 104–12, on the difference between the Cassiciacum dialogues and the later works on this account.

[28] I adopt the translation for officium or καθῆκον that has become conventional in studies on Stoicism.

[29] *eius enim propheta veracissimus ait: mihi autem adhaerere deo bonum est. de fine boni namque inter philosophos quaeritur, ad quod adipiscendum omnia officia referenda sunt. nec dixit iste: mihi autem divitiis abundare bonum est, aut insigniri purpura et sceptro vel diademate excellere, aut, quod nonnulli etiam philosophorum dicere non erubuerunt: mihi voluptas corporis bonum est; aut quod melius velut meliores*

Augustine is relying on the well-known fact that while all men agree that the final end is happiness, the nature of the supreme good that guarantees happiness is highly controversial among them.[30] He quotes and dismisses the definitions of the final end or *telos* formulae first of vulgar hedonistic materialism, then of the Epicureans and finally of the Stoics. Following the traditional division of the goods, the three definitions centre on external, bodily, and internal goods respectively.[31] Each of them fails because it conceives of the supreme good as purely immanent; therefore, they are superseded by the formula of the Psalmist who alone has grasped the transcendent character of the absolute good and rightly puts God at the centre of his definition.[32] Augustine often criticizes the idea that a man's inner virtue is his good as illusory and as characteristic of the philosophers' pride (*superbia*) or excessive self-love. Even though the Stoic sage does not care for glory and human applause, still, precisely because of the illusion of autarchy he cherishes, he is more concerned to please himself than to please God and thus falls under the verdict that those who wish to please men cannot be the servants of God (Gal 1. 10).[33]

In order to better understand what exactly Augustine is rejecting here, we should turn to the version of the Stoic paradox put forward by Cicero in the *Tusculan disputations*. In the proem of the fifth book, he programmatically states that whoever thinks that it makes sense to do philosophy at all is of necessity committed to the principle of self-sufficiency:

And if by them [i.e. those who first betook themselves to the study of philosophy] virtue was first discovered and brought to maturity, and if virtue provides all the security that is needed for living happily, who would think that the task of philosophy had not been admirably laid down by them and taken up by us? But if virtue, subject to varied and uncertain chances, is a slave to Fortune and is not strong enough to protect herself, I am afraid that we must not so much pursue the hope of living happily in reliance on virtue as say our prayers. (*Tusc.* 5. 2)[34]

Cicero claims, (1) that philosophy as a way of life is chosen for the sake of happiness, (2) that this goal can only be reached if the philosopher becomes independent from everything that cannot be influenced by himself, primarily external goods that are

---

dicere visi sunt: *mihi virtus animi mei bonum est; sed: mihi, inquit, adhaerere deo bonum est.* Translation adapted from Wiesen (1968).

[30] Cf. *trin.* 13. 8; Sen. *v. beat.* 1. 1.

[31] For the three kinds of goods (*tria genera bonorum*) cf. e.g. Cic. *Tusc.* 5. 24; Wacht (1986).

[32] There can be little doubt that Augustine regarded Ps 72. 28 as the *telos* formula, not just of the Old Testament, but of Scripture in general. Cf. e.g. *ep.* 155. 3; *ep. Io. tr.* 10. 5; *mor.* 1. 24; 26.

[33] Cf. *civ.* 5. 20. For 'pleasing oneself' (*sibi placere*) as a biblical expression for superbia cf. *civ.* 14. 13 and 2 Petr 2. 10. Gal 1. 10 is often quoted, cf. e.g. *s. dom. m.* 1. 18 (with parallels from Scripture).

[34] *quodsi ab is inventa et perfecta virtus est, et si praesidii ad beate vivendum in virtute satis est, quis est qui non praeclare et ab illis positam et a nobis susceptam operam philosophandi arbitretur? sin autem virtus subiecta sub varios incertosque casus famula fortunae est nec tantarum virium est, ut se ipsa tueatur, vereor ne non tam virtutis fiducia nitendum nobis ad spem beate vivendi quam vota facienda videantur.* We may safely assume that these words struck Augustine as typical for the philosophers' pride. Translations from the *Tusculans* are quoted from Douglas (1990).

governed by fortune, but also, he seems to imply, the help of the gods,[35] (3) that this independence is achieved through virtue or even identical with it. As becomes clear later on, Cicero conceives of happiness primarily as a state of mind free from fear, anxiety, lust, and the affections in general and characterized by tranquillity and inner peace. Virtue is understood as that mental attitude by which freedom from the affections is ensured; it is equated with the Stoic ideal of *apatheia*.[36] If we possess courage, we will be free from fear, if we possess temperance, we will be able to control lust and desire, and so on.[37] Cicero's position is thus quite exactly captured by the formula Augustine rejects in the passage quoted above, that 'virtue of the mind' is the supreme good.[38] In Augustine's view, this philosophical ideal of inner freedom and autarchy is both pretentious and illusory. As long as we are in this life, our inner life will be in a state of continuous war; our 'carnal' and our 'spiritual' parts will always lie in conflict with one another, and the only thing virtue can do is to try to prevent our carnal desires from becoming dominant and leading us. Just as Adam refused to obey God's commandment, our reason is unable to secure the stable obedience of our appetites; our inability to achieve inner peace by ourselves is part of God's just punishment for original sin.[39] There are even several passages in which Augustine neatly separates 'living well' (*bene vivere*, which he agrees with Cicero is equivalent to virtue)[40] from 'living happily' (*beate vivere*).[41] It seems that on such occasions he is

[35] For a more explicit statement to the same effect, see *ND* 3. 86–7, where Cotta the Academic states that no one has ever thanked the gods for virtue because it was a particularly human achievement and because otherwise it could not be the object of moral praise.

[36] Cf. *Tusc.* 5. 17: 'So if there is someone who regards as endurable the power of Fortune and all the human lot, whatever can befall, so that neither fear nor anxiety affects him, if he lusts after nothing, is carried away by no meaningless mental pleasure, on what grounds is he not happy? And if this is brought about by Virtue, on what grounds does Virtue of itself alone not make people happy?' (*quodsi est qui vim fortunae, qui omnia humana, quae cuique accidere possunt, tolerabilia ducat, ex quo nec timor eum nec angor attingat, idemque si nihil concupiscat, nulla ecferatur animi inani voluptate, quid est cur is non beatus sit? et si haec virtute efficiuntur, quid est cur virtus ipsa per se non efficiat beatos?*). Cf. the image of the calm sea immediately before in *Tusc.* 5. 16.

[37] Cf. *Tusc.* 5. 40–1.

[38] The term *virtus/virtutes animi* is frequent in the *De finibus*, cf. e.g. 4. 16; 5. 38.

[39] *civ.* 19. 4, quoting Gal 5. 17. For Adam's disobedience and its consequences, cf. *civ.* 14. 24. I think the notion of punishment is a sufficient answer to the worry of Buddensiek (2009), 77–9 that Augustine's insisting on the misery of this world is not fully consistent with his conviction that the *ordo* of this world is perfect. Being just, even an order of punishment is perfect, even though it is not agreeable for the punished.

[40] Cf. *lib. arb.* 2. 50 'the virtues thanks to which we live rightly' (*virtutes . . . quibus recte vivitur*); *trin.* 12. 21; *civ.* 9. 4; 15. 22; and the approving quotation of an ancient definition in *civ.* 4. 21: 'Virtue has explicitly been defined by the ancients as the art of living well and rightly' (*ars quippe ipsa bene recteque vivendi virtus a veteribus definita est*). A formal definition of this kind is not extant, but Augustine may have in mind such passages as Cic. *inv.* 1. 93; *Tusc.* 1. 95; 5. 18.

[41] *mor.* 1. 10: 'God, then, remains: If we follow him, we live well, but if we reach him, we live not only well but also happily' (*deus igitur restat quem si sequimur, bene, si assequimur, non tantum bene sed etiam beate vivimus*). Cf. *trin.* 13. 10; *mor.* 1. 18; 22 and, for a fuller but aporetic discussion of the relationship between *bene vivere* and *beate vivere*, *beata v.* 19–20.

directly contradicting the argument for self-sufficiency of the fifth book of the *Tusculans*, where Cicero more than once vigorously asserts the identity of the two.[42]

2. Self-sufficiency and the Redefinition of Virtue as Love of God

But while Augustine obviously rejects Cicero's strong claim that virtue and happiness are one and the same thing, he sides with him against his Hellenistic opponents— Peripatetic or otherwise—in denying external and bodily things all relevance for happiness.[43] He accepts the paradox that virtue is sufficient for happiness in such a way as to regard its converse as true, that is, he is committed to the claim that whatever is relevant for happiness is virtue. It remains however to be determined what exactly this amounts to. It has been maintained that by splitting up the Ciceronian unity of virtue and happiness Augustine reduces virtue to an instrumental status, making it a mere means to an end.[44] There may be some truth to this verdict, but its justification rests on the assumption that Cicero's and Augustine's notion of virtue is more or less the same, which is obviously not the case. Though he takes it from Cicero, Augustine understands the term 'living well' in a different and more dynamic manner than Cicero himself. In Cicero and the Stoics, virtue had been a mental disposition in accordance with right reason that was able to guarantee a peaceful and undisturbed mind. Augustine famously redefines it as love of God:

If, then, virtue leads us to a happy life, I should assert that virtue is nothing other than the greatest love of God. For if virtue is said to have four parts, this is so, as far as I can tell, because the passion[45] of love itself is to some extent manifold. So I would not hesitate to define the well-known four virtues…as follows: Temperance is love that preserves itself uncontaminated for its beloved; courage is love that easily tolerates all hardships for the beloved; justice is love that serves its beloved alone and therefore also rightly dominates; prudence is love that sagaciously distinguishes things that help it from things that hinder it. But as we said, this love is not love for anything but love for God, i.e. the supreme good. (*mor.* 1. 25)[46]

---

[42] *Tusc.* 5. 53: 'And if there is in Virtue sufficient guarantee for living well, there is enough for living happily too' (*Atque si in virtute satis est praesidii ad bene vivendum, satis est etiam ad beate*). Cf. *Tusc.* 3. 37; 5. 12; *fin.* 5. 88.

[43] See above note 5.

[44] Thus Müller (2010), 34.

[45] *affectu*: it is difficult to tell whether this means 'passion, emotion' or more neutrally 'disposition' (= *affectio*). In the combination with *amor* I find the first option more likely; moreover I cannot find an unambiguous passage in Augustine where *affectus* means 'disposition' and not (also) 'emotion'.

[46] *quod si virtus ad beatam vitam nos ducit, nihil omnino esse virtutem affirmaverim nisi summum amorem dei. namque illud quod quadripartita dicitur virtus, ex ipsius amoris vario quodam affectu, quantum intellego, dicitur. itaque illas quatuor virtutes… sic etiam definire non dubitem, ut temperantia sit amor integrum se praebens ei quod amatur, fortitudo amor facile tolerans omnia propter quod amatur, iustitia amor soli amato serviens et propterea recte dominans, prudentia amor ea quibus adiuvatur ab eis quibus impeditur sagaciter seligens. sed hunc amorem non cuiuslibet sed dei esse diximus, id est summi boni.* See Rist (1994), 161.

The inspiration for this move is probably both biblical and Platonic. Already here in the *De moribus* (written in 388), Augustine takes his guidance for the interpretation of virtue from the biblical double commandment of love (Mt 22. 37 and 39: 'You shall love the Lord your God with all your heart, with all your soul, and with all your mind; [and] you shall love your neighbour as yourself'), which, at least as far as the love of God is concerned, he tends to read in terms of the ascending *eros* of the Platonic tradition.[47] The redefinition of virtue as love of God has two important consequences. The first is Augustine's well-known internalization of moral value. If virtue is essentially love of God, the criterion that allows us to determine whether a given action is virtuous or not is whether it is performed out of love of God. In other words, the moral value of an action lies not with its material content but with its inner motivation, that is to say, its final end. To say that an action is motivated either by love (*caritas*) or by pride (*superbia*) is equivalent to saying that the action is referred either to God or to the self as the final good which the agent pursues. Identical actions may thus have a fundamentally different moral status.[48] It has often, and rightly, been pointed out that in reorienting the moral judgement from the outer to the inner world Augustine followed the lead of the Stoics.[49] But it is of course no marginal change that in his ethical theory love or will replaces reason as the criterion of morality. The result is, among other things, a certain scepticism about the moral judgement as such: For Augustine, nobody can ever be sure of the purity of his own intentions, let alone those of others; or at least God knows man's intentions infinitely better than man himself does.[50] The second consequence is even more important for our present purposes. The fundamental difference between Ciceronian virtue, which is identical with right reason, and Augustinian virtue, which is love, is that the latter is by its very nature intentional. The relationship of virtue to God is that between love and beloved, which, it would seem, is a much closer relation than that of a means to an end. As the lover, in a sense, always already possesses the object of his love—which, on the assumptions of the Neoplatonic interpretation of Plato's Eros, is especially true if the 'object' of love is immaterial[51]—the lover of God can be said to 'have God', which, it will be remembered, is precisely the definition of happiness.

---

[47] Cf. the whole development of *mor.* 1. 13–24 and esp. *mor.* 1. 22: 'If, then, we ask what is means to live well, i.e. to strive for happiness by living well, the answer will surely be that it means to love virtue, wisdom and truth, and to love virtue with all your heart, with all your soul, and with all your mind' (*si ergo quaerimus quid sit bene vivere, id est ad beatitudinem bene vivendo tendere, id erit profecto amare virtutem, amare sapientiam, amare veritatem, et amare ex toto corde, et ex tota anima, et ex tota mente virtutem etc.*). Virtue is the object of love here itself because it is viewed as the second person of the Trinity after 1 Cor 1. 24 (*Christum dei virtutem et dei sapientiam*). Cf. *ep.* 155. 15; *civ.* 10. 3. Love of the neighbour, about which Augustine is somewhat reticent in the *De moribus*, raises some extra problems which cannot be addressed here; see Rist (1994), 159–68; Brechtken (1975), 85–155; Holte (1962), 275–81; O'Donovan (1980), 112–36.

[48] For an impressive statement to this effect, cf. *ep. Io. tr.* 8. 9, where even the actions prescribed in the Sermon on the Mount—clothing the naked, feeding the hungry, etc.—are said to be performed by love as well as by pride.

[49] Cf. e.g. Rist (1994), 168.   [50] *civ.* 1. 28 with my remarks in Tornau (2006a), 201–3.

[51] Cf. *lib. arb.* 2. 33, following Plot. VI 5. 10. 1–11; O'Connell (1968), 52–7.

And the virtuous person, as we have seen, is by definition a lover of God. Because of this dynamic and 'loving' character of virtue (as opposed to its Stoic equation with right reason), I would suggest, Augustine is entitled to use the more static term 'having God' and the more dynamically sounding biblical expression 'clinging to God' interchangeably as formulae for the *telos* or supreme good.[52] Thus even though virtue and happiness are no longer identical, the principle that virtue is self-sufficient for happiness has acquired a new and unexpected validity.

It might be objected here that this reading brings the Augustinian lover of God dangerously close to the sceptic who incessantly searches for, and in this sense loves, truth but must be deemed unhappy because truth is unintelligible to man.[53] The difference is however that the Christian lover of God may legitimately hope to see God 'from face to face' one day, and together with his love this hope will surely contribute to his happiness. At this point, we should inquire more closely into the eschatological character of Augustine's notion of happiness.

3. Self-sufficiency and Eschatology

As we have seen, Augustine limits true happiness to eternal bliss and thinks that we cannot but be wretched during our life on earth. It remains therefore to be determined, (1) how exactly the relation of virtue and happiness must be conceived of in the future life, (2) why virtue can be said to guarantee happiness in this life, even if it is unable to overcome the inherent misery of the latter. It would of course be possible to say that virtue belongs only to this life and happiness only to the next one, but from what we have found so far, it would not seem that this neat but over-simple separation is what Augustine has in mind. To understand how exactly he conceives of the validity of the principle of self-sufficiency on each side of the *eschaton*, let us return to his interpretation of what he regarded as the Scriptural *telos* formula: *mihi adhaerere deo bonum est* (Ps 72. 18).

Letter 155, written in 413/14 to Macedonius, a Christian imperial officer who was interested in the *City of God*, contains a critical discussion of the philosophers' pretension at their virtue's self-sufficiency.[54] In the course of his argument, Augustine repeatedly lists definitions of the four cardinal virtues which are reminiscent of the above-cited definitions from the *De moribus* and which consider virtue from a

---

[52] For the present purpose, these general remarks on the basic structure of Augustinian love must suffice. In reality, Augustinian love is of course a more complex phenomenon. Four aspects at least can be distinguished: (1) love as desire in the traditional eudaemonist framework (this aspect is most prominent in the *De moribus*); (2) love as a passion in the Platonic sense; (3) love as will (this comes close to the first two aspects, since Augustine famously rehabilitates the affections by redefining them as forms of the will; cf. *civ.* 14. 6–9 and Wetzel (1992), 98–111); (4) love as humility (being, according to *civ.* 15. 22, 'ordered love', virtue loves everything according to its true value and hence loves God more than the self; cf. *civ.* 14. 28).

[53] For a similar discussion, cf. *beata v.* 14; 20–1; van Geest (2004), 541.

[54] *ep.* 155. 3 with the traditional image of Phalaris' bull (cf. Cic. *Tusc.* 5. 75; Plot. I 4. 5. 6–7).

variety of perspectives: virtue in everyday life (especially politics),[55] virtue as love in terms of the biblical commandment,[56] and the role of virtue in our contemplation of God in eternal bliss.[57] The ultimate background of this development is, it seems, the Neoplatonic theory of the degrees of virtues.[58] It was introduced by Plotinus and systematized by Porphyry in order to solve the puzzle that while the Platonic *telos* formula urged man to become similar to god through virtue, it was far from clear how, and if, god himself could be considered to have virtue—the social virtues, at any rate, did not seem suitable for a transcendent being.[59] The Neoplatonists' answer was to introduce additional grades or definitions of virtue in such a way as to suit each ontological level; the social virtues were thus supplemented with 'kathartic', 'para-digmatic', and other virtues. Augustine wants to solve an analogous puzzle.[60] There did not seem to be much need for such virtues as justice or temperance in eternal bliss; similarly the Pauline virtues—love, faith, and hope—could be thought to be constitutive of our earthly life, when we see God only 'through a glass darkly', and to become superfluous when we will contemplate him 'face to face'.[61] While Augustine does admit this for faith and hope,[62] he argues that the four cardinal virtues persist after the resurrection as various forms of the redeemed men's 'clinging to God':

And those virtues will be true virtues and, by the help of him by whose bounty they were given, they will grow and become perfect so that they will without any doubt bring you to the truly happy life, which is none other than eternal life. In it prudence will not distinguish evil, which will not exist, from what is good, nor will courage endure adversity, because we will find there only what we love, not what we endure, nor will temperance bridle desire where we will not feel its enticements. Nor will justice aid the needy with help where we will have no one poor and needy. In that life there will be only one virtue, and it will be both virtue and the reward of virtue, something that one who loves this says in the holy writings, 'But for me it is good to cling to God' (Ps 72. 28). There this will be complete and everlasting wisdom, and this same wisdom will also be the truly happy life. It is, of course, the attainment of the eternal and highest good, and to cling to it for eternity is the goal that holds all our good. This might be called prudence because it will with perfect foresight cling to the good that will not be lost. It

---

[55] *ep.* 155. 10; 12.　　[56] *ep.* 155. 13; 16.　　[57] *ep.* 155. 12.

[58] For an interpretation of *ep.* 155 in these terms see Tornau (2013b).

[59] Aristotle had pronounced himself famously against virtue in god (*EN* VII 1, 1145a25-7; X 8, 1178b8-18), and some Middle Platonists had followed him (Alcin. *Did.* 181. 43-5). For the background, cf. Whittaker (1990), 138-9.

[60] It is generally agreed that the Neoplatonic grades of virtue were familiar to him. Cf. esp. *an. quant.* 70-6; Schissel von Fleschenberg (1928), 81-94.

[61] 1 Cor 13. 12. For the problem, cf. *trin.* 14. 12 where Augustine quotes and discusses Cicero who seems to have argued that the cardinal virtues could be dispensed with in a hypothetical state of immortality and bliss (*Hort.* fr. 110 Grilli = 101 Straume-Zimmermann). Cf. furthermore *mus.* 6. 50-5; *en. Ps.* 83. 11. Becker (2002) cites and discusses the relevant texts.

[62] See *Gn. litt.* 12. 31. 59 on faith, hope, and patience. *Pace* Horn (1999), 188 patience here should not too readily be equated with love. On faith, see *trin.* 14. 4. For hope see the frequent antithesis of (present) *spes* and (future) *res* (e.g. *div. qu.* 67. 7, quoting Rm 8. 24). For the persistence of love of God and the neighbour in the future life, cf. *ench.* 121. In *sol.* 1. 12 all three Pauline virtues seem to have a preparatory and 'kathartic' function, but Augustine does not say that they will cease to exist in eternal bliss.

might be called courage because it will most firmly cling to the good that will not be torn away. It might be called temperance because it will most chastely cling to the good by which it will not be corrupted. And it might be called justice because it will with full righteousness cling to the good to which it is rightly subject. (*ep.* 155. 12)[63]

Two points emerge from this passage. First, 'clinging to God', the Augustinian *telos* formula, has an eschatological meaning. In this life, we cling to God by practicing virtue, which is none other than the love of God; in the next life, we will do the same with the sole difference that our clinging will last forever. The four cardinal virtues that will persist in the future life are defined as four different ways of *adhaerere deo* in exactly the same way as, in the *De moribus*, the four cardinal virtues we practice in this life are defined as varieties of love. Under the scriptural label of 'clinging to God', the virtues are fully incorporated in Augustine's definition of the *summum bonum*.[64] This means that they are an integral part of what he understands by happiness; and since 'clinging to God' describes the supreme good of the Christian both in his present and in his future life, it will, if practised, ensure happiness on both sides of the *eschaton*—even though it remains to be determined how this can be true under the miserable conditions of the earthly life which Augustine so often emphasizes. Second, the self-sufficiency of virtue for and even its identity with happiness is fully reinstated: In eternal bliss, Augustine says, virtue and the reward of virtue will be one and the same thing. The resurrected Christian's happiness consists in his virtue, that is to say, his eternal, peaceful and undisturbed love of God. This may fairly be regarded as Augustine's Christianized version of Cicero's immanent Stoicizing ideal of the peaceful virtuous mind[65]—with the important difference that the distance between the Creator and the created human mind persists even in the happy state of the resurrected. God and the mind are not, as in Stoicism and perhaps Plotinianism,

---

[63]   *et verae illae virtutes erunt et illius opitulatione, cuius largitate donatae sunt, ita crescent et perficien-tur, ut te ad vitam vere beatam, quae non nisi aeterna est, sine ulla dubitatione perducant, ubi iam nec prudenter discernantur a bonis mala, quae non erunt, nec fortiter tolerentur adversa, quia non ibi erit, nisi quod amemus, non etiam, quod toleremus, nec temperanter libido frenetur, ubi nulla eius incitamenta sentiemus, nec iuste subveniatur ope indigentibus, ubi inopem atque indiguum non habebimus. una ibi virtus erit et id ipsum erit virtus praemiumque virtutis, quod dicit in sanctis eloquiis homo, qui hoc amat: mihi autem adhaerere deo bonum est. haec ibi erit plena et sempiterna sapientia eademque vita veraciter iam beata; perventio quippe est ad aeternum ac summum bonum, cui adhaerere in aeternum est finis nostri boni. dicatur haec et prudentia, quia prospectissime adhaerebit bono, quod non amittatur, et fortitudo, quia firmissime adhaerebit bono, unde non avellatur, et temperantia, quia castissime adhaerebit bono, ubi non corrumpatur, et iustitia, quia rectissime adhaerebit bono, cui merito subiciatur.* The text of *ep.* 155 is quoted from Goldbacher (1904), translations are quoted or adapted from Teske (2003). For a similar argument, cf. *en. Ps.* 83. 11, where the unified virtue of the future life is, on the grounds of 1 Cor 1. 24, equated with Christ. On *ep.* 155. 12 cf. Horn (1999), 180; 187.

[64]   The same goes for Augustine's definition of happiness in *trin.* 13. 8: 'For he lives happily … who lives as he wishes and who does not wish anything badly' (*ille quippe beate vivit, … qui vivit ut vult nec male aliquid vult*).

[65]   Cf. the discussion of Stoic ἀπάθεια in *civ.* 14. 9: Freedom from irrational affections is desirable but unattainable in this life; it will only exist 'when there will be no sin in man' (*quando peccatum in homine nullum erit*).

ultimately identical. This, it seems, is the reason why the relationship of the Christian to God before and after the resurrection can be described with the same formula—the two states seem to differ by degree rather than in principle.

This brings us back to the question how, and if, virtue guarantees happiness already in this life. Augustine certainly insists that it is impossible to become happy in a world that has been arranged by God in such a way as to work as a punishment for original sin.[66] However, he equally insists on the essential identity of virtue in this life and in the next one, even if under earthly conditions it is less effective than it will be in its free and unhindered future state: 'For the same virtues are practiced here and will have their results there' (ep. 155. 16).[67] If virtue were just a means to an end and if it could be reduced to, say, the social practice of giving each his due or to the control of the passions, this sentence might well be taken to imply that during this life that end—whatever it is—can only be pursued but not reached. It is certain that God cannot be seen 'face to face' in this life; and even if, following Cicero, we granted that virtue pursues more intrinsic and immanent aims, such as perfect inner tranquillity, Augustine is convinced that this goal cannot be reached on earth either. If, in essence, the virtues were no more than our ability and willingness to struggle with the external hardships and internal conflicts that mark our earthly existence, they might indeed be regarded as indicators of our misery rather than as a way to happiness[68] and be dispensed with as soon as these hardships and conflicts cease to exist. However, we have seen that Christian or saintly virtue primarily denotes a positive relationship to God and that the scriptural expression for this relationship, 'clinging to God', is a suitable description of the Christian's supreme good on both sides of the eschaton. It is hard to see how this formula, on the one hand, can denote the intimate connection of virtue and happiness in the life of the blessed but, on the other, be wholly unrelated to happiness when it is applied to the saint's life on earth. If we possess true virtue, our struggling with affections and inner conflicts immediately expresses our 'clinging to God'; because we love God, we resist the temptation of other, lesser objects of love, including our own self. If this were otherwise, Cicero and other pagans who identified virtus animi with the supreme good were simply guilty of confusing means and ends. In reality, their resisting temptations and controlling passions expresses not their love of God but their love of self and, hence, is not virtue at all, except in a purely external sense that reduces virtue to a certain way of acting and abstracts from its basic character as love.[69] The problem, I would suggest, is not so

---

[66] Cf. e.g. civ. 22. 22.

[67] hic enim sunt eaedem virtutes in actu, ibi in effectu.

[68] As Augustine puts it in civ. 19. 4 (testimonia miseriarum). His characterizations of the earthly virtues often centre on their importance for the struggle against the adversities of this life; cf. trin. 13. 9; ep. 155. 10.

[69] It should be noted that this abstraction is sometimes used by Augustine himself when he wants to safeguard the notion of natural or 'pagan' virtue. See Tornau (2006b).

much that in our present condition Christian virtue is unable to attain its goal. It is rather the fact that we are inevitably sinners—'If we claim that we are without sin, we deceive ourselves, and truth is not in us', as an often-quoted biblical saying has it[70]—and that our moral self-knowledge is haunted by uncertainty. Even if we are virtuous, we cannot be sure that our virtue is untainted by pride or excessive self-love or that we will persevere in it until we die.[71] If we could rely on our virtue, we could also rely on our happiness; but it is of course part of the Christian's virtue that he realizes its fragility.[72]

It remains to be asked what this provisional happiness consists in. As should by now have become clear, love of God, which in a sense already 'has' God, is an essential part of it. Another part is hope. Augustine frequently says that the Christian is 'happy in hope' (spe beatus), and I think that this phrase should be taken seriously.[73] Of course, being 'happy in hope' falls short of being 'really happy' (re beatus), but it is equally opposed to being wretched.[74] That this happiness is provisional but real, and that the Christian virtues are sufficient to attain it even under the most adverse earthly circumstances, is proven by the example of the Christian martyrs whom Augustine styles as the legitimate successors of the Stoic sage who remains happy even when he is roasted in the bull of Phalaris.[75] He adds, admittedly, that if the pains and torments of the martyrs were to last forever, they would beyond doubt have to be deemed miserable, regardless of how great their virtues were. Part of our earthly happiness is the certainty that our life is going to end. We might say, then, that two of the Pauline virtues, love (caritas) and hope (spes) (and, presumably, faith), are the ingredients of the Christian's happiness even before he sees God 'face to face'.

---

[70] 1 John 1. 8, quoted about 50 times in Augustine, mostly in the anti-Pelagian work; cf. pecc. mer. 2. 8; c. Iul. imp. 1. 98 etc.

[71] Cf. Mt. 10. 22 = 24. 13: 'He who perseveres to the end will be saved', quoted e.g. at corrept. 10; persev. 2.

[72] To trust in one's own virtue (Ps 48. 7: qui confidunt in virtute sua) is in fact a mark of the proud Pelagian (c. Iul. imp. 1. 41 and about 20 quotations in the same work).

[73] Cf. e.g. trin. 13. 9–10 and above note 62.

[74] Cf. conf. 10. 29: 'there are some who are happy in hope of becoming so. The kind of happiness they have is inferior to those who have the real thing. But they are better than those who are happy neither in reality nor in hope' (et sunt, qui spe beati sunt. inferiore modo isti habent eam quam illi, qui iam re ipsa beati sunt, sed tamen meliores quam illi, qui nec re nec spe beati sunt; translation adapted from Chadwick (1991). Cf. Doignon (1987), 354–5. One might also compare mus. 6. 52, where the virtues in this life—here interpreted as the Plotinian 'kathartic' virtues—are said to enable us to 'taste' the 'sweetness' of the Lord (quoting Ps 33. 9).

[75] ep. 155. 16: 'And so all good and holy people, even amid torments of every sort, supported by God's help, are called happy because of the hope for that end, the end in which they will be happy. For, if they were always in the same torments and the fiercest pains, no sound mind would doubt that they were miserable no matter what virtues they had' (itaque omnes boni et sancti etiam in tormentis quibuslibet divino fulti adiutorio spe illius finis beati vocantur, quo fine beati erunt; nam si in eisdem tormentis et atrocissimis doloribus semper essent, cum quibuslibet virtutibus eos esse miseros nulla sana ratio dubitaret).

4. Conclusion: Self-sufficiency and Grace

But what follows from all this for the relationship of virtue and grace?[76] Augustine fully endorses the traditional ideal of the sage's—or the saint's—independence from everything external and bodily. Divine grace, however, is by definition beyond the reach of human control. To claim that one does not depend on it, as 'the philosophers' do, would be as futile as it would be pretentious. Did Augustine then, after having come to consider the Stoic attempt at self-sufficiency as illusory, simply put grace at the place traditionally occupied by fortune, so as to replace a blind and arbitrary entity with a just and benevolent, albeit not fully intelligible, one?[77] Two reasons, it seems to me, speak against this interpretation. First, it would entail a synergistic view of grace. Happiness would be the sum of virtue and grace, with virtue attaining happiness as far as it is within the reach of human endeavour and grace supplying (or denying) the rest by granting (or refusing) virtue its reward. Not only is this clearly foreign to Augustine's thought, but it would make him an easy target for his critics—Pelagian, humanist, or otherwise—who could claim that his God lacks justice because he does not give virtue its due. Second, it would amount to sacrificing the principle of virtue's self-sufficiency, which, as we have seen, Augustine accepts for the Christian saint. In order to understand this more clearly, let us have a look at a paradoxical but lucid statement on the relationship of virtue, happiness, and grace:

Let us ask the Lord our God, who made us, for the virtue to conquer the evils of this life and for the happy life that we may enjoy after this life in his eternity. In that way both in virtue and in the reward of virtue, as the apostle says, 'let one who boasts boast in the Lord'. (ep. 155,9, quoting 2 Cor 10,17)[78]

This is best taken to mean that while they are as closely related to one another as in Cicero and the classical tradition, virtue and happiness together depend on grace. This means that grace is not the reward of virtue but rather its presupposition; therefore, the Augustinian claim that whatever is relevant for happiness is virtue cannot be refuted by pointing to grace except in the sense that virtue itself comes from grace. However, its general dependence on the creator notwithstanding, virtue remains something distinctly human. Augustine agrees with Cicero that the only means at the disposal of humankind to attain happiness is personal endeavour and

---

[76] Secondary literature on Augustine's doctrine of grace abounds. For an overview, see Drecoll (2004–2010). For philosophical discussion, see e.g. Wetzel (1992), 112–218; Kirwan (1989), 104–28; Müller (2009), 355–61.

[77] For a similar view, see Wetzel (1992), 54–5: 'Although he comes to the very unstoic conclusion that virtue and beatitude never coincide in the *saeculum*, he also refuses, in a very Stoic way, to admit that virtue and beatitude could ever accidentally coincide. To get virtue and beatitude reunited again, divine agency rather than fortune must on his view serve as the impetus for reunion.' Cf. also Horn (1999), 181.

[78] *ac per hoc a domino deo nostro, a quo facti sumus, et virtutem petamus, qua huius vitae mala superemus, et beatam vitam, qua post istam vitam in eius aeternitate perfruamur, ut et in virtute et in praemio virtutis, sicut apostolus dicit, qui gloriatur, in domino glorietur.* Cf. *trin.* 14. 21; *ep.* 194. 6; *Io. ev. tr.* 3. 10.

commitment. We cannot simply sit down and wait for divine grace to raise us to heaven. But he does not follow Cicero in claiming that it is simply a matter of decision to convert to philosophy and lead a virtuous life. Augustine thought, and probably made the experience, that we are most urgently dependent on God's assistance when we begin to form the will to adopt a way of life that radically changes our habits but that—as we know—will eventually make us happy.[79] Or to put it slightly differently: Augustine inherited the idea of human responsibility inherent in the Stoic principle of self-sufficiency and highlighted in Cicero's aphorism that if that principle were not true, we had better renounce philosophy and say our prayers.[80] But Augustine was acutely aware that it is not a matter of course to take up that responsibility and to live a truly human life. This possibility may have been open to the first couple in paradise before sin entered the world.[81] Since then, however, human nature is vitiated and can only be restored by God's grace.

[79] The most impressive account of this phenomenon is, of course, Book 8 of the *Confessions*.
[80] *Tusc.* 5. 2, quoted in Section 1, this chapter.
[81] Cf. Rist (1994), 176.

Bibliography

Ackrill, J. L. (1997). 'Aristotle's Distinction between Energeia and Kinēsis', in J. L. Ackrill, *Essays on Plato and Aristotle*. Oxford: Oxford University Press, 1997. Originally published in R. Bambrough (ed.), *New Essays on Plato and Aristotle*. London: Routledge, 1965.

Adkins, A. W. H. (1960). *Merit and Responsibility: A Study in Greek Values*. Oxford: Clarendon Press.

Alesse, F. (2000). *La stoa e la tradizione socratica*. Naples: Bibliopolis.

Allen, J. (2010). 'Pyrrhonism and medicine', in R. Bett (ed.), *The Cambridge Companion to Ancient Scepticism*. Cambridge: Cambridge University Press, 232–48.

Andersen, Ø. (2011). 'Happiness in Homer'. *Symbolae Osloenses* 85: 2–16.

Annas, J. (1977). 'Plato and Aristotle on Friendship and Altruism'. *Mind* 86: 532–54.

Annas, J. (1993). *The Morality of Happiness*. Oxford: Oxford University Press.

Annas, J. (1999). *Platonic Ethics Old and New*. Ithaca: Cornell University Press.

Annas, J. (2002a). 'Democritus and Eudaimonism', in V. Caston and D. Graham (eds.), *Presocratic Philosophy: Essays in Honor of Alexander Mourelatos*. Burlington, VT: Ashgate, 169–80.

Annas, J. (2002b). 'My Station and Its Duties: Ideals and the Social Embeddedness of Virtue'. *Proceedings of the Aristotelian Society* ns 102: 109–23.

Annas, J. (2006). 'Virtue Ethics', in D. Copp (ed.), *The Oxford Companion to Ethical Theory*. Oxford: Oxford University Press, 515–36.

Annas, J. (2011). *Intelligent Virtue*. Oxford: Oxford University Press.

Archie, J. P. (1984). 'Callicles' Redoubtable Critique of the Polus Argument in Plato's *Gorgias*'. *Hermes* 112: 167–76.

Armstrong, A. H. (1966–1988). *Plotinus, Ennead I–VI*. Text with an English translation, 7 vols. Cambridge MA/London: Harvard University Press.

Armstrong, J. M. (2004). 'After the Ascent: Plato on Becoming Like God'. *Oxford Studies in Ancient Philosophy* 26: 171–83.

Baker, S. H. (2014). 'Defining the Human Good: Aristotle's *Ergon* Argument'. PhD dissertation, Princeton University.

Baltzly, D. (2004). 'The Virtues and "Becoming Like God": Alcinous to Proclus'. *Oxford Studies in Ancient Philosophy* 26: 297–321.

Barnes, J. (1992). 'Diogenes Laertius IX 61-116: The Philosophy of Pyrrhonism', in H. Haase (ed.), *Aufstieg und Niedergang der Römischen Welt* II.36.6. Berlin: de Gruyter, 4241–301.

Barnes, J. (1999). 'An Introduction to Aspasius', in A. Alberti and R. Sharples (eds.), *Aspasius: The Earliest Extant Commentary on Aristotle's Ethics*. Berlin: de Gruyter, 1–50.

Barney, R. (2007). 'The Carpenter and the Good', in D. Cairns, F.-G. Herrmann, and T. Penner (eds.), *Pursuing the Good: Ethics and Metaphysics in Plato's Republic*. Edinburgh Leventis Studies 4. Edinburgh: University of Edinburgh Press, 293–319.

Barney, R. (2008). 'Aristotle's Argument for a Human Function'. *Oxford Studies in Ancient Philosophy* 34: 293–322.

Becchi, F. (1994). 'Aspasio, commentatore di Aristotele', *Aufstieg und Niedergang der römischen Welt* II. 36(7): 5365–96.

Becker, M. (2002). 'Augustinus über die Tugenden in Zeit und Ewigkeit', in W. Blümer, R. Henke, and M. Mülke (eds.), *Alvarium: Festschrift für C. Gnilka*. Münster: Aschendorff, 53–63.

Beierwaltes, W. (1967). *Plotin Über Ewigkeit und Zeit. Enneade III 7*. Übers., eingel. und kommentiert von W. Beierwaltes. Frankfurt am Main: Klostermann.

Beierwaltes, W. (1981). *Regio Beatitudinis: Augustine's Concept of Happiness. The Saint Augustine Lecture 1980*. Villanova: Villanova University Press.

Berman, S. (1991). 'Socrates and Callicles on Pleasure'. *Phronesis* 36: 117–40.

Blackburn, S. (1984). *Spreading the Word*. New York: Oxford University Press.

Bloomfield, P. (2011). 'Justice as a Self-Regarding Virtue'. *Philosophy and Phenomenological Research* 82: 46–64.

Blundell, M. W. (1989). *Helping Friends and Harming Enemies*. Cambridge: Cambridge University Press.

Bordt, M. (1998). *Platon. Lysis*. Göttingen: Vandenhoeck und Ruprecht.

Bouffartigue, J., and M. Patillon (tr. and introduction) (1977/1995). *Porphyre: De l'abstinence*, ii. Paris: Les Belles Lettres.

Boyle, M. (2012). 'Essentially Rational Animals', in G. Abel and J. Conant (eds.). *Rethinking Epistemology*, ii. Berlin: de Gruyter, 395–428.

Boyle, M. (n.d.). 'Additive Theories of Rationality: A Critique', unpublished article.

Brechtken, J. (1975). *Augustinus Doctor Caritatis: Sein Liebesbegriff im Widerspruch von Eigennutz und selbstloser Güte im Rahmen der antiken Glückseligkeits-Ethik*. Meisenheim: Hain.

Brennan, T. (2005). *The Stoic Life. Emotions, Duties, and Fate*. Oxford: Oxford University Press.

Brickhouse, T. C. (2003). 'Does Aristotle Have a Consistent Account of Vice?' *The Review of Metaphysics* 57: 3–23.

Brisson, L. (2006). 'The Doctrine of the Degrees of Virtues in the Neoplatonists: An Analysis of Porphyry's Sentence 32, Its Antecedents, and Its Heritage', in H. Tarrant and D. Baltzly (eds.), *Reading Plato in Antiquity*. London: Duckworth, 89–105.

Broadie, S. (1991). *Ethics with Aristotle*. New York: Oxford University Press.

Broadie, S. (2002). 'Introduction', in C. Rowe (ed.), *Aristotle: Nicomachean Ethics*. New York: Oxford University Press, 9–91.

Broadie, S. (2003). 'Aristotelian Piety'. *Phronesis* 48: 54–70.

Broadie, S. (2009). '*Nicomachean Ethics* VII. 8–9 (1151^{b}22): *Akrasia*, *enkrateia*, and Look-Alikes', in C. Natali (ed.), *Aristotle: Nicomachean Ethics, Book VII, Symposium Aristotelicum*. Oxford: Oxford University Press, 157–72.

Brown, L. (2007). 'Glaucon's Challenge, Rational Egoism and Ordinary Morality', in D. L. Cairns, F.-G. Herrmann, and T. Penner (eds.), *Pursuing the Good*. Edinburgh: Edinburgh University Press, 42–60.

Buddensiek, F. (2009). 'Augustinus über das Glück', in C. Mayer (ed.), *Augustinus: Ethik und Politik*. Würzburg: Echter, 63–85.

Burkert, W. (1985). *Greek Religion*. Cambridge, MA: Harvard University Press. Originally: (1977). *Griechische Religion der arkaischen und klassischen Epoche*. Stuttgart: Kohlhammer.

Burkert, W. (1987). *Ancient Mystery Cults*. Cambridge, MA: Harvard University Press.

Burnyeat, M. (1980). 'Aristotle on Learning to be Good', in A. Rorty (ed.), *Essays on Aristotle's Ethics*. Berkeley: University of California Press, 69–92.

Burnyeat, M., and M. J. Levett (1990). *Plato: Theaetetus*. Indianapolis: Hackett.

Cairns, D. L. (1993). Aidōs: *The Psychology and Ethics of Honour and Shame in Ancient Greek Literature*. Oxford: Clarendon Press.

Cairns, D. L. (2011). 'The Principle of Alternation and the Tyrant's Happiness in Bacchylidean Epinician'. *Symbolae Osloenses* 85: 17–32.

Caluori, D. (2011). 'Reason and Necessity: The Descent of the Philosopher-kings'. *Oxford Studies in Ancient Philosophy* 40: 7–28.

Chadwick, H. (1991). *Augustine: Confessions*, trans. H. Chadwick. Oxford: Oxford University Press.

Charles, D. (1984). *Aristotle's Philosophy of Action*. Ithaca: Cornell University Press.

Chazán, P. (1998). *The Moral Self (The Problems of Philosophy)*. London: Routledge.

Chekola, M. (2007). 'Happiness, Rationality, Autonomy and the Good Life'. *The Journal of Happiness Studies* 8: 51–78.

Claus, D. B. (1981). *Toward the Soul*. New Haven and London: Yale University Press.

Clay, J. S. (2003). *Hesiod's Cosmos*. Cambridge: Cambridge University Press.

Cooper, J. M. (1975). *Reason and Human Good in Aristotle*. Cambridge, MA: Harvard University Press.

Cooper, J. M. (1985). 'Aristotle on the Goods of Fortune'. *The Philosophical Review* 94: 173–96.

Cooper, J. M. (1996). 'Reason, Moral Virtue, and Moral Value', in Frede and Striker (1996), 81–114. Reprinted in Cooper (1999), 253–80.

Cooper, J. M. (1998). 'The Unity of Virtue'. *Social Philosophy and Policy* 15: 233–74.

Cooper, J. M. (1999). *Reason and Emotion: Essays on Ancient Moral Psychology and Ethical Theory*. Princeton: Princeton University Press.

Cooper, J. M. (2004). 'Plato and Aristotle on "Finality" and "(Self)-Sufficiency"', in *Knowledge, Nature, and the Good: Essays on Ancient Philosophy*. Princeton: Princeton University Press, 270–308.

Cooper, J. M. (2005). 'The Emotional Life of the Wise'. *The Southern Journal of Philosophy*, Special Issue: Ancient Ethics and Political Philosophy, suppl. 43: 176–218.

Cooper, J. M. (2010). 'Political Community and the Highest Good', in J. G. Lennox and R. Bolton (eds.), *Being, Nature, and Life in Aristotle*. Cambridge: Cambridge University Press, 212–64.

Cooper, J. M. (2012). *Pursuits of Wisdom. Six Ways of Life in Ancient Philosophy from Socrates to Plotinus*. Princeton: Princeton University Press.

Corcilius, K. (2011). 'Aristotle's Definition of Non-rational Pleasure and Pain and Desire', in J. Miller (ed.), *Aristotle's* Nicomachean Ethics: *A Critical Guide*. Cambridge: Cambridge University Press, 117–43.

Currie, B. (2005). *Pindar and the Cult of the Heroes*. Oxford: Oxford University Press.

Curzer, H. J. (2012). *Aristotle and the Virtues*. Oxford: Oxford University Press.

Darwall, S. L. (2002). *Welfare and Rational Care*. Princeton: Princeton University Press.

Darwall, S. L. (2013). 'Grotius at the Creation of Modern Moral Philosophy', in *Honor, History, and Relationship: Essays in Second-Personal Ethics II*. Oxford: Oxford University Press, 157–88.

Decleva Caizzi, F. (1981). *Pirrone: Testimonianze*. Naples: Bibliopolis.

Decleva Caizzi, F., and M. S. Funghi (1988). 'Un testo sul concetto stoico di progresso morale (PMilVogliano inv. 1241)', in *Aristoxenica, Menandrea, Fragmenta philosophica, Studi e testi per il Corpus dei papiri filosofici greci e latini*. Florence: L. S. Olschki, 3: 85–124.

Deichgräber, K. (1965 [1930]). *Die griechische Empirikerschule*. Berlin: Weidmann.

Devereux, D. (1981). 'Aristotle on the Essence of Happiness', in D. O'Meara (ed.). *Studies in Aristotle*. Washington, DC: University of America Press, 247–60.

Dewald, C. (2011). 'Happiness in Herodotus'. *Symbolae Osloenses* 58: 52–73.

Dihle, A. (1973). 'Posidonius' System of Moral Philosophy'. *The Journal of Hellenic Studies* 93: 50–7.

Dillon, J. (1996). 'An Ethic for the Late Antique Sage', in L. Gerson (ed.), *The Cambridge Companion to Plotinus*. Cambridge: Cambridge University Press, 315–35.

Dimas, P. (2002). 'Happiness in the *Euthydemus*'. *Phronesis* 47: 1–27.

Dimas, P. (2014a). 'Knowing and Wanting in the *Hippias Minor*'. *Philosophical Inquiry* 38: 106–18.

Dimas, P. (2014b). 'Our Death'. *Rhizomata* 2: 52–79.

Dodds, E. R. (1951). *The Greeks and the Irrational*. Berkeley: University of California Press.

Doignon, J. (1987). 'Saint Augustin et sa culture philosophique face au problème du Bonheur'. *Freiburger Zeitschrift für Philosophie und Theologie* 34: 339–59.

Dombrowski, D. A. (1987). 'Porphyry on Vegetarianism: A Contemporary Philosophical Approach'. *Aufstieg und Niedergang der römischen Welt* II. 36(2): 774–91.

Donini, P., and B. Inwood (1999). 'Stoic Ethics (VIII–XI)', in K. Algra, J. Barnes, J. Mansfeld, and M. Schofield (eds.), *The Cambridge History of Hellenistic Philosophy*. Cambridge: Cambridge University Press, 705–38.

Douglas, A. J. (1990). *Cicero: Tusculan Disputations II and V, with a Summary of III and IV*, edited and translated by A. E. Douglas. Warminster: Aris & Phillips.

Dover, K. (1994 [1974]). *Greek Popular Morality in the Time of Plato and Aristotle*. Indianapolis: Hackett.

Drecoll, V. H. (2004–2010). 'Gratia', in C. Mayer (ed.), *Augustinus-Lexikon*, iii. Basel: Schwabe, 182–242.

Drummond, J. (2014). 'Husserl's Phenonemological Axiology and Aristotelian Virtue Ethics', in M. Tuominen, S. Heinämaa, and V. Mäkinen (eds.), *New Perspectives on Aristotelianism and its Critics* (Brill's Studies in Intellectual History 233). Leiden: Brill, 179–95.

Emilsson, E. K. (2011). 'Plotinus on Happiness and Time'. *Oxford Studies in Ancient Philosophy* 40: 239–59.

Farwell, P. (1995). 'Aristotle and Complete Life'. *History of Philosophy Quarterly* 12: 247–63.

Finley, M. I. (1979 [1954]). *The World of Odysseus*. Harmondsworth: Penguin.

Flasch, K. (1994). *Augustin: Einführung in sein Denken*. 2nd ed. Stuttgart: Reclam.

Flasch, K. (1995). *Logik des Schreckens. Augustinus von Hippo: De diversis quaestionibus ad Simplicianum* I 2. 2nd ed. Mainz: Dieterich.

Fossheim, H. (2006). 'Habituation as *Mimesis*', in T. Chappell (ed.), *Values and Virtues: Aristotelianism in Contemporary Ethics*. Oxford: Oxford University Press, 105–17.

Fränkel, H. (1960 [1955]). 'Ephemeros als Kennwort für die mennschliche Natur', in *Wege und Formen frühgriechischen Denkens*. München: Beck, 23–9.

Frede, M. (1988). 'The Empiricist Attitude Towards Reason and Theory', in R. J. Hankinson (ed.), *Method, Medicine and Metaphysics: Studies in the Philosophy of Ancient Science. Apeiron* 21: 79–97.

Frede, M. (1996). 'Introduction', in Frede and Striker (1996), 1–28.

Frede, M. (1997). 'Euphrates of Tyre', in R. Sorabji (ed.), *Aristotle and After. Bulletin of the Institute of Classical Studies* suppl. 68: 1–11.

Frede, M., and G. Striker (eds.) (1996). *Rationality and Greek Thought*. Oxford: Oxford University Press.

Freudenthal, G. (1995). *Aristotle's Theory of Material Substance: Heat and Pneuma, Form and Soul*. Oxford: Clarendon Press.

Garland, R. (1990). *The Greek Way of Life: From Conception to Old Age*. London: Duckworth.

Gauthier, R. A., and Jolif, J. Y. (1970). *L'Éthique à Nicomaque*, ii, 2nd edn. Louvain/Paris: Publications universitaires.

van Geest, P. (2004). 'Stoic against His Will? Augustine on the Good Life in De beata vita and the Praeceptum'. *Augustiniana* 54: 533–50.

Gerber, D. E. (1999). *Greek Elegiac Poetry*. Loeb Classical Library. Cambridge, MA: Harvard University Press.

Giannopoulou, Z. (2011). 'Socrates and Godlikeness in Plato and Theaetetus'. *Journal of Philosophical Research* 36: 135–48.

Gill, C. (2006). *The Structured Self in Hellenistic and Roman Thought*. Oxford: Oxford University Press.

Goldbacher, A. (1904). *Augustinus: Epistulae*, iii: Epistulae CXXIV–CLXXXIVA, edited by A. Goldbacher. Wien: Tempsky (CSEL 44).

Goldschmidt, V. (1979). *Le système stoïcien et l'idée de temps*. Paris: J. Vrin.

Gosling, J. C. B., and Taylor, C. C. W. (1982). *The Greeks on Pleasure*. Oxford: Oxford University Press.

Gourinat, J.-B. (2009). 'Stoicism Today'. *Iris* 1: 497–511.

Graeser, A. (1972). *Plotinus and the Stoics*. Leiden: Brill.

Graham, D. W. (2010). *The Texts of Early Greek Philosophy*. Part I. Cambridge: Cambridge University Press.

Grant, A. (1874). *The Ethics of Aristotle*, ii. London: Methuen.

Graver, M. (2007). *Stoicism and Emotion*. Chicago: University of Chicago Press.

Griffin, J. (1980). *Homer on Life and Death*. Oxford: Clarendon Press.

Griffith, M. (2009). 'Greek Lyric and the Place of Humans in the World', in F. Budelmann (ed.), *The Cambridge Companion to Greek Lyric*. Cambridge: Cambridge University Press, 72–94.

Grönroos, G. (2007). 'Listening to Reason in Aristotle's Moral Psychology'. *Oxford Studies in Ancient Philosophy* 32: 251–71.

Grönroos, G. (2015). 'Wish, Motivation, and the Human Good in Aristotle'. *Phronesis* 60: 60–87.

Hadot, P. (1987). Plotin, *Traité 38 (VI 7)*, Introduction, traduction, commentaire et notes. Paris: Cerf.

Hadot, P. (1995a). *Philosophy as a Way of Life: Spiritual Exercises from Socrates to Foucault*, trans. M. Chase. Oxford: Oxford University Press.

Hadot, P. (1995b). '"Only the Present is Our Happiness": The Value of the Present Instant in Goethe and in Ancient Philosophy', in Hadot (1995a), 217–37.

Hadot, P. (2004). *What Is Ancient Philosophy?* Cambridge, MA: Harvard University Press.

Hagendahl, H. (1967). *Augustine and the Latin Classics.* Gothenburg: Acta Universitatis Gothoburgensis.

Haybron, D. M. (2008). *The Pursuit of Unhappiness. The Elusive Psychology of Well-Being.* Oxford: Oxford University Press.

de Heer, C. (1968). *MAKAR-EUDAIMŌN-OLBIOS-EUTYCHÉS A Study of the Semantic Field Denoting Happiness in Ancient Greek to the End of the 5th Century BC.* Amsterdam: Hakkert.

Heinämaa, S. (2014). 'Husserl's Ethics of Renewal: A Personalistic Approach', in M. Tuominen, S. Heinämaa, and V. Mäkinen (eds.), *New Perspectives on Aristotelianism and its Critics* (Brill's Studies in Intellectual History 233). Leiden: Brill, 196–212.

Heinimann, F. (1961). 'Eine vorplatonische Theorie der *technē*'. *Museum Helveticum* 18: 105–30.

Heylbut, G. (ed.) (1889). *Aspasii in Ethica Nicomachea quae supersunt commentaria* (CAG IXX 1). Berlin: Reimer.

Holte, R. (1962). *Béatitude et sagesse: Saint Augustin et le problème de la fin de l'homme dans la philosophie ancienne.* Paris: Études augustiniennes.

Horn, C. (1998). *Antike Lebenskunst: Glück und Moral von Sokrates bis zu den Neuplatonikern.* Munich: C.H. Beck.

Horn, C. (1999). 'Augustinus über Tugend, Moralität und das höchste Gut', in T. Fuhrer and M. Erler (eds.), *Zur Rezeption der hellenistischen Philosophie in der Spätantike.* Stuttgart: Teubner, 173–90.

Huffman, C. (2009). 'The Pythagorean Conception of the Soul from Pythagoras to Philolaus', in D. Frede and B. Reis (eds.), *Body and Soul in Ancient Philosophy.* Berlin: de Gruyter, 21–43.

Ierodiakonou, K. (1999). 'Aspasius on Perfect and Imperfect Virtues', in A. Alberti and R. W. Sharples (eds.), *Aspasius: The Earliest Extant Commentary on Aristotle's Ethics.* Berlin/New York: de Gruyter, 142–61.

Igál J. (1982). *Porfirio: Vida de Plotino, Plotino: Ennéadas I–II.* Introducciones, traducciones y notas par Jesús Igál. Madrid: Editorial Gredos.

Inwood, B. (1985). *Ethics and Human Action in Early Stoicism.* Oxford: Oxford University Press.

Inwood, B. (1999). 'Rules and Reasoning in Stoic Ethics', in K. Ierodiakonou (ed.), *Topics in Stoic Philosophy.* Oxford: Oxford University Press, 95–127.

Irwin, T. H. (1979). *Plato: Gorgias.* Oxford: Clarendon Press.

Irwin, T. H. (1985a). *Aristotle: Nicomachean Ethics,* trans. with intro. and notes. Indianapolis, IN: Hackett Publishing.

Irwin, T. H. (1985b). 'Permanent Happiness: Aristotle and Solon'. *Oxford Studies in Ancient Philosophy* 3: 89–124.

Irwin, T. H. (1995). *Plato's Ethics.* Oxford: Oxford University Press.

Irwin, T. H. (2001). 'Vice and Reason'. *The Journal of Ethics* 5: 73–97.

Irwin, T. H. (2004). Review of White (2002). *Ethics* 114: 848–58.

Irwin, T. H. (2006). 'Stoic Naturalism and Its Critics', in B. Inwood (ed.), *The Cambridge Companion to the Stoics.* Cambridge: Cambridge University Press, 345–64.

Irwin, T. H. (2007). *The Development of Ethics: A Historical and Critical Study,* ii: *From Socrates to the Reformation.* Oxford: Oxford University Press.

Irwin, T. H. (2008). *The Development of Ethics: A Historical and Critical Study,* ii: *From Suarez to Rousseau.* Oxford: Oxford University Press.

Janáček, K. (1972). *Sextus Empiricus' Sceptical Methods*. Prague: Charles University.

Jenks, R. (2007). 'The Sounds of Silence: Rhetoric and Dialectic in the Refutation of Callicles in Plato's *Gorgias*'. *Philosophy and Rhetoric* 40: 201–15.

Johnson, C. N. (1989). 'Socrates' Encounter with Polus in Plato's *Gorgias*'. *Phoenix* 43: 196–216.

Jost, L. J. (2002). 'Introduction', *Eudaimonia and Well-Being–Ancient and Modern Conceptions*, special issue of *Apeiron* 35: ix–xxiv.

Kahn, C. H. (1979). *The Art and Thought of Heraclitus: An Edition of the Fragments with Translation and Commentary*. Cambridge: Cambridge University Press.

Kahn, C. H. (1985). 'Democritus and the Origins of Moral Psychology'. *American Journal of Philology* 106: 1–31.

Kahn, C. H. (1996). *Plato and the Socratic Dialogue: The Philosophical Use of a Literary Form*. Cambridge: Cambridge University Press.

Kahn, C. H. (1998). 'Pre-Platonic Ethics', in S. Everson (ed.), *Companions to Ancient Thought 4: Ethics*. Cambridge: Cambridge University Press, 27–48.

Kidd, I. (1978). 'Moral Actions and Rules in Stoic Ethics', in J. Rist (ed.), *The Stoics*. Berkeley/ Los Angeles/London: University of California Press, 245–58.

Kirwan, C. (1989). *Augustine: The Arguments of the Philosophers*. London: Routledge.

Kitto, H. D. F. (1951). *The Greeks*. London: Penguin Books.

Klosko, G. (1984). 'The Refutation of Callicles in Plato's *Gorgias*'. *Greece and Rome* 31: 126–39.

Konstan, D. (1997). *Friendship in the Classical World*. Cambridge: Cambridge University Press.

Konstan, D. (2006). *Aspasius: On Aristotle's* Nicomachean Ethics *1–4, 7–8* (trans. with introduction and notes). (Ancient Commentators on Aristotle). London: Duckworth.

Korsgaard, C. (2008). *The Constitution of Agency: Essays on Practical Reason and Moral Psychology*. Oxford: Oxford University Press.

Kraut, R. (1979). 'Two Conceptions of Happiness'. *Philosophical Review* 88: 167–97.

Kraut, R. (1989). *Aristotle on the Human Good*. Princeton: Princeton University Press.

Kraut, R. (1997). *Aristotle Politics Books VII and VIII*. Oxford: Clarendon Press.

Kube, J. (1969). Technē *und* Aretē*: Sophistisches und platonisches Tugendwissen*. Berlin: de Gruyter.

Lännström, A. (2011). 'Socrates, the Philosopher in the Theaetetus Digression (172c–177c), and the Ideal of Homoiōsis Theōi'. *Apeiron* 44: 111–30.

Lavere, G. J. (2000). 'Virtue', in A. D. Fitzgerald (ed.), *Augustine through the Ages: An Encyclopedia*. Grand Rapids: Eerdmans, 871–4.

Lear, G. R. (2004). *Happy Lives and the Highest Good: An Essay on Aristotle's* Nicomachean Ethics. Princeton: Princeton University Press.

Lear, G. R. (2006). 'Aristotle on Moral Virtue and the Fine', in R. Kraut (ed.), *The Blackwell Guide to Aristotle's* Nicomachean Ethics. Oxford: Oxford University Press, 116–36.

LeBar, M. (2010). 'Prichard vs Plato: Intuition vs. Reflection', in S. Black and E. Tiffany (eds.), *Reasons to be Moral Revisited. Canadian Journal of Philosophy* Suppl. Vol. 33. Calgary: University of Calgary Press, 1–32.

Linguiti, A. (2007). *Plotin: Traité 36, I. 5*. Introduction, traduction, commentaire et notes par Alessandro Linguiti. Paris: Les éditions du Cerf.

Lloyd-Jones, H. (1971). *The Justice of Zeus*. Berkeley: University of California Press.

Lloyd-Jones, H. (1990). 'Pindar' [1982], in *Greek Epic, Lyric, and Tragedy: The Academic Papers of Sir Hugh Lloyd-Jones*. Oxford: Clarendon Press, 57–79.

Long, A. A. (2004). 'Eudaimonism, Divinity, and Rationality in Greek Ethics'. *Proceedings of the Boston Area Colloquium in Ancient Philosophy* 19: 123–43.

Long, A. A. (2009). 'Heraclitus on Measure and the Explicit Emergence of Rationality', in D. Frede and B. Reis (eds.), *Body and Soul in Ancient Philosophy*. Berlin: de Gruyter, 87–109.

Long, A. A. (2011). 'Aristotle on *Eudaimonia*, Nous, and Divinity', in J. Miller (ed.), *Aristotle's Nicomachean Ethics: A Critical Guide*. Cambridge: Cambridge University Press, 92–114.

Long, A. A., and Sedley, D. N. (1987). *The Hellenistic Philosophers*. 2 vols. Cambridge: Cambridge University Press.

MacIntyre, A. (1981). *After Virtue*, South Bend, IN: Notre Dame University Press.

Mahoney, T. (2004). 'Is Assimiltaion to God in the *Theaetetus* Purely Otherworldly?' *Ancient Philosophy* 24: 321–37.

McGroarty, K. (2006). *Plotinus on Eudaimonia: A Commentary on Ennead I.4*. Oxford: Oxford University Press.

McMahon, D. (2006). *The Pursuit of Happiness: A History from the Greeks to the Present*. Harmondsworth: Penguin.

McPherran, M. L. (2006). 'The Gods and Piety of Plato's *Republic*', in G. Santas (ed.), *The Blackwell Guide to Plato's Republic*. London: Blackwell, 84–103.

Mele, A. R. (1984). 'Aristotle on the Roles of Reason in Motivation and Justification'. *Archiv für Geschichte der Philosophie* 66: 124–47.

Merki, H. (1952). Homoiōsis theōi: *Von den platonischen Angleichung an Gott zur Gottähnlichkeit bei Gregor von Nyssa*. Freiburg, Switzerland: Paulusverlag.

Mitsis, P. (1993). 'Seneca on Reason, Rules, and Moral Development', in J. Brunschwig and M. Nussbaum (eds.), *Passions and Perceptions*. Cambridge: Cambridge University Press, 285–312.

Morison, B. (2015). 'What Is a Perfect Syllogism?' *Oxford Studies in Ancient Philosophy* 48: 107–66.

Moss, J. (2011). '"Virtue Makes the Goal Right": Virtue and *Phronesis* in Aristotle's Ethics'. *Phronesis* 56: 204–61.

Moss, J. (2012). *Aristotle on the Apparent Good*. Oxford: Oxford University Press.

Most, G. W. (2006). *Hesiod: Theogony; Works and Days; Testimonia*. Loeb Classical Library. Cambridge, MA: Harvard University Press.

Müller, J. (2009). *Willensschwäche in Antike und Mittelalter: Eine Problemgeschichte von Sokrates bis Johannes Duns Scotus*. Leuven: Leuven University Press.

Müller, J. (2010). '"Glücklich ist, wer Gott hat": Beatitudo beim frühen Augustinus', in J. Disse and B. Göbel (eds.), *Gott und die Frage nach dem Glück: Anthropologische und ethische Perspektiven*. Frankfurt am Main: Knecht, 14–59.

Murray, A. T., and W. F. Wyatt (1999). *Homer: Iliad*, i–ii. Loeb Classical Library. Cambridge, MA: Harvard University Press.

Nagel, T. (1979). 'Death', in *Mortal Questions*. Cambridge: Cambridge University Press, 1–10.

Nagel, T. (1980). 'Aristotle on *Eudaimonia*', in A. O. Rorty (ed.), *Essays on Aristotle's Ethics*. Berkeley and Los Angeles: University of California Press, 7–14.

Nikolsky, B. (2001). 'Epicurus on Pleasure'. *Phronesis* 4: 440–65.

de Noronha Galvao, H. (1986–1994). 'Beatitudo', in C. Mayer (ed.), *Augustinus-Lexikon*. Basel: Schwabe, 624–38.

North, H. (1966). *Sophrosyne: Self-Knowledge and Self-Restraint in Greek Literature*. Ithaca: Cornell University Press.

Nozick, R. (1974). *Anarchy, State, and Utopia*. New York: Basic Books.

Nussbaum, M. (2001 [1986]). *The Fragility of Goodness*. Cambridge: Cambridge University Press.

O'Connell, R. J. (1968). *St. Augustine's Early Theory of Man*. Cambridge MA: Belknap.

O'Donovan, O. (1980). *The Problem of Self-Love in St. Augustine*. New Haven, CT: Yale University Press.

O'Meara, D. J. (1995). *Plotinus: An Introduction to the Enneads*. Oxford: Clarendon Press.

O'Meara, D. J. (2003). *Platonopolis: Platonic Political Philosophy in Late Antiquity*. Oxford: Oxford University Press.

O'Meara, D. J. (2013). 'Aristotelian Ethics in Plotinus', in J. Miller (ed.), *The Reception of Aristotle's Ethics*. Cambridge: Cambridge University Press, 53–66.

Pakaluk, M. (1998). *Aristotle: Nicomachean Ethics Books VIII and IX*. Oxford: Oxford University Press.

Passmore, J. (1970). *The Perfectibility of Man*. London: Duckworth.

Pearson, G. (2012). *Aristotle on Desire*. Cambridge: Cambridge University Press.

Pizzolato, L. F. (1987). 'Il De beata vita o la possibile felicità nel tempo', in G. Reale (ed.), *L'opera letteraria di Agostino tra Cassiciacum e Milano: Agostino nelle terre di Ambrogio*. Palermo: Edizione Augustinus, 31–112.

Polito, R. (2014). *Aenesidemus of Cnossus: Testimonia*. Cambridge: Cambridge University Press.

Price, A. W. (1980). 'Aristotle's Ethical Holism'. *Mind* 89: 338–52.

Price, A. W. (1995). *Mental Conflict*. London: Routledge.

Prichard, H. A. (2002a). 'Does Moral Philosophy Rest on a Mistake?' in J. McAdam (ed.), *Prichard: Moral Writings*. Oxford: Oxford University Press, 1–20.

Prichard, H. A. (2002b). 'Duty and Interest', in J. McAdam (ed.), *Prichard: Moral Writings*. Oxford: Oxford University Press, 21–49.

Race, W. H. (1979). 'Shame in Plato's *Gorgias*'. *Classical Journal* 74: 197–202.

Race, W. H. (1997). *Pindar*, i–ii. Cambridge, MA: Harvard University Press.

Raz, J. (1999). *Engaging Reason: On the Theory of Value and Action*. Oxford: Oxford University Press.

Van Riel, G. (2000). *Pleasure and the Good Life. Plato, Aristotle, and the Neoplatonists*. Leiden: Brill.

Rist, J. M. (1967). *Plotinus: The Road to Reality*. Cambridge: Cambridge University Press.

Rist, J. M. (1980). 'Epicurus on Friendship'. *Classical Philology* 75: 121–9.

Rist, J. M. (1994). *Augustine: Ancient Thought Baptized*. Cambridge: Cambridge University Press.

Robertson, D. (2010). *The Philosophy of Cognitive-Behavioural Therapy (CBT): Stoic Philosophy as Rational and Cognitive Psychotherapy*. London: Karnac Books.

Robinson, T. M. (2008). 'Presocratic Theology', in P. Curd and D. W. Graham (eds.), *The Oxford Handbook of Presocratic Philosophy*. Oxford: Oxford University Press, 485–98.

Rogers, K. (1993). 'Aristotle's Conception of *To Kalon*'. *Ancient Philosophy* 13: 355–71. Reprinted in L. P. Gerson (ed.) (1999), *Aristotle: Critical Assessments*, iv. London: Routledge, 337–55.

Roloff, D. (1970). *Gottähnlichkeit, Vergöttlichung und Erhöhung zu seligem Leben: Untersuchungen zur Herkunft der platonischen Angleichung an Gott*. Berlin: de Gruyter.

Roochnik, D. (1996). *Of Art and Wisdom: Plato's Understanding of Technē*. University Park, PA: Penn State Press.

Roochnik, D. (2007). 'Aristotle's Account of the Vicious: A Forgivable Inconsistency'. *History of Philosophy Quarterly* 24: 207–20.

Rosenbaum, S. E. (1990). 'Epicurus on Pleasure and the Complete Life'. *The Monist* 73: 21–41.

Roskam, G. (2005). *On the Path to Virtue: The Stoic Doctrine of Moral Progress and its Reception in (Middle-)Platonism*. Leuven: Leuven University Press.

Ross, W. D. (1984). *Metaphysics*, in *The Complete Works of Aristotle*, trans. J. Barnes (ed.). Princeton: Princeton University Press.

Ross, W. D., and L. Brown (2009). *Aristotle: Nicomachean Ethics*. Oxford: Oxford University Press.

Rowe, C. (2002). *Aristotle: Nicomachean Ethics*, trans. with commentary by S. Broadie. New York: Oxford University Press.

Rue, R. (1993). 'The Philosopher in Flight'. *Oxford Studies in Ancient Philosophy* 11: 71–100.

Russell, D. (2005). *Plato on Pleasure and the Good Life*. Oxford: Clarendon Press.

Russell, D. (n.d.). 'Why the Stoics think there is no right way to grieve', unpublished article.

Rusten, J. S. (1985). 'Two Lives or Three? Pericles on the Athenian Character (Thucydides 2.40.1–2)'. *Classical Quarterly* 35: 14–19.

Schafer, J. (2009). *Ars Didactica: Seneca's 94th and 95th Letters*. Hypomnemata 181. Göttingen: Vandenhoeck & Ruprecht.

Schissel von Fleschenberg, O. (1928). *Marinos von Neapolis und die neuplatonischen Tugendgrade*. Athens: Sakellarios.

Schneewind, J. B. (1998). *The Invention of Autonomy*. Cambridge: Cambridge University Press.

Schniewind, A. (2003). *L'éthique du sage chez Plotin: Le paradigme du spoudaios*. Paris: Vrin.

Schniewind, A. (2014). 'Plotin et les émotions nobles: un accès privilégié par les vertus supérieures', in B. Collette and S. Delcominette (eds.), *Unité et origine des vertus dans la philosophie ancienne*. Brussels: Ousia, 321–37.

Schofield, M. (1984). 'Ariston of Chios and the Unity of Virtue'. *Ancient Philosophy* 4: 83–96.

Schofield, M. (1986). '*Euboulia* in the *Iliad*'. *Classical Quarterly* 36: 6–31. Reprinted in: (2001), *Oxford Readings in Homer's Iliad*, edited by D. L. Cairns. Oxford: Oxford University Press, 220–59.

Schofield, M. (2003). 'Stoic Ethics', in B. Inwood (ed.), *The Cambridge Companion to the Stoics*. Cambridge: Cambridge University Press, 233–56.

Schwyzer, H.-R. (1951). 'Plotinos', in Wissowa, G. (ed.), *Paulys Realencyclopädie der classischen Altertumswissenschaft*, t. XXI. Stuttgart: Druckenmüller; col. 471–592 (and Supplementband 15, 1978; col. 311–27).

Sedley, D. N. (1999). 'The Ideal of Godlikeness', in G. Fine (ed.), *Plato 2: Ethics, Politics, Religion, and the Soul*. Oxford: Oxford University Press, 309–28.

Sedley, D. N. (2003). 'The School, from Zeno to Arius Didumus', in B. Inwood (ed.), *The Cambridge Companion to the Stoics*. Cambridge: Cambridge University Press, 7–32.

Sedley, D. N. (2004). *The Midwife of Platonism: Text and Subtext in Plato's Theaetetus*. Oxford: Clarendon Press.

Sedley, D. N. (2007). *Creationism and Its Critics in Antiquity*. Berkeley: University of California Press.

Sedley, D. N. (2013). 'Socratic Intellectualism in the Republic's Central Digression', in G. Boys-Stones, D. El Murr, and C. Gill (eds.), *The Platonic Art of Philosophy*. Cambridge: Cambridge University Press, 70–89.

Segvic, H. (2000). 'No One Errs Willingly: The Meaning of Socratic Intellectualism'. *Oxford Studies in Ancient Philosophy* 19: 1–45.

Sellars, J. (n.d.). 'Philosophy as Medicine: Stoicism and Cognitive Psychotherapy', unpublished article.

Smith, A. (2005). 'Action and Contemplation in Plotinus', in A. Smith (ed.), *Philosopher and Society in Late Antiquity*. London: University of Wales Press, 65–72.

Soll, I. (1998). 'On the Purported Insignificance of Death', in J. Malpas and R. C. Solomon (eds.), *Death and Philosophy*. London: Routledge, 22–38.

Solmsen, F. (1949). *Hesiod and Aeschylus*. Ithaca: Cornell University Press.

Sorabji, R. (1993). *Animals Minds and Human Morals: The Origins of the Western Debate* (Cornell Studies in Classical Philology). Ithaca, NJ: Cornell University Press.

Sorabji, R. (1997). 'Is Stoic Philosophy Helpful as Psychotherapy?' in R. Sorabji (ed.), *Aristotle and After: Bulletin of the Institute of Classical Studies* suppl. 68: 197–209.

Stauffer, D. (2002). 'Socrates and Callicles: A Reading of Plato's *Gorgias*'. *The Review of Politics* 64: 627–57.

Stewart, J. A. (1892). *Notes on the* Nicomachean Ethics. Oxford: Oxford University Press.

Stocker, M. (1976). 'The Schizophrenia of Modern Ethical Theories'. *The Journal of Philosophy: On Motives and Morals* 73: 453–66.

Strawson, G. (2004). 'Against Narrativity'. *Ratio* (new series) 17: 428–52.

Striker, G. (1990). 'Ataraxia: Happiness as Tranquillity'. *Monist* 73: 97–110. Reprinted in: *Essays on Hellenistic Epistemology and Ethics*. Cambridge: Cambridge University Press, 183–95.

Striker, G. (1991). 'Following Nature: A Study in Stoic Ethics', *Oxford Studies in Ancient Philosophy* IX: 1–73.

Striker, G. (1998). 'Greek Ethics and Moral Theory', in *Essays in Hellenistic Epistemology and Ethics*. Cambridge: Cambridge University Press, 169–82.

Sumner, W. (1996). *Welfare, Happiness, and Ethics*. Oxford: Oxford University Press.

Svavarsson, S. H. (2002). 'Pyrrho's Dogmatic Nature'. *Classical Quarterly* 52: 248–56.

Svavarsson, S. H. (2011). 'Two Kinds of Tranquility: Sextus Empiricus on Ataraxia', in D. E. Machuca (ed.), *Pyrrhonism in Ancient, Modern, and Contemporary Philosophy*. Dordrecht: Springer, 19–32.

Svavarsson, S. H. (2013). 'Tranquility: Pyrrho and Democritus', in S. Marchand and F. Verde (eds.), *Épicurisme et Scepticisme*. Rome: Sapienza, 3–32.

Svavarsson, S. H. (2014). 'Sextus Empiricus on Persuasiveness and Equipollence', in M.-K. Lee (ed.), *Strategies of Argument: Essays in Ancient Ethics, Epistemology, and Logic*. New York: Oxford University Press, 356–73.

Taylor, C. (1989). *Sources of the Self: The Making of the Modern Identity*. Cambridge, MA: Harvard University Press.

Teske, R. J. (2003). *The Works of Saint Augustine: A Translation for the 21st Century*, part II, vol. 2, Letters 100–55, translated by R. J. Teske. New York: New City Press.

Tieleman, T. (2007). 'Panaetius' Place in the History of Stoicism with Special Reference to his Moral Psychology', in A. M. Ioppolo and D. N. Sedley (eds.), *Pyrrhonists, Patricians, Platonizers. Hellenistic Philosophy in the Period 155–86 BC*. Naples: Bibliopolis, 103–42.

Tornau, C. (2006a). *Zwischen Rhetorik und Philosophie: Augustins Argumentationstechnik in De civitate Dei und ihr bildungsgeschichtlicher Hintergrund*. Berlin: de Gruyter.

Tornau, C. (2006b). 'Does Augustine Accept Pagan Virtue? The Place of Book 5 in the Argument of the City of God', in F. Young, M. Edwards, and P. Parvis (eds.), *Studia Patristica XLIII: Papers presented at the XIVth International Conference on Patristic Studies held in Oxford 2003*. Leuven: Peeters, 263–75.

Tornau, C. (2013a). '"Die Tugend ist hinreichend zur Erlangung der Glückseligkeit": die stoische Autarkie-Formel im kaiserzeitlichen Platonismus', in C. Pietsch (ed.), *Ethik des antiken Platonismus: Der platonische Weg zum Glück in Systematik, Entstehung und historischem Kontext*. Stuttgart: Steiner, 141–58.

Tornau, C. (2013b). 'Augustinus und die neuplatonischen Tugendgrade: Versuch einer Interpretation von Augustins Brief 155 an Macedonius', in F. Karfík and E. Song (eds.), *Plato Revived: Essays on Ancient Platonism in Honour of Dominic O'Meara*. Berlin: de Gruyter, 215–40.

Vegetti, M. (1998). *La Repubblica*, ii. Naples: Bibliopolis.

Velleman, D. (1991). 'Well-Being and Time', *Pacific Philosophical Quarterly* 72: 48–77.

Vlastos, G. (1946). 'Solonian Justice'. *Classical Philology* 41: 65–83. Reprinted in (1995), *Studies in Greek Philosophy*, i: *The Presocratics*, edited by D. Graham. Princeton: Princeton University Press, 32–56.

Vlastos, G. (1967). 'Was Polus Refuted?' *American Journal of Philology* 88: 454–60.

Vogt, K. (2010). 'Desiring the Good: A Socratic Reading of Aristotle', manuscript at <http://katjavogt.com/pdf/katja_vogt_motivation.pdf> accessed 11 April 2015.

Wacht, M. (1986). 'Güterlehre', in T. Klauser (ed.), *Reallexikon für Antike und Christentum*, xiii. Stuttgart: Hiersemann, 59–150.

Walzer, R. and M. Frede (1985). *Galen: Three Treatises on the Nature of Science*. Indianapolis: Hackett.

West, M. L. (1978). *Hesiod: Works and Days*. Oxford: Clarendon Press.

Wetzel, J. (1992). *Augustine and the Limits of Virtue*. Cambridge: Cambridge University Press.

White, N. P. (2002). *Individual and Conflict in Greek Ethics*. Oxford: Oxford University Press.

White, N. P. (2005). *A Brief History of Happiness*. Oxford: Blackwell.

Whittaker, J. (1990). *Alcinoos: Enseignement des doctrines de Platon*, edited by J. Whittaker and translated by P. Louis. Paris: Les Belles Lettres.

Wiesen, D. S. (1968). *Augustine: The City of God against the Pagans*, iii, Books VIII–XI, translated by D. S. Wiesen. London: Heinemann.

Williams, B. (1973). 'The Makropoulos Case: Reflections on the Tedium of Immortality', in *Problems of the Self*. Cambridge: Cambridge University Press, 82–100.

Williams, B. (1993). *Shame and Necessity*. Berkeley: University of California Press.

Williams, B. (1997). 'Stoic Philosophy and the Emotions: Reply to Richard Sorabji', in R. Sorabji (ed.), *Aristotle and After. Bulletin of the Institute of Classical Studies* suppl. 68: 211–13.

Woods, M. (1992). *Aristotle: Eudemian Ethics Books I, II, and VIII*. Oxford: Oxford University Press.

Woolf, R. (2009). 'Pleasure and Desire', in J. Warren (ed.), *The Cambridge Companion to Epicureanism*. Cambridge: Cambridge University Press, 158–78.

Zeyl, D. J. (2000). *Plato: Timaeus*. Indianapolis: Hackett.

Index Locorum

Alcinous, *Didaskalikos* (*Did.*)
  180.39–41 267*n20*
  180.41f. 266*n10*
  181.43–5 275*n59*

Alexander Aphrodisiensis
  De anima libri mantissa (*De an. mant.*)
    159–68 267*n19*
  De fato
    199.14–22 184*n2*, 189

Ammonius, *In Porphyrii isagogen sive quinque*
    voces (*Isag.*)
  98.3–7 184*n3*

Aristotle
  Analytica Priora (*An. Pr.*)
    I 1, 24b23f. 143
  De anima (*DA*)
    II 2, 413a 220*n45*
    II 4, 416a6–9 117
    II 5, 417a17f. 228
    II 7, 1108a11 253
    III 7
      431a6f. 227
      431a8–12 150
    III 9
      432b5 150
      432b6 150
    III 10, 433b8–10 150
  Categoriae (*Cat.*)
    8b27–9a13 186
    13a23–9 163*n32*
  Ethica Eudemia (*EE*)
    I 2, 1214b6–11 95*n15*, 110
    I 6, 1215b15–18 156
    I 7, 1217a21–9 137
    II 1
      1219a8 129*n2*
      1219a35–b9 195*n31*
      1219a35–b8 130
      1219b1–3 215*n11*
      1219b7f. 136
    II 10, 1227a18–31 158*n24*
    II 11, 1227b23–5 102*n26*
    VII 2
      1235b24–6a15 151*n14*
      1235b26f. 159
    VII 6, 1240b11–15 149
  Ethica Nicomachea (*EN*)
    I 1
      1094a1–3 156

1094a1f. 89
I 2
  1094a8f. 90
  1094a10–14 90
  1094a18–22 90, 92
  1094a19f. 92
  1094a22–6 111*n36*
  1094a22–4 103*n26*
  1094a25f. 90
  1094a26f. 90
  1094a28–b2 90
  1094b4–7 90
  1094b7–11 17
  1094b7–10 91
  1094b11–27 111*n36*
  1094b14–18 91n
I 4
  1095a14–22 110
  1095a14–17 90
  1095a18–20 2, 7*n19*, 95, 131
  1095a20–6 156
  1095a21–6 110
  1095a22–5 143
I 5
  1095b17 9
  1095b22f. 36
  1095b23 9
  1095b26–31 36
  1096a4 9 n. *29*
  1096a5–7 129*n2*
I 7
  1097a16–22 90
  1097a25–b5 92
  1097b5–8 246
  1097b6–16 18
  1097b8 246
  1097b8–16 125*n36*
  1097b8–13 17
  1097b14f. 93
  1097b15–21 93
  1097b22–8a20 96
  1097b22–33 97*n18*, 105
  1097b26 105
  1097b33–8a5 97
  1098a3f. 97, 103
  1098a4f. 102
  1098a8–12 99
  1098a16–20 129, 138
  1098a16f. 97, 103, 233
  1098a16 7

Aristotle (*cont.*)
1098a17f. 195*n31*
1098a18–20 249
1098a21–33 111*n36*
I 8
1098b10 95
1098b12–18 95
1098b18–20 225
1098b20f. 95, 215*n11*
1098b30 95
1098b31–99a1 140
1098b33 95
1099a3–7 127
1099a7 95
1099a22 95
1099a31–b7 131
1099a31f. 95
I 9
1099a33–b2 255
1099b4–7 125
1099b32–1100a2 137
1099b32–1100a5 136
1100a2 131
1100a4–9 225
I 10
1100a4 195*n31*
1100a11 113*n2*
1100b12–17 140
1100b15 140*n18*
1100b35–1101a8 132*n6*
1101a4–9 133
1101a9–13 226f
1101a9–10 133
1101a11–13 135, 139
1101a11–16 129
1101a11f. 133
1101a14–21 226
1101a14–19 133, 139
I 12, 1102a1–4 103
I 13, 1102a5f. 195*n31*
II 2
1103b26–31 22, 103*n28*
1103b34–4a11 111*n36*
II 4, 1105a32f. 140, 142
III 1, 1110b30–11a2 159
III 3
1112b11–15 92
1112b27f. 18*n41*
III 4
1113a15–33 156
1113a33–b2 155, 158f
III 5, 1113b12–19 163*n31*
III 8, 1118a32–b1 120*n23*
III 9, 1117b9–13 137
IV 5, 1126a7f. 120
V 1
1129b26f. 251*n37*

1129b30–33 251*n37*
VI 5
1140a25 106
1140a28 131
VI 8, 1141b23f. 91
VI 9
1142b18–20 154
1142b28–33 154
VI 11, 1143b13f. 115
VI 12
1144a7–9 102*n26*
1144a23–36 154
VI 13
1144b1–17 162
1144b1–9 195*n31*
1145a5–7 102*n26*
VII 1
1145a15–18 146*n2*
1145a25–7 275*n59*
VII 3, 1146b19–24 155
VII 4
1148a4–11 148
1148a16f. 148
VII 7
1150a16–22 155*n20*
1150a19–21 154f
1150a21–3 150
VII 8
1150b29–36 150
1151a5–7 148
1151a15–19 102*n26*
VII 14, 1154b9–15 155
VIII 1, 1155a3f. 142
VIII 3
1156a28–31 254*n46*
1156b25–34 141
VIII 5, 1157b14–16 117
VIII 6, 1158a2–11 117
VIII 8, 1159b7–9 153
VIII 12
1161b14–16 254
1161b15 254*n48*
IX 2
1164b27–33 111*n36*
1165a12–14 111*n36*
IX 4
1166a19–23 156
1166b2–26 149
1166b5 149
1166b7f. 150
1166b8–11 149
1166b8–10 149
1166b11–14 149
1166b11–13 147
1166b11 149
1166b12 147*n3*
1166b19–22 147*n3*, 140

1166b22–5 161
1166b23–5 149
1166b23f. 150n10
1166b24–8 147
1166b25f. 161
IX 8
    1168b15–23 155
    1169a22–5 138
IX 9
    1169b13–22 247
    1170b8–10 147
X 2
    1172b35f. 156
    1173a2–4 157
    1173a4f. 157, 162
X 4
    1174a14–23 227
    1174a19–29 134
    1174a19 233
    1174b19–23 147n4
X 7
    1177a12–b34 29
    1177a19–b31 34
    1177a32–b1 247
    1177a34 254n44
    1177b4–15 132n6
    1177b24–6 130, 139
X 8
    1178a34–b3 134
    1178b8–18 275n59
    1178b8–15 33
    1178b18–20 140n17
    1178b24 137
    1179a16–22
X 9, 1179a33–b4 103n28
De generatione animalium (GA)
IV 4, 770b3 118n16
Historia animalium
I 1
    487b33–8a14 19n42
    488a7f. 19n42
Metaphysica (Met.)
V 16, 1021b13f. 134
VII 7, 1072a27f. 159
IX 6
    1048b23–8 227
    1048b26 228
XI 9, 1066a20–21 227
De motu animalium (MA)
700b23–8 150
700b28f. 159
De partibus animalium (PA)
650b28f. 118
651b10 118n16
Physica (Phys.)
III 2
    201b31f. 227

201b31 228
VIII 5, 257b8 228
Politica (Pol.)
I 2
    1252b28–30 91n7
    1253a2–5 247
    1253a7–8 247
I 8, 1256b5 129
I 13, 1260a9–14 110n33
II 9, 1270b38–71a1 125
III 1
    1274b38 19 n. 44
    1275a17–23 124
III 3, 1276b1–15 19n44
III 9, 1280a31f. 91n7
III 12, 1282b14–18 91n7
IV 1, 1289a15–18 19n44
VII 8, 1328a35–7 91n7
VII 9
    1329a13–34 137
    1329a28–35 124
VII 13, 1332a1–28 132n6
VII 15, 1334a10–40 132n6
VII 16, 1335a30 124n33
VII 17, 1336a32–4 118
Problemata
II 11
    867a38f. 118
    867a39–b1 118
XXX 1, 954b12ff. 118
Rhetorica (Rhet.)
I 5, 1361b7–14 137
I 10, 1368b37–9a7 150n12
II 13
    1389b15–18 115n11
    1389b21f. 115n11
    1389b30 118
    1389b31f. 118
    1389b31 118
    1390a4f. 121
    1390a11–14 120f
II 14, 1390b9–11 115n9
Topica (Top.)
I 10
    104a22 251
    104a30 251
IV 5, 126a13 150
VII 8, 146a36–b9 158n24

Aspasius, In ethica Nicomachea
        commentaria (Eth. Nic.)
19.8–10 249
19.9 249
23.7–9 252
24.9–11 18
24.9 255n50
24.10f. 255

Aspasius, *In ethica Nicomachea*
    commentaria (Eth. Nic.) (cont.)
24.10 255
52.26–30 253
53.34–4.1 254
121.4 254
121.6 254
171.27–32 253
171.30 254n44
171.31–32 254
175.19 254
175.21 254
177.20 254
181.16 254
183.26–8 254
183.27f. 255
184.1f. 254n48
184.13 254

Atticus, *Fragmenta*
2.9–17 267n20

Augustine
De animae quantitate (an. quant.)
70–76 275n60
De beata vita (beata v.)
5 266n13
11 265n5f
14 274n53
19f. 271n41
20f. 274n53
23–9 265n4
De civitate Dei (civ.)
1.28 273n50
5.20 270n33
8.8 265n3, 266nn7, 10
9.4 271n40
10.1–3 265n6
10.3 265n3, 273n47
10.18 269
10.29 266n15
11.13 265n5, 270n33
14.1 266n13
14.6–9 274n52
14.9 276n65
14.24 271n39
14.28 274n52
15.22 271n40, 274n52
19.4 266nn11, 15, 271n39, 277n68
22.22–30 266n11
22.22 277n66
22.29 266n12
Confessiones (conf.)
7.26 266n15
10.7 266n12
10.29 278n74
Contra Iulianum opus imperfectum
    (c. Iul. imp.)

1.41 278n72
1.98ff. 278n70
3.76f. 268n23
6.11 265n2
De correptione et gratia (corrept.)
10 278n71
De diversis quaestionibus octoginta tribus
    (div. qu.)
67.7 275n62
Enarrationes in Psalmos (en. Ps.)
31.1.1 266n13
83.11 275n61, 276n63
Enchiridion de fide, spe et caritate
    (ench.)
121 275n62
Epistolae (ep.)
155.2 266n15
155.3 270n32, 274n54
155.5 268n25
155.9 266n14, 279
155.10 275, 277
155.12 275f
155.13f. 268n25
155.13 275
155.15 273n47
155.16 275, 277, 278n75
194.6 279n78
In epistulam Iohannis ad Parthos tractatus
    decem (ep. Io. tr.)
8.9 273n47
10.5 270n32
De Genesi ad litteram (Gn. litt.)
12.31.59 275n62
In Iohannis evangelium tractatus (Io. ev. tr.)
3.10 279n78
De libero arbitrio (lib. arb.)
2.33 273n51
2.35 266n8
2.50 271n40
De moribus ecclesiae catholicae (mor.)
1.4–61 265n6
1.5 265nn4f
1.10 265n6, 271n41
1.13 273n47
1.18 271n41
1.22 271n41, 273n47
1.24ff. 265n3
1.24 265n6, 270n32
1.25 272
1.26 266n9, 270n32
1.35 266n9
De musica (mus.)
6.50–55 275n61
6.52 278n74
De peccatorum meritis et remissione
    (pecc. mer.)
2.8 278n70

De perseverantia (*persev.*)
 2 278*n71*
Retractiones (*retr.*)
 1.2 266*n11*
 1.4.3 266*n11*
 1.7.4 266*n11*
De sermone domini in monte (*s. dom. m.*)
 1.18 270*n33*
 22.39 273
Soliloquia (*sol.*)
 1.12 275*n62*
 1.14 266*n11*
De trinitate (*trin.*)
 12.21 271*n40*
 13 266*n15*
 13.6–25 265*n6*
 13.7 265*n2*
 13.8 270*n30*, 276*n63*
 13.9–10 278*n73*
 13.9 277*n68*
 13.10 266*nn7, 11*, 271*n41*
 14.4 275*n62*
 14.12 275*n61*
 14.21 279*n78*

Aulus Gellius, *Noctes Atticae*
 11.5.5 202

The Bible
 Ecclesiastes (Ecli)
  10.13 266*n14*
 First Epistle to the Corinthians (1 Cor)
  1.24 273, 276*n63*
  13.12 266, 275*n61*
 Second Epistle to the Corinthians (2 Cor)
  10.17 279
 Epistle to the Galatians (Gal)
  1.10 270
  5.17 271*n39*
 First Epistle of John (1 John)
  1.8 278*n70*
 The Gospel of Matthew (Mt)
  10.22 278
  22.37 273
 Second Epistle of Peter (2 Petr)
  2.10 270*n33*
 Book of Psalms (Ps)
  33.9 278*n74*
  48.7 278*n72*
  72.18 274
  72.28 266*n9*, 269, 270*n32*, 275
 Epistle to the Romans (Rm)
  8.24 275*n62*

Boëthius, *In Categorias Aristotelis* (*Cat.*)
 257b–c 185

Cicero
 Academica
  1.44 203
 De finibus ((*De*) *fin.*)
  1.19 230
  1.29 265*n3*
  1.33–47 230
  3.12 267*n18*
  3.20 192
  3.46 232
  3.47 232, 239
  3.48 185
  4.16 271*n38*
  4.21 188
  4.55 188
  4.56 190
  4.64 185
  4.65 189
  5.38 271*n38*
  5.88 272*n42*
 Hortensius (*Hort.*)
  fr. 58 265*n2*
  fr. 110 275*n61*
 De inventione (*inv.*)
  1.93 271*n40*
 De natura deorum (*ND*)
  3.86f. 271*n35*
 De officiis
  1.153 254*n44*
  3.37–9 58*n21*
 Tusculanae Disputationes (*Tusc.*)
  1.95 271*n40*
  3.37 272*n42*
  5.1 267*n16*
  5.2 270, 280*n80*
  5.12 272*n42*
  5.16 271*n36*
  5.17 271*n36*
  5.18 271*n40*
  5.24 270*n31*
  5.40f. 271*n37*
  5.53 272*n42*
  5.75 274*n54*

Clemens Alexandrinus, *Stromata* (*strom.*)
 4.52.1–3 257*n20*
 5.96.5 257*n20*

Diodorus Siculus, *Bibliotheca historica*
 2.19.5 209*n19*
 16.35.5 209*n19*

Diogenes Laërtius (DL), *Vitae philosophorum*
 II.28 11
 II.89 238
 IV.33 202
 VII.88 183
 VII.89 231
 VII.116 216
 VII.120 185
 VII.127 187
 VII.129 257*n54*

Diogenes Laërtius (DL), *Vitae philosophorum*
(*cont.*)
    IX.61 201
    IX.63 200
    IX.65 200
    IX.66 200
    IX.107 203, 205
    IX.108 205
    IX.116 205
    X.3 169
    X.137 169

Epictetus
  Dissertationes ab Arriano digestae (*Diss.*)
    2.22 17n37
    3.2 231
    3.10 231
    3.24.84–7 191
    4.1.111–13 191
  Enchiridion (*Ench.*)
    3, 7, 11, 15, 26 191

Epicurus
  Epistula ad Menoeceum (*Ep. Men.*)
    25f. 237
    32.4 238
    127.8–11 177
    127.10–11 176
    128.1–11 170
    128.11–9.1 175
    129 168n8
    130.5 177
    132.7 179
    132.9–11 179
    135 29n7
  Key Doctrines (*KD*)
    3 174
    4 237
    18 172, 174
    19 230
    20 230

Eusebius Pamphili, *Praeparatio evangelica* (*PE*)
    14.5.13 202
    14.18.1–5 199
    14.18.19 200

Galen
  De methodo medendi
    10.163.14 210n21
  *De propriorum animi cuiuslibet affectuum
      dignotione et curatione*
    8 249
  De sectis ad eos qui introducuntur
    5.11.8–5 211n22
  Subfiguratio empirica
    2.44.13f. 210n21

Pseudo-Galen, *De historia philosophia*
    116.2 209n19

Gregorius Nazianzenus, *Epistulae* (*ep.*)
    32 267n20

Herodotus, *Historiae*
    I.32.5 226

Hesiod, *Works and Days*
    190–92 39n33
    280–88 40
    286–92 40
    826 34n19

Homer, *Iliad*
    9.496–8 36
    11.783f. 36n25
    12.310–12 38
    15.642 36n24
    17.446f. 35

Marcus Aurelius, *Τὰ εἰς ἑαυτόν*
    11.34 191

Philo Judaeus, *De ebrietate*
    200 267n20

Photius, *Bibliotheca*
    169b21–30 203
    170b30–5 204

Pindar
  Isthmia
    3.18 43n48
    4.6f. 44n49
    8.24 43n47
  Nemea
    6.1–7 43
  Olympia
    2.30–36 44
    2.51–6 44
    2.56–72 44
    10.20–22 44
  Pythia
    5.1–4 44
    5.12–14 44
    5.122f. 43
    7.19–21 44n49
    8.95 43
    9.76f. 44n49
  Fragmenta
    131b 43
    133 43

Plato
  Euthydemus
    278e–82e 50n6, 52n12
  Gorgias (*Gorg.*)
    445d–e 68
    452e1–4 67
    452e9–3a3 67
    454d4 67
    454d6f. 67
    454e9–5a2 67

455a1 67
455a8–d5 68
456b–c 68
456c–7c 68
458e–9a 69*n5*
459c8–e 69
459e 69
460a2f. 69
460b f. 73
460b8–c6 71
464b2–6a3 72
465b–d 73
466d7–e2 75
467b2–10 156
467d–8c 74
468c5–7 74
469a 73
470a9–12 75
470a10–12 74
470d1 85
470e 75f
470e8–11 75
470e8 76
471e1–2d4 85
472c f. 90*n6*
473a f. 76
473d3 54*n16*
473e6–4b5 85
474c f. 76
474c7–d2 77
475 b–d 76
476a7–b2 76
476b3–d4 76
476d5–7a4 77
476e3–7a4 77*n13*
477a5–7 77*n13*
477a7f. 77
477c2–5 77*n13*
480e 77
482c4 78
483a 78
484c 78
487e–8a 90*n6*
491e6–2a1 80*n14*
492b2–8 80*n14*
492d 9, 85, 90*n6*
492e 79
493c–d 81
493e 6–4a3 149
494c2f. 80f., 83
494d1 82
495a2–4 82
495a5f. 82
495d4f. 82
498a1–5 82
498b7–c3 82
498c2f. 82

498e5–8 82
499a1f. 82
499b4–8 83
500c f. 90*n6*
500d6–8 83
502a–3a 83
503c f. 86
503d3 87
505d 84
506c–7e 87
519a 68*n4*
Ion
    541e–2b 56*n18*
Laws
    II, 659d 125*n37*
    III
        678e9–9e4 54
        679e2f. 54
    IX, 875a5–b1 149
    XI, 931a, 125*n37*
Meno
    80a–b 64*n27*
    99b–d 56*n18*
Phaedrus
    247d 217
    252d–53c 29*n3*
Philebus
    20b–23a 50*n6*, 52*n12*
    34e ff. 175
    60a–61a 50*n6*
    64c–66c. 9
Republic (Rep.)
    I
        328e6 123*n31*
        329b f. 123
        329d 90*n6*
        329e 90*n6*
        344e 90*n6*
        345e–6e 94*n12*
        347e 90*n6*
        348c5–d2 53
        351e 10–2a9 153
        352d 9, 90*n6*
    II
        357b4–8a3 57*n19*
        358e3 85
        359e–60d 85*n19*
        360c6–d7 55
        260e1–61d3 58
        361c1–4 61
        363a 85
        363e4–4a4 61
        366c3–d4 55
    V
        462a8–b1 149
        464c 7f
    VI, 519c–d 32

Plato (*cont.*)
  VII, 538d6–e5 63
  IX
    580a ff. *7n18*, 9
    588b1–92b5 *49n3*
    588b1–4 49
  X
    608e 3f. *257n52*
    613a 32
    613a f. *29n3*
  Statesman
    276e 10–12 246
    277a 246
  Symposium
    204e–5a *52n12*
    206a ff. 128
    207d–9e *29n3*
  Theaetetus
    175c5–6b1 16
    176a–b *261n66*
    176a5–e4 28
    176b 32
    176b1f. 16
  Timaeus
    29e 32
    90c 28
    90a–d *29n3*
Plotinus, *Enneades*
  I.2 13, *261n66*
  I.4 237
  I.4.1.1–3 *214n10*
  I.4.1.5–10 215
  I.4.1.8–10 215
  I.4.2.1f. 218
  I.4.2.3–6 218
  I.4.2.4f. 218
  I.4.2.4 218
  I.4.2.8–13 218
  I.4.2.13–15 218
  I.4.2.15–19 218
  I.4.2.21–3 218
  I.4.2.26 218
  I.4.2.35–43 219
  I.4.3 236
  I.4.3.18–20 220
  I.4.3.24–8 220
  I.4.3.26–30 214
  I.4.3.33f. 220
  I.4.3.33–7 220
  I.4.4.23–5 *267n20*
  I.4.5–6 234
  I.4.5.6f. *274n54*
  I.4.12 216
  I.4.18–23 220
  I.4.22–30 220
  I.5 232
  I.5.1 233
  I.5.5.1–3 233

  I.5.5.4–8 234
  I.5.6.1–8 234
  I.5.6.13f. 235
  I.5.6.16–18 234
  I.5.6.18f. 235
  I.5.7 234–6
  II.2.3.12–15 217
  IV.3.32.1–6 216
  V.9.1 *219n43*
  VI.5.10.1–11 *273n51*
  VI.7 217
  VI.7.24.4–9 216
  VI.7.25.16–32 216
  VI.7.30.17f 217
  VI.7.34.36–8 217
  VI.7.35.20–29 217
  VI.7.35.24–6 217
Plutarch
  De communibus notitiis adversus Stoicos (De comm. not.)
    1061F 231
    1063A f. 185
    1076A f. 188
  De esu carnium
    996A *260n64*
  Quomodo quis suos in virtute sentiat profectus (De prof. in virt.)
    75C 188
    82F 200
  Septem sapientium convivium
    159B *258n60*
  De Stoicorum repugnantiis (De Stoic. rep.)
    1046E f. 191
    1048E *184n2*, 189
  De virtute morali (De virt. mor.)
    440F–41A 191
Pseudo-Plutarch, *Placita philosophorum (Plac.)*
  874E 194
  906E4 *209n19*
Polybius, *Historiae*
  9.6.5 *209n19*
  28.7.1 *209n19*
Porphyry
  De abstinentia (de abst.)
    1.1.1–13 256
    2.2.1–16 259
    2.12.14–18 259
    2.12.14–17 259
    2.12.16–2.13.1 *258n57*
    2.3.3–5 263
    2.47 262
    3.1.1f. 260
    3.1.20–22 257
    3.1.22–5 258
    3.1.5–10 260
    3.18.3–20.6 *260n62*
    3.18.16–30 258

3.19.7–10 258n57
3.20.7–20.5 260n62
3.25 260n62
3.26f. 260
3.26.12f. 258n57
3.26.27–33 260
3.26.47f. 258
3.26.48–50 258
3.26.59–63 257, 261
3.26.69–27.1 262
3.27.27 262
4.27.40–44 262
4.27.43f. 262
In Aristotelis categorias expositio per interrogationem et responsionem (Cat.)
137.23–8.32 185

Seneca
Epistulae Morales ad Lucilium (Epist.)
3 17n37
9 17n37
92.3 29n7, 231
94.11 193
94.21 193
94.50 192
95 193
132 232
De *vita beata* (*v. beat.*)
1.1 270n30

Sextus Empiricus (SE)
Adversus mathematicos (M)
7.432 184
11.20 201
11.42 204
11.181 184
11.200f. 187
Pyrrhoniae hypotyposes (PH)
1.12 206f
1.21–4 211
1.25 206f
1.25–30 206
1.26 206
1.27f. 208
1.29 205, 208
1.91 184
1.232 202
1.234 202n7, 10
3 208n17
3.235 205n14
3.236 208n17
3.280 209

Simplicius, *In Aristotelis categorias commentarium (Cat.)*
237.25–238.29 231
237.29–8.1 186
284.12–5.8 185
286.35–7.5 186

Solon, *Fragmenta*
14 41
15 42
24 42

Stobaeus, *Eclogues (Ecl.)*
2.63.6–10 191
2.77 231
2.113.18–23 190
2.113.24–14.3 186
5.906.18–7.5 187

Stoicorum Veterum Fragmenta (SVF)
I.187 267n16
I.206 215n16
III.17 215n13
III.29–45 267n17
III.49–67 267n16
III.55 231
III.431 216n18
III.586 267n20

Theognis, *Elegiae*
1.129f. 42
1.131f. 41
1.765–8 41
1.933–5 42
1.1067f. 41

Torquatus, *De finibus (De fin.)*
1.29 168n8, 171
1.30 168n8
1.37 168n8, 173f
1.66 180
1.67 180
1.68 182

Xenophanes, *Fragmenta*
B2 45
B7 45
B11 45
B12 45
B13–16 45
B14 45
B18 45
B23 45
B23–5 45
B25f. 45
B26 45
B32 46
B41 46
B79 46
B82f. 46
B94 46
B112 46
B119 46
B189 46n55

Xenophon, *Memorabilia*
2.1.21–34 8n26

General Index

Achilles 36
Ackrill, J. L. 228
activity, *See energeia; praxis*
Adeimantus 55f, 61, 85, 245
Adkins, A. W. H. 36*n24–6*, 39*n35*
Aenesidemus 199f, 202–5, 209
agathon, to (the good)
aidōs (shame) 36, 40, 76–9
aisthēsis (sensation, perception) 67, 97f, 168,
    173f, 182, 217–20, 258, 259
akolasia (intemperance, self-
    indulgence) 120*n23*, 152, 154f
akrasia (weakness of will) 110*n33*, 122–4,
    148–50, 152f, 160–3
Alcinous 29*n3*, 266*n10*, 267*n20*, 275*n59*
Alesse, F. 191*n17*
Alexander Aphrodisiensis 184*n2*, 188–90, 249,
    267*n19*
Allen, J. 205*n12*, 211*n22*
Alteration (Principle of) 8, 9, 38, 42, 44
altruism 241–64
Ammonius 184*n3*
Anaxarchus 200
Andersen, Ø. 7*n20*, 37*n31*
andreia (courage, bravery) 33, 79, 81–3, 119,
    136–8, 271f, 275f
anger 120
Annas, J. 2*n2*, 5, 6*n16*, 19, 20*n46*, 22*n49*, 24–5,
    29*n3*, 31*n12*, 47*n58*, 49*n4*, 147*n5*, 149*n8*,
    150*n11*, 165*n1*, 172*n19*, 179*n31f*, 180*n33*,
    192*n19*, 196*n34*, 242*n2f*, 243*n6f*, 244*n11*,
    248*n22f*, 251*n36f*, 265*n3*, 267*n16*
apatē (deception (concerning)) 159–61
Apelles 209
apparent and true 74f, 150f, 155–63, 218
    derivative, instrumental 165, 168–70, 173,
        177–80, 201, 204, 208
    external 30, 41f, 44, 50, 95, 129–32, 144, 183f,
        226f, 231, 237, 242, 245, 255, 257, 262, 270
    highest, ultimate, greatest, final 77, 88, 90–3,
        95f, 102f, 110, 111, 129*n2*, 131, 134, 136,
        140, 144, 151, 154–6, 158f, 164, 171f, 179f,
        245, 265, 275
    identification of 73–5, 156, 218
    intrinsic, natural 61f, 161, 165, 168–73, 178,
        180–2
appetite, *See epithumia*
Arcesilaus 202f
Archie, J. P. 76*n12*
aretē (virtue, excellence)

cardinal 33, 43, 274–6
change in meaning 47
compared to *olbia* (prosperity) 42
degrees of 184–96 *passim*, 231
distinction between ethical and
    intellectual 12f, 102
ethical (of character) 15, 30, 241f, 247, 253
etymology 36
intellectual 46, 102, 106, 115, 247
kuria (full) 162
natural (*phusikē*) 162
necessity for *eudaimonia* 50, 97, 241
stability 119, 140–5, 227
sufficiency for *eudaimonia* 14, 27, 44, 46f, 50,
    131, 136, 197, 231
teachability 194
teleology 179, 183
theoretical 13, 29–34, 134, 179
unity of 191
voluntariness 40, 119, 122, 266
Aristo of Chios 191
Aristocles of Messene 199f, 204
Aristotle 28f, 32–6, 49, 52, 63, 67, 70, ch. 4–7,
    182, 183, 185f, 195, 197, 199, 213, 215,
    220*n45*, 223–9, 233f, 236–55, 259, 263,
    266*n10*, 275*n59*
Armstrong, A. H. 212*n4*, 217*n27*, 233*n7*
Armstrong, J. M. 29*n3*
art, *See technē*
Aspasius 14, 18, ch. 13
asteia, ta (noble emotions) 216
ataraxia (calm, tranquillity) 10, 13, 171f,
    174–7, 184, 197–211, 224, 230f, 266*n11*,
    271, 277
    etymology 198
Augustine 2, 14, ch. 14
autarkeia (self-sufficiency) 17, 34f, 47, 93f, 107,
    125f, 177, 197, 229, 246–8, 257, 262

Baker, S. H. 229*n2*, 130*fn3*
Baltzly, D. 29*n3*
Barnes, J. 117, 199*n3*, 225*n3*, 249*n24–7*, 253*n42*
Barney, R. 92*n8*, 97*n18*, 99*n20*, 105*n29*
Becchi, F. 249*n25*
Becker, M. 275*n61*
Beierwaltes, W. 233, 265*fn1*, *6*, *8*
Bentham, J. 3*n7*
Berman, S. 83*n17*
Blackburn, S. 21*n47*
Bloomfield, P. 21*n47*

Blundell, M. W. 18*n39*
Boëthius 185
Bordt, M. 18*n40*
Bouffartigue, J. 158*n58*, 60, 160*n63f*
boulēsis ((rational) wish, desire) 75, 92, 101*n23*,
    120f, 146–63 *passim*, 148, 150, 157, 216
Boyle, M. 98*n19*, 100*n22*
bravery, *See andreia*
Brechtken, J. 265*n1*, 273*n47*
Brennan, T. 187*n8*
Brickhouse, T. C. 149*n8*, 150*n11*, 152, 154, 160
Brisson, L. 195*n32*
Broadie, S. 8*n24*, 9*n30*, 93*n11*, 112*n37*, 113*n1*,
    125*n35*, 141*n19*, 149*n8*, 150*n11*, 162*n29*
Brown, L. 29*n5*, 51–64 *passim*
Buddensiek, F. 265*n1*, 271*n39*
Burkert, W. 45*n50*, 46*n56*
Burnyeat, M. 28*n1*, 110*n34*, 162*n30*

Cairns, D. L. 7*n20*, 8*n22*, 36–9*n24*, 28f, 35
Callicles 66f, 78–87, 123
calm, *See ataraxia*
Caluori, D. 245*n17*
carnivorism 256–64
Chadwick, H. 278*n74*
chance, *See tuchē*
change, *See kinēsis*
chara (joy) 174, 216
Charles, D. 146*n1*
Chazán, P. 243f, 245*n15*
Chekola, M. 222f, 229, 240
Chrysippus 184*n5*, 187, 189, 194, 257*n54*
Cicero 17f, 121, 188–90, 202f, 230, 232, 267,
    269–73, 276f, 279f
Claus, D. B. 46*n53*
Clay, J. S. 39*n34*-6
Cleanthes 187, 194
Cleisthenes 80
cleverness, *See deinotēs*
Cooper, J. M. 1*n1*, 7*fn17*, 24, 19*n43*, 66*n2*,
    88*n2*, 93*n10*, 110*n32*, 120*n21*, 132*n6*,
    150*n12*, 165*fn1-3*, 171*n17*, 190–2*n15*, 17,
    19, 195*n30*
Corcilius, K. 158*n24*
courage, *See andreia*
craft, *See technē*
Croesus 34*n19*, 223f
Currie, B. 41*n39*
Curzer, H. J. 110*n34*
Cyrenaïcs 2*n2*, 10, 11, 176

daimōn 28, 39–41, 43, 46, 183
Darwall, S. L. 3*n4*, 21*n48*
Decleva Caizzi, F. 185*n5*, 199, 200, 201
Deichgräber, K. 210*n20f*
deinotēs (cleverness) 154
desire, *See epithumia*

Devereux, D. 100*n22*
Dewald, C. 7*n20*, 226
diathesis (disposition, state of character) 186f,
    190, 192, 195, 230f, 237
Dihle, A. 193*n24*
dikaiosunē (justice) 28, 32, 37, 42–4, 53, 88, 101
    connection with happiness 75f, 86
    definition 53, 57, 72, 87, 258–61, 264
    divine 33, 35, 37, 39f, 45f
    intrinsic value 61–3, 151, 179, 245
    knowledge of 66–87
    legal 78f
    motivation 49–65, 179
    natural (*phusikē*) 78f, 82, 162f
    scope 251, 254–64
    utility 21, 153, 179
Dillon, J. 212*n2*
Dimas, P. 14, 19, 24, 26, 71*n8*, 75*n11*
Diogenes Laërtius 170, 174, 199, 200, 203, 205f,
    209, 216, 231
disposition, *See diathesis, hexis*
divine, the 8, 16, 56, 201
    dependence on 34f, 39, 41, 43, 265–80
    imitation of 28–48, 125, 256f, 261–4
Dodds, E. R. 39*n35*
Doignon, J. 265*n1*, 267*n21*, 278*n74*
Dombrowski, D. A. 258*n57*
Douglas, A. J. 270*n34*
Dover, K. 34*n19*, 114*n6*
Drecoll, V. H. 279*n76*
Drummond, J. 20*n45*

education, *See upbringing*
egoism 51f, 56–60, 62*n25*, 164f, 181f, 242–6
Emilsson, E. K. 6, 11, 13, 27, 128*n1*, 237–8
empeiria (experience) 114–6, 121, 145, 162
empiricism, medical 199, 205, 209–11
energeia (activity) 7, 12, 19, 29, 32f, 34, 96*n17*,
    129–32, 134–45, 224–9, 233, 240
enkrateia (strength of will) 122–4, 160
Epictetus 194, 231
Epicureanism 10f, 14f, 29*n7*, 58, 203f, 213, 215,
    218, 224, 229f, 235, 237–9, 270
Epicurus 16, 52, 57f, ch.9, 229f, 232, 237
epithumia (desire, appetite) 79–84, 85–7, 98,
    100–2, 110, 113, 119–24, 126, 119–24, 119f,
    146–63 *passim*, 150, 216; *See also boulēsis*
    anankaia (necessary) 177
    conflict with *boulēsis* (wish) 146–63 *passim*
    definition 150
    empty (*kenē*) 178
    natural (*phusikē*) 177
    object 150, 176, 265
ergon (function, work, task) 91, 96–100,
    102–11, 129*n2*, 136, 137*n14*, 139, 215
    argument 89, 96–103, 104ff
    thesis 105–7

ethismos (habituation) 13, 115f, 122, 162
euboulia (excellence in deliberation,
    prudence) 36*n27*, 53, 154
eudaemonism 49–65, 88f, 96, 104–9, 172,
    265–7
    definition 88, 183
    hedonistic 164
    rational 51
eudaimonia; See also happiness
    ambiguity 8
    attainability 184–96, 237
    definition 7, 10, 95f, 97, 214, 225, 231
    degree 119, 185f, 189–91, 195, 231–7, 275
    duration 127–45, 222–40, 249f
    etymology 7, 127
    experience of 146, 148
    Homeric 35–8
    inclusivist conception of 130f, 137*n14*
    intellectualization of (condition of) 30–5, 45f
    internalization of (condition of) 30–5,
        41–6, 224
    popular conception 95f
    stability 11f, 225, 236f
    teleios (perfect, complete) life
        requirement 127–45, 222–40, 249f
    translation 7, 49*n1*, 88*n2*, 127, 146, 222
    ultimacy 92, 94, 103
    unity 31, 191, 272
    universal wish for, pursuit of 50, 75f, 98, 127,
        156–9, 222, 265, 270
    voluntariness 30–3, 38, 39f, 44–7, 95,
        122, 266
Eudoxus 157
euētheia (simplicity) 53–5
eupatheiai (good feelings) 215–17
Euphrates of Tyre 194
Eusebius Pamphili 199f, 202*n10*
excellence, *See aretē*
experience, *See empeiria*

Farwell, P. 134*n10*
Fates, the 38
Finley, M. I. 35*n23*
Flasch, K. 268*n23*
Foot, Ph. 137
Fossheim, H. 6, 12, 25, 122*n27*, 155*n18*, 163*n32*
Frede, M. 14*n35*, 194, 210f*n20–2*, 226*n4*
free will 100f, 104, 108f
friendship, *See philia*
function, *See ergon*

Galen 209f, 211*n22*, 249
Garland, R. 114*n4*, 123*n29*, 31
Gauthier, R. A. 149
van Geest, P. 266*n13*, 274*n53*
Gerber, D. E. 41*n38*
Giannopoulou, Z. 29*n3*

Gill, C. 191*n17*, 196*n35*
Glaucon 49–65 *passim*, 85, 248
Glaucus 38
god, *See* divine, the
Goldbacher, A. 276*n63*
good, the, *See agathon, to*
Gosling, J. C. B. 80*n15*
Graeser, A. 215
Graham, D. W. 45*n51*
Grant, A. 157*n23*
Graver, M. 190*n15*
Griffin, J. 35*n21*
Griffith, M. 41*n40*
Grönroos, G. 13, 150*n12*, 158*n24*
Gyges, Ring of 57f

habit, *See hexis*
habituation, *See ethismos*
Hadot, P. 1*n1*, 195*n30*, 217*n31*, 238
Hagendahl, H. 267*n21*
hairesis (rational choice) 164, 166, 172
happiness
    in the ancient sense, *See eudaimonia*
    in the modern sense 50, 222, 223
    objectivist conception 3–7, 21, 10, 95, 147f,
        198, 223
    subjectivist conception 3–7, 21, 147f, 223f
Haybron, D. M. 4, 21*n48*
hēdonē (pleasure) 37f, 41, 81–7, 95, 110, 120,
    146–63 *passim*
    cause 169ff
    connection with friendship 180–2
    connection with virtue 179f
    degrees of 172–4
    katastematic and kinetic 170–8
    kenē (empty), *See pathos*
hedonism 41, 57, 67, 79–84, 110, 146–63,
    155*n19*, 164–82, 230, 244*n12*, 245, 270
    ethical and psychological 164–8
de Heer, C. 8*n25*, 34*n20*, 37–41*n31*f, 36, 42
Heinimann, F. 8*n23*
Heraclides 205
Heraclitus 44–6
Herodotus 34*n19*, 223f, 226
hexis (habit, disposition) 12, 140–5, 162,
    186, 248
Heylbut, G. 157*n22*, 249*n29*, 250
Holte, R. 265*n1*, 273*n47*
Homer 28–48 *passim*, 114, 127f
Horn, C. 1*n1*, 265*n1*, 269*n26*, 275*n62*, 276*n63*,
    279*n77*
Huffman, C. 46*n56*
Hume 198

Ierodiakonou, K. 10, 26, 184*n3*, 195*n31*
immortality, desire for 128, 230
intellect, *See nous*

intemperance, *See akolasia*
intuitionism 64f
Inwood, B. 183, 185, 187, 190, 193*n22*, 194, 196*n33*
Irwin, T. H. 3*n4f*, 29*n6*, 32*n15*, 54*n15*, 74*n10*, 83*n17*, 115, 134*n11*, 135*n12*, 141*n20*, 147*n3*, 149*n8*, 150*n11*, 153*n16*, 154, 155*n18*, 183, 242*n2*, 244

Janáček, K. 207*n15*
Jenks, R. 83*n17*
Johnson, C. N. 76*n12*
Jolif, J. Y. 149
Jost, L. J. 147*n5*
joy, *See chara*
justice, *See dikaiosunē*
justification 61–5, 92, 103

Kahn, C. H. 31*n10*, 46*n53*, 66*n2*, 83*n17*, 85*n18*, 197*n2*
kalon, to (the noble, fine, beautiful) 45, 61, 95, 115, 116*n12*, 119–21, 144
Kant 21*n47*
Kantianism 60
kenon (empty) 170, 177f
Kidd, I. 193*n22*
kinēsis (change, process, motion) 96*n17*, 134f, 138, 144f, 173f, 227–9
Kirwan, C. 279*n76*
Kitto, H. D. F. 223*n1*
Klosko, G. 83*n17*
Konstan, D. 18*n39*, 255
Korsgaard, C. 21*n47*
Kraut, R. 5*n13*, 7*n17*, 88*n2*, 115*n10*, 125*n34*, 147*n5*
Kube, J. 8*n23*

Lavere, G. J. 269*n26*
Lear, G. R. 6, 8*n24*, 11, 93, 120, 131*n4f*, 132*n7*, 150*n12*
LeBar, M. 64*n28*
Levett, M. J. 28*n1*
life, lives (*bios, zōē, zēn*)
  choice of 8f, 59f, 95f
  compared to circumstances 60
  difference between *bios* and *zōē* 130
  to eu zēn (living well) 106, 214f, 220
  impact on others 58–61
  judgement of 58–61
  political 29, 35f, 124, 144
  teleios (perfect, complete) life requirement, *See eudaimonia*
  theoretical 29, 124, 140, 144
Linguiti, A. 233, 236*n8*
Lloyd-Jones, H. 37*n30*, 39*n35*, 43*n46*
logon didonai (giving a reason) 61–5
  different senses 101f

logos (speech, reason, etc.) 19, 88, 97, 100–3, 108–11, 218f, 257
Long, A. A. 29*n6f*, 30, 33, 46*n54*, 166*n4*, 188f, 191, 194, 215*n16*, 216, 230f
luck, *See tuchē*
Lysias 62

MacIntyre, A. 35*n23*, 89*n3*, 128*n1*, 229*n6*
Mahoney, T. 29*n3*
makar (blessed) 34, 38, 39, 41, 46, 175
Marcus Aurelius 191, 194, 253
McGroarty, K. 213, 215*n13*, 220*n50*
McMahon, D. 3*n6*
McPherran, M. L. 33*n17*
Mele, A. R. 162*n30*
Merki, H. 29*n3*
metriopatheia (moderate affection) 205–8
Mill, J. S. 3*n7*
Mitsis, P. 193*n22*
mochthēros, ho (the wretched, bad) 146–63, 149
Morison, B. 144*n22*
Moss, J. 102*n26*, 150*n12*, 158*n25*
Most, G. W. 39*n33*
Murray, A. T. 35*n22*

Nagel, T. 100*n22*, 128*n1*
naturalism 88f, 103*n27*, 165, 183, 148*n22*
  naturalisitc fallacy 89, 104, 107
Neoplatonism 195, 224, 243, 245, 273, 275
nihilism 197, 201
Nikolsky, B. 172*n20*
noble emotions, *See asteia, ta*
de Noronha Galvao, H. 265*n1*
North, H. 37*n29*
nous (intellect, reason) 214, 217, 218, 219, 220, 236–8
Nozick, R. 22*n50*
Nussbaum, M. 29*n7*, 32*n14*, 244

O'Connell, R. J. 273*n51*
O'Donovan, O. 273*n47*
offspring 125f, 127
olbia (prosperity) 34, 38–44, 46f, 223*n2*
O'Meara, D. J. 13*n34*, 195*n32*, 214*n7*, 241*n1*, 245*n17*
One, the 214, 217, 245

paganism 267, 277
pain 76, 78, 81–4, 120, 137, 155, 164–78, 216*n17*, 224, 234, 237, 258*n57*
Pakaluk, M. 161*n28*
Panaetius 193
Passmore, J. 29*n3*
pathos (passion, affection, emotion, feeling) 120, 122f, 168, 215f, 218f
Pearson, G. 150f*n12f*, 155*n19*, 158*n25*
Peisistratus 80

perception, *See aisthēsis*
Pericles 68, 80
philia (friendship) 17f, 20, 72, 88, 117, 126,
   141–3, 168–82, 246–8, 249, 251, 254–6, 267
Philo of Larissa 199, 202
Photius 203f
phronēsis (practical wisdom, prudence) 79,
   81f, 88, 102, 106, 119, 131, 144, 177, 179f,
   184, 204
Pindar 41–4, 46
Pizzolato, L. F. 269*n27*
Plato 28f, 31–4, 42, ch. 2f, 88, 90*n6*, 94*n12*, 96,
   119, 123, 125, 127f, 149, 153f, 156, 175,
   185f, 188, 190, 195, 197, 202*n10*, 213,
   215*n14*, 216f, 223*n2*, 226, 241f, 243, 245f,
   250f, 261, 263
Platonism 29*n3*, 185, 229, 241f, 245*n17*,
   261, 266
pleasure, *See hēdonē*
Plotinus 128*n1*, 185, 195, ch. 11, 229–40, 241f,
   245, 246*n17*, 261*n66*, 275f, 278*n74*
Plutarch 174, 188–90, 200, 231f
pneuma ('vital heat') 116–26 *passim*
poiēsis 106f
poiotēs (quality) and *poion* (quale) 184–6
polis 17f, 91, 125f, 247f
Polito, R. 204f*n11, 13*
Polus 54*n16*, 66f, 66–87
Polybius 209
Porphyry 185f, 195, ch. 13, 275
Posidonius 193f, 257*n54*
praxis (activity) 89–112 *passim*
precepts, Stoic 192–4
Priam 133*n9*, 225f
Price, A. W. 141*n19*, 150*n12*
Prichard, H. A. 51–3, 63–5
principles of action 90, 103, 110; *See also*
   precepts
pronoia (providence) 189
prosperity, *See olbia*
providence, *See pronoia*
prudence 180; *See also deinotēs; euboulia;*
   phronēsis
psuchē (soul), parts of the 97, 102, 150f, 154,
   156, 160f
Pyrrho of Elis 197, 199f, 202–4
Pythagoras 45f, 258

Rabbås, Ø. 16, 19
Race, W. H. 43*n45*, 72*n9*
rationalism 88
rationality 30, 32, 74–6, 88f, 100–12 *passim*,
   122, 183f, 219f, 239, 257–9
Raz, J. 21*n47*
realism, ethical 103
remorse 147–50, 152f, 161–3
rhetoric 66–73

van Riel, G. 216, 217*n26*, 30
Rist, J. M. 180*n35*, 217, 236, 265*n1*, 269*n26*,
   272fn46f, 49, 280*n81*
Robertson, D. 195*n30*
Robinson, T. M. 45*n52*
Rogers, K. 120*n21*
Roloff, D. 30*n9*
Roochnik, D. 8*n23*, 153*n15*
Rosenbaum, S. E. 178*n29*
Roskam, G. 185*n5*, 190*n15*, 192*n20*
Ross, W. D. 29*n5*, 134
Rowe, C. 89*n4*, 90*n5*, 140, 141*n20*
Rue, R. 29*n3*
Russell, D. 29*n3*, 192*n19*
Rusten, J. S. 9*n27*

sage, Stoic 184f, 187f, 192f, 200, 212f, 216, 231,
   237–9, 270, 279
Sages, Seven 114
Sarpedon 38
sceptic non-assertion 200
scepticism 10, 197–211, 273
Schafer, J. 193*n24*
Schissel von Fleschenberg, O. 275*n60*
Schneewind, J. B. 3*n4*
Schniewind, A. 6, 13, 212*n3*, 5, 216*n22*,
   245*n17*
Schofield, M. 36*n27*, 191, 195*n30*
Schwyzer, H.-R. 214*n10*, 236
Sedley, D. N. 29*n3*, 30, 33*n16*, 166*n4*, 188f, 191,
   193*n25*, 194, 195*n32*, 215*n16*, 216, 230f
Segvic, H. 67*n3*, 76*n12*
self-constraint, *See enkrateia*
self-indulgence, *See akolasia*
self-knowledge 141–5
self-restraint, *See sōphrosunē*
self-sacrifice 137f
self-sufficiency, *See autarkeia*
Sellars, J. 195*n30*
Seneca 192f, 231f, 238
sensation, *See aisthēsis*
Sextus Empiricus 197, 199, 201f
Sidgwick, H. 3*n7*
Simplicius 185f
skopos (aim) 95, 110f
Smith, A. 117, 246*n17*
Socrates 31, 33, 127, 191, 194, 203, 226
Soll, I. 148*n6*
Solmsen, F. 42*n44*
Solon 34*n19*, 41–6, 113, 130, 132, 136, 223–7,
   229, 240
sōphrosunē (temperance, self-restraint) 33, 37,
   40, 46, 61, 120, 152, 271, 275f
Sorabji, R. 195*n30*, 256*n51*
Stauffer, D. 66*n1*, 83*n17*
Stewart, J. A. 157*n23*
Stobaeus 186*n6*, 187, 190, 191

Stocker, M. 5*n14f*, 244
Stoicism 31, 33, 52, 60, ch. 9, 203, 213, 215–8,
    224, 229–32, 235, 237–9, 242–4, 251, 253f,
    257–9, 264, 267, 269–80
    as way of life or therapy 194f
Strawson, G. 11*n32*
Striker, G. 11*n31*, 31*n11*, 197*n1*, 209*n18*
Sumner, W. 4*n12*
Svavarsson, S. H. 8, 10, 13, 113*n1*, 201 n. 5,
    208*n16*, 211*n22*

Taylor, C. 229*n6*
Taylor, C. C. W. 80*n15*
technē (art, craft) 72f, 83f, 89–92, 94f, 97*n18*,
    105–8, 116, 132*n6*, 186
teleology 89–94, 97–100, 103f, 176–9,
    197f, 206
telos (end, goal) 88–112 *passim*, 130–45
    passim, 150f, 154–63 *passim*, 170–9
    passim, 183, 203–10, 225f, 240, 269f,
    274–6
temperance, *See sōphrosunē*
Teske, R. J. 276*n63*
Themistocles 68
Theophrastus 258*n57*, 259, 260*n62*
Thompson, M. 103*n27*, 137
Thrasymachus 53–6, 153, 245
Thucydides 9
thumos 113, 119–24, 126, 150*n12*
Tieleman, T. 193*n25*
timē (honour) 34–44 *passim*
Timon of Phlius 199f
Tithonus 124
Tornau, C. 3, 14, 267*n20*, 273*n50*, 275*n58*,
    277*n69*
Torquatus 167, 171, 180f
tranquillity, *See ataraxia*
tuchē (chance, luck) 31f, 132f*n6*, 9, 143, 197,
    207–11

Tuominen, M. 13, 18, 19, 163*n32*

unhappiness 79, 189, 216, 225, 234f, 237, 240
upbringing 64, 109, 118, 121, 193f, 262

value, *See agathon, to*
vegetarianism 256–64
Vegetti, M. 56*n18*
Velleman, D. 11*n32*, 128*n1*, 229*n6*
vice 146–63, 183–96 *passim*
virtue, *See aretē*
'vital heat', *See pneuma*
Vlastos, G. 42*n43*, 76*n12*
Vogt, K. 151*n14*

Wacht, M. 270*n31*
Walzer, R. 210*n20*
weakness of will, *See akrasia*
welfare 83, 125
West, M. L. 39*n36*
Wetzel, J. 265*n1*, 267*n22*, 274*n52*, 279*n76f*
White, N. P. 3*n6*, 51, 53–5, 61, 64
Whittaker, J. 266f*n10*, 20, 275*n59*
Wiesen, D. S. 270*n29*
Williams, B. 37*n28*, 89*n3*, 128*n1*, 135*n12*, 192
wisdom 45f, 114f, 184, 194f, 197, 212f, 216, 232,
    266; *See also* sage
    practical, *See phronēsis*
wish, *See boulēsis*
Woods, M. 110*n32*
Woolf, R. 175*n26*, 188
Wyatt, W. F. 35*n22*

Xenophanes 30, 44–6

youth 118f

Zeus 30, 31, 35, 37f, 39f, 42f, 46
Zeyl, D. J. 28*n2*